The PHOTO SHOP 4 WOW! BOOK

Tips, Tricks, & Techniques for Adobe Photoshop 4

Linnea Dayton & Jack Davis

Peachpit Press

The Photoshop 4 Wow! Book, Windows Edition

Linnea Dayton and Jack Davis

Peachpit Press
1249 Eighth Street
Berkeley, CA 94710
(510) 524-2178
(510) 524-2221 (fax)

Find us on the World Wide Web at:
http://www.peachpit.com

Peachpit Press is a division of Addison Wesley Longman.

Cover design: Jack Davis
Book design: Jill Davis
Production and prepress: Jonathan Parker
Imposition and imagesetting: Adage Graphics

ISBN 0-201-68857-3

0 9 8 7 6 5 4 3 2 1

Printed and bound in the United States of America.

To Victor Gavenda, Editor
Extraordinaire

— Linnea Dayton

To our latest edition,
Rachel Marin

— Jack and Jill Davis

ACKNOWLEDGMENTS

This book would not have been possible without a great deal of support. First, we would like to thank the Photoshop artists who have allowed us to include their work and describe their techniques in this book; their names are listed in the Appendix. We are also grateful to many Photoshop artists whose work does not appear in the book but who have passed along some of their Photoshop knowledge and experience; among them are Russell Brown, Kai Krause, Jeff Girard, and Ellie Dickson. We appreciate the support of the folks at Adobe Systems, Inc., who kept us up to date on the development of Photoshop and other Adobe programs, supplied us with software, and answered our technical questions. Thanks also to the people who helped us test our techniques, including Tommy Yune, Geno Andrews, Rob Keele, and our editor at Peachpit Press, Victor Gavenda. We'd also like to thank Karen Fishler and Jennifer Loflin of *adobe.mag,* who have been supportive in many ways.

We are grateful to Jill Davis, whose book design made the writing and illustrating much easier; to Cher Threinen-Pendarvis, who helped us with research and contributed her knowledge of Photoshop painting techniques; to Jonathan Parker, who once again made room in his design studio's schedule to produce this edition, "tweaking" the layouts, running prepress checks, and automating the separation of color images through Aldus PrePrint. Special thanks also to Doug Isaacs at Adage Graphics in Los Angeles, who imposed and output our pages in eight-page flats using a Scitex Dolev 800 imagesetter. We highly recommend Doug and Adage.

We'd like to thank the friends, family, colleagues, and coworkers, including those at Peachpit Press, who have so far supported us through six editions of this endeavor.

And finally, we'd like to thank those readers of previous editions who have let us know that *The Photoshop Wow! Book* has been useful and important to them, as well as those who have just quietly used and appreciated it. Thanks also for pointing out where we could improve the book so all of us can get the most "Wow!" from our favorite tool — Photoshop.

CONTENTS

WELCOME TO *THE PHOTOSHOP 4 WOW! BOOK*

ADOBE PHOTOSHOP IS ONE OF THE MOST POWERFUL visual communication tools ever to appear on the desktop. The program has expanded the visual vocabulary of designers and illustrators to include color photo imagery, making photos the "raw material" for creative expression. It also lets photographers do their magic in the light, without chemicals! And it makes it much easier to do the resizing, cropping, and basic color correction of production work. Beyond that, it provides a laboratory for synthesizing textures, patterns, and special effects that can be applied to photos, graphics, video, or film.

As our time spent using the program began to exceed 90% of the work day, as we watched others experiment, and as we saw the nearly miraculous transformations that appeared on-screen, the tools the program provided, the shortcuts for carrying out complicated changes, and the ways people combined the things Photoshop could do, the response we continuously heard was "Wow!" So when we needed a title for this book we were planning, it just sort of came naturally — *The Photoshop Wow! Book*. Photoshop 4 has only increased the "Wow!" factor, with the addition of numerous new features like Adjustment layers for applying color and tone corrections that you can edit later, and Actions for automating everything from routine production tasks to graphics special effects.

HOW TO USE THIS BOOK

For those who have enjoyed the earlier editions of this book, this one — though it's completely revised and expanded — works basically the same way. The text for the separate Macintosh and Windows editions of the book has been carefully tailored to fit the platform, with the appropriate keyboard shortcuts and tips. But, apart from Chapter 1, which requires platform-related illustrations, the screen captures in the rest of the book are a mixture of Windows and Mac. No matter which platform you work on most, you'll be able to see that Photoshop now looks virtually the same on both.

You'll find five kinds of information in the body of this book: (1) basic information about how Photoshop's tools and functions work, (2) short tips for making your work quicker and easier, (3) step-by-step techniques for particular kinds of projects, (4) galleries of work done by experienced Photoshop artists, and (5) illustrated lists of resources — including the Wow! Actions on the CD-ROM that comes with the book, as well as filters, images, and other products that can make Photoshop even more valuable and easier to use.

1

2 SELECT AND MOVE

In Photoshop 4 the selecting and moving functions have been separated. After making a selection, hold down the Ctrl key to turn any tool (except the pen) into the move tool so you can move the selected material.

3

Complex Crystal

H2O

The "Solarizing" Action on the Wow! CD-ROM automates the solarizing process, giving you several Curves settings to mix and match.

An "Action indicator" at the beginning of a technique section tells you that you can find similar effects, automated as a Photoshop Wow! Action, on the CD-ROM that comes with the book. In addition to the ones marked in the book, the disc holds many others.

1 You'll find the **Basics** sections at the beginning of each of the nine chapters of this book. They tell how Photoshop's functions work. *The Photoshop 4 Wow! Book* wasn't designed to be a substitute for the *Adobe Photoshop User Guide,* which has always been an excellent reference manual and has continued to improve with version 4 of the program. Instead we've gathered and condensed some of the most important of the basics, and in some cases explained a little further, with the idea that understanding how something works can make that knowledge easier to remember and to apply in new ways. Our goal is to provide an "under-the-hood" look at Photoshop that will help you maximize the program's performance and your own productivity with it.

Most of the chapter introductions are short, with most of the meat of the chapter in the techniques sections that follow. The exceptions are Chapters 1 and 2. Since these two introductions cover the fundamentals of using Photoshop 4 — setting up your system for efficiency, understanding how Photoshop deals with color, getting the hang of scanning and resolution, and choosing the best ways to make, use, and store selections — it's a good idea to read these two sections before you start in on the techniques. They aren't "required reading," mind you, but if you don't read them to begin with, you may want to turn back to them later to pick up some basic underpinnings to anchor the techniques presented in the rest of the book.

2 To collect the kind of hands-on information that can make you instantly more efficient, flip through the book and scan the **Tips**. You can easily identify them by the gray title bar on top. The tips are a kind of hypertext — linked bits of information that we've positioned alongside the basics and techniques wherever we thought they'd be most helpful. But each one also stands on its own, and you can pick up a lot of useful information quickly by reading them.

3 Each **Technique**, presented in 1 to 4 pages, is designed to give you enough step-by-step information so you can carry it out in Photoshop. Our goal was to provide enough written and pictorial instructions so you wouldn't have to hunt through the *Adobe Photoshop User Guide* to follow the steps. But to spare you a lot of repetition, we've assumed you know the basic Mac or Windows interface — how to open and save files, for instance — and we've focused on specific techniques in some cases, rather than explaining every detail of every method used in a particular project. Some of the techniques are simple and introductory; others are more advanced and challenging. If something isn't clear to you, go back to review Chapters 1 and 2.

Some techniques are presented with artwork created specifically for the demonstration. Other techniques are descriptions of the methods artists used to create particular illustrations or parts of illustrations. Some of the examples shown in the book were done with earlier versions than 4.0. In those cases we've updated the techniques so they're current.

Photoshop 4 works virtually identi-
cally on Macintosh, Power Mac,
and Windows machines. So if
you're running Photoshop 4 on a
Macintosh computer, you can use
the techniques described in this book
by substituting the **Command** key for
the Ctrl key, and the **Option** key for
the Alt keyin almost all cases. Where
the instructions call for pressing the
right mouse button, hold down the
Mac's **Control** key instead.

The step-by-step techniques consist of numbered, illustrated
instructions. The first step of each technique tells, briefly, how to get
to the starting point for the project. If you need to know more about
some process described in step 1, check the index at the back of the
book for references to other sections.

The techniques sections are more like recipes than like micro-
wave dinners — you supply your own "fresh ingredients," follow the
directions, and "season to taste." When you want the equivalent of
a microwavable meal, turn to the **Wow! Actions** on the CD-ROM
in the pocket at the back of the book. After you've enjoyed a no-
fuss-no-muss Action effect, you can dissect the Action to learn about
that particular technique and about making Actions in general.

As you work with Photoshop 4, you'll notice that there seem to
be at least a dozen ways to do everything — you can choose from a
menu, use a keyboard shortcut, or click in the new customizable
Actions palette; you can cut and paste, or drag and drop; you can
montage images with layer masks or load selections from alpha
channels and then cut and paste; you can make color adjustments
directly or add Adjustment layers to do it. Because of the variety of
possibilities, you'll find varied approaches used in the techniques
sections, so you'll get a broad exposure to the different ways Photoshop can work. But, in general, the methods presented are the ones
that seem to be the most efficient and effective — approaches that
will save you time and produce high-quality results.

4 The images in the **Galleries** are for inspiration, and their captions
include a lot of useful information about how the artwork was produced. Many of the methods mentioned in the Galleries are described more fully elsewhere in the book. Again, check the index if
you need help finding a particular technique.

5 Throughout the book, and especially in Chapter 5, "Using Filters,"
and in the Appendixes at the back, is information you can use to
locate the kinds of **Resources** Photoshop users need to know about,
such as stock photo images, plug-in filters, and "how-to" references.
And at the very back, after the index, is the **Actions Index,** a "catalog" of some of the effects you can produce with the Wow! Actions.

Experiment! The aim of this book is to get you started using the
tools if you're new at it, and to give you some new insight and ideas
if you're an old hand. As you read the book and try out the tips,
techniques and Actions, we hope you'll use them as a jumping off
place for your own fearless experimentation.

And don't miss the Wow! CD-ROM — in addition to the
Actions, it's filled with images and plug-ins, from leading filter and
photo stock resources, as well as demo versions of programs that
complement Photoshop.

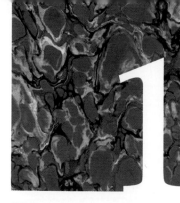

PHOTOSHOP BASICS

A view box in Photoshop 4's Navigator palette lets you see exactly how the view in your working window relates to the entire image. Drag the box to scroll around the image, or move the slider to zoom in or out.

Adjustment layers let you modify the color of a layer below without actually changing the image itself.

IF YOU'RE NEW TO PHOTOSHOP, this chapter is designed to give you some general pointers on using the program more easily and efficiently. But it won't replace the *Adobe Photoshop User Guide* or the *Tutorial* as a comprehensive source of basic information. If you're experienced with earlier versions of the program, this chapter will help bring you up to date on some of the changes in Photoshop 4.

WHAT'S NEW?

Here's a quick look at some of the things that are new or different in Photoshop 4 and where in this book you can find out more about them. One of the big improvements you'll notice is that Photoshop **works faster on bigger documents**, making **better use of your computer's RAM**.

In addition, Photoshop now has a **Navigator palette** that makes scrolling and zooming easier, quicker, and more precise. (See "Changing Your View" later in the chapter.) And a system of viewable but nonprinting **Grid and Guides**, as well as the new **Position** function in the **Layer**, **Transform**, **Numeric** command, let you control placement of selected parts of images precisely. The Grid and Guide colors and the Grid spacing are set up by choosing File, Preferences, Guides & Grid, and Guides are dragged onto the image from the rulers, which can be displayed by pressing Ctrl-R. Grid and Guides as they relate to selections and paths are described in Chapter 2, and their use with painting tools is described in Chapter 6.

You'll also find new tools for building yourself a "safety net," so you effectively have more "Undo" options. **Adjustment layers**, which represent one more step toward multiple Undo's in Photoshop, fit in among Photoshop's image layers. But instead of image pixels they store color-adjustment

continued on page 6

LOCKED OR UNLOCKED?

To keep Guides from being jarred out of place accidentally, you can lock them (choose View, Lock Guides). But with Guides locked, they won't be repositioned to match if the image is resized. So you'll have to unlock them (choose View, Lock Guides again) before resizing.

Guides provide a way to visually or automatically align elements in an image. If you lock them, be sure to unlock before resizing the image.

Actions can be quite elaborate. This one turns a simple white-on-black graphic (top) into a beveled 3D object with a brushed chrome surface.

instructions and a mask through which these instructions are applied to layers below them in the stack.

Another improvement that gives you the flexibility to back up a few steps, especially in making montages, is **"Big Data"**: You can now leave parts of layers sticking out beyond the boundaries of your image — like the lettuce in a tuna sandwich — without having the outlying pixels "bitten off" when you make changes to the file. You can even save and close the file, and when you open it the image material will still be there in case you want to move the layer again. There's more about Adjustment layers, Big Data, and related improvements in the "Layers, Layer Masks, and Adjustment Layers" section of Chapter 2, and you'll see them applied in techniques throughout the book.

The **Actions palette** replaces the Commands palette and also makes it easier to "automate" color correction and production tasks — everything from correcting for a scanner-introduced color cast that affects every image you scan, to applying a special effect to graphics, to preparing images for the World Wide Web. You can set up buttons to make single menu choices as you could before in the Commands palette, but you can also string together a series of commands, running the whole series with a single button. The "Automating with Actions" section at the end of this chapter tells how to use the Actions palette with single images or batches of files, and the Wow! CD-ROM that comes with this book provides "Actions" versions of many of the techniques presented in the book, as well as other effects.

The **Free Transform** command in the Layer menu reduces the wear and tear on a file when you apply a series of transformation operations, like those necessary to skew and foreshorten a manufactured shadow and align it with the base of the object that casts it. Instead of carrying out these transformations one by one with potential image degradation at every step, Free Transform lets you perform Scale, Rotate, Skew, Distort, and Perspective manipulations — in any combination you want — until

RELATIVE TO WHAT?

By default the numbers entered in the Position boxes in the Numeric Transform dialog box are distances measured from the current location of the element you're transforming. But if you deselect the Relative box, the element will be moved relative to the 0,0 point of the image, which is always at the upper left corner, regardless of where the 0,0 point for the Rulers is set.

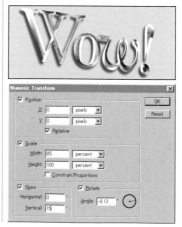

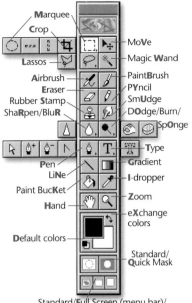

Marquee
Crop
Lassos
Airbrush
Eraser
Rubber Stamp
ShaRpen/BluR

MoVe
Magic Wand
PaintBrush
PYncil
SmUdge
DOdge/Burn/
SpOnge

Type
Pen
LiNe
Paint BucKet
Hand

Gradient
I-dropper
Zoom
eXchange
colors

Default colors

Standard/
Quick Mask

Standard/Full Screen (menu bar)/
Full Screen (no menu bar)

*Single-key commands (shown here in red)
activate tools and toggle between tools that
occupy the same space in the palette. The
key command is often the first letter of the
tool's name, or if that letter is already taken,
another important letter within the word.
(The pencil tool got stuck with "Y.")*

the selected area is oriented exactly as you want it. You can preview the entire process, watching every step, but the image data isn't actually changed until you've completed all the transformation operations and hit the Enter key (or double-clicked inside the selection). Since the image is redrawn only once, deterioration is minimized. The **Numeric Transform** dialog box (made available by choosing Layer, Transform, Numeric) also gives access to several transformations at once (Scale, Skew, and Rotate), but instead of having an interactive preview like Free Transform, it accepts numbers only.

Never far behind what digital artists wanted to do next, Photoshop has expanded its ability to prepare graphics for the **World Wide Web,** with new file formats for saving graphics that store smaller and download quicker. The new formats are described briefly in the "File Formats" section of this chapter, and Chapter 9, "3D, Multimedia and the Web," provides tips and techniques for creating Web graphics.

In addition to the obvious improvements in Photoshop 4, you'll notice some places where the new version hasn't really added new functions but has moved the old ones to new places or changed the keyboard shortcuts. For instance, the **toolbox** has been rearranged and some of the single-key access commands for the tools have changed. The selection tools (marquees, lasso, magic wand, and move tool) are grouped at the top, the viewing tools (zoom and hand) are at the bottom, and the painting and editing tools are in between. The multi-tasking tools (the ones with little triangles in the lower right corner of the icon), now have **pop-out palettes** you can choose from.

Tool variations have been moved to pop-outs from a separate palette (as in the case of the path tools, for instance) or from the tool Options palettes (as in the case of the single-row and single-column marquee tools). Note that the **cropping tool** has been closeted away on the palette that pops out from the marquee tool.

One of the biggest changes in the tools themselves is that **selecting has become more clearly distinguished from moving.** The "Moving Selections" section of Chapter 2 points out the changes in the way selection tools and the move tool work. The functions of the lasso and type tool have been split into two tools (using the **lasso and polygon lasso** is covered in "Selecting by Shape" in Chapter 2; techniques for using the standard **type tool** and the **type selection tool** are described in "The Type Tools," also in Chapter 2. The **gradient tool** has taken a big jump in versatility, and it now provides many more options for customizing color blends, as described in "The Gradient Tool" in Chapter 6.

The **single-letter keyboard shortcuts** for selecting tools from the palette are largely the same as they have been, so you can type the first letter (or another important letter) of the tool's name

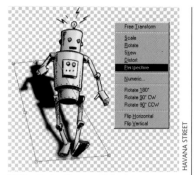

With a tool active or a dialog box open, press the right mouse button to pop out a context-sensitive menu. The menu for the Free Transform command makes all the transformation options available instantly.

USING FILE INFO

Choosing File, File Info opens a dialog box where you can permanently store information in the form of text. The scrollable Caption field can hold a large text block. When you save the file, Photoshop will warn you if the File Info can't be preserved in the format you've chosen.

to switch to that tool or to toggle to another tool on the same pop-out. Changes include **"P" for pen**, which has moved back into the toolbox; **"T" for type**; and **"Y" for pencil**.

The **menus** have also changed a bit. A new one called **Layer** has been added, for example, and **Mode** has become a submenu under Image. In addition to the standard menus at the top of the Photoshop window and the pop-out menus available from the various palettes, there are now **context-sensitive menus** of choices you might like to have available when using a particular tool or command — choices that may let you avoid a mouse-trip to the tool's Options palette or to the program's menu bar. To pop out a context-sensitive menu for the current tool or command, click the right mouse button.

Many keyboard shortcuts that used to include the Ctrl key — for subtracting from a selection, for example, or stepping through the layers of a file — now use the **Alt key** instead. If you've become a whiz at keyboard shortcuts in earlier versions of the program, you may notice that some of the new key commands actually make it a little harder for your fingers to do the walking. But the shortcuts are now more consistent among Adobe's graphics programs — for instance, Photoshop, Illustrator, and PageMaker. And the freed-up **Ctrl key** can now be used to **turn any tool (except the pen) into the move tool,** which is very handy once you get used to it.

CPU, RAM, AND ACCELERATION

Photoshop files tend to be large — a lot of information has to be stored to record the color of each of the thousands or millions of pixels that make up an image. So it can take quite a bit of computer processing just to open a file (which brings that information into the computer's memory, or RAM) or to apply a special effect (which can involve complicated calculations that change the color of every pixel in the image). Photoshop needs a lot of RAM to hold an image while it works on it. Although you can do good Photoshop work on a smaller, slower, less powerful computer system, the program works best if you have a fast computer, a great deal of RAM, a monitor displaying full 24-bit photorealistic color, and a very large, fast hard disk with plenty of free space.

The **minimum system required** for running Photoshop 4 under Windows 95 or Windows 3.1 is an i486 or faster PC running Microsoft Windows 3.1 and DOS 5.0 or higher, or Windows 95 or Windows NT 3.5.1 or later. The computer must have at least 16 MB of RAM available for Photoshop. (The **minimum system recommended** by Adobe for decent Photoshop performance, though, is a Pentium or Pentium Pro processor running Windows 95 or Windows NT 3.5 or later and at least 32 MB of available RAM.)

A CD-ROM drive is also required, and also a hard disk drive with at least 25 MB of free space. Adobe recommends a 24-bit color

To optimize space on your hard disks, run the Scan Disk program and then run Disk Defragmenter. Both can be found by choosing Start, Programs, Accessories, System Tools. Disk Defragmenter collects all the small pieces of storage space that result when a disk is used and reused over time. The goal is to join all the free disk space into a single large block. That way, when you store a file, it can stay together instead of being broken into smaller parts that have to be sought out separately when Photoshop works on the file.

Before defragmenting, the empty space (indicated by white, above) is in many small blocks. Afterwards, the empty space is as contiguous as possible.

monitor setup (millions of colors), although 16-bit color (thousands of colors) may be adequate for much color work.

Accelerator products designed specifically to support some of Photoshop's calculation-intensive functions, such as running filters or resizing images, are available. Look for the Adobe-Charged logo to be sure they will significantly improve Photoshop's performance.

VIRTUAL MEMORY

If Photoshop doesn't have enough room to handle a file entirely in RAM, it can use hard disk space for memory — that's *virtual memory*, or in Photoshop parlance *scratch disk*. In that case, two factors become important: first, the amount of empty hard disk space (you'll want at least as much space as you have RAM and at least three to five times the size of any file you work on) and second, the transfer rate of the disk drive (the speed at which data can be read off a disk).

WORKING SMART

Once your system is set up with lots of RAM and a fast hard disk drive, here are some other things you can do to reduce the time you spend in "hourglass land" as you work on high-resolution full-color images:

Opening several files together. You can open several files at once from the desktop by Shift-clicking their icons or names to select them all and then dragging them onto the Photoshop icon or a Photoshop shortcut icon. The files need not be Photoshop files to be opened in this way, as long as they are a format Photoshop can open.

Starting out in low resolution. For some images you can do your planning and "sketching" in a lower-resolution file than you will ultimately need for output. (See "Resolution, Pixel Depth, and File Size" and "Setting Up a Scan"

For large graphics files stored on a relatively unfragmented hard disk, the disk's *access time* (how fast it can find and begin to read a file) is generally less important than its *transfer rate* (how fast it reads a file once it's found). Some hard disks are composed of two drives linked in a dual array to double the speed of data transfer — it's kind of like using two fire hoses instead of one to put out a fire.

A Photoshop "shortcut" icon can sit out on the desktop so it's easy to open the program by double-clicking it or by dragging image file icons onto it. Meanwhile, the real Photoshop stays in its appropriate location. You can make a shortcut this way: Locate the **Photoshp.exe** icon (you can use the Find command from the Start menu if you need help) and drag it out onto the desktop.

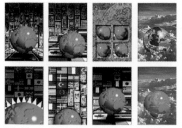

Working at low resolution saves time and disk space. Several designs for the Healthy Traveler *book cover were worked out at 72 dpi before one was chosen for development at high resolution.*

later in the chapter for a discussion of how to determine the resolution you need.) Working at low resolution will reduce processing time for changes you make to the image. Although you'll have to make the changes again on the higher-res file, some of the changes you make at the lower resolution can be saved as Adjustment layers and then dragged and dropped from the Layers palette of the low-resolution image into the bigger file. For instance, settings for four of the most useful functions of the Image, Adjust submenu — Levels, Curves, Hue/Saturation, and Color Balance can be applied through an Adjustment layer, as can Brightness/Contrast, Selective Color, Invert, Threshold, and Posterize. (If a mask is constructed in an Adjustment layer, however, the layer might not be able to be successfully dragged and dropped to the higher-resolution file because it will be too small. However, if it's a soft-edged mask, you may be able to resize the planning file to a larger

Things that you're likely to do again and again, like correcting a color cast introduced by a scanner or converting files to GIF or JPEG for use on the World Wide Web are great candidates for Actions. In Button mode the Actions palette looks like the Commands palette of Photoshop 3.

ADDING TO THE START MENU

To list Photoshop in the top level of the Start menu in Windows 95, drag its program icon (or a shortcut icon; see "Making a Shortcut" on page 9) onto the Start button. Now when you press the Start button, the Photoshop (or Photoshop shortcut) icon will appear in the list at the top of the pop-up menu.

size and then drag and drop the Adjustment layer.) Settings for some other Image, Adjust commands, such as Variations and Replace Color, which can't be applied as Adjustment layers, can be saved and loaded again later, using the Save and Load buttons in their dialog boxes.

Working with Adjustment layers. Storing color adjustment information in Adjustment layers (as described in Chapter 3) until you've finalized your image allows you to readjust without having to start over and without degrading the original image by reworking it. Adjustment layers also let you save settings that you can't normally save, such as Color Balance, because they don't have Save buttons in their dialog boxes.

Using Free Transform. When you want to perform some combination of scale, rotate, skew, distort, or perspective, use the Layer, Free Transform command (**Ctrl-T**) rather than making the individual transformations with the Layer, Transform command. This makes the transformation process much more interactive, since you can work back and forth between the different transformations until you get exactly what you want, and it keeps the image from being degraded by each separate transformation (for more about Free Transform, see page 6).

Recording your actions. Any time you make changes to an image that you think you might someday want to make to other files, record the process using the **Actions palette** (see "Automating with Actions" later in this chapter). The process of recording doesn't take extra time or RAM, and it may very well produce a useful Action. You may have to go back and rerecord some steps in slightly different ways in order to make the Action work smoothly, since not everything you can do in Photoshop 4 can be recorded in an Action. But you'll have a framework for building a useful "macro."

Blending a "processed" image with the original. Use the new **Fade** command, which is found in the Filter menu but which also applies to the Image, Adjust commands and to painting in version 4.0.1 and later, to interactively adjust the effects of the filters, color adjustments, and paint you apply. When you choose Filter, Fade and then move the Fade dialog box's Opacity slider or change its blending mode, it's as though the effect had been applied to a copy of the image that was then stacked on top of the original; changing Opacity or blending mode produces the same result as it would in that top layer. But the Fade command is available only immediately after you apply an effect. So if you can afford the memory overhead, you may want to apply your effect to a copy in a separate layer, and then you'll be able to "fade" with the Opacity slider or change the blending mode long after you applied the effect. An Adjustment layer is a still better solution for those effects that can be applied that way; again, the Adjustment layer's Opacity slider lets you "fade" the effect anytime you want to.

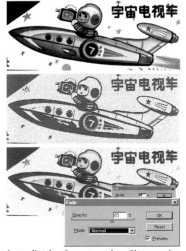

Immediately after you apply a filter or color adjustment (or painting strokes in version 4.0.1 or later), the Filter, Fade command lets you reduce the effect (with the Opacity slider) and change the blending mode, as if the effect had been applied to a copy of the image in a layer of its own. Here we applied the Notepaper filter (Filter, Artistic, Notepaper; center) and then faded it to 65% Opacity (bottom).

Building a file in stages. If you plan to modify and combine images, do the modifications on the separate, smaller parts first, and then combine them into a larger file. Instead of having a separate layer for every piece of the image, consider building an illustration in "modules": Build one component of several layers, then copy those layers into a single layer; create other components the same way; then layer the merged copies to make the final image. (Chapters 2 and 4 tell more about copying and merging layers.)

Saving selections as you work. If you're making a complex selection, save it periodically in an alpha channel, a layer mask, or an Adjustment layer. (Making selections and using alpha channels and layer masks are discussed in Chapter 2; Adjustment layers are

When you choose File, New, you can base the new file size on any document that's open in Photoshop: Instead of filling in the dimensions called for in the New File dialog box, pull down the Window menu and choose from the files listed at the bottom to open a new file with the same dimensions, resolution, and color mode as the one you chose. This trick also works with the Canvas Size dialog box.

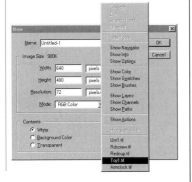

covered in Chapter 3.) With a backup version of the selection saved, if you accidentally drop the selection, you won't have to start over from the beginning. Having the selection stored in a channel also lets you use the painting and editing tools to clean up the selection boundaries, as described in Chapter 2. Be sure to save the selection when it's finally finished, so you can reselect exactly the same area if you need to later.

If you're using the pen tool to create a selection outline, save the selection as a path rather than as an alpha channel. It takes much less disk space this way.

"Emptying" the clipboard and other caches. If you cut or copy something to the clipboard or use the Take Snapshot or

The palettes for Layers, Channels, Info, Tool Options/Brushes, and colors can be stored on-screen, ready to use, without taking up much space. Click the small box in the upper right corner of each palette to toggle between its collapsed version with only its tab showing and its expanded, functional version. (Some palettes have a two-stage collapse/expand function, and you have to Alt-click to collapse the palette all the way down to its tab alone.) When you click to expand a palette, it pops *into* the window. So even if you store the collapsed palettes at the very bottom of the screen, they'll be fully visible when they expand. Shift-click on a palette's title bar to snap it to the nearest edge of the screen; or Shift-drag to move it around the edge of the screen. (For an uncluttered view with all palettes available, consider an inexpensive second monitor for palettes alone.)

IMAGES: PLANET ART

Here's one way to set up a 1024 x 768-pixel screen for working efficiently in Photoshop, with most of the palettes available. The Actions palette is stretched along the edge of the screen so its buttons are always available. The Channels and Layers palettes are separated so both can be open at the same time; the Brushes palette is nested with the Tool Options palette so it's available for use with any tool, and Swatches is the third palette in this nest; the Info palette is present, nested with the Navigator palette, which shows the whole image and makes it easy to scroll with the close-up view in the main window. The Document Size/ Scratch Size window can show information about memory, file size, and image resolution.

Although it's powerful for generating macros, the Actions palette in Photoshop 4 isn't as compact or easy to edit as its predecessor the Commands palette in Photoshop 3. So you might want to rely on the default function key assignments that come with the program. There's a complete list of keyboard shortcuts on the Adobe Photoshop Quick Reference Card that comes with the program, but here are some especially useful toggles for showing palettes or hiding them to free up some screen real estate:

Brushes palette	F5
Color palette	F6
Layers palette	F7
Info palette	F8
Actions palette	F9

If a palette doesn't appear on the first press of the function key, try again. It may have been obscured behind another palette, so the first press turned it off, and the second will bring it back and place it in front of the others.

To **hide the currently open palettes** or to bring them back into view, press **Tab**.

To **hide all the open palettes** *except the toolbox* or to bring them back, press **Shift-Tab**.

Define Pattern command, the stored material is retained in RAM even after you've pasted a copy in place, or used the Snapshot or Pattern. In addition, Photoshop always remembers what the image was like before your last change, in case you decide to use Edit, Undo (Ctrl-Z). Since some of Photoshop's commands can be carried out only in RAM (not in virtual memory), it's good strategy to release the RAM from a large clipboard selection, a Snapshot, a Pattern, or a step you know you won't need to Undo. Photoshop 4's new Purge command makes it really easy. Just choose **Edit, Purge**; any choices that aren't grayed out have something stored and are available to be purged. Consider making the **Edit, Purge All** command into an Action so you can release RAM quickly with one click of an on-screen button or by pressing a single keyboard shortcut (see "Automating with Actions" later in this chapter).

Cleaning up virtual memory. If Photoshop tells you it can't complete an operation because there isn't enough space in virtual memory, simply closing another file that's open on-screen may not release all the space you need. After you close extra files, **save a document in Photoshop format** to get the hard disk to clean up its virtual memory allocation. If that doesn't do the trick, you can **Quit** the program and start up again. Or check the Trash for Photoshop temporary files, and **empty the Trash** to delete them.

Closing other applications. As you work, if you find that you need more RAM, close any other programs you've opened. Even if you aren't doing anything with them, open applications reserve their assigned amount of RAM, which may cut down on the amount available to Photoshop.

Saving "thumbnail" files. When you've finished a multi-layered image, and you've flattened a copy and printed it, you may not want to store the original in its layered, memory-hog form. Still, you'd like to be able to go

continued on page 15

If RAM is limited, there are several ways you can copy and paste a selection, a layer, a channel, or an entire image without using the clipboard, which requires RAM.

• **To copy and paste a selection in the same file,** hold down the Alt key and drag the selection with the move tool; then click the New Layer icon at the bottom of the Layers palette. Or float a copy as a new layer (Ctrl-J).

• **To duplicate the content of a layer,** drag its name or thumbnail to the New Layer icon. Or use Duplicate Layer from the Layer menu.

• **To copy and paste a selected area or a layer from one file to another,** drag and drop with the move tool from one document to the other. Or use the Layer, Duplicate Layer command.

• **To copy a channel from one image to another,** drag the channel from the Channels palette into the other image.

• **To duplicate an entire image into a new file,** choose Image, Duplicate.

To preserve access to all the blending mode, opacity, Adjustment layer, and masking information that you used to build a montage, use the Image Size command to store a very small copy of the file before you flatten the original for printing. Sized for a 6-inch-wide postcard at 225 dpi (a total of 1350 pixels wide, top), this multilayered file would occupy 13.2 MB of storage space. But a small "thumbnail" version (center), reduced to 100 pixels wide, takes only 158K and retains all the information you need to recall how the montage was put together.

LITTLE BOXES

The small box in the lower left corner of the Photoshop window holds a lot of information:

• **How big is the file?** In Document Sizes mode the box shows the current open size of the file with all its layers and channels (the number to the right of the slash) and the size it would be if it was flattened to one layer with all alpha channels removed (to the left of the slash) — that is, the amount of data that will be sent to the printer or other output device.

• **Is the scratch disk being used?** In Scratch Sizes mode the box shows how much RAM is available for Photoshop to use (right) and how much memory is currently tied up by all open Photoshop files, the clipboard, Snapshot, and so on (left). If the left-hand figure exceeds the right-hand figure, it means Photoshop is using virtual memory to carry out its functions.

• **Would more RAM help?** You can watch the Efficiency indicator to see how much Photoshop is using RAM alone, rather than swapping data with the scratch disk. A value near 100% means the scratch disk isn't being used much, so adding more RAM probably wouldn't improve performance. A value less than about 75% means that assigning more RAM would probably help.

• **How long did that take?** In Timing mode, the box tells how long the last operation took. So you can walk away from your computer leaving it to filter a large file, and find out when you return how long it took, so you'll know for future filtering.

• **How will it print?** Pressing on the numbers themselves opens a box that shows the size of the image relative to the page size currently selected in File, Page Setup.

• **How is it organized?** Holding down the Alt key while pressing the numbers shows the dimensions (in pixels and in the current unit of measure), the resolution (in pixels per inch), the color mode, and the number of channels in the image file.

Holding down the Ctrl key while pressing the numbers shows the number and size of the rectangular "tiles" that make up the image. The tiles are the blocks of information Photoshop uses to store the image. (In a large file you can see them appear one by one as the screen is redrawn when you work on a file.) The amount of additional memory required by each layer depends on how many of these tiles its pixels occupy. For instance, in a nine-tile file, a layer with a small circle of pixels at the center of each tile would require more memory than a layer with all the small circles aggregated in one tile.

back someday and see how you accomplished the look you got in the final printed piece — how the elements were layered and what blending modes, Opacity settings, layer options, layer masks, alpha channels, Adjustment layers, and clipping groups you used — in case you want to get a similar effect in another image later. To save all this information, use Image, Image Size to reduce a copy of the layered file to a small, low-res version. You could never use it for print, but it will store the layer information in much less space.

CHANGING YOUR VIEW

When Photoshop 4 opens a file, it stores information for a number of standard views, such as 33.33%, 50%, 66.67%, 100%, and 200%, up to 1600%. The result is that zooming in and out and scrolling are much smoother operations than before — you can zoom to those views or scroll around in them very quickly, since the program has already calculated all the screen pixels it needs in order to change the display. In addition, Photoshop's new Navigator palette makes it easier to move different parts of the image into the work window and to change magnification.

What Percentages Mean

Changing the percentage (displayed in the file's title bar and the lower left corner of the Navigator palette) doesn't change the pixels in the image file — it just changes your on-screen view of them.

- When you view a Photoshop image at **100%**, it doesn't mean you're viewing it at the dimensions it will print. It means that every pixel in the image file is represented by 1 pixel on-screen.

- **Higher percentages** mean that more than 1 screen pixel is being used to represent 1 pixel of the image file. For instance, 200% means that each pixel in the file is being shown as a 2 x 2-pixel square on-screen; at 300% it's a 3 x 3-pixel square, and so on.

- **Lower percentages** mean just the opposite: 1 on-screen

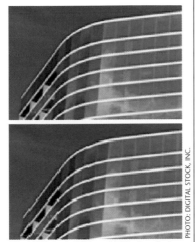

The 100% (top), 50%, and 25% views look much smoother on-screen than other settings, such as the 104% view (bottom).

OPENING THE NAVIGATOR

Photoshop 4.0 doesn't have a built-in keyboard shortcut for displaying the Navigator palette. But if you leave it nested with the Info palette, you can use the default Info palette toggle — the F8 key — to bring the Navigator palette to the screen so you can activate it by clicking its top tab.

Or you can assign a function-key toggle to show and hide the Navigator palette itself: Choose Window, Show Actions and then choose New Action from the Actions palette's pop-out menu, assign a function key (and a color, if you like, for when the Actions are displayed in Button mode), name the Action, and click Record. Choose Insert Menu Item (also from the pop-out menu); choose Window, Show Navigator; and click OK. Finally, click the square stop button at the bottom of the Actions palette to stop recording and complete the Action.

Sometimes it can be helpful to see full-size "footprints" of the tools, so you can instantly visualize the brush size. To see cursors up to 300 pixels in diameter, choose File, Preferences, Display & Cursors and then choose Brush Size in the Painting Cursors section of the dialog box. The cursor grows or shrinks as you increase or decrease magnification, so it's always the right size relative to the image. (If it gets too big to be practical, it switches back to the standard tool icon; if it gets too small to show up, it becomes crosshairs.)

pixel represents more than 1 pixel in the image file. For instance, at 50% each pixel on-screen represents a 2 x 2 block of pixels in the image file; at 33.33% each on-screen pixel represents a 3 x 3-pixel block in the file, and so forth.

Zooming

As you work with Photoshop, you'll want to change your view fairly often:

- In close-up (zoomed-in) views you can work on fine detail.
- In a 100% view, the screen shows the details of your image most accurately, so it's the best resolution for precise viewing or image editing.
- A zoomed-out view makes the image small, so you can get it out of the way, for example, or get a full view of a large file.

Of course, you can choose one of the **Zoom functions** from the **View menu.** But you'll save time and mousing effort if you learn how to zoom with the Navigator palette or, better yet, with keyboard shortcuts, alone and with the zoom tool.

To zoom with the Navigator palette:

- Click the big (or small) **mountains icon** to zoom in (or out) to the next standard magnification.
- Move the **slider** at the bottom of the palette for intermediate magnifications. Move right to zoom in, left to zoom out.
- Hold down the **Ctrl key and drag** diagonally in the Navigator window to view the dragged-over area at the **largest size that will fit in your working window.**
- Enter a **specific magnification** percentage in the box at the lower left corner of the palette and press Enter.
- Hold down the **Ctrl key and click** in the Navigator window to zoom to the **maximum magnification** (1600%).

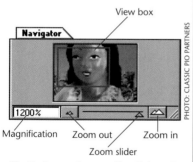

PHOTO: CLASSIC PIO PARTNERS

The Navigator palette provides all the tools you need for managing your view of an image.

To zoom from the keyboard:

- **Ctrl-+** (really Ctrl-= because you don't need the Shift key, but Ctrl-+ is an easier way to remember it) **zooms in, without resizing the window**.
- **Ctrl-Alt-+** zooms in and **enlarges the window at the same time.**
- **Ctrl-minus** (that's Ctrl-hyphen), **zooms out, without resizing the window.**
- **Ctrl-Alt-minus** zooms out and **resizes the window as well.**
- **Ctrl-0** enlarges the image to **fit the available screen space.**
- **Ctrl-Alt-0** sizes the view to **100%.**

Palette Options, from the Navigator palette's pop-out menu, lets you change the color of the view box for good contrast with any picture.

• **Ctrl-spacebar** (held down) toggles the current tool to the **zoom-in** version of the zoom tool (see below), and **Alt-spacebar** toggles to the zoom-out version.

The toolbox offers several ways to zoom in or out:

With the zoom tool (the magnifier from the toolbox) you can pick the area you want to magnify. Whether the window is resized depends on whether Resize Window To Fit is chosen in the Zoom Tool Options palette.

• **Click to zoom in.** The new view will be centered on the clicked spot.

• **Alt-click to zoom out.**

• **Drag diagonally** to **enlarge the area** you drag over to fill the window.

• **Double-click** the tool in the toolbox to get the **100%** view, or click the **Actual Pixels button** in the Zoom Tool Options palette (opened by pressing Enter while the zoom tool is active).

With the hand tool, double-click the tool in the toolbox **to make the image as big as the available screen space.**

Navigating

Photoshop 4 offers vast improvements over the standard Mac scroll bars for getting around in an image. Use the interactive Navigator palette to see where in the image any move will take you. Or, to change your view without mousing, use keyboard controls.

To scroll with the Navigator palette:

• **Check the view box** to see where in the image you're working.

• **Drag the view box** to scroll from one place to another in the image.

To navigate with an extended keyboard:

• **Page Up** (or **Page Down**) moves your view **one screenful up** or **down**).

• **Shift-Page Up** (or **Shift-Page Down**) **nudges** your view **10 pixels up** or **down.** (Those are image pixels, not screen pixels.) **This can be helpful for scrolling with control.**

• **Home** shows the **upper left corner.**

• **End shows the lower right corner.**

To see your image in an uncluttered black window, press the "F" key twice to hide the menus and turn the background black, and press the Tab key once to hide the palettes.

You can change the "window filler" from the default gray to the Foreground color by Shift-clicking the gray with the paint bucket.

- **Spacebar** (held down) toggles the current tool to the **hand** tool.

From the toolbox, drag with the **hand** tool to **scroll** the image. Double-click to fit the image to the available screen space.

Other Viewing Options

Here are two other viewing possibilities that can be helpful for evaluating your image without desktop clutter or as it will appear on a particular background color:

- **To hide the clutter of the desktop and all open windows except the active one** and center the image at its current size on a black screen, click the right-hand window control at the bottom of the tool palette (or, starting with the default window setup press "F" twice). This automatically closes the menu bar. To close the palettes as well, press Tab (or to close all but the toolbox, press Shift-Tab). You can reopen the palettes by pressing Tab (or Shift-Tab) again.

- **To change the color of the normally gray apron** that surrounds the image if it doesn't fill the window, choose a Foreground color (click the Foreground square and choose from the Color Picker, or click on a color in the Color palette or Swatches palette), and then choose the paint bucket tool and Shift-click in the gray area. The change applies to all open windows until you change the color again.

RECOVERING

Officially, Photoshop 4 provides only one level of Undo — the familiar Macintosh **Ctrl-Z** affects only your last operation. However, the program provides several ways to work backwards if you need to. Here are some suggestions:

Use Adjustment layers. By applying the effects of the Image, Adjust menu through Adjustment layers, you can go back and change the settings, simply by double-clicking the layer's circular icon in the Layers palette to reopen the dialog box. And if you decide that a different type of adjustment would be better, you can drag the Adjustment layer to the trash can at the bottom of the Layers palette and add a new Adjustment layer in its place.

Record and play an Action. Besides letting you automate a multistep process so you can apply it to other files, recording an Action while you work can provide a way to go back and reapply the series of changes, modifying intermediate steps that would be unreachable with the Edit, Undo command. Double-clicking a step in the Actions palette (or choosing Record "..." Again from the palette's pop-out menu) opens up the step so you can change dialog box settings. Then run the edited Action on another copy of your original file. **Note:** Not all of Photoshop's many operations

In a dialog box like Color Balance, where there are a number of settings that can be adjusted, use Ctrl-Z to undo the last slider setting. You can also hold down the Alt key to change the Cancel button to a Reset button, restoring the default values for all sliders in the box.

Starting with a scanned photo (top), we added a Color Balance Adjustment layer to brighten the gold tones. A masked Hue/Saturation Adjustment layer changed the color of the walls and ceiling. These modifications were made without permanently changing the photo, which remained intact in the Background layer.

and settings are "actionable" (able to be recorded in an Action), so an Action may not include everything you need in order to backtrack and re-create an effect. For tips on how to work so that non-actionable operations such as drawing selection boundaries with the lasso or pen tool, or painting with a brush, are stored and available to be reused, see "Saving selections as you work" on page 12 and "Make a 'repairs' or 'painting' layer" on page 20.

Use "Undo" inside a dialog box or palette. When you're working inside a dialog box that has more than one entry box or slider, you can use **Ctrl-Z** (or Edit, Undo) to undo the last setting you changed. This also works for entry boxes — but not sliders — in tool palettes.

Reset a dialog box. In any dialog box that lets you enter at least one value and that has a Cancel button, holding down the **Alt** key while you click **Cancel** leaves the box open but resets all the settings to the state they were when you first opened the box.

Save intermediate versions. By using the **Duplicate** function, you can save several intermediate versions of a file under different file names. Choose Image, Duplicate to make a copy of the file in its current condition. The copy will become the active file, leaving the original file open on-screen as well, easily accessible (but also tying up RAM, of course). You can reduce the file size of the duplicate by choosing to merge the visible layers and discard the invisible ones. (Merging is covered in Chapter 2.)

In contrast to the Duplicate method, if you use File, **Save A Copy** (**Ctrl-Alt-S**), the duplicate file is stored (closed, not using any RAM). And you have several storage options: You can merge all the layers into one, save the file without its alpha channels, or save in a different file format.

Using the File, **Save As** command (**Ctrl-Shift-S**) and giving the file a new name is another way to save an intermediate version. With this method the original file is closed and stored in the form that it was before you last saved, and the Saved As (current) version remains open and active. Save As before you start to work on a scanned image, and then use Save As or Save A Copy often during the editing process. Then if you decide to change something that you did halfway through the development of the image, you can open one of the saved versions.

Revert to the last saved version. Choose File, **Revert** to keep the file open but eliminate all the changes you've made since you last saved it.

Restore part of the last saved version. Use the **magic eraser,** which is the eraser tool either with the Alt key held down or with Erase To Saved checked in the Eraser Options dialog box. Or

Holding down the Alt key makes the eraser operate in Revert mode (right), restoring the last saved version of the image.

To focus attention on a particular feature of an image, the file can be blurred (left) and then Edit, Fill, Saved can be used to restore the original sharp version to an area selected with a feathered lasso.

Rubber Stamp Options

| Normal ▼ | Opacity: | 100% |

Option: From Snapshot ▼

- Clone (aligned)
- Clone (non-aligned)
- Pattern (aligned)
- Pattern (non-aligned)
- ✓ From Snapshot
- From Saved
- Impressionist

Storing a current image or selection in a Snapshot buffer by choosing Edit, Take Snapshot makes it possible to restore it later with the rubber stamp tool.

PHOTO: DIGITAL STOCK, INC.; JOSHUA ETS-HOKIN

The image was copied as a new layer before the Impressionist rubber stamp and the Lighting Effects filter were applied experimentally.

use the **rubber stamp tool in From Saved mode.** Both the rubber stamp method and the magic eraser give hand-held control of the restoration process. The rubber stamp, however, has the added advantage of being able to change the painting mode if you want to. Or make a selection of the area you want to restore; choose **Edit, Fill,** and choose **Saved** from the Contents list in the Fill dialog box. With any of these methods, the changes are made to the active layer only; you can control which channels of the active layer are affected — turn them on or off in the Channels palette (see Chapter 2 for more about activating layers and channels).

Save intermediate steps. The **Snapshot** is a buffer, or storage space, in which you can store one intermediate stage of an image — either the entire image or a selected part of it. Choose Edit, Take Snapshot to store the active layer or current selection in the buffer. Or choose Edit, Take Merged Snapshot to store the entire image or a selection from it, as if the image were flattened. (You can make the Snapshot selection with any selection tool; the buffer will save a rectangular area that includes your entire selection.) Then you can restore the selected area later by using the rubber stamp tool in From Snapshot mode or the Edit, Fill command with Snapshot selected from the Contents list. Keep in mind that, like the clipboard, the Snapshot ties up RAM.

Duplicate a layer. If you want to make changes to a particular layer but you want an "escape hatch" to get back to the previous version, copy the layer and work on the copy. You can do this by dragging the layer name in the Layers palette to the New Layer icon at the bottom of the palette.

Make a "repairs" or "painting" layer. If you're using the sharpen/blur, smudge, or rubber stamp to make repairs to an image, you can add the repairs to a separate, transparent top layer, making sure that Sample Merged is selected in the tool's Options palette so that the sharpening, blurring, smudging, or stamping strokes use a composite of all layers of the image to make the repairs.

With a repairs layer the new work doesn't actually get mixed into the image. So if you want to undo part of your repair work, you can select that part (with the lasso, for instance) and remove it from the layer, leaving intact the rest of the repairs, as well as the layers beneath.

Besides repairs, you can use a separate layer for adding brush strokes to a painting without messing up the work you've already done. When you're sure you like the new work, you can merge it with the layer below (Ctrl-E), then add another new layer and experiment with more brush strokes.

Since tool strokes are a kind of Photoshop operation that isn't captured when an Action is recorded, keeping repairs or new painting on

After this image was rotated to level the horizon, a "repairs" layer was added and the rubber stamp tool was used in Clone (Aligned) mode to fill in the corners and to add plants to the beach. Turning on Sample Merged made it possible to keep the top layer active for repair work while sampling from the layer below.

To turn a flattened copy of the repaired photo into a painting, a transparent layer was added and the smudge tool was applied with Sample Merged turned on to pick up paint from the layer below.

separate layers gives you the flexibility of reworking an image by recording your work as an Action and then replaying it on a new copy of the original image, bringing in the non-actionable repairs or painting by dragging and dropping layers from your current file.

AUTOMATING WITH ACTIONS

New in Photoshop 4, the Actions palette replaces the Commands palette. But it not only allows you to make single-click buttons as the Commands palette did; it also offers a way to record a series of Photoshop operations and play them back in order, on a single file or a whole folderful. Actions provide a great way to record processes that you'll want to carry out again and again, even on batches of files (see "Correcting a Batch of Scans" on page 47 for an example of such an Action).

Knowing What's "Actionable"

To someone who isn't an Adobe engineer, the logic of which Photoshop commands can be recorded as part of an Action isn't always apparent. But this section lists some things that, at least with the first update of Photoshop 4 (version 4.0.1), you can and cannot automate with Actions. (Adobe is still developing the Actions function; future updates of Photoshop will be able to record more commands than you can record now, as well as capture settings that can't currently be fully automated as part of an Action.)

"Actionable" commands tend to be **items that can be chosen from the main menu or its submenus.** Handwork done with tools, such as making brush strokes or drawing selection borders, can't be included. And some commands, such as changing Preferences or Color Settings, showing a CMYK Preview or Gamut Warning, zooming your view, turning Snap To Guides on or off, or opening or closing a tool's Options palette, won't record directly as part of a multistep Action. Instead they have to be recorded with the Insert Menu Item command as described in "The Recording Process" on page 23.

- **Painting, drawing, and editing:** Although you can't record strokes made with the painting tools (paintbrush, pencil, airbrush, paint bucket, line, gradient, or eraser) or editing tools (blur/sharpen or dodge/burn/sponge), you can still use the Edit, Stroke and Edit, Fill commands to automate standard stroke and fill tasks. For example, you can stroke a selection with the Foreground color or fill it with Foreground, Background, black, white, 50% gray, the last-saved version of the image, a Snapshot (an intermediate version of the image stored with Edit, Take Snapshot or Take Merged Snapshot), or a stored pattern.

- **Selecting:** You can't draw selection boundaries with the marquee, lasso, magic wand, or pen tool. But you can make selections by color with Select, Color Range. And you can load a

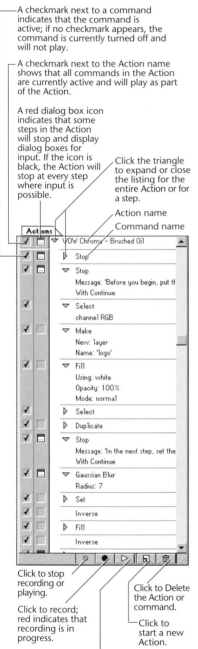

A checkmark next to a command indicates that the command is active; if no checkmark appears, the command is currently turned off and will not play.

A checkmark next to the Action name shows that all commands in the Action are currently active and will play as part of the Action.

A red dialog box icon indicates that some steps in the Action will stop and display dialog boxes for input. If the icon is black, the Action will stop at every step where input is possible.

Click the triangle to expand or close the listing for the entire Action or for a step.

Action name

Command name

Click to stop recording or playing.

Click to record; red indicates that recording is in progress.

Click to Delete the Action or command.

Click to start a new Action.

Click to play a selected Action or to play from a selected command onward; Ctrl-click to play only the selected command and then stop.

mask (a layer mask, a transparency mask, an alpha channel, or even a color channel) as a selection as you record by dragging its name in the Channels palette to the Make Selection icon at the bottom of the palette, or by holding down the Ctrl key as you press the appropriate mask designator. (See Chapter 2 for more about selecting and masks.)

A current selection can be feathered, expanded, or contracted as part of an Action by recording the appropriate command from the Select menu.

- **Palette operations:** You can't automate commands that can only be found in pop-out menus in the palettes (for instance, the Define Brush command from the Brushes palette). But some commands that once were found only in the palette pop-outs have now also been added to the standard menus, so they can be included in Actions (for example, from the Layer menu, Duplicate Layer and Delete Layer).

  But note that another command from that menu, Layer Options, *doesn't* record, so you can't use it to rename a layer or change its blending mode or Opacity setting. Choices from the blending mode list and changes in the Opacity slider setting in the Layers palette can't be recorded either. So the only way to set the blending mode or Opacity of a layer completely automatically is to do it when you first create the layer, either by choosing Layer, New Layer (or Layer, New Adjustment Layer), or by Alt-clicking (or Ctrl-clicking) the New Layer icon at the bottom of the Layers palette. (See "Layers" in Chapter 2 for more about layers and the Layers palette.)

  You can use the icons at the bottoms of the Layers and Channels palettes in recording an Action, but not the Paths palette icons.

  You can use keyboard shortcuts for some palette operations — for instance, to change the active layer in the Layers palette (see "Layers Shortcuts" in Chapter 2), but not for others — for instance, to change brush tips in the Brushes palette.

- **Meeting the requirements of the command:** Of course, your Action will only work if the conditions of the file you're working on will allow it to work. For instance, if your Action includes a step to add a layer mask, you won't be able to do that if the layer that's active when that step is played is the *Background* layer, which can't have a mask, or if it's a transparent layer that already has a layer mask. Likewise, if the step requires an active selection (as the Select, Modify, Contract command does), it won't work unless something is selected when the step is played.

- **Putting Actions within Actions.** It would be nice if you could simply select, copy, and paste one Action into another in order to include it, but that isn't the case. You can, however, nest

In its single-column format the Button mode of the Actions palette is
less compact than the Commands
palette of Photoshop 3, since the
minimum width of the Buttons is
wider. But if you use a multicolumn
layout for the palette — which you
can do just by dragging a corner to
reshape the palette — the individual
buttons get narrower, and the palette takes up less space per button.

Actions	
Play Me First!	Save to Folder
Button Mode	Actions that wo...
Wow!-Text Panel	Wow!-Blur Bac...
Wow!-Drop Shadow	Wow!-Drop Sha...
Wow!-Cast Shadow	Wow!-Photo Gl...
Wow!-Photo Gl...	Actions that Wo...
Wow!-Graphic ...	Wow!-Graphic ...
Wow!-Graphic ...	Wow!-Graphic ...

QUICK CHANGES

To make it easy to go back and
forth between the Actions palette's
list mode and Button mode, use
"Button" in the Wow! Actions on
the CD-ROM that comes with this
book. Or make your own Action for
choosing Button mode: Working in
list mode, choose New Action from
the palette's pop-out menu. Name
the Action "Button Mode," choose
a color and keyboard shortcut, and
click Record. Choose Insert Menu
Item from the pop-out menu, and
then choose Button Mode, and
click OK. Finally, click the square
black Stop button at the bottom of
the palette to stop recording. Now
the quickest way to get to Button
mode is to use the keyboard shortcut. When you're working in Button
mode, either use the shortcut or click
your button to get back to list mode.

Actions	
Unsharp Mask	
Button Mode	

a finished Action within the one you're currently recording by
playing it as you record. Click in the Actions list to select the
Action you want to include, then press the Play button. This
Action will be added as a step in the one you're recording.

The Recording Process

The Actions recording process differs, depending on whether you
want to make a clickable button to choose a single menu item or
whether you want to record a multistep process.

To turn any Photoshop command into a clickable device
that chooses a command (the same way the Commands palette did
in Photoshop 3), open the Actions palette (Window, Show Actions)
and click the New Action icon at the bottom of the palette. Name
the Action and assign a color or function key shortcut if you like;
then click Record. Choose Insert Menu Item from the pop-out
menu and select the command you want from a menu or
submenu, or type in the command's name as it's listed in the
menu. Then click the square Stop button at the bottom of the palette to complete the recording.

Now whenever you click that Action in the Actions palette,
Photoshop should respond as if you had chosen the command
from its menu. And if the command includes a dialog box, the box
should open so you can enter the settings you want, just as it would if
you were choosing it from the menu. But the process may not
always work perfectly. So another way to record a single command
is to set up a file that will allow you to carry out the command you
want as you record. Now click the New Action icon and click
Record in the New Action dialog box, then carry out the command
on the file, and finally click the Stop button. Expand the Action listing by clicking the triangle in front of the name of your command,
and click in the dialog box column next to the command. Now
when you click on your new Action, the Action will pause and the
box will open so you can enter settings.

To record a multistep operation so you'll be able to apply the
whole series of commands again, open a file like the ones you want
to work on, click the New Action icon at the bottom of the Actions
palette, name the Action, and start performing operations, tailoring
your choices within the limitations of "actionable" operations
mentioned in "Knowing What's Actionable" earlier in this section.
The round Record button at the bottom of the Actions palette will
stay red (indicating that recording is in progress) until you press the
square black Stop button to end the recording session.

If you want your multistep Action to include an operation that
can't be recorded as part of an Action — like changing the blending
mode or opacity of an existing layer — the Insert Menu Item command provides a way. As you record the Action, choose Insert

A useful Action is one that will choose the Select, Load Selection command, opening a dialog box so you can choose which of the available selections (alpha channels, layer masks, or transparency mask) you want to load, and whether you want to add it to, subtract it from, or create the intersection of the current selection if there is one. In the first release of Photoshop 4, if you tried to set up such a command using the Insert Menu Item command from the Actions palette's pop-out menu, it wouldn't work right. But the problem was fixed in the 4.0.1 update. (Updates can be downloaded from **www.adobe.com**.)

To make an Action for loading a selection, click the New Action icon at the bottom of the Actions palette, name the Action "Load Selection," click Record to close the dialog box, and choose Insert Menu Item from the palette's pop-out menu. Choose Select, Load Selection. Now when you play the Action, it will open the Load Selection dialog box, offering you whatever options are available for the particular file you're working on.

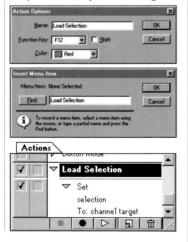

Menu Item from the palette's pop-out menu, and then enter the command you want to insert. For instance, to insert the Layer Options command to pause the action and open the Layer Options dialog box so the user can reset the blending mode or Opacity of a layer, choose Layer, Layer Options, or type "Layer Options" into the Find box in the Insert Menu Item dialog box. Any step you record with Insert Menu Item won't have any effect at the time it's recorded. But when the Action is run later, this step will be carried out. Often when you insert a command this way, it's a good idea to include a Stop just before it, to display instructions for the step.

Playing an Action

Once you've recorded an Action or loaded one recorded by someone else (see "Saving and Loading Actions" later in this section), you can play it back on a single file or on all the files in a folder. Before you run an Action, it's a good idea to duplicate your image file and store the original for safekeeping, since **Undo works only on the last executed step** of an Action, not on the entire Action.

- **To run an Action,** click its name in the Actions list and click the triangular Play button at the bottom of the palette.
- **To play an Action from a specific step** forward, select that step in the Actions list and then click the Play button.
- **To play a single step** of an Action, click on that step to select it, and then Ctrl-click the Play button.
- **To run an Action on a whole batch of files**, use the Batch command from the palette's pop-out menu.

Editing Your Actions

After you've finished recording an Action and have tried playing it, you may need to go back and change its steps, especially in cases where some experimentation was involved while you recorded. For example, you may need to work in a "nonactionable" way (play with settings that won't record) to get the result you want while you're recording the Action, and then go back and rerecord parts of the process so you can play the Action successfully. For instance, setting the blending mode or Opacity for a layer may be a trial-and-error process. But since none of this experimentation can be recorded, you can go back to the step in the Action where the layer was created and replace it with a step that creates a new layer with the final Opacity and blending mode settings you liked.

As usual in Photoshop, when it comes to editing an Action, there are several ways to do it. But here are some easy methods:

- **To remove a step** (or even an entire Action) from the Actions list, click its name and Alt-click the trash can at the bottom of the Actions palette; or drag it to the trash can; or choose "Delete [Action's name]" from the palette's pop-out menu.

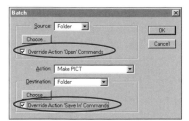

If you click on the name of an Action in the Actions palette's list mode and then choose the Batch command from the palette's pop-out menu, your Action will be applied to all the images in the folder you choose as the Source, and then the treated files will be saved. The Batch dialog box gives you the chance to turn off these built-in Open and Save As commands if they also exist as part of your Action.

- **To change dialog box settings** for a step that opens a dialog box, double-click the command's name in the Actions palette, enter new settings, and click OK.

- **To insert a new step** (or steps) in the Actions list, click the step you want the new command to come after. Then click the Record button, record the new command(s), and click the Stop button.

- **To change the order of steps,** drag their names up or down to new positions in the Actions list.

- **To completely change a step,** first click on the step above it and choose Insert Stop from the pop-out menu. Start from a fresh copy of a file like the one the Action is meant to be used on, and play the entire Action from the beginning. The Stop you inserted will pause the Action when it gets to the step you want to replace. Then follow the directions above for inserting a new step. (The reason for playing the entire Action from the beginning when you want to rerecord one or more steps is to ensure that you've given the Action a chance to create the conditions that will be needed — layers and channels, for instance — when you get to the step you're redoing.) Then remove the old version of the step, as described above.

- **To duplicate a step** in an Action, hold down the Alt key and drag the step's name to the point where you want the copy in the Actions list.

- To make your Action **pause between steps** and provide instructions for a nonrecordable step that the user must carry out, or to insert tips about settings for an upcoming dialog box, click the command in the Actions list that you want the pause to come after. Then choose Insert Stop from the palette's pop-out menu, and type the message. Select the Allow Continue option if you want the user to be able to proceed with the Action after reading the message. Leave this box unchecked if you want the user to have to click the next step in the Actions list and then click the Play button in order to continue. Make the latter choice anytime some handwork has to be done before the Action can proceed. When you've finished making entries in the Record Stop dialog box, click OK.

- To make the Action **pause within a step** so the user can choose whether to change the settings in a dialog box or continue with its current settings (by pressing OK), click in the column just to the left of the command's name. A dialog box icon will appear in the column to show that the command will pause with its dialog box open. Clicking again in this column toggles the box's pause function off.

- To **temporarily disable a step** so it isn't carried out when you play an Action, without permanently removing the step

from the Action (or to disable an Action without permanently
removing it from the palette), click off the checkmark in the farthest left column of the Actions palette. Click in this column
again to re-enable the step.

Saving and Loading Actions

When you finish recording and editing an Action, it remains part
of the current Actions palette, even if you don't go through a saving process. Even if you quit and restart Photoshop, your new
Action will still appear in the palette. You can, however, preserve
the entire Actions palette with a name of its own by choosing Save
Actions from the palette's pop-out menu.

There are some real advantages to saving an Actions palette. For
one thing, you may want to divide your list of Actions among different palettes that you load for different kinds of jobs — maybe
one for special effects, one for correcting color and sharpening
scanned images, one for artistic filter treatments, and so on.
Another advantage of saving Actions palettes is that you won't lose
your Actions if you ever have to delete Photoshop's Preferences file,
which is where the current Actions palette is stored.

You can't save individual Actions — only entire Actions palettes.
So to save some Actions without others, you'll need to first save the
current palette with all its Actions, then delete any individual
Actions you don't want in that palette (see "Editing Your Actions"
on page 24), and save the modified palette under a new name.

You can load a saved Actions palette either as an addition to the
current palette (choose Load Actions from the palette's pop-out
menu as described earlier), or you can load it *instead of* the current
palette (choose Replace Actions). Note: Before you replace Actions,
make sure you've saved the current set so you'll be able to retrieve
it again.

COLOR IN PHOTOSHOP

Photoshop's interface for choosing and mixing color includes the
Image, Mode submenu, the Foreground/Background color squares,
the Color Picker, the color palettes (Color and Swatches), the eyedropper tool, and the gradient.

Color Modes

Photoshop employs several different systems of color representation. These systems — Bitmap, Grayscale, Duotone, Indexed Color,
RGB Color, CMYK Color, and Lab Color — can be selected through
the Mode menu. Each color mode has a different *gamut,* or range of
colors that can be produced in that color system.

CMYK Color. In any color system the *primary colors* are the
basics from which all other colors can be mixed. In *four-color process
printing,* which is the type of printing most often used for reproduc-
ing the photos, illustrations, and other works created in Photoshop,

In a subtractive *color model (represented by the top illustration), cyan, magenta, and yellow inks combine to make a dark, nearly black color. In* additive *color (bottom), red, green, and blue light combine on-screen to make white light.*

the primaries (called *subtractive primaries*) are cyan, magenta, and yellow, with the potential for adding black to intensify the dark colors and details. Adding black makes dark colors look crisper than darkening with a heavier mix of cyan, magenta, and yellow. Darkening with black also requires less ink; this can be important because a press has an upper limit to the amount of ink it can apply to the printed page before the ink will no longer adhere to the paper.

RGB Color. The CRT monitors used in computers and TV generate primary colors of light (called *additive primaries*) by bombarding the phosphor coating of the screen with electrons. The mix of red, green, and blue light that results is perceived by the eye as color. When all three colors are turned on at full intensity, the result is white light; when all are turned off, black results. Different intensities of energy excite the phosphors to different degrees, and the various brightnesses of the three colors mix visually to form all the colors of the RGB spectrum.

Because of the architecture of typical computer hardware and software, there are theoretically 256 different levels of energy that can be applied to each of the three primary colors of the computer's RGB system; this means that there are 256 x 256 x 256 (or more than 16 million) colors that can be mixed. This gamut provides enough colors to very realistically represent the world we see.

It takes 8 bits of computer data (a bit is a 1 or a 0, an ON or OFF signal) to represent 256 different energy settings ($2^8 = 256$); to represent three sets of energy settings takes 24 bits ($2^8 \times 2^8 \times 2^8 = 2^{24} = 16.7$ million). So full color as displayed on the computer screen is called 24-bit color.

Indexed Color. Some computers aren't equipped to display 24-bit color. Instead, they can display only 256 (or fewer) colors at once, or 8-bit color. In such a system, 256 colors are stored in a *color look-up table* (or *CLUT*) whose storage addresses are identified by numbers between 0 and 255. The process of assigning 256 colors to represent the millions of colors potentially in a full-color image is called *indexing*. When you choose Mode, Indexed Color in Photoshop, you can choose to index the colors to:

- An **Exact** palette (if the image includes 256 or fewer colors)

- A **System** palette (either **Macintosh** and **Windows**). The System palettes are the sets of 256 colors that are used on each of these platforms to provide a good color representation of all parts of the RGB gamut).

- An **Adaptive** palette (a set of 256 colors chosen to best represent the parts of the spectrum used in a particular image). Adaptive palettes also automatically include black and white. When you convert an image to an Adaptive palette, you can make Photoshop assign more of the 256 colors to particular parts of

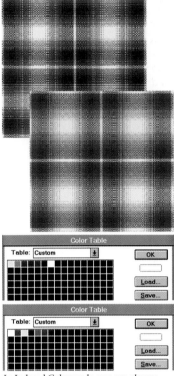

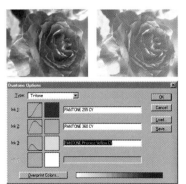

In Indexed Color mode, you can change colors quickly by clicking on the cells of the Color Table. Peter Kaye used this method to try different colorways in this fabric design.

Photoshop's Duotone mode provides curves that store information for printing a grayscale image in one to four ink colors. The program comes with several sets of preset duotone, tritone, and quadtone curves. Or you can shape the curves yourself. By drastically reshaping curves as in this tritone, you can make different colors predominate in highlights, midtones, and shadows.

the spectrum. For instance, you may want to weight the color choices in a portrait toward flesh tones and away from the clothing or background colors.

- A **Uniform** palette (a set of colors sampled evenly from all areas of the spectrum). In a Uniform palette there are approximately equal numbers of reds, greens, blues, cyans, magentas, and yellows. The Uniform palette can be set for as many as 256 colors or as few as 2 by entering the number of Colors you want.

- The **Web** palette (a set of 216 colors that the most popular Web browsers use to represent color). Every color in this palette is found in both the Macintosh and the Windows System palettes. Using the Web palette helps ensure that the color in your image will look the same, regardless of whether it's seen on a Mac or a Windows machine, with Netscape or the Microsoft Internet Explorer.

- A **Custom** palette (a set of colors selected for some particular purpose). Choosing Mode, Indexed Color, Custom opens the Color Table dialog box, where you can choose one of several Custom palettes that are supplied with the program or make your own color table by clicking the individual squares of the table and choosing new colors to fill them. As long as your file is in Indexed Color mode, you can choose Mode, Color Table and change the table.

- The **Previous** palette (the set of colors that was used the last time, within the current Photoshop session, that a file was indexed with a Custom or Adaptive palette). This option is useful for converting a number of images so they share a single custom palette.

"SHAPING" ADAPTIVE PALETTES

If you select an area of the image that contains the important colors before you make the conversion to Indexed Color, the choice of the 256 colors of the Adaptive palette will be weighted in favor of the parts of the spectrum in that selection.

INDEXED TO INDEXED

There are two ways to change a color file from one Indexed Color palette to another. The method you use will depend on whether you know in advance what palette you want to change to.

- If you know the existing color palette you want, choose **Image, Mode, Color Table** and Load the palette you want to change to.

- If you want to create a new Indexed palette — for instance, if you want to try reducing the number of colors to make an image file smaller for use on the World Wide Web — you first have to go back through the RGB Color mode: Choose Image, Mode, RGB Color and then choose Image, Mode, Indexed Color and pick Exact, Adaptive, or Uniform. Keep in mind that choosing RGB Color after indexing merely changes the color mode — it does not restore the original RGB color of the file.

The Overprint Colors button in the Duotone dialog box lets you make the on-screen display of your duotone look more like it will when it's printed. Clicking any of the color squares in the Overprint Colors dialog box opens the Color Picker so you can change the display of that color mix to match a printed sample that shows your ink colors overprinted solid. (Letraset publishes samples of overprinted Pantone Matching System inks.) For color accuracy, you need to have a calibrated monitor (see "Calibration and Color Matching" later in the chapter).

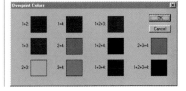

In Duotone mode you can't see the individual color plates that will be used for printing. To look at them you can convert the file to Multichannel mode temporarily, open a second window, and view a different channel in each window. Follow these steps exactly: Open the Channels palette (Window, Show Channels) and open a second view of the image (View, New View). Then choose Image, Mode, Multichannel. Activate a different Channel (by clicking on its name in the Channels palette) for each window. View both plates, but don't try to edit or you won't be able to convert back to Duotone. Then choose Edit, Undo to go back to Duotone mode.

Lab Color. Instead of being separated into three colors (plus black in the case of CMYK color), color can be expressed in terms of a brightness component and two hue/saturation components. Photoshop's Lab Color mode uses such a system. So does Kodak Photo CD (its Photo YCC color system) and so does color television. Because its gamut is large enough to include the CMYK, RGB, and Photo YCC gamuts, Photoshop's Lab Color mode serves as an intermediate step when Photoshop converts from RGB to CMYK or from Photo YCC to RGB.

Grayscale. A Grayscale mode image, like a black-and-white photo, includes only *brightness* values, no data for *hue* or *saturation,* the other two components of color. Only 8 bits of data are required for storing the 256 shades (black, white, and grays) in the Grayscale gamut.

Duotone. Even though a Grayscale image can include 256 levels of gray, most printing processes can't actually produce that many different tones with a single ink color. But with two inks (or even one color of ink applied in two passes through the press) it's possible to extend the tonal range. By adding a second color in the highlights, for example, you increase the number of tones available for representing the lightest tones in an image. Besides extending tonal range, the second color can "warm" or "cool" a black-and-white image, tinting it slightly toward red or blue. Or the second color may be used for dramatic effect or to visually tie a photo to other design elements.

In Photoshop's Duotone mode, a set of *gamma curves* determines how the grayscale information will be represented in each of the ink colors. Will the second color be emphasized in the shadows but omitted from the highlights? Will it be used to color the midtones? The Duotone image is stored as a grayscale file and a set of curves that will act on that grayscale information to produce two or more separate plates for printing. Duotone mode also includes tritone and quadtone options, for producing three or four color plates.

Bitmap. The least "bulky" mode in Photoshop is Bitmap, which uses only 1 bit of "color" data to represent each pixel. A pixel is either off or on, producing a gamut of two colors — black and white. Photoshop's several methods for converting Grayscale images to Bitmap mode provide useful options for printing photos with low-resolution, one-color printing methods, as well as some interesting graphic treatments (see Chapter 3, "Enhancing Photos").

In addition to the color modes themselves, the Image, Mode submenu includes two more choices: Multichannel and Color Table. Multichannel mode can be useful for viewing the plates of a Duotone image, as shown at the left.

To convert an image to Duotone mode, it needs to be in Grayscale first. If the file is in any other mode, choose Image, Mode, Grayscale and then Image, Mode, Duotone.

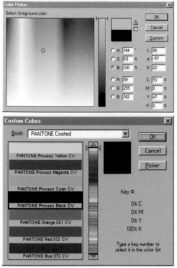

Photoshop's default Color Picker (shown at the top in Brightness mode) lets you enter numeric values to mix colors in the RGB, CMYK, Lab, and HSB (hue, saturation, brightness) modes. Or you can click one of the round buttons to switch between color models. Clicking on Custom lets you choose from several custom color matching systems (bottom).

The Color palette has a color bar from which colors can be sampled. The gamut of the bar can be changed by choosing Color Bar from the palette's pop-out menu or Ctrl-clicking on the bar to open the Color Bar dialog box. Or Shift-click on the bar to toggle through the four color bar choices: RGB Spectrum (A), CMYK Spectrum (B), Grayscale Ramp (C), and Current Colors (Foreground To Background) (D).

Color Views

CMYK Preview, found in the View menu, lets you see how an RGB image will look if you convert it to CMYK mode with the current Separation Setup parameters. (Separation Setup is discussed in "Getting Consistent Color" later in this chapter.) Opening a second view of your RGB file (View, New View) and choosing View, CMYK Preview lets you see the file in both RGB (the original file) and CMYK (the new view) at the same time. Unlike choosing Mode, CMYK Color, the CMYK Preview option doesn't actually make the conversion, so you don't lose the RGB color information and therefore you still have the full RGB color gamut to work with.

Gamut Warning, also chosen from the View menu, identifies the colors in your RGB image that will be adjusted to bring them inside the printable color range if you change to CMYK mode with the current Separation Setup settings.

Using the Color Picker and Color Palettes

The **Foreground and Background color squares** in the toolbox show what color you'll get when you paint on any layer (the

GETTING INTO GAMUT

Once you choose View, Gamut Warning to identify the colors that will change when an RGB file is converted to CMYK mode, the CMYK Preview and the sponge tool can help bring the out-of-gamut colors into gamut. Most RGB colors can be brought into the smaller CMYK gamut by reducing their saturation. So you can proceed this way: Open another window in CMYK Preview mode (choose View, New View; then choose View, CMYK Preview for this window). Looking at the new window, you may decide that Photoshop's Separation Setup will do an acceptable job of bringing the color into CMYK gamut. But If you see a few areas of out-of-gamut colors that won't look good when converted, you may want to do some desaturation by hand: "Paint" the out-of-gamut areas with the sponge tool set to Desaturate at a fairly low Pressure. Use a soft-edged brush to prevent sharp color breaks, brushing over the out-of-gamut areas to desaturate them just until the indicator color is removed. Be careful that you don't desaturate some areas more than necessary or cause streaking where your brush strokes overlap.

PHOTO: DON COCHRAN

The Gamut Warning (from the Mode menu) uses a medium gray (top) to indicate colors that may change when the file is converted to CMYK mode, as shown here (bottom). The gray disappears on-screen as you bring colors into gamut. If gray doesn't work well for a particular image, you can change the indicator color by choosing File, Preferences, Transparency & Gamut, clicking the color square, and choosing a new color.

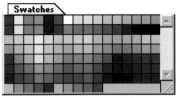

Choose Replace Swatches from the Swatches palette's pop-out menu to replace the default Photoshop Swatches (above) with a custom "swatch book" like the Web palette described in Chapter 9. If you want to add swatches to the existing palette instead of replacing the palette, choose Load Swatches. A number of swatch sets are found in the **Palettes** directory on the Adobe Photoshop 4.0 CD-ROM. You can always reset to the default Photoshop Swatches palette by choosing Reset Swatches from the palette's pop-out menu.

The Scratch palette of earlier versions of Photoshop no longer exists in version 4. But you can make your own small file for mixing colors from airbrush dabs or image selections dragged into the file with the move tool.

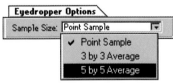

The eyedropper tool can sample color by clicking on any open file or palette; the sampled color becomes the Foreground color. Alt-clicking sets the Background color. The Sample Size, set in the Eyedropper Options palette lets you pick up the color of a single pixel or the average color from a 3 x 3- or 5 x 5-pixel area around the cursor's "hot point." The sample size of the eyedroppers in the Levels and Curves dialog boxes is also controlled by the setting in the Eyedropper Options palette.

Foreground color) or erase on the *Background* layer (the Background color; but erasing on a transparent layer produces transparency rather than the Background color). You can choose Foreground and Background colors simply by clicking on one of the squares to open the **Color Picker** and then choosing or specifying a color. Beyond the Color Picker, the two **color palettes** (Color and Swatches) can be left open on-screen and are ideally suited for certain ways of choosing colors:

The **Color palette**, with its different modes and sliders, lets you mix colors scientifically (by reading the numbers as you move the sliders) or "by feel," or by sampling from the Color Bar at the bottom of the palette.

By default the **Swatches palette** shows a set of 122 color samples. You can click a swatch to select a Foreground color or Alt-click to select a Background color. The palette can be expanded to hold a scrolling preset palette of colors, such as the System or Pantone colors in the **palettes** directory.

GETTING CONSISTENT COLOR

If you've done color artwork on the computer and then printed it out, you may have noticed some fundamental differences in the way color is represented on-screen and on the printed page. There are several contributing factors.

- **First of all,** transmitted (additive) **color from a monitor looks brighter** than the color produced by light reflected from ink on paper (subtractive color).

- Second, because the RGB gamut (the range of available colors) is bigger than the CMYK gamut, **not all the colors that can be displayed on-screen can be printed,** so it's possible to mix colors in RGB files that can't be reproduced on the printed page.

- Third, because you're moving from a three-color to a four-color system in which black can partially substitute for mixes of the other three colors, **there are many different ways to represent a particular RGB color in the CMYK system,** and because of the way ink pigments interact, the results of all these ways can look slightly different from each other.

- And finally, **variations** in film output, paper, ink, presses, and press operators also affect the color in the final printed product.

When To Make the RGB-to-CMYK Conversion

If you're preparing an image for print, unless you use one of a few desktop color printers that can't handle CMYK files, the image will eventually need to be turned into CMYK separations. This can be done at several different stages in the development of the image. For instance:

- You can choose CMYK Color mode when you first create a new Photoshop file (File, New).

Photoshop's gradient tool now allows multiple colors and transparencies. Its use is described in Chapter 6.

Setting the parameters for converting RGB to CMYK color. (Unless you understand the technical aspects of working with color separation curves, use the default setting or get advice from your printer.)

- Some scanning services (and even some desktop scanning software) can make the CMYK conversion for you. The quality of the result depends on the sophistication of the software and the suitability of its settings for the kind of printing you want to do, or on the skill of the professional scan operator. (For more about scanning, see "Image Input" and "Setting Up a Scan" later in this chapter.)

- You can choose Photoshop's Mode, CMYK Color at any point in the development of an image. But **once you make the conversion you can't regain the original RGB color** by choosing Mode, RGB Color. The out-of-gamut colors will have been permanently "dulled down" to CMYK-printable versions.

- Or you can keep the file in RGB Color mode, place it in a page layout, and allow the page layout or color separation utility to make the separation.

How do you decide when to convert from RGB to CMYK? Here are some tips to help you choose:

- The single advantage of working in CMYK from the beginning is that it prevents last-minute color shifts, since it keeps the image within the printing gamut during the entire development process.

- But if you're working in CMYK mode and your printing specifications change (a different paper may be chosen for the job, for instance), the CMYK specifications you chose may no longer apply. In that case, you'll have to start over from an RGB version or compensate manually (see "There's No Going Back" at the left.)

- Working in RGB and putting off the CMYK conversion to the last possible moment allows more freedom, so you can get just the color you want on-screen and then work with Photoshop's Hue/Saturation, Levels, or Curves adjustments to tweak out-of-gamut colors to get CMYK alternatives that are as close as possible to your original colors.

- Another very significant advantage of working in RGB is that some of Photoshop's finest functions (for example, the Lighting Effects filter described in Chapter 5) don't work in CMYK mode.

- With CMYK Preview and Gamut Warning available, **it makes sense to work in RGB, preview CMYK in a second window, and do the actual RGB-to-CMYK conversion at the end of the process.**

- You may be able to bow out of the conversion process altogether for many jobs. **Your page layout program or** the **separation utility** used by your imagesetting service bureau **may do an excellent job of converting most of your RGB images to CMYK.** If that's the case, you can save yourself some time and angst by using this method. It's often worth the money

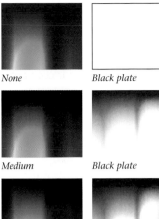

None   Black plate

Medium   Black plate

Maximum   Black plate

Part of the full-spectrum palette (provided on the CD-ROM that comes with this book) converted to CMYK with three different Black Generation settings

The default settings for the Printing Inks Setup dialog box covers the most common paper, ink, and press conditions used for printing color images. If you're going to do your own RGB-to-CMYK conversions, get advice about the Dot Gain setting from your printer, or from your imagesetting service bureau, since technicians there may be more familiar with Photoshop than the printer is; better yet, have the printer and service bureau technician talk to each other and then let you know how to set the Dot Gain. Specify that the dot gain compensation needs to be from the film stage to the final press sheet, not from proof to press sheet. The Dot Gain value is for the 50% point.

to run a test file through film separation to laminate proof to check the result.

- **In some cases doing the conversion to CMYK yourself may be the only way to control color** — for example, when you won't have the opportunity to review laminate proofs of the film separations and you don't have a printed sample to send along as a color-match target (or you don't trust the production team to use the target appropriately even if you do send one). This may be the case if you're providing a photo-illustration to a publication produced by someone else. But you'll need to know quite a bit about how the piece will be printed (the dot gain and maximum ink coverage, for instance) in order to make the right settings in the Printing Inks Setup and Separation Setup dialog boxes (see "Making the Conversion," next).

Making the Conversion

At whatever point you make the conversion, the Monitor Setup, Separation Setup, and Printing Inks Setup functions (under File, Color Settings) all affect the final result. Chapter 5 of the *Adobe Photoshop 4.0 User Guide* that comes with the program walks you through the process of producing a CMYK separation in Photoshop.

To make the appropriate settings in the Separation Setup and Printing Inks Setup dialog boxes, you need certain information about the printing process that will be used to put the image on paper. For instance, you need to know the maximum ink coverage and the expected dot gain. **Dot gain** is a change from the expected size of the tiny dots of ink used for printing, which can cause changes in color. There can be a gain or loss as your go through the process of making printing plates from film or the process of transferring ink from the printing plate to the paper, depending on the paper's absorbency, the type of ink, and the line screen. Photoshop's dot gain settings seem to be on the high side. So when you get advice about settings, it's good to ask someone who not only knows how your job will be printed, but also understands how Photoshop works. If you make an RGB-to-CMYK conversion without knowing these things, you're just guessing about the outcome.

Calibration and Color Matching

In order for your computer monitor to be as accurate as possible in showing how an image will look when it's printed, each part of the display and print production system must be *calibrated*, adjusted so it produces color consistently over time. And then all the parts of the system have to be coordinated with each other.

"Olé! No Moiré" provides fine-tuned color and good shadow detail so you can be confident the image is right, as well as standard color swatches that your imagesetting service bureau can check with a densitometer.

The SpectroCalibrator, part of the Colortron color measurement system for Windows 95 and Macintosh, is an example of a hardware-and-software device for monitor calibration.

USING THE INFO PALETTE

If you can't get a proof in advance of printing, or if you can't confidently rely on the monitor as a predictor of printed color, learn to use the Info palette to see how the color changes you make will affect printing. With a dialog box open, you can set up the Info palette to show you the before and after values for RGB and CMYK color composition so you can see how the Image adjustments you're considering will affect color.

The Gamma control panel utility that comes with Photoshop helps with basic system calibration. Chapter 5 of the *Adobe Photoshop 4.0 User Guide* tells how to use Gamma and the Monitor Setup dialog box to calibrate your monitor. Once the monitor is adjusted, it's a good idea to lock the brightness and contrast knobs in place with tape to keep them from being changed accidentally.

To get consistent color, the viewing environment has to be maintained constant also, because changes in lighting conditions can change your perception of colors on the screen. Position the room's light source above and behind the monitor, and keep it dimmed and constant. If your room lighting is controlled by a rheostat, mark the knob and the base plate so you can always restore the lighting to the same level. Also, wear neutral colors when you sit in front of the monitor, to minimize color reflections from your clothes onto the screen.

Standardizing the monitor and its environment doesn't finish the job of getting your system ready to show you predictable color. Assuming that your output process is also kept consistent over time (you don't let the inkjets get clogged up in your desktop printer and you can count on the service bureau to keep its imagesetting equipment tuned up and its processing chemicals fresh), you can do a sort of "backwards calibration" to make sure your screen display is an accurate predictor of the color you'll get in a print or proof. Here's a way to do it:

1 Print or proof a color file; this could be an image of your own, but you may also want to include the "Olé! No Moiré" image **Testpict.psd** in **Goodies/Calibrat** on the Adobe Photoshop 4.0 CD-ROM. You might also include a "step wedge" like the one described in "Correcting a Batch of Scans" later in this chapter. The 21 gray levels in such a scale will show you what's happening to the highlight and shadow tones in your image. Either:

- print the file on the same system you'll use for final printing,

- print the file on a proofing printer that your press operator assures you will be a good predictor of final printed color,

- or produce film and a laminate proof that your printing press operators can check and assure you they can match on press. Going all the way to printing a proof on the press, rather than stopping at a laminate proof, is even better, but it usually isn't possible.

2 In your controlled-light environment, open the file on-screen. Hold the print or proof up to the screen to compare color.

3 Readjust your monitor with the Gamma control panel until the on-screen image looks like the printed piece, and use the Save Settings button in the Gamma panel to save the settings for future use

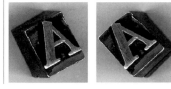
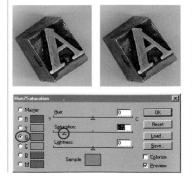
in projects that will use the same printing process. The back-to-front system calibration process depends on changing the display characteristics of the monitor, not the file itself at this point. So don't do any work in Photoshop during the process — that is, *don't change the file.*

Once your monitor has been readjusted so the on-screen image matches the print or proof, you can assume that for files you produce in the future, when the image looks the way you want it on-screen, the print or proof will look the same.

Note: Chapter 5 in the *Adobe Photoshop User Guide* recommends that you adjust Monitor Setup and Printing Inks Setup rather than Gamma to do back-to-front calibration. However, that assumes that you will be doing the RGB-to-CMYK conversion for all your images in Photoshop, since both Monitor Setup and Printing Inks Setup affect *the file itself,* not just the on-screen display. Using Gamma instead works for both Photoshop-separated images and those handled by a different separation utility, such as one designed to work with a page layout program.

IMAGE INPUT

Scanners — desktop, mid-range and high-end — turn photos into image files that can be manipulated in Photoshop. An inexpensive desktop flatbed scanner can capture photographic prints, other hard copy, and even some three-dimensional objects to make files you can use for photo-illustration (for tips see "Setting Up a Scan" later in this chapter). Desktop slide scanners and some transparency adapters for flatbed scanners (though the quality of transparency adapters varies greatly) make it possible to capture images from transparencies in sizes from 35 mm to 8 x 10 inches.

Another input option is to **have your images scanned by a service bureau** or a color separation house using scanners with optical-mechanical systems that are more precise than those of desktop scanners. Keep in mind that the quality of a service bureau scan depends not only on the quality of the scanning equipment, but also on the operator's willingness to calibrate and maintain it, and on his or her understanding of color, and skill in operating the machine.

Besides inputting images by scanning, you can also buy collections of photos and other artwork already scanned and provided on **CD-ROM**. Many stock images, patterns, and textures are now available on CD-ROM, with a variety of arrangements for use and payment (you can find examples in Appendix A).

Kodak Photo CD technology makes it easy and inexpensive to have images from film (35 mm negatives or slides) stored on a compact disc. The easiest and least expensive way to get your images in Photo CD format is to take your film to a photofinisher who offers the Photo CD service and get the disc back along with the finished

To open a Photo CD file in Photoshop 4:

1 Choose File, Open, and then choose the Photo CD disc; within the disc, choose the PHOTO_CD folder, and within that folder choose IMAGES. Choose the number of the image you want — you can find the number by looking at the index print that comes in the Photo CD jewel case with the disc — and double-click (A).

2 When the image dialog box opens (B), you can choose the Resolution (which of the five or six files sizes you want). Also, click the Image Info button to find out what kind of film was scanned to make the file.

3 Note the Medium Of Original and Product Type Of Original (C), and click OK to close the box.

*4 Back in the Image dialog box (B), click on the Source button. Choose Kodak Photo CD for the Device (unless a special device profile is supplied for the disc) and select the appropriate film description from the list (D). If the Medium Of Origin (in step 3) was Color Negative, choose **Color Negative V3.0 Input**; for slide film (called "Color Reversal" in the Image Info box), choose **Universal Kodachrome V2.0 Input** if the Product Type starts with "116/"; for all other Color Reversal film, use **Universal Ektachrome V2.0 Input**.*

prints or slides. The images on the disc are relatively high-quality scans, very efficiently compressed, and stored in Kodak's Image Pac format, which provides each image in five different resolutions, or file sizes. Pro Photo CD discs include the five file sizes used for Photo CD plus a bigger size that can accommodate larger film formats (up to 4 x 5 inches).

Photo CD images are scanned in RGB color and then translated to Kodak's Photo YCC color system because it's compatible with television (Photo CD was originally designed to "play" to a TV screen), and it allows efficient compression of data so the images can be stored in less space without losing image quality. To use Photo CD, you need a CD ROM-XA (eXtended Architecture) drive and software that can retrieve the Photo CD images and convert them to a form that Photoshop can use. For this purpose Photoshop includes an automatically installed plug-in module that lets you open Photo CD files with the File, Open or Open As command, as described at the left.

Digital cameras, which bypass film altogether and record images as digital files on disk, are another potential source of images for manipulation in Photoshop. **Video** — from video camera, videocassette, or videodisc — can be brought into Photoshop through the File, Import command, using a plug-in module provided with the *video frame grabber,* a hardware-software combination designed to acquire and enhance the video images. The image quality that can be achieved with relatively inexpensive digital cameras or with video is not nearly as good as film. But if an image is to be extensively manipulated for a photo-illustration or is to be used only at low resolution — for instance, for placement in a World Wide Web page — the convenience of having the "photo" instantly available may outweigh the quality difference.

PHOTO CD FILE SIZES

The five file sizes in the Photo CD Image Pac (six sizes in Pro Photo CD) are as follows. Print sizes are for high quality at halftone line screens of 150 lines per inch. Many Photo CD files can be printed bigger than the sizes listed if the photo doesn't include hard edges or if the halftone line screen used for printing is lower than 150 lpi; the lower the line screen, the more the image can be enlarged.

Base/16	128 x 192 pixels	For thumbnail sketches
Base/4	256 x 384 pixels	For position only in layouts
Base	512 x 768 pixels	For TV, for on-screen computer presentation, or for high-quality print up to about 2 x 3 inches
4•Base	1024 x 1536 pixels	For HDTV or for print up to about 3½ x 5 inches
16•Base	2048 x 3072 pixels	For print up to about 7 x 10 inches
64•Base*	4096 x 6144 pixels	For print up to about 14 x 20 inches

* Available with Pro Photo CD only

Some digital cameras come with plug-ins for Photoshop that allow you to open images chosen from a "contact sheet."

For imitating traditional art media such as the paintbrush, pencil, airbrush, or charcoal, a **pressure-sensitive tablet** with stylus has a more familiar feel than a mouse and also provides much better control. Photoshop's painting tools (see Chapter 6) are "wired" to take advantage of pressure sensitivity.

STORAGE AND TRANSPORT OF FILES

With Photoshop, of course, you can never have enough RAM; as soon as you get more, you need *even more.* But even if you have enough RAM so you rarely need to use virtual memory, a fast large-capacity hard disk will be vital. First of all, Photoshop requires that you have scratch disk space available, as described in "Virtual Memory" earlier in this chapter. And second, you'll need space to store the files you work with. For archiving (long-term storage of files you don't expect to need to work on often), digital audio tape (DAT) backup provides a solution that's relatively compact and inexpensive. But tape usually can't be used as a working storage medium; files have to be copied from tape to disk to be loaded into Photoshop.

Bernoulli systems and SyQuest removable-cartridge disks in several have given way to Zip and Jazz disks for transporting large files. As desktop CD-ROM writers become less expensive, CD-ROM is becoming popular for transport and storage, since the medium is inexpensive and stable, and the format is well-established and widely readable.

FILE FORMATS

Photoshop can save or export images in 20 different file formats. Here are some tips for saving files, depending on what you want to do with them:

For the most flexibility in what you can do with the file in the future, save in Photoshop format. It keeps all the layers (the number of layers you can create is limited only by your computer's RAM) and alpha channels (you can have up to 25 channels, including both color channels and alpha channels).

Also, for images that will be opened in a program that can't accept Photoshop layers, save in Photoshop format. By default the Photoshop format includes a flattened copy that can be opened in Photoshop 2.5 or 2.5.1, with all of the layers merged into one. If a file has more than 16 channels, though, it won't open in Photoshop 2.5 or 2.5.1.

File, Acquire, Quick Edit lets you open part of any file saved in Photoshop 2.0, uncompressed TIFF, or Scitex CT format. After you've worked on the part, choose File, Export, Quick Edit Save to return it to exactly the same place in the larger file. The modifiable Grid makes it possible to open and replace non-overlapping sections of an illustration, one by one, so you can modify a large image with much less RAM than you would need to work with the whole image at once.

To save a very large image in a format that will let you open a part of it with the File, Import, Quick Edit command so that not as much RAM is required, save in Photoshop 2.0, Scitex CT, or uncompressed TIFF formats. Although these formats all require flattening the file to a single opaque layer, the files can include alpha channels.

For files you can use with Adobe Illustrator, save as Photoshop EPS or TIFF, or simply drag and drop from an open Photoshop file to an open Illustrator file (see Chapter 7 for more about using Photoshop with Illustrator).

For files you can use with Macromedia FreeHand, save in TIFF format.

For files to be viewed with Adobe Acrobat Reader, save as PDF.

To place images on pages in PageMaker or QuarkXPress for color separation to make film for printing, it's a good idea to check with your imagesetting service bureau to see how they suggest saving and placing the Photoshop files. But here are some general tips:

- **Both PageMaker and QuarkXPress can accept images in Bitmap, Grayscale, Duotone, RGB Color and CMYK Color modes,** although not all modes can be handled in all file formats, as described below. (Color modes, specified in the Image, Mode submenu, are described in "Color in Photoshop" earlier in this chapter.)

- **If you want to produce color separations directly from PageMaker** without using a separation utility program, save color Photoshop files in CMYK mode (see "Making the Conversion" earlier in this chapter) before you save in TIFF format.

- **If your PageMaker files will be separated with a utility such as Adobe TrapWise,** you can save color images as TIFFs in RGB mode and rely on the separation software to do the conversion to CMYK (the Photoshop files are smaller this way, and you don't have to figure out the appropriate Separation Setup settings). That's the way this book was done, because we found that the separation algorithms in an old version of Aldus PrePrint worked very well, the process entailed less work for us.

- **If you need to silhouette an image when you place it in PageMaker,** you can use either Photoshop EPS format or TIFF with a clipping path that

Among the plug-ins in Photoshop 4's Filter menu is one that's designed to help you protect your work by applying to the image a "watermark" — an identifiable pattern of noise, customized and associated with your name as the originator. We found that, especially for small images, at the higher, more durable watermark settings that are designed to remain recognizable through cropping, filtering, and so on, the noise can be noticeable. And the watermark can't stand up to some filters, such as Despeckle or the Artistic filters. The **Digimarc** filter *can* be useful, though. For instance:

- To include a © symbol in the title bar of any file, choose Filter, Digimarc, Embed Watermark, move the Watermark Durability slider all the way to the left (Less Visible, Less Durable), and click OK. The © mark tells anyone looking at the file in Photoshop that the originator of the image cares about rights of ownership.

- To include the © mark and also let a viewer of the image know that you are the copyright owner, it's necessary to register with Digimarc. You can do this by clicking the Personalize or Change button in the Embed Watermark dialog box and following the registration instructions. (A three-month trial registration has been offered free to registered Photoshop 4 owners; after the trial period there is an annual fee for the service.) Once you register, whenever you use Filter, Digimarc, Embed Watermark, a viewer of the image can read the watermark to get a code number and then, via Digimarc's site on the World Wide Web, match that code with your name and, if you choose to include contact info, can find out how to get in touch with you.

makes the silhouette. (To designate a path as a clipping path, select the path and choose Clipping Path from the Paths palette's pop-out menu.)

- **For images to be placed in QuarkXPress for separation,** save files that are in Bitmap, Grayscale, or CMYK mode in Photoshop EPS format or in TIFF.

To save a Bitmap image whose white parts will be clear instead of opaque white when you place it in an application such as Illustrator, PageMaker, or QuarkXPress, save in Photoshop EPS format, choosing the Transparent Whites option.

   To save a Duotone file for placement in an application such as Illustrator, PageMaker, or QuarkXPress, save in EPS format.

   For images to be used for on-screen presentations other than on the World Wide Web, save in PICT File format, remembering to set Resolution (in the Image Size dialog box) to 72 dpi to match the screen. PICT can accommodate one alpha channel, which many multimedia design and production programs can interpret as a mask. PICT files are quite compact and can be made even smaller by using the JPEG compression options built into the PICT saving process. "To compress a finished image" (on page 40) tells more about JPEG.

   To save a file for use on the World Wide Web, you can save in JPEG or PNG format or export as GIF89a. Chapter 9 tells about how to choose from these formats and how to use them to best advantage.

   Adobe Premiere can save QuickTime movies in Filmstrip format, which can be opened in Photoshop. **To resave Premiere files after you've opened and worked on them in Photoshop,** use the Filmstrip format so they can be brought back into Premiere.

   To save files to be opened in paint programs on DOS- or Windows-based computers, the BMP, PCX, Amiga IFF, TIFF, and TGA formats work in many instances. Before choosing a file format, check to see what format(s) will work with a particular hardware-software-operating system combination.

   To pass files to other computer systems such as Scitex, Amiga, or Pixar, use the special format provided for that system. Pixar files can include an alpha channel, which can be used as a mask.

   To compress a finished image — in order to send it by modem or to fit it on a floppy

To make an image that fills the screen behind any open windows on your Windows 95 desktop, save your picture in **.BMP** format in the **Windows** directory. Then open the Display control panel (Start, Settings, Control Panel, Display). Locate the file in the scrolling Wallpaper list. Select it and choose Tile (to make a small image repeat as a pattern, or a very large image fill the screen, starting at the upper left corner of the picture) or Center. Then click OK to close the Desktop window, and enjoy your new view.

In scans and screen displays, images are made up of pixels. The pixels are all the same size but vary in color, with over 16 million color possibilities.

Many printed images are composed of overlaid screen patterns of halftone dots. These dots vary in size, but the number of lines of halftone dots per inch remains constant and the number of ink colors is often limited to four: cyan, magenta, yellow, and black. The spectrum of printed colors results from the visual "mix" of the dots of color.

Stochastic screening is another way of using a visual mix to print color. The "cells" of the stochastic screen pattern, instead of containing halftone dots that vary in size, contain very tiny dots that are in randomized patterns. The number of tiny dots in a region is what makes the color more intense (many dots) or less intense (few dots). Because the tiny dots within a "cell" are spread randomly instead of being clumped together to make larger dots, no halftone pattern is generated, and so more image detail can usually be seen.

disk for transport, for instance — you can use the JPEG format (Save As, JPEG). Photoshop's own JPEG plug-in provides a sliding scale of compression, with 10 preset levels. In compressing a file, the JPEG routines start by eliminating detail data that's likely to be lost in the printing process anyway. So compression at the Maximum Quality level (the "10" setting, least compressed) usually produces acceptable results for emergency archiving or transmitting of CMYK images that will eventually go to print. The most compressed (the "0" setting, which makes the smallest file size and is called Low Quality) shows the most image degradation. The reduction in file size that JPEG provides depends on the compression setting and the content of the image; a typical compressed size for a 900K image might be 59K for the Low setting and 169K for the Maximum setting.

JPEG compresses by averaging the color of blocks of pixels. The greater the compression, the more pixels per block. As a result, the color in JPEGged images can look "chunky," especially at the lower quality compression settings. To cut down on chunkiness, choose Baseline Optimized in the JPEG Options dialog box instead of the default Baseline Standard. (Another JPEG option, Progressive, is important for display of images on the World Wide Web and is discussed at the beginning of Chapter 9.)

It's now possible in some cases to place images in JPEG format into page layouts for separation and printing. But the standard procedure is still to **open JPEGged files in Photoshop and resave them in an appropriate format, such as TIFF or Photoshop EPS, before you place them** in a page. **Don't recompress** an image that has been stored in JPEG format and then opened; repeated compression degrades the image.

OUTPUT: PROOFING AND PRINTING

Like other desktop color files, Photoshop images can be printed on inkjet, thermal transfer, or dye sublimation printers, color photocopiers that can accept digital input, or film recorders (as negatives or positive transparencies). Typically, inkjet, thermal transfer, or dye sublimation printing is used to show generally how the image and the color will look when printed on an offset press, or to achieve a particular kind of art print quality. Photoshop files can also be produced as color-separated film for making plates for offset printing, using imagesetters or high-end color-separation systems such as Linotype-Hell or Scitex systems. And they can be output direct-to-plate (which bypasses film), or even direct-to-press, which bypasses both film and plates. Output to film recorders produces color transparencies, which can then be reproduced by traditionally available photographic printing options.

When color separations for offset printing are made by the traditional halftone screening method, the *contract proof,* which a

With stochastic screening it's possible to get good prints from smaller file sizes than with halftone screening. Because there's no halftone dot pattern with stochastic to interfere with the edges and detail in the image, these smaller files can produce sharper images.

But there are also some things to watch out for:

- Without extra dot gain compensation, images printed with stochastic screens tend to be darker overall and show higher contrast. This is because the dots used for stochastic screening are extremely tiny — very much smaller than halftone dots — so dot gain can be much more significant. The "spread" of the dot can be a much bigger fraction of the original dot size than it is for the larger halftone dots, and so the change in color due to dot gain is more drastic than for halftone printing.

- The tiny size of the dots in stochastic screening also means that it's much harder for press operators to make the kinds of adjustments they use to correct color during a print run.

- Since dot gain can be so important, and since an ordinary laminate proof doesn't accurately show dot gain, a special, alternative proofing method may be needed.

If you plan to use stochastic screening, be sure to get advice from both your printer and your service bureau. The service bureau should have an imagesetter equipped with a *RIP* (raster image processor) that uses stochastic screens, such as Adobe Brilliant Screens, Agfa's Crystal Raster technology, or Linotype-Hell's Diamond Screening. Have the service bureau run a test to separated film, and then ask the printer to check the film to make sure it will work for printing.

printer and client agree is the color standard to be matched on the printing press, is usually a laminate made from the film that will be used to make the printing plates. However, as stochastic screening (see "Using Stochastic Screening" at left), direct-to-plate, and direct-to-press printing technologies replace halftone film for some printing jobs, the "soft" proof (often made by an inkjet printer) becomes more important.

RESOLUTION, PIXEL DEPTH, AND FILE SIZE

Resolution is the term used to describe the **amount of data**, or color information, in a scan, a stored image file, a screen display, or a printed image. Typically, the more data, the more you can enlarge the image before it starts to look pixelated and lose detail.

Resolution is sometimes expressed as the number of dots, pixels, or ink spots per unit of measure (inch, centimeter, or pica, for example). Or resolution may be stated as pixel dimensions — 640 x 480 pixels, for instance — giving a more direct report of how much data is present, independent of the measured height and width of the image.

The terminology used to discuss resolution is a hodgepodge of words from printing, computer graphics, and prepress services. For consistency and to reduce confusion, this book uses resolution terminology the same way it's used in the *Adobe Photoshop 4.0 User Guide*. Our discussion of resolution starts with *screen frequency* because that's the piece of information you need to know first, in order to figure out how much information to collect in a scan or build into an image file in order to get the best printed image at the size you want. If you can help it, you don't want to find yourself in the opposite position: faced with a finished file and wondering how big you'll be able to print it without losing image detail and quality.

Screen frequency refers to the resolution or density of halftone screens, which are the patterns of ink dots used for printing most of the pages that come off presses today. Screen frequency is expressed in terms of **how many rows of halftone dots there are per linear inch,** called *lines per inch* (lpi). The higher the lpi, the less obvious the halftone dot pattern and therefore the more image detail you can see in the print.

In a printed image, the screen frequency (lpi) is the same in all areas of the image — it's the same where the color is pale as it is where the color is intense. The main characteristic that changes the intensity of the color is the *halftone dot size*. For example, in an image printed with a 150 lpi screen, an area of pale yellow is printed with 150 very small dots of yellow ink per inch, and perhaps no dots of cyan, magenta, or black, the other three process printing colors. Because quite a bit of bare white paper shows through between the tiny dots, the color looks pale. A bright red, on the other hand, might be made up of magenta and yellow dots, printed on top of each

On a 72 dpi monitor you can use the 25% or 33% view of an image file as a rough check of how big the image can be printed with a 150 or 133 lpi halftone screen without losing image quality.

other and as large as the 150 lpi screen density allows. Since these larger dots fill up the space, no white shows through, and the color is intense. Screen frequency, along with height and width of the printed image, determines how much information is *needed* to print the image without its showing pixels.

Image resolution — set in the Resolution field of the Print Size section of Photoshop's Image Size dialog box — is expressed as **pixels per inch** or pixels per centimeter. Image resolution, along with the image Height and Width in the Print Size section, determine how much information is stored in the file.

- **The image resolution you need for an image that will be printed** depends on the screen frequency (see "Getting Enough Information" on page 43).

- **The image resolution you need for an image that will be displayed on-screen** (in a multimedia presentation, for example) is typically 72 pixels per inch, which is a standard monitor resolution. Or it may be expressed directly as pixel dimensions — 640 x 480 pixels for instance.

Instead of being expressed as pixels per inch or pixel dimensions, **image resolution can be expressed as file size** (in K or MB), which also takes into account the height and width of the image. Both pixel dimensions and file size indicate how much information (or, relatively, how much image detail) is stored in the file.

Scan resolution is usually expressed as the number of ***samples per inch,*** *pixels per inch* (ppi), or sometimes *dots per inch* (dpi) **recorded by the scanner.** Scan resolution, along with the height of the scanned area and its width, determines how much information is *collected* for the image file. The more information the scan collects, the more image detail is recorded. With more image detail, the scan can be printed at a higher screen frequency or at a larger size. Like image resolution, scan resolution is sometimes expressed as file size (K or MB) or as pixel dimensions, which can be computed by multiplying the height and width of the image by the samples per inch.

Display resolution — or monitor resolution — is determined only by the monitor itself and the software that runs it. Some monitors have more than one setting and can display at a higher resolution than the standard 72 pixels per inch. Here are some important things to remember about display resolution:

- **When you view a Photoshop image at 100% magnification** (shown in the title bar of the image), every pixel in the image is represented by a pixel on-screen. So you're seeing it *not at the final printed size,* but at the monitor's display resolution, usually 72 to 85 pixels per inch.

There may be some instances when you *want* the individual square pixels to be obvious in your final printed image, providing a kind of "digital grain." If you want the square pixels to show, you need only decide how big you want them to be — 72 to the inch or 50 to the inch, for instance. Then set your scan or file resolution at that number, and set its dimensions (height and width) at the final size you want the image to be.

You may also want to set your Interpolation method to Nearest Neighbor (choose File, Preferences, General). That way, Photoshop won't try to hide the "jaggies" when you scale or rotate an image. Just be sure to remember to set Interpolation back to Bicubic when you've finished your "computer look" project.

The terms 4K and 8K are often used to describe scans made from 35 mm and larger transparencies. These terms mean that about 4000 or about 8000 samples are taken by the scanner across the long dimension of the image. For a 35 mm slide, a 4K scan takes about 4000 samples across the 35 mm width of the slide. So the scanned image is about 4000 pixels wide, enough to support enlargement to about 10 inches if you're printing at a screen frequency of 200 lpi. (See "Getting Enough Information" on this page for more about the relationship of image resolution to screen frequency.) The calculation works this way:

At a 2:1 ratio of image resolution to screen frequency, you need 400 pixels per inch to print at 200 lpi.

approx. 4000 pixels ÷ 400 ppi = approx. 10 inches

- In general, **the size that an image appears on-screen shouldn't be used as a predictor of the size it will be when it's printed.** However, if you display an image in a 25% view, you can safely assume that it contains enough data to print at the size it looks on-screen or smaller if you print at a halftone screen resolution of 150 lpi or less (133 lpi and 150 lpi are the screen frequencies typically used for printing books and magazines).

Besides the dimensions (length and width) and the resolution (number of pixels per inch), **pixel depth** is the other factor that affects the amount of information stored in an image. Pixel depth is the **amount of computer data required to store the color information for each pixel** in the image.

- A **grayscale** image includes only brightness data; each pixel requires 8 *bits* (also called 1 *byte*) to store this brightness information.

- A typical **color scanner** picks up 8 bits of brightness information for each of the three colors of light in the additive color model — red, green, and blue. So **a color scan** requires 8 x 3 = 24 bits of information per pixel. (Some scanners collect more color data; see "Super Scans" on page 45.)

Getting Enough Information

When you're trying to decide on a resolution for scanning or creating an image, the goal is to gather (or create) enough image information to print the image successfully — keeping the color transitions smooth and the details sharp. If your scan doesn't collect enough image information (or you create your artwork file too small), Photoshop's Image Size command can interpolate to increase the file size to the amount needed for printing. This may produce a better image than having the output device do the interpolation. But still, **an interpolated image won't look as good as if you had collected (or painted) the right amount of information in the first place.**

Although you want to be sure to use a high enough scan resolution, you don't want to overdo it — because the higher the scan resolution, the bigger the file size. The bigger the file size, the more disk space you need to store it, the more RAM and Scratch Disk space you need to work on it in Photoshop, and the longer it takes to open, work on, save, and print. So the real goal in scanning is to capture enough information to make your final print or slide look great, but no more.

To determine the appropriate resolution, the first thing you need to know is how much information will be required for printing, and that depends on the printed size of the image and the screen frequency. If the picture will be printed by the four-color printing process (like most color books and magazines), it will be printed with halftone screening. To get consistently

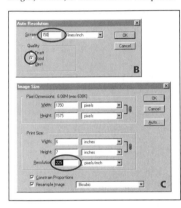

Steps 1 and 2 *To figure out how big to make a scan file, start by opening a dummy file in Photoshop and setting the color mode. You don't have to worry about setting the Height, Width, or Resolution at this point.*

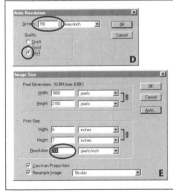

Steps 3 and 4 *Open the Image Size dialog box, set the Print Size dimensions to the units you want, and click Auto. In the Auto Resolution box enter the halftone screen frequency that will be used to print, and choose either Good (which uses a 1.5:1 ratio) or Best (which uses 2:1) (B). Then click OK to return to the Image Size box (C). The Resolution value is set automatically, based on your entry in Auto Resolution. The Pixel Dimensions value tells how large (in K or MB) the scan file will have to be. Either a larger Screen value or a higher Quality setting (D) will increase the Resolution, which increases the Pixel Dimensions size (E).*

good results for printing with halftone screens, your **scan resolution should be 1.5 to 2 times the print resolution**: 1.5 can work well for natural scenery without geometric patterns, sharp color boundaries, or fine details; 2 works well for everything, including man-made structures, which tend to have straight lines and sharp color breaks. Above 2, you increase file size without making the picture look any better.

SETTING UP A SCAN

In your quest to collect enough image data in a scan, the scan resolution setting (in pixels per inch) and the height and width (in inches or cm) or scale (in percentage) can vary, as long as enough information is collected.

To figure out the scan resolution you need to specify, you can start with the size and resolution you want for the printed piece and use Photoshop to calculate the size of the file you'll need.

1 Setting pixel depth. One of the things that will affect the amount of information collected is pixel depth, determined by the color mode used for the scan. Open a new file (File, New). This file will not be used to make an image, only to calculate scan resolution. The first step is to set the mode (see figure A at the left):

- For both color and grayscale images, the mode used for scanning should be RGB Color; grayscale images typically turn out better if you collect the color information in the scan and then convert to Grayscale in Photoshop. (See the beginning of Chapter 3 for tips on converting from RGB to Grayscale.)

- Use Grayscale mode for scanning black-and-white line art; line art usually turns out better (with smoother, more consistent lines) if it's scanned in Grayscale mode and then perfected with Image, Adjust, Levels. ("Colorizing Line Art" in Chapter 6 demonstrates this method.)

With the mode set, click OK.

2 Setting the dimensions. The amount of scan data you need depends on the printed size and the halftone screen frequency. Choose Image, Image Size. In the Print Size section of the Image Size dialog box, enter the dimensions (Height and Width) you want for the final printed image (refer to figure A).

3 Factoring in the screen frequency. Now you'll account for the halftone screen. In the Image Size dialog box, make sure the Resample Image box is checked, so Photoshop will be able to adjust the Resolution without changing the dimensions.

With the Height and Width already set by your entry in step 2, to get the Resolution setting, click the Auto button. In the Auto Resolution dialog box set the Screen (halftone screen frequency)

Step 5 *When your scanner shows you a preview of your image, use the scanning software's cropping tool to identify the area you want to scan (F).*

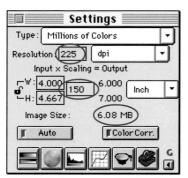

Step 6 *Adjust your scanner's scale setting until the image size (K or MB) matches or slightly exceeds the Pixel Dimensions file size number that you wrote down in step 4 (G). Then complete the scan. (The interface shown here is that of the Microtek ScanWizard desktop scanning software.)*

you and your printer agree on. Then choose Good (1.5 times the screen value, for natural, organic images) or Best (2 times the screen, for images with hard-edged elements or fine detail). Click OK.

4 Reading the file size. Back in the Image Size dialog box, note the new file size number in the Pixel Dimensions section of the box (write it down). This is the file size (in K or MB), in other words the amount of data the scanner will need to gather to support the size and halftone screen you've chosen. You now know the dimensions, resolution, and resulting file size that you need.

5 Defining the area to scan. Put your original in the scanner. If your scanner has a plug-in module for Photoshop, activate the scanner by choosing it from the File, Acquire submenu. Use the scanner's Preview function to show you the image you'll be scanning, and use its cropping box to select the area to scan. Be sure you crop to an area with the same proportions, if not exactly the same dimensions, as the Width and Height you set in the Image Size dialog box. That is, if the final printed size will be 6 x 7 inches, the scan crop should have the same proportions: for instance, 3 x 3.5 inches, or 12 x 14 cm.

6 Sizing the scan. Now find the place in the scanner interface that tells what the file size will be (in K or MB) for the scan you've set up. If this value is different than the new file size value you wrote down from the Pixel Dimensions section of the Image Size dialog box, and if the scanner allows you to enter a file size value, enter the number you wrote down. But if the scanner won't let you enter a file size value (most won't), adjust the scanner's Scale setting until the file size is close to that value: If the scan file size is too small, increase the Scale factor above 100% until the file size is right. On the other hand, if the scan file size is larger than you need, you can reduce the Scale below 100% to save on the file size. (If your scanner doesn't have a scale option, change the Resolution of the scan until the file size matches the size you wrote down.)

Other circumstances. You may not always know in advance exactly how big to make your scan. Here are some approaches you can take if you don't have all the info you need for steps 1 through 5:

- **If you don't know the screen frequency for printing,** guess high. Enter the Screen value in step 3 as 150 lpi or higher.

- **If you don't know the final printed dimensions of the image,** go for the "optimal scan": Scan the image at its full original size either at the Resolution in the Print Size section of the Image Size box or the scanner's default, whichever is larger. If this would make the file too big to work with, scale it down to the biggest file size you can manage.

Some scanners have built-in descreening algorithms for eliminating the moiré that can result from scanning a page that was printed using halftone screens. Shown here are scans made with Microtek ScanWizard desktop scanning software with (bottom) and without (top) the descreening function.

- **If the image you're scanning will be only a small part of a composite,** you can either: Estimate the final printed size of that element and use those dimensions in the Image Size dialog box in step 1. Or, if you really don't know how big you want to use the element, scan it at its full original size at the Resolution in the Print Size section of the Image Size box or the scanner's default (as above). Place the scanned element on its own layer in your composite file. If you need to size it up or down, use Layer, Free Transform to size it relative to the other components of the image.

RESAMPLING IN PHOTOSHOP

Regardless of how well you plan there are likely to be times when you need to *resample* — either resample down or resample up — in Photoshop. *Resampling down* means decreasing the file size. You might do it because you have more information than you need for printing and you want to reduce the bulk of the file. *Resampling up* is increasing the file size. You might do this in order to have enough information to reproduce the image at the size and screen frequency or display resolution you want.

To resample, use the Image Size dialog box. Make sure that both the Constrain Proportions and the Resample Image box are checked and that Bicubic is chosen from the Resample Image pop-out list. Then:

- **To change the image dimensions,** enter a new value in the Height or Width field. The other dimension will change automatically and so will the file size. The Resolution will stay the same.

- **To change the image resolution,** set Height and Width units to anything but pixels. Then enter a new value in the Resolution field. The dimensions will stay the same but file size will change. *Wow!*

Correcting a Batch of Scans

Overview *Make a grayscale step wedge; laser print it; scan it; check the scan for a color cast; record an Action as you correct the color with Levels, Curves, or Color Balance; play back the Action on a batch of scanned images.*

PHOTODISC: PEOPLE, LIFESTYLES, & VACATIONS

IF YOUR SCANNER ADDS A COLOR CAST to the images you scan, that color will have to be removed from each one. So, as much as possible, scanner software should be adjusted to avoid introducing a color cast. Follow steps 1 and 2 below to assess whether your scanner is adding color, even after you've adjusted it. Steps 3 and 4 tell how to record and play back an Action for "neutralizing," if necessary, all the scans done on that machine. (You may find from step 2 that your scans don't need to be corrected for a scanner-introduced color cast. If so, you can use steps 3 and 4, along with "Automating with Actions," starting on page 21, as a reference for recording a different Action and playing it back on a batch of files. For instance, you may need to correct a bluish color cast from changes in old film, or a greenish cast from using the wrong film indoors under fluorescent lighting.)

1 Making a step wedge. A 21-step gray scale can be made as follows: Set up a wide rectangular file (File, New, Grayscale, 7 inches × 1 inch, 72 dpi). With black as the Foreground color and white as the Background color (press "D" to restore the default colors) double-click the gradient tool to open its Options palette, and set up a Foreground To Background Linear gradient in Normal mode. Hold down the Shift key to constrain the gradient to horizontal, and drag the gradient tool from one edge of the file to the other. Then choose Image, Adjust, Posterize and set up 21 steps. This will produce bands in steps of 5%, from 100% black to white (0% black). Print the step wedge file in black only (on a laser printer, for example) on bright white paper.

2 Scanning and checking for a color cast. Now scan your printed step wedge in full color (RGB) mode. You may have to experiment with color balance if your scanning software allows it, to get the most neutral representation of the steps in the gray scale. If you end up with a moiré (an unwanted interference pattern) in the bands of your scan, you can use a slight Gaussian blur to smooth the grays (Filter, Blur, Gaussian Blur).

Whether or not you think you see a color cast in your scan file, the only way to tell the exact nature of the problem is to open the Info palette (Window, Show Info), move the cursor onto your scan,

1a

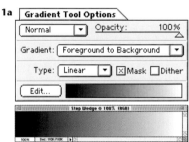

Filling a file with a black-to-white gradient

1b

Posterizing the gradient file

2

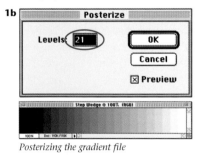

Scanning the step wedge introduced a slight pinkish cast.

3a

Starting the recording process

3b

After using the neutral gray eyedropper in the Levels dialog box, final adjustments were made by adjusting color balance for Highlights and Shadows.

3c

The Info palette shows color composition before and after the current adjustments.

3d

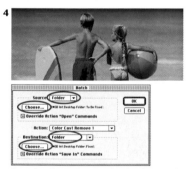

The recorded Action

4

Running the Action on a batch of scanned images corrects the scanner-introduced color change. (The color cast in this image was not present in the beautifully color-balanced PhotoDisc original; we made a print and introduced the color with a desktop scanner for purposes of demonstration.)

COLOR, YES — TONES, NO

Since a laser-printed step wedge is black toner on white paper, if a scan of the print shows color, you can figure it was introduced in scanning. But you can't use the step wedge to check for contrast and brightness changes made by the scanner, since the variation might have been caused by expansion of the laser printer dots on the page.

and move it around as you watch the R, G, and B values in the Info palette. At any point, if the gray is neutral, the R, G, and B values will be equal. If the values are more than a few points different from one another, a color cast has been introduced. Your first course of action should be to adjust your scanner software as well as you can to reduce the cast. Then rescan and recheck with the Info palette.

3 Recording the neutralizing process. If you couldn't completely avoid a color cast, now you'll turn on Photoshop's "recorder" while you remove the color, so you can play the steps back on files scanned on the same machine with the same settings. Open the Actions palette (Window, Show Actions) and click the New Action button at the bottom of the palette. In the dialog box that appears, name the Action and click Record. Move the Info palette to a spot that's visible but out of the way. Then make adjustments to remove color from the grays. A good way to start is to open the Levels dialog box (Image, Adjust, Levels) and, with the Preview turned on, use the middle (gray, neutral) eyedropper to click the middle band of the step wedge — the 50% gray band — in an attempt to neutralize the medium gray, and click OK. Now move the cursor over the gray bands checking the R, G, and B values before (original; on the left) and after (as they will be if you accept the current Levels settings by clicking OK; on the right). You may find that the R, G, and B values are now balanced for each band.

If the new values are not balanced, you can probably balance them now by adjusting Levels or Curves in the individual color channels or with Image, Adjust, Color Balance. Since we used the Levels neutral dropper to take the color out of the midtones, we started using Color Balance with the Highlights and Shadows settings. If the R value for a very light or very dark band was high in the Info palette, we moved the Cyan-Red slider toward Cyan. If R was low, we moved the slider toward Red. We did the same for the other two sliders, checking the Info values as we adjusted. (Color Balance changes that are made to the Highlights and Shadows have overlapping effects on the whole range of tones, so you may have to work back and forth in Highlights, Shadows, and even Midtones to get the entire range neutralized.) When the color had been balanced, we clicked OK, and then clicked the Stop button at the bottom of the Actions palette to stop recording.

4 Playing the Action on a batch of files. To play your Action on a number of files, first put all the images in a single folder and set up another (empty) folder. Then click on the name of the Action in the Actions palette and choose Batch from the palette's pop-out menu. In the Batch dialog box, choose the folder with the scans as the Source and the empty folder as the destination. When you click OK, Photoshop will automatically open each of the files, run the Action, and save the modified file in the destination folder. *Wow!*

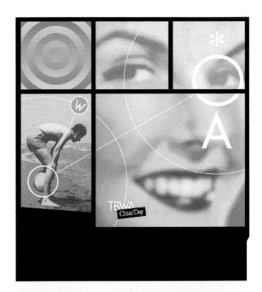

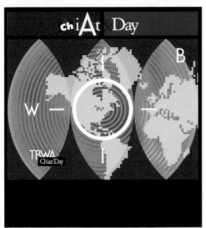

Louis Fishauf** created the *TBWA Chiat/ Day window murals* for a ground-floor all-purpose space that housed reception, employee lockers, lunch tables and meeting areas at the company's headquarters in Toronto. The 7-foot-high door (above right) shows the scale of the murals; the black areas outline the mostly rectangular panes of glass.

The murals were assembled in Photoshop from scanned imagery from Fishauf's clip art collection, with type set in Adobe Illustrator. Where exact placement was critical, Fishauf saved his Photoshop image in EPS format, opened it in Illustrator, and created crop marks to exactly fit the outline of the image. After setting the type to fit and saving the Illustrator file in EPS format, he used Photoshop's File, Place command to render the type, aligned automatically by the crop marks, exactly in position in the Photoshop file. For type whose placement

was less critical, he dragged and dropped from Illustrator to Photoshop.

The large-format inkjet process that was used to print the window-covering film introduced a dithering effect that allowed the images to be printed from relatively low-resolution files. Fishauf kept the files as small as possible, varying the resolution depending on the content of the panels and using smaller files for soft-focus images like the woman's face shown at the upper right. The largest file — the girl riding the fish — was only 70 MB.

Files were output in 54-inch-wide strips, first as proofs on paper and then on a thermal transfer material that was laminated onto three different kinds of window-marking film. From inside the building some parts of the mural are visible and others look like clear or smoked glass. From the outside, all parts of the mural are visible, as shown at the right.

The white curves, generated in Adobe Illustrator, were applied in a highly reflective opaque material, produced with a computer-driven cutting machine.

To put together the opening scene for the movie *The Mask*, **Eric Chauvin** of Industrial Light & Magic started with a shot of the Pacific coastline above Malibu (shown at the right) and concept art by Doug Chang. The photo dictated the lighting; taken on a gray, overcast day, it had no strong shadows. Chauvin shot photos of individual buildings in San Francisco, in one case crawling out a window onto a fire escape and from there onto the roof to get the angle he wanted for a photo. He composited the building photos with the beach scene, and then built and rendered the other buildings he needed in a 3D program, adding them to the composite. "It was difficult to figure out the vanishing points," says Chauvin. "There was a lot of guesswork involved in making things look correct." Chauvin's approach to Photoshop composites is to use a big, fast system; bring the individual elements into separate layers in one file; do all the color correction and other editing in place; and "save a billion copies" as the image develops so he can go back to previous stages if the client requests a change. When he had finished painting the dismal scene, the only thing moving in the sequence was the water. To help establish scale and add a bit more life, Chauvin animated 3D cars on the overpass (itself a 3D model), added smoke coming out of the smokestacks, and put small birds in the sky (squiggly lines moved along a "flight path").

PHOTO: BELA BORSODI / MODEL: APRIL PALASTNY – I'M NY

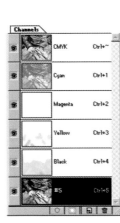

Eric Reinfeld created *Debutante Wilding*, a three-color tinted photo, as one of a series of fashion illustrations for New York's *Paper* magazine. He began with a CMYK scan of a black-and-white photo. Working in the main channel (#0), he selected all and copied. Then he activated the Black channel (#4) and pasted the copied image into the channel. Next he activated each of the other three channels — Cyan, Magenta, and Yellow — in turn and filled them with white. Reinfeld viewed all the channels together as he modified one at a time. He left the Cyan channel white, since no cyan ink would be used to print the image. In the Magenta channel he applied black paint with soft brush strokes at a low Opacity setting (about 10 to 15%) to some parts of the skirt. He filled the Yellow channel with black at a low opacity and then used the paintbrush and white paint to erase the tint in the area of the leather jacket; he painted with black, again at a low Opacity, onto the skirt and other areas of the image. In the Black channel, he used the dodge and burn tools to lighten and darken folds in the skirt and other parts of the image. In all channels Reinfeld kept his painting light in order to accommodate the dot gain that would occur when the images were printed on *Paper's* relatively soft stock.

SELECTIONS, MASKS, LAYERS, AND CHANNELS

WHETHER YOU'RE WORKING ON GRAPHICS for the World Wide Web or for print, creating images with Adobe Photoshop almost always depends on isolating some part of the image so you can paint it, filter it, move it, or make it part of a montage. Isolating part of an image this way is called *selecting*. To work effectively with Photoshop, you need to know about selections: how to make them, how to store them, how to activate them again from storage, and how to combine them.

Selections are ephemeral. When you make a selection, a flashing boundary (sometimes referred to as "marching ants"), lets you see what part of the image is selected. But the selection boundary disappears if you click outside it with a selection tool or press Ctrl-D or choose Select, None. The selection disappears forever when you deselect it, unless you have first stored it — by turning it into a Quick Mask (described in "Quick Mask" on page 62), an alpha channel (page 65), a pen path (page 55), a layer of its own (page 66), a layer mask (page 71), or an Adjustment layer (page 72).

MAKING SELECTIONS

Selections can be made with choices from the Select menu, with selection tools, with the pen tool, with the type tools, or by modifying a copy of one of the file's color channels — for instance, the Red, Green, or Blue channel of an RGB image. In general, selections that are made *procedurally* — that is, by using information like color or brightness that's intrinsic to the image — rather than by drawing a selection boundary by hand, can be faster and more accurate.

The tool or command that works best for making a selection depends on what you want to select. Each of the selection tools and commands has its own advantages and disadvantages. To decide which to use, you need to analyze the area you want to select — Is it organic or geometric? Is it fairly uniform in color, or is it multicolored? — and choose the tool, command, or combination of techniques that will do the job.

SELECTING BY SHAPE

If the subject you want to select is not distinctly different in color from its surroundings, you'll need to select it by shape. In that case the marquee tools, the lasso, and the pen are the tools you'll need to choose from.

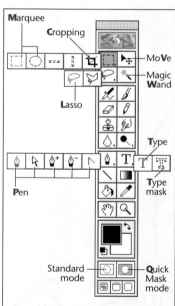

One of the biggest changes to the selecting process in Photoshop 4 is that the tasks of making and moving selections have been separated. Selection tools draw and move selection boundaries, but to actually move pixels you have to use the move tool, always accessible with the Command key.

continued on page 54

For a vignette effect with a hard or soft (feathered) border, use the rectangular or elliptical marquee.

To select an area that has a complex outline and shares colors with its surroundings so it's hard to select by color, use the lasso tool.

Holding down the Alt key lets you switch between dragging the lasso in its freeform mode and clicking it as a polygon lasso. The Alt key also prevents closing the selection border if you accidentally let go of the mouse button.

HYBRID SELECTIONS

To make a selection that's partly sharp-edged and partly feathered, set the Feather in the Options palette and make the feathered selection first; then set the Feather to 0 and add the unfeathered selection by holding down the Shift key as you select. (If, instead, you make the sharp-edged selection first and then the feathered, the feather softens the junction of the two selections.)

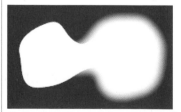

Feathered selection made first; sharp-edged selection added

Selecting Geometric Shapes — The Marquees

To "frame" a selection, use one of the marquee tools: the rectangular marquee or the ellipse. The marquee tools offer a variety of options for selecting.

- The default mode for the marquee tools is to start the selection from the edge. But many times you have better control of exactly what you select if you draw the selection from the center out. **To start a selection at its center,** press and hold the Alt key at any time during the selection process. If the selection frame turns out to be the right size but it still doesn't encompass exactly what you want, you can drag to move the selection border itself into place, without moving any of the pixels inside it.

- **To select a square or circular area,** constrain the rectangular or elliptical marquee by holding down the Shift key as you drag.

- **To make a selection of a particular height-to-width ratio,** double-click on either of the marquee tools to open the Marquee Options palette, choose Constrained Aspect Ratio for the Style, and set a particular height-to-width ratio. Now the marquee will make selections of those proportions.

- **To make a selection of a specific size:** If you want to make a selection of a specific measurement in inches or centimeters, build the selection boundary in the upper left corner of the image: Turn on the ruler (Ctrl-R), and drag Guides into the image from the rulers and align them at the measurements you want. For instance, if you want a horizontal 3 x 2-inch selection, drag a Guide from the top ruler and align it with the 2-inch mark on the vertical ruler; drag a guide from the side ruler and align it with the 3-inch mark on the horizontal ruler. Turn on Snap To Guides (View, Snap To Guides) and drag the marquee from the upper left corner of the image until it snaps to the

FEATHERING A SELECTION

Feathering is a way of softening the edges of a selection so it blends into the surrounding image. This kind of edge can be useful for making a "seamless" change when part of an image is selected, modified, and then released back into its original unmodified surroundings. Feathering extends the selection outward but at less than full opacity so that some of the surrounding image is included. At the same time the opacity of the image is also reduced for a distance inside the selection border. It's the Feather Radius that determines how far into and outside the selection border this transition extends.

- **To feather a lasso or marquee selection as you make it,** first double-click the tool in the toolbox to open its Options palette so you can enter a Feather setting. Then make the selection.

- If you forget to set the Feather ahead of time, or if the selection method you used didn't have a Feather option, **you can feather the selection after you've made it** (but before you move or change it): With the selection active choose Select, Feather and set the Feather Radius.

Antialiasing smooths a selection's edge by making the edge pixels partially transparent so you don't get "stairsteps" in the selection border. When the antialiased selection is pasted into its new surroundings, these partly clear pixels pick up color from the ones they're pasted on top of, so they end up being a blend of the colors on the two sides of the selection border. Of the selection tools, the rectangular marquee, with its straight-sided selections, doesn't need antialiasing. For the elliptical marquee, lasso, and magic wand you can turn antialiasing on or off.

Antialiasing (right) looks blurry close up, but it smooths the appearance of edges.

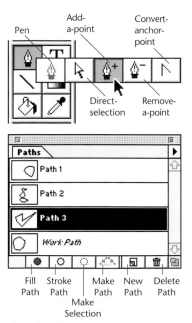

The path tools pop-out toolbar (top) with tools for drawing and adjusting paths; and the Paths palette (bottom) for storing and stroking paths and converting selections to paths and vice versa

Guides. Now turn off Snap To Guides and drag the selection boundary until it surrounds the area you want to select.

If you want to make a selection with specific measurements in pixels, choose Fixed Size for the Style in the Marquee Options palette and specify the Width and Height in pixels.

Selecting Irregular Shapes — The Lassos

To select a multicolored area with a complex boundary, especially if the thing you want to select shares colors with its surroundings, you may have to hand-draw the selection border with one of the two lasso tools — the plain one or the polygon. Here are some tips for using the lasso tools:

- Clicking a **series of short line segments with the polygon lasso** is often an easier and more accurate way **to define a smooth curve** than trying to trace the edge by dragging the lasso.

- Holding down the **Shift key** as you use the **polygon lasso** restricts its movement to **vertical, horizontal, or 45° diagonal.**

- Holding down the **Alt key** lets you **operate the tool as either** the lasso or the polygon lasso.

Selecting with Curves — The Pen Tool

The pen tool has a pop-out toolbar for choosing from the five path drawing and editing tools. Pressing the "P" key cycles through these five tools. The Paths palette (opened by choosing Window, Show Paths) includes everything necessary to name these smoothly curving paths (called Bezier curves), and to save them so they can be recalled later, to fill or stroke them, turn them into selections, combine one with an existing selection, or turn a selection into a path. The filling, stroking, and selecting functions are found in the icons at the bottom of the palette, along with icons for creating a new path from a selection and for removing a path. Every-

Photoshop 4's new nonprinting Grid makes it easy to create geometric selections that were difficult in the past. For instance, with the Grid it's easy to draw a set of same-size, aligned selections by using marquee tools: Choose View, Show Grid to display the grid, and View, Snap To Grid to make the Grid "sticky" so the motion of the tools will be controlled by the grid. Choose a marquee tool, line up its cursor with a grid point, and drag to draw from a corner, or Alt-drag from a center point, to draw a selection boundary. To draw another selection, line up the selection tool with another Grid point, hold down the Shift key so the old selection will also stay active while you add this new one, and drag again.

thing you can do on the palette itself you can also do by choosing from the palette's pop-out menu; in addition, the menu lets you designate a **clipping path** for "clipping" away the surrounding image to silhouette the selection for export to a page layout program, for example.

Clicking to make corner points

Dragging to make smooth points

Closing a path

Adding a point

Deleting a point

Changing the type of point

To be able to see the next segment of the pen path as you're drawing it, you can put the pen tool into "rubber band" mode: Double-click the pen in the toolbox to open the Pen Tool Options palette; click the Rubber Band checkbox (A). Now when you draw you'll be able to see how the curve is shaping up before you click to place the next point (B). If you're just learning how Bezier curves work, this can be a big help.

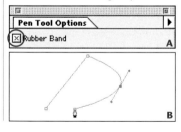

One of the advantages the pen tool has over using the lasso is that you can move the anchor points and manipulate their handles to adjust the shape of a selection border. This fine-tuning process can be quite a bit easier than making lots of little additions to or subtractions from a lasso selection.

The shape of the Bezier curve drawn by the pen tool is controlled by the positions of anchor points and direction lines, or "handles," which direct the curve as it comes out of the anchor points. The *Adobe Photoshop User Guide* explains how to work the pen tool, but here are some quick tips for using it.

Drawing a path (either an open-ended path or a closed shape) with the pen tool is done by placing a series of anchor points:

- **To place a corner point** where the line can change direction abruptly without a curve, click with the pen. Placing two corner points one after another draws a **straight line**.

- **To create a smooth (curve) point,** position the pen tool's cursor where you want the point and then hold the mouse button down and drag to position the handles that control the curve as it approaches and leaves the point.

- **To constrain the position of the next corner or smooth point** to any 45- or 90-degree angle, hold down the Shift key as you place the point.

- **To close a path,** move the pen icon close to the starting point; when you see a little circle to the right of the pen icon, click.

- **To end a path without closing it** so you can start to draw a new path, hold down the Ctrl key to turn the pen into the direct-selection arrow, move the cursor away from the path and click. This will end the path, and releasing the Ctrl key brings back the pen tool so you can start again.

To reshape a path after it's drawn, you can:

- **Move a point:** Drag it with the direct-selection tool (the arrow).

- **Select a control point or a curve segment so you can move it:** Click with the direct-selection tool. Shift-click to select more.

- **Add a point:** Click on the curve with the pen+ tool.

- **Remove a point:** Click on that point with the pen– tool.

- **Turn a corner into a smooth point or vice versa:** Click it with the convert-anchor-point tool (the caret).

- **Reshape a curve by moving one handle independently of its mate:** Drag on the handle with the convert-direction-point tool. If you then want to move the other handle, use the direct-selection tool.

You can Copy (Ctrl-C) or **cut** (Ctrl-X) a path to the clipboard and then **paste** it (Ctrl-V) into the same or a different file.

To duplicate a path, hold down the Alt key, and drag with

With a selection active, choosing Make Path from the Paths palette's pop-out menu brings up a dialog box that lets you set Tolerance, to specify how closely the Bezier curve will trace the selection boundary when the selection is converted to a path. A tolerance of "0" means the path must trace every little nook and cranny in the selection; this makes a very accurate and tight-fitting, though possibly "jaggy" path, but it can also make for a very complex and calculation-intensive path. The higher the Tolerance value, the looser and smoother the path and the sloppier the selection it will make, but the less likely it is that the path will create a limitcheck error on output if it's exported to another program.

Make Work Path

Tolerance: `2.0` pixels   OK   Cancel

Kern type with the magic wand as follows: In the Magic Wand Options palette, set Tolerance to 255. Click and Shift-click to select letters. Hold down the Ctrl key and Shift-drag or press the arrow keys to move the type.

the direct-selection tool to position the copy where you want it. Hold down the Shift key as well to constrain the motion.

To activate a path, click its name in the Paths palette.

To move a path, with the path active (click it with the direct-selection tool or click its name in the Paths palette to make it active), Alt-click with the direct-selection tool to select all the points in the path. Then release the Alt key and drag the path to move it without duplicating it or changing its shape.

To save a Work Path, double-click its name in the palette.

To convert a selection to a path, click the Make Path icon, third from the right at the bottom of the palette.

To convert a path to a selection (or add it to or subtract it from an existing selection), activate the path and click (or Shift-click or Alt-click) the Make Selection icon, third from the left at the bottom of the palette. Or, with any tool but a painting tool active, press the Enter key (or Shift-Enter or Alt-Enter).

To stroke a path with the Foreground color, choose a painting tool and press the Enter key or click the Stroke Path icon, second from the left at the bottom of the Paths palette.

To fill a path with the Foreground color, click the Fill Path icon, farthest left at the bottom of the Paths palette.

The Type Tools

Photoshop's type tool provides access to fonts, so you can incorporate type into images. Like the lasso, the type tool has two forms:

- The **plain type tool** sets type on its own layer.

- The **type mask,** or **type selection, tool** makes a type-shaped selection. You can then manipulate the selected part of the image, or turn the selection into a new layer (Ctrl-J), or cut the type out (Ctrl-X), or cut the type out and make the cutout into a new layer (Ctrl-Shift-J).

When you choose either type tool and click in an image, the Type Tool dialog box opens. In the Type Tool dialog box you can specify typeface, style, and spacing, and enter the text you want to set. Clicking OK returns you to the image, where the type appears,

The pen tool snaps to the Grid — both for placing points and for positioning direction lines. This makes possible elements like symmetrical scalloped and wavy borders. And the elusive round-cornered rectangle, popular for interactive buttons can now be very easily constructed: For each corner, click to place the first point where you want the curved corner to begin and drag at matching the around-the-corner point to make the curve. You can control the roundness of the corners by adjusting the Grid size (File, Preferences, Guides & Grid). Use a larger grid for bigger, rounder corners, a smaller grid for tighter, squarer ones.

Increasing the Font Cache in the *atm.ini* file from its default 256K can help with smoothing type.

OutBack

OutBack

OutBack

OutBack

Dramatic "inline-outline" type effects can be accomplished in Photoshop by setting type, blurring it to get a full range of tones, and then putting a number of "switchbacks" into the Curves dialog box. Colorizing the type with Image, Adjust, Hue/Saturation before adjusting Curves gives even wilder results.

SAVE THAT SELECTION!

Any selection border that's more complex than a simple marquee and that wasn't created as a pen path should be stored in a layer or as an alpha channel in its original file in case you need the selection border again later.

• If you cut or copy the selection, filled with the selected image material, to a layer of its own, you don't need to do anything more; the selection border will automatically be stored as the transparency mask for the layer (see "Transparency Masks" on page 70).

• If you don't turn the selection into a layer, store the selection boundary as an alpha channel: With the selection active, choose Select, Save Selection, New. (Alpha channels are discussed on page 65.)

either as a layer or a selection, depending on which form of the tool you used. You can move the type around without disturbing the image underneath: For type set as its own layer, use the move tool. To move the selection boundary for type set with the type selection tool, drag with the type tool or any other selection tool. Here are some tips for using type in Photoshop:

• If you're using PostScript fonts, make sure you have **Adobe Type Manager** (atm.ini) installed so Photoshop has access to smooth PostScript-based type outlines. If it's installed but you're still having problems with jagged type, open the **atm.ini** file and increase the size of the Font Cache.

• Unless you want stairstepped, jaggy type for some reason, always select the **Anti-aliased** Style option in the Type Tool dialog box to smooth the edges.

• When you set type on its own transparent layer, Preserve Transparency is automatically turned on, so you can **change the fill** (color, pattern, or image) of the type without having the fill extend into the transparent area. **Note:** Be sure to *turn off* Preserve Transparency if you want to blur the type.

• Putting type on its own transparent layer also lets you **hand-kern the type** (adjust spacing between letters) fairly easily: Double-click the magic wand tool to open the Magic Wand Options palette. Set the Tolerance at 255 (the highest possible setting). Then click the magic wand on the letter you want to move; you'll have complete freedom to drag it around with the move tool, which turns it into a floating selection temporarily. (If you want to move two or more letters at once, Shift-click with the magic wand to add characters to the selection.) To keep the type on its original baseline, press and hold the Shift key as you drag it.

• To use **type as a mask** — in a layer mask or an alpha channel, for example — activate the mask or channel by clicking on its icon in the Layers palette or Channels palette, use the type selection tool to set the type, and fill with white or black (Edit, Fill), depending on whether you want the type part of the mask to be transparent and the rest of the mask opaque, or vice versa.

• Type set on its own transparent layer can also be used to **mask several layers at once** (see "Clipping Groups" later in the chapter).

SELECTING BY COLOR

Cleanly silhouetting a subject by color can help you grab elements such as a purple flower among pink ones, or a brown dog on a green lawn. Selecting by color is a *procedural* method. It uses the image's hue, saturation, or brightness information (or some

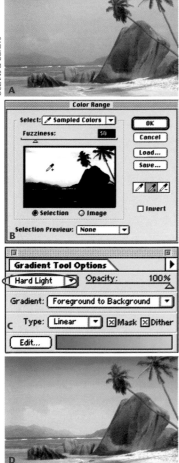

Use the Select, Color Range command in Sampled Colors mode to select a broad expanse of closely related colors. Here the challenge was to add drama to the sky without having to make a manual selection in a photo (A) with a subtle gradation at the hazy horizon and complex shapes (the palms) that had to be excluded. The Color Range eyedropper was dragged across the sky to select a range of blues. Then the Alt key was held down and the eyedropper was clicked on the colors we wanted to exclude. Fuzziness was adjusted between 15 and 30 — a good range for Fuzziness in general — to antialias the selection around the palms and "feather" the horizon area (B). The selection was stored as an alpha channel for safekeeping (Select, Save Selection). With the selection active, the gradient tool was used in Hard Light mode (C) to add a color ramp to the sky while retaining some of the subtle cloud structure in the original (D).

combination of these) to define the selection. To make a selection of all the pixels of a similar color, you can use the magic wand tool or the Select, Color Range command, or develop a selection from one of the color channels — for instance, the Red, Green, or Blue channel of an RGB image.

Using the Magic Wand

One advantage of the **magic wand** tool is that it's quick and easy. It's good for selecting one uniformly colored area or a small number of similarly colored areas in an image where there are other areas of the same color that you don't want to select.

- **To make a selection with the magic wand,** just click it on a pixel of the color you want to select. It selects that pixel and all similar neighboring pixels for as far as that color continues.

- **To specify how broad a range of color the magic wand should include in a selection,** double-click the wand in the toolbox to open the Magic Wand Options palette and set the Tolerance value to a number between 0 and 255. The lower the number, the smaller the range of colors.

- **To control whether the selection is based on the color of only a single layer or from all visible layers** combined, turn Sample Merged off or on in the Magic Wand Options palette.

Selecting by Color Range

The **Select, Color Range** command is complex, but it's well worth learning to use. In many cases it offers much more control of what's selected than the wand does — you can select pixels from many parts of an image at once, for example — and it shows the extent of the selection much more clearly.

The little **preview window** in the Color Range dialog box shows a grayscale image of the selection. White areas are selected; gray areas are partially selected, with the degree of selection decreasing as you go toward black, which is completely deselected. This picture is much more informative than the marching ants you see when you use the selection tools from the toolbox.

The **Fuzziness** is like the magic wand's Tolerance setting, but it's easier to work with, since the entire range is spread out on a slider scale and the preview window instantly shows the effect of changing it. Try to keep the setting above 16 to 32 to prevent jagged edges in the selection.

TOLERANCE VALUES

The Tolerance for the magic wand also controls the range of Select, Similar and Select, Grow. If there is a lot of color variation and contrast in the original selection, you may not get exactly the results you expect when you choose Grow or Similar. If so, you can try again by undoing the Grow or Similar function (Ctrl-Z), resetting the Tolerance lower, and choosing Grow or Similar again.

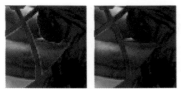

Sometimes you don't notice a "fringe" of background pixels surrounding a silhouetted subject until you've layered it on top of a new background. But it isn't too late to remove it. Choose Layer, Matting, Defringe before you merge the layer with the composite. The Defringe command pushes color from the inside of the selection outward to replace the edge pixels, thus eliminating the fringe.

The **"Select" field** at the top of the box lets you choose the color selection criteria:

- **To select based on colors sampled from all visible layers of the image as if they were merged,** choose Sampled Colors, then choose the dialog box's leftmost eyedropper tool and click on the image, just as you would with the magic wand. One difference between using the magic wand and using the Color Range eyedropper is that the selection extends throughout the image (or the existing selection, if there is one), as if you had made a magic wand selection and then chosen Select, Similar.

- **To select based on color sampled from a single layer**, first make all other layers invisible by clicking off their "eye"

CROPPING

Cropping is trimming an image to the size and proportions you want. In Photoshop, cropping is done by selecting the part of the image you want to preserve, and then removing everything outside the selected part. You can use either the rectangular marquee or the crop tool.

If you have an **active, unfeathered rectangular selection** and you choose **Image, Crop**, the image will be cropped to that shape, and its window will automatically shrink to fit the new dimensions.

For some situations the **cropping tool** provides an advantage over using the rectangular marquee because you can move the cropping borders in, out, up, or down by dragging on the side or corner handles; you can rotate the cropping frame by dragging just outside the cropping frame; and you can trim and resample an image in one step. Press the Enter key or double-click inside the crop box to accept the crop, or press Ctrl-period to release it so you can start over.

With Fixed Target Size turned on, the crop tool can cause an image to be resampled (averaging pixels to shrink the image or manufacturing new pixels to enlarge it; see "Resampling" in Chapter 1), and this resampling can make the cropped image appear fuzzy. You need to understand how the cropping tool works so you don't unknowingly resample.

Double-clicking the cropping tool in the toolbox opens the Cropping Tool Options palette. If you click on Fixed Target Size and then on Front Image, the dimensions and resolution of the image appear in the Width, Height, and Resolution fields.

- If you **set the Width and Height values** but delete the number in the Resolution field so the field is blank, and then drag the crop tool, the cropping frame will hold the proportions you set in Width and Height. When you click inside the selected area to accept the crop, the Resolution will be set at a value that won't cause resampling (adding or averaging pixels).

- If you leave the Height and Width fields empty but **set the Resolution**, you can drag the cropping frame to any proportions you want. And when you click to accept the crop, the dimensions will be adjusted and no resampling will occur.

- But if instead you set the **Width and Height** *and* enter a value for Resolution, the image will be resampled as it's cropped, so that it will come out to the dimensions and resolution you specify. Then you'll probably need to apply the Unsharp Mask filter to repair the fuzziness that resampling will have introduced.

A one-step crop and rotation of a selection

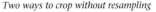

Two ways to crop without resampling

Cropping with resampling

The Color Range command makes it easy to "subselect" by color criteria, sort of like searching a database using several key words: "Select everything *red* that's *in this one area of the image* so I can change the color to green." The key to subselecting is that Color Range makes its selections *within the current selection.*

To select within a color family *and* within a particular area of the image, use a selection tool to surround the general area you want to change (A). Then choose Select, Color Range; choose the color family from the "Select" list (Reds in this case) (B). (If the color family you need doesn't appear in the list — like orange, for example — leave the Select setting on Sampled Colors.) Click OK to close the dialog box, and "marching ants" will show the selection. Press Ctrl-H to hide the selection border so you can see what you're doing. Then use Image, Adjust, Variations or Hue/Saturation to adjust the color (C).

icons in the layers palette (see "Layers, Layer Masks, and Adjustment Layers" later in this chapter for more about the Layers palette). Then choose Select, Color Range and click with the eyedropper.

- **To extend or reduce the range of colors in the current selection,** click or drag with the + or – eyedropper to add new colors or to subtract colors. Or click or drag with the plain eyedropper, with Shift (to add) or Alt (to subtract). You can also expand or contract the selection by adjusting the Fuzziness.

- **To select a family of colors,** choose from the color blocks in the "Select" list. The color families are predefined — you can't change the Fuzziness or use the eyedroppers to expand or shrink the range.

- **To Select only the light, medium, or dark colors,** choose Highlights, Midtones, or Shadows. Again, there's no opportunity to make adjustments to these ranges.

- **To bring *small areas* of RGB color that can't be reproduced with CMYK inks into the printable range,** use the Out-Of-Gamut selection criterion. See the "Getting Into Gamut" tip on page 30 for information about selecting and correcting out-of-gamut colors.

The **Invert box** provides a way **to select a multicolored subject on a plain background:** Use the Color Range eyedropper to select the background, and then click the box to reverse the selection.

Using a Color Channel as a Starting Point

Photoshop stores color information in individual color channels, such as the Red, Green, and Blue values of an RGB image. Often the contrast between a subject and its surroundings is a lot more pronounced in one of the color channels than in the others.

To use a color channel as a starting point for making a selection, look for a channel where the subject is very light and the surrounding area very dark, or vice versa. Then copy that channel to make an alpha channel and use the Levels command and black and white paint to increase the contrast between the areas you want to select and those you want to leave unselected. (This technique is illustrated on page 65.)

MAKING SPECIALIZED SELECTIONS

Photoshop's toolbox and Select and Edit menus provide what you need for specific selecting tasks:

To select a border area around some part of an image, select that part of the image and then choose Select, Modify, Border and specify the width you want the border to be. Once you make a border around a selection, you can modify it or fill it to create a frame. Or turn it into an alpha channel and use it with Lighting Effects to form a beveled edge, as shown at the beginning of Chapter 8.

Quick Mask lets you store a selection temporarily while you edit it. By making a selection and then clicking the Quick Mask icon (on the right side near the bottom of the toolbox), you can turn the selection into a clear area in a semitransparent mask. The Quick Mask remains stable as you use the painting tools to edit it. Switching back to Standard mode by clicking the Standard mode icon (to the left of the Quick Mask icon) turns the mask into an active selection again.

Quick Mask has three features that make it better for some selecting tasks than using a layer mask or an alpha channel:

- It's quick — just click the icon to turn a selection into a mask.

- You don't store the selection permanently, so it saves on space.

- You can see both the image and the mask at the same time, which can be helpful if you're doing some fairly subtle mask painting.

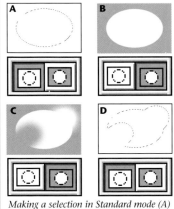

Making a selection in Standard mode (A) converting to Quick Mask mode (B), changing the selection mask by adding to the mask with black paint and removing from the mask with white paint (C), and turning the altered mask back into a selection (D)

To select an object with a very complex boundary (such as a person's hair) **or with many parts** (such as the leaves of a tree), it's often easier to select the background and then invert the selection by choosing Select, Inverse (or pressing Ctrl-Shift-I).

Unless you make a selection in an image, many of Photoshop's functions act as if the entire image were selected; for instance, if there's no active selection, paint can be applied anywhere on an image. But for some commands — such as Edit, Copy or any of the Image, Transform commands (Scale, Skew, Distort, or Perspective) — there has to be an active selection for it to work. **You can select the entire image,** including parts that extend beyond the current window, by choosing Select, All (or press Ctrl-A).

To select nothing — that is, to drop any active selection, even if it's hidden or is outside the current window — choose Select, None or use the keyboard shortcut, Ctrl-D (for "deselect"). Try this if painting, filtering, or some other function doesn't seem to work. There may be a selected area off-screen or a selection hidden with Ctrl-H, and dropping it will allow the function to work on the entire image.

ADDING AND SUBTRACTING

Photoshop provides several ways to extend a selection or to remove parts of it. The **Shift key** (for adding to the current selection) and the **Alt key** (for subtracting from the current selection) play an important role in many of these methods.

Expanding a Selection

You can enlarge a selection in any of the following ways:

- **To add more area to the current selection,** hold down the **Shift key** and use any selection tool to surround the area you want to add. The addition doesn't have to be connected to the first selection area — it can make a new selected patch somewhere else in the image.

- **To expand a selection outward,** picking up more pixels at the edge, choose Select, Modify, Expand, and enter a pixel value for the distance you want the selection to expand.

- **To add pixels that are similar in color and adjacent to the current selection,** you can choose Select, Grow. The selection will continue to grow as you repeat the command. Each time you use the command, the range of colors selected gets larger; the amount the range grows is controlled by the Tolerance setting in the Magic Wand Options palette.

- **To add all pixels in the image that are similar in color** to the pixels in the current selection, choose Select, Similar.

- **To add the contents of an alpha channel, a layer mask, or a layer's transparency mask to an existing selection,**

With a selection active, if you hold down the Shift or Alt key as you choose Select, Color Range, the selection you make will be added to or subtracted from the current selection.

```
Select
   All          ⌘A
   None         ⌘D
   Inverse     ⇧⌘I
─────────────────────
   Color Range...
```

The Alt key turns the lasso into a "superlasso" that can operate as either a regular (dragging) lasso or the polygon (clicking) lasso, but the Alt key also subtracts a new selection from an existing one. So using the superlasso to make a subtracted selection is a bit tricky. How will the lasso know whether you just want to subtract, or whether you want to subtract and also use the superlasso? Here's how you tell it: Press the Alt key and begin the subtraction by dragging the lasso or clicking with the polygon lasso; then release the Alt key and *press it again and hold it* as you continue with your lasso work.

To add to a selection with the superlasso, press the Shift key to start the addition, then press and hold the Alt key; once you've started selecting, you can release the Shift key.

For most purposes, smooth anti-aliased edges on silhouetted subjects are ideal. So it's a good idea to turn on the Anti-aliased feature in the selection tools' Options palettes before making selections. But for some World Wide Web applications, antialiasing can lead to unwanted color fringes around silhouetted images.

choose Select, Load Selection, Add To Selection, and choose the Document and Channel in the Source section of the Load Selection dialog box. (The discussion of alpha channels and layers later in the chapter includes **keyboard shortcuts** for adding channel and layer contents to or subtracting them from selections.)

Subtracting from a Selection

- **To remove part of the current selection,** press the **Alt key** (you don't need to hold it down) and use any selection tool to surround the area you want to remove. Or choose Select, Load Selection, choose the Source (an alpha channel, layer mask, or transparency mask), and choose Subtract From Selection.

- **To select the intersection of the current selection and a new selection**, hold down the **Alt and Shift keys** together as you drag to make the new selection. The rest of the original selection will be removed, and only the intersection will remain selected. Or choose Select, Load Selection, choose the Source (an alpha channel, layer mask, or transparency mask), and choose Intersect With Selection.

- **To deselect some parts of a multipart selection but keep others selected,** which is actually a special case of selecting an intersection, hold down the **Alt and Shift keys** and use the lasso or marquee to surround the parts you want to keep.

- **To contract a selection inward,** dropping the edge pixels, choose Select, Modify, Contract and enter a pixel value.

- **To subtract the contents of an alpha channel, a layer mask, or a layer's transparency mask to an existing selection,** choose Select, Load Selection, Subtract From Selection, and choose the Document and Channel in the Source section of the Load Selection dialog box. (The discussion of alpha channels and layers later in the chapter includes **keyboard shortcuts** for adding or channel and layer contents to or subtracting them from selections.)

CLEANING UP A SELECTION

Sometimes, despite the most careful selecting, a selection retains some background color, visible around the edge. To get rid of this unwanted "fringe," you can use the commands of the Layer, Matting submenu. Note that these commands work only after a selection is separated from its surrounding pixels, by being copied and pasted, or by being floated, or moved.

- **To eliminate an "edging" picked up by an image selected from a black (or white) background,** choose Layer, Matting, Remove Black Matte (or Remove White Matte).

Pixelated edges on a mask (A) can be cleaned up by blurring (B) and then using Image, Adjust, Brightness/Contrast to sharpen up the edge. First adjust the Contrast to reduce the blur to an antialiasing effect (C). Then move the Brightness slider to the right to enlarge the white part of the mask (so it will make a larger selection) (D) or to the left to shrink it (E).

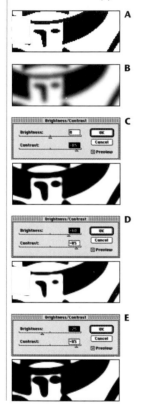

To move a selection more than 1 image pixel at a time with the arrow keys, zoom out to a magnified view. If you're working in a 100% view, 1 screen pixel is the same as 1 actual image pixel; but in a 50% view, 1 screen pixel represents 2 image pixels, so a press of an arrow key moves a selection 2 actual pixels, and so on.

Photoshop lightens dark pixels (or darkens light pixels) that it finds at the edges of the selection.

- **To remove edging in a color other than black or white,** try the Layer, Matting, Defringe command on the floating selection. This will "push" color from inside the selection into the edge pixels. Be careful, though. Using a Defringe setting of more than 1 or 2 pixels can create "spokes" or "rays" of color at the edge.

- Besides the Layer, Matting command, **another way to remove color edging is to "choke" the selection,** to shrink the selection border just slightly before copying, moving, or floating, so what's causing the edging is excluded. You can do that if you've saved the selection as an alpha channel or as a layer of its own. Load the selection border from the alpha channel or load the layer's transparency mask as a selection. Then choose the Select, Modify, Contract command to shrink the selection, then invert the selection (Ctrl-Shift-I) and press Backspace to remove the troublesome edge. (Alpha channels and layers are described later in this chapter.)

MOVING SELECTIONS

In Photoshop 4 the tasks of making and moving selections have been separated. Selection tools draw and move selection boundaries. The move tool is what moves pixels. It can move selected pixels if there's a selection active. Or it can move an entire layer — or a set of linked layers — if there's no active selection.

- **To move the selection boundary (the marching ants) without moving any pixels,** with any selection tool active, move the cursor inside the selection boundary and drag.

- **To move the selected pixels,** regardless of what tool is active at the moment, press the "V" key to switch to the move tool, and drag. Or hold down the Ctrl key to toggle to the move tool temporarily, drag to move the selected pixels, and release the Ctrl key to switch back to the tool you were using.

- **To constrain the movement of the selection border or selected pixels to horizontal, vertical, or a 45° diagonal,** use the Shift key. This technique works with either the marquee pointer or the move tool. But if you use it with the marquee pointer, you have to press the Shift key *after* you start the dragging process.

- **To move a selection boundary or selected pixels 1 screen pixel at time,** choose the move tool or a selection tool and use the arrow keys on the keyboard. Hold down the Shift key with the arrows to move a selection **10 screen pixels at a time**.

FIXED AND FLOATING SELECTIONS

Photoshop has two kinds of selections: *fixed* and *floating*. A **fixed selection** is still part of the image around it. A **floating**

To start a mask to select the surgeon, we found that the Red channel showed good contrast between the subject and the background. So we duplicated it to make an alpha channel.

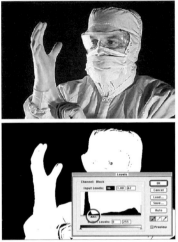

Contrast was increased in the alpha channel by adjusting the Input Levels (Image, Adjust, Levels). The airbrush and paintbrush tools were used to touch up the mask with black and white paint, getting rid of unwanted gray pixels.

The completed alpha channel was loaded as a selection, and Image, Adjust, Variations was used to change the overall color and lighting.

selection, on the other hand, hovers "above" the plane of the image.

When you make a selection with a selection tool or command, it's a fixed selection. But it turns into a floating selection if you hold down the Alt key and drag, or drag with the move tool. When a selection is floating, you can apply the Opacity and blending mode controls in the Layers palette. But if you want more control of the way it will combine with the image underneath, you have to turn it into a layer so you can control it with the Layer Options dialog box (see "Layers" later in the chapter, and "Using Layer Options" in Chapter 4).

STORED SELECTIONS: ALPHA CHANNELS

Photoshop's alpha channels provide a kind of subfile for storing selection boundaries so you can load them back into the image and use them later. A selection stored in an alpha channel becomes a mask, with white areas that can be loaded as an active selection, black areas that protect parts of the image where changes shouldn't apply, and gray areas that expose the image to changes proportionally to the lightness of the gray.

You can store any type of selection boundary in an alpha channel. A Photoshop file can have as many as 25 channels in total. So an RGB file, for example, since it has four channels tied up in the main channel and the three individual colors, can have up to 21 alphas, each providing a way to recall a particular selection independently of any other selection. A grayscale file can have up to 24 alphas, and a CMYK file can have as many as 20.

To make an alpha channel from a selection:

- Choose Select, Save Selection.

- Or Choose Window, Show Channels and then click the mask icon, second from the left at the bottom of the Channels palette. To name the channel as you make it, Alt-click the icon to open the Channel Options dialog box, where you can also choose whether you want the selection to be the white (transparent) part of the alpha channel (the default "Selection" setting) or the black (opaque) part (the "Mask" setting).

To load an alpha channel as a selection:

- Choose Select, Load Selection and, if more than one alpha channel exists, choose the channel's number.

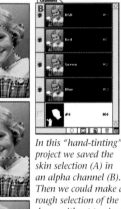

In this "hand-tinting" project we saved the skin selection (A) in an alpha channel (B). Then we could make a rough selection of the dress, without tracing the neck or arm (C). We Ctrl-Alt-clicked the alpha channel in the Channels palette to subtract it from the rough selection.

- Or click the Load Channel As Selection icon at the bottom left of the Channels palette; it's a dotted circle inside a white square.
- Or Ctrl-click the channel's name in the palette.
- Or use the keyboard shortcut: Ctrl-Alt-channel number.

To add to, subtract from, or **make an intersection** with the current selection, apply the Shift, Alt, or Shift and Alt keys as you either Ctrl-click the channel's name in the palette or click the Load Channel As Selection icon.

Combining alpha channels. The Image, Calculations command opens the very powerful Calculations dialog box. It operates like a logic puzzle, allowing you to pick any channel — alpha or color or layer mask or transparency mask or even luminosity (called Gray) — from any layer in the active document or from any other open document with the same pixel dimensions, and combine it (Add, Subtract, or use any of nine blending modes) with any other channel, through a mask of your choice. Then you can store or load the result in any qualifying open document or a new one that will be created at the same size. The Calculations command has tremendous potential for blending channels to make composite masks. Better yet, with an existing selection active you can add, subtract, or make an intersection with any other alpha channel by holding down the appropriate modifier key (Shift, Ctrl, or Shift-Ctrl) and dragging the channel's name to the Make Selection icon in the channels palette.

LAYERS, LAYER MASKS, AND ADJUSTMENT LAYERS

Photoshop image files can have as many *layers* as the RAM on your computer will allow. Layers act like a stack of transparent acetate sheets, ready to accept pixels that are painted onto them or pasted or dragged in from another source. Layers let you keep individual parts of an image separate — and to manipulate them singly — as you build a composite image. Once you're sure you like the image, you can combine the layers into a single layer. Although layers can be "memory-hungry," they provide amazing flexibility in building composite images.

To help you manipulate and keep track of the layers in an image, the Layers palette (Window, Show Layers) shows them in their stacked order. A layer can have several parts:

- **Nontransparent (opaque or partly opaque) pixels,** where there is image information
- **Transparent areas,** where there's no image information
- A **transparency mask** (a mask that will make a selection boundary that will select all nontransparent pixels)
- A **layer mask** (a mask that affects how the pixels of only that layer contribute to the composite)

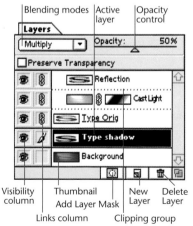

Blending modes | Active layer | Opacity control

Visibility column | Thumbnail | Add Layer Mask | New Layer | Delete Layer | Links column | Clipping group

The Layers palette provides many options for controlling how the layers of an image interact.

In Photoshop 4 you can drag a copy of a selection boundary, a selection, or a layer across your computer's screen from one open Photoshop window to another.

- **To copy a layer from the** *active file* **into another file,** use the move tool. Start the drag either from the active image's working window (in which case you'll be dragging the *currently active* layer) or from its Layers palette (in which case you can drag any layer you want). Drop the layer into the other file; it will appear in the stack above the currently active layer, and it will become the active layer.

- **Linked layers will be dragged and dropped together.**

- **To copy selected image material from the** *active file* **into another file,** use the move tool. When you drop the selection into the other file, it will become a new layer.

- **To copy** *a selection boundary* **into another file,** drag with any selection tool.

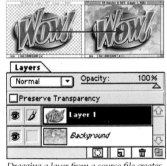

Dragging a layer from a source file creates a new, active layer in the target file

To help you keep track of the layers, the Layers palette shows them in their stacked order.

Here's a quick summary of what you can do with a layer.

- **Change it independently** of other layers by clicking on its name in the Layers palette to target it as the active layer and then painting on it or filtering it or otherwise modifying it. Only one layer can be active at a time.

- **Make it visible or invisible** by turning on or off its eye icon in the visibility column. Any or all layers can be visible at once.

- **Protect it from change** by making a different layer active in the Layers palette.

- **"Slide" it around independently** of the rest of the image by dragging with the move tool.

- **Link it to other layers** so they move together, by clicking in the column to the right of the eye column.

- **Control its overall transparency** with the Opacity slider.

- **Control how its colors blend** with the layers below by choosing a blending mode.

- **Include or exclude pixels from the blend** based on their colors and the colors of the pixels in layers below with the composite controls in the Layer Options dialog box (for more about Layer Options, see the beginning of Chapter 4.

- **Hide parts of it** by creating a layer mask.

- **Turn it into a mask** for layers above it by including it as the bottom layer in a clipping group.

The tools and commands you need for adding and removing layers, and changing the way they blend with the other layers in the composite are found in the Layers palette itself or in the palette's pop-out menu, or in the main Layer menu. "Exercising Layers," starting on page 74, will give you an opportunity to apply the basics of layer operations before tackling the techniques presented later in the book.

There's more than one way to add a layer to an image:

- Make a blank (completely transparent) layer by clicking or Alt-clicking the New Layer icon at the bottom of the palette.

- Duplicate an existing layer by dragging its thumbnail in the Layers palette to the New Layer icon.

- Create a layer from the contents of the clipboard with the Edit, Paste command (Ctrl-V).

- Copy several layers into a single merged layer by turning on the eye icons in the Layers palette for the layers you want to copy and choosing Edit, Copy Merged (Ctrl-Shift-C) and then Edit, Paste (Ctrl-V).

- Use the move tool to drag a layer in from another Photoshop file.

- Set type with the type tool.

- Drag an object from an open Adobe Illustrator file or import an EPS graphic using File, Place (see Chapter 7).

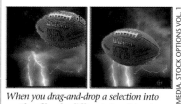
Transparency

Photoshop artists are used to thinking of each pixel in a Grayscale file as having a brightness level (a shade of gray) and each pixel in an RGB file as having three color values, representing its red, green, and blue components. In addition to these brightness and color values, each pixel in each layer of a Grayscale or RGB file also has an Opacity value.

Transparency is the essence of layers. Except for the *Background*, an opaque layer at the bottom of the stack, all layers automatically start out transparent. (Even the bottom layer can start out transparent if you set it up that way when you start the New file, or if you open an EPS file that has no background.) You can see a representation of transparency if you view any layer but the *Background* by itself (by Alt-clicking its eye icon to turn its visibility on while turning off visibility for the other layers). The transparent parts of the layer are represented by a checkerboard pattern, which Photoshop uses to distinguish transparency from a solid white background.

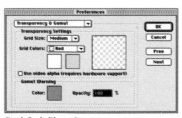

By default Photoshop represents transparency on-screen with a gray checkerboard pattern so you can differentiate a transparent background from a solid white one. But you can change the color, size, and tone of the pattern by choosing File, Preferences, Transparency & Gamut.

The transparent parts of a layer let the layer underneath show through unmodified. If there are no transparent (checkerboard) areas in a layer, it blocks underlying layers from view, or at least modifies the way they look.

When you paint on a layer, the transparent pixels are replaced by ones that have color and opacity values. You can measure the opacity if you open the Info window (Window, Show Info), set one of the color readouts for Grayscale, RGB, HSB, or Lab, and note the "Op:" (opacity) reading at the bottom of the list of color characteristics. As you move a cursor over a layer, you can watch the change in color and transparency values in the Info window. If the Opacity slider for the layer is set at less than 100, or if the edge of the element is antialiased or feathered, the Opacity value falls below 100 — antialiasing and feathering make the pixels at the edge partly transparent.

The Opacity for the layer as a whole can be controlled with the Opacity slider at the top right side of the Layers palette. The effect of the Opacity setting is cumulative with whatever opacity is already built into the pixels in the layer. For example, if you paint a stroke with the Opacity slider in the Paintbrush Options palette set at 50% and then set the layer's Opacity at 50% also, the stroke will have an effective Opacity of 25%. (See Chapter 6 for more about paintbrush controls.)

Blending Modes

Along with the Opacity slider, the blending modes affect how a whole layer interacts with the layers below it in the stack.

Normal mode's name speaks for itself. The color acts normal and doesn't change in relation to the layers underneath.

At full opacity, **Dissolve** mode is just like Normal, but reducing the Opacity setting, instead of pushing all the pixels toward transparency, makes a dither (randomized) pattern, with some pixels completely transparent and others at full opacity. The lower the Opacity setting, the more pixels disappear.

The effect of **Multiply** mode is like putting two slides together in the same slide projector and projecting them. Where both of the slides have color, the projected color is darker than either. White is neutral in Multiply mode; that is, the white parts of a layer are like the clear parts of a slide — the white has no effect on the layers below. Some of the things Multiply is good for are: increasing the density of overexposed images (see the beginning of Chapter 3), applying shadows without completely eliminating the color of the shaded areas in the layers underneath, layering line work over color (as described in "Coloring Line Art" in Chapter 6), and combining an image with a simulated paper or canvas texture when you want it to appear that the paint is pooling in the recesses of the texture.

Screen mode is like projecting two slides, from separate slide projectors, onto the same spot on the wall, or overlapping colored

Normal

Dissolve, 75% Opacity   *Multiply*

Screen   *Overlay*

Soft Light   *Hard Light*

Color Dodge   *Color Burn*

Lighten   *Darken*

Difference   *Exclusion*

Hue   *Saturation*

Color   *Luminosity*

Photoshop's blending modes — available in the Layers palette, the Calculations and Apply Image dialog boxes, and the painting tools and Fill function — provide many ways to composite images.

spotlights. The result is to lighten the composite. Black is a neutral color in Screen mode, causing no effect. Screen mode is good for applying highlights to an image (see Chapter 8).

Overlay, Soft Light, and **Hard Light** provide three different complex combinations of Multiply and Screen, acting differently on dark colors than on light colors. For all three, 50% gray is neutral, which makes them good for embossing with the Emboss filter, since the flat surfaces of an embossed image are 50% gray. These modes are useful in general for applying special effects (see Chapter 8).

Color Dodge and **Color Burn** increase contrast of the image underneath, intensifying the color by changing the hue and saturation. Color Dodge lightens as it brightens, and Color Burn darkens. With Color Dodge, light colors affect the composite more. With Color Burn, dark colors have more effect.

Lighten mode compares pixels in the overlying layer and the image underneath, channel by channel — that is, it compares the Red channels of both, the Blue channels, and the Green channels — and chooses the lighter channel component in each case.

Darken mode makes the same comparison as Lighten does, but chooses the darker channel component in each case.

Difference mode does a complex calculation to compare the overlying layer and the image underneath, generally resulting in more intense colors. Black results if there is no difference in the pixel colors, and black is also the neutral color for Difference mode, causing no change in the image underneath. Difference is good for creating psychedelic color effects. It's also good for comparing two images to see if there is any difference between the two. **Exclusion** is like a subdued, grayed-back version of Difference.

Hue, Saturation, and **Luminosity** modes each apply only one of the three attributes of the pixels in the overlying layer. **Hue** is good for shifting color without changing brightness or value. **Saturation** is good for desaturating selectively based on a shape. **Luminosity** is the mode to use if you want to transfer the light-and-dark information from a texture onto an image underneath.

Color mode is like a combination of Hue and Saturation modes. The layer contributes all the information except Luminosity (the brightness information). Color mode is good for applying color in painting (see Chapter 6).

Transparency Masks

If you create a layer — by choosing New Layer from the Layers palette's pop-out menu or by clicking the New Layer icon at the bottom of the palette — the layer that's added (above the currently active layer) will consist of nothing but the transparent sheet. But as soon as you paint on it or add something (by dragging and dropping or pasting, for instance), the layer has three components — transparency, pixels, and a transparency mask.

Here are some tricks for managing layer masks by using the layer mask thumbnail in the Layers palette:

To make changes to a mask, click the mask thumbnail. A little mask icon to the right of the eye column shows that the mask is active. You'll still be viewing the image rather than the mask, but any painting, filtering, or other functions you do will affect the mask, not the layer.

To make the *mask* **visible** instead of the layer, Alt-click the mask thumbnail.

To turn the mask off temporarily so it has no effect, Shift-click the mask thumbnail. A red "X" on the thumbnail shows that the layer is turned off. Shift-click again to turn the mask back on.

To load the layer mask of the active layer as a selection, press Ctrl-Alt-\.

Making a selection and choosing Edit, Copy (Ctrl-C) copies pixels only from the active layer. But you can copy pixels from all visible layers as if they were merged by choosing Edit, Copy Merged (Ctrl-Shift-C).

The transparency mask is a stored selection boundary that defines the edge between a layer's opaque pixels and its transparent ones. Where there are semitransparent pixels — for instance, at the antialiased edge of the opaque element — the mask will be semitransparent also. If you move an element around on its layer, its transparency mask moves with it. If you change the element by scaling it, blurring it, or painting on it, for instance, the transparency mask changes to fit.

You can make a layer's transparency mask into an active, visible selection by Ctrl-clicking the layer's thumbnail in the Layers palette. This selection, evidenced by the typical "marching ants" border, will now operate in whatever layer you activate in the stack. That is, once a transparency mask is loaded as a selection, if you choose another layer in the Layers palette, the selection you loaded will still be active in this different layer.

Layer Masks

Besides its pixels, its transparent area, and its built-in transparency mask, each transparent layer you create can also have its own nondestructive layer mask, which you add by clicking the mask icon (the circle inside the gray square) at the bottom of the Layers palette. A layer mask provides a way to affect how the layer contributes to the composite image, without permanently changing the layer. For instance, instead of erasing part of the layer, you can leave it intact but block it with a layer mask. (The *Background* layer at the bottom of the file doesn't have the option for transparency, and it can't have a mask.)

When a layer mask is created, three things happen in the Layers palette to tell you how the mask relates to the image in the layer:

- A **mask icon** appears in the narrow column next to the "eye" column to let you know that whatever you do will be done to the mask instead of the image. (The mask icon replaces the paintbrush icon, whose job it is to tell you that the image, not the mask, will be the target of whatever you do next.)

- A **mask thumbnail** appears beside the image thumbnail.

- A **link icon** appears between the two thumbnails, to show that if you move the layer or the mask the other one will move along with it. (You can unlink by clicking the link icon so you can move one without the other.)

A layer mask is a grayscale entity that can have up to 256 shades of gray, from white to black. Where the mask is white, it's transparent, and it allows the image on its layer to show through and contribute to the composite. Where the mask is black, it's opaque, and the corresponding portion of the image is blocked (masked out). Where the mask is gray, it's partly transparent — the lighter the gray, the more transparent — and the corresponding pixels in the layer's image make a semitransparent contribution to the composite. A layer mask affects only its own layer — it doesn't mask the layers above or the layers below.

To control the way a layer combines with the layers underneath, you can fill the mask with a gradient, paint in it, or paste in an image. Layer masks are important in making montages, covered in Chapter 4.

Adjustment Layers

Adjustment layers are layers without any image pixels. New in Photoshop 4, Adjustment layers are can carry two kinds of information. First, they store directions for color and tonal adjustments; second, they can include a mask. An Adjustment layer's mask can be completely clear, in which case the layer's adjustments are applied to visible pixels in all the layers beneath it in the stack. Or, like a layer mask, it can contain grayscale information that restricts its contribution to certain areas. Like layer masks, Adjustment layers are nondestructive. That is, their effects can be applied without actually changing the pixels in the image. Chapter 3 tells how to put Adjustment layers into action.

Clipping Groups

Another nondestructive compositing element, a clipping group is a group of layers, the bottom layer of which acts as a mask. The bottom layer clips all the associated layers so only the parts that fall within the shape of its own transparency mask can contribute to the image.

You can make a clipping group by Alt-clicking on the borderline between the names of two layers. The lower of the two layers — its name is now underlined in the palette and the borderline becomes dotted — is the clipping mask, and the other layer is clipped. Working your way up the palette clicking more borderlines adds clipped layers to the group. To be members of a clipping group, layers have to be together in the stack.

A clipping group can also be set up or added to when a layer is added to the stack, by checking the Group With Previous Layer box in the New Layer dialog box.

```
New Layer...
New Adjustment Layer...
Duplicate Layer...
Delete Layer

Layer Options...

Merge Down
Merge Visible
Flatten Image

Palette Options...
```

The Merge commands available in the Layer menu or in the Layers palette's pop-out menu vary depending on which layers are active and visible.

Clipping groups are "high-overhead" items. They take more computation than layer masks or alpha channels. So if you can think of another way to accomplish the "clipping" you want, you might be better off doing that instead of making a clipping group.

Merging and Flattening

When you've finished working on a set of layers and it produces exactly the effect you want, you may decide that you no longer need to keep all the parts of the image on separate layers. Reducing the number of layers reduces the amount of RAM needed for the image and can make Photoshop work faster To reduce the number of layers, you can merge or flatten them. *Merging* combines visible layers of a file into one layer. But there are at least six different possibilities for merging. Four of them — Merge Down, Merge Visible, Merge Linked, and Merge Group — can be found in the Layers palette's pop-out menu and the Layer menu, and the others in the Edit and Image menus. **A "merger" has to include the active layer.** If the active layer isn't visible, you won't be able to merge layers.

- **Merge Down** combines the active layer with the layer just below it in the stack shown in the Layers palette. Both must be visible.

- **Merge Visible** combines all visible layers (those with their eye icons showing in the Layers palette) and keeps invisible ones.

- **Merge Linked** combines the active layer and any visible layers linked to it, discarding any hidden linked layers.

- **Merge Group,** available when the bottom layer of a clipping group is the active layer, combines all visible layers of the group, discarding its hidden layers.

- **Copy Merged** (from the Edit menu; Ctrl-Shift-C) makes a copy of all visible layers. Then Edit, Paste (Ctrl-V) can be used to make a new layer.

- **Duplicate** (from the Image menu) offers the Merged Layers Only option, which makes a copy of the file with invisible layers discarded and visible ones merged into a single layer.

When layers are merged, the new combined layer takes its name, blending mode, opacity, and place in the layers stack from the bottom layer of the merging group.

Flattening not only combines all visible layers into a single layer, discarding the invisible ones, but it also takes away the option for transparency, making a *Background* layer. Any areas that were transparent in the combined layers become white in the flattened file.

- **Flattening discards the hidden layers** in the process of combining the visible ones into one remaining Background layer. (A dialog box warns you about this so you can reconsider.)

- When you merge or flatten, **layer masks are applied** (their effects are made permanent) and then discarded from the file.

- **Alpha channels are retained** in merging or flattening.

Exercising Layers

Overview *Duplicate the Liz and Elaine files from **goodies\dressup** on the Wow! CD-ROM. Work with the Layers palette to learn its functions.*

TOMMY YUNE, © 1995 URSUS STUDIOS

1

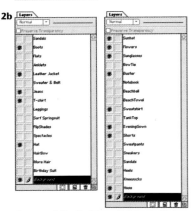

*Liz (left) and Elaine (holding Buster) as you find them in **dressup***

Turning off the thumbnails in the Layers palette to save screen space and RAM

2a

2b

Layers palettes for Liz and Elaine in their original condition; refer to these if you accidentally turn off layers and need to reset visibility or stacking order.

INSPIRED BY A LAYERS DEMO featuring "Barbie/GI Joe" and presented by Russell Brown of Adobe Systems, Inc., we asked Tommy Yune, creator of the *Buster the Amazing Bear* comic books (see more of his work in Chapter 6), to put together a file that could be used for an elementary demo of how layers work. On the Wow! CD-ROM open the **goodies** directory to find two Photoshop files in the **dressup** directory — Elaine (above on the right) and Liz, two heroines from the *Buster* series. Then follow the steps on these four pages to get the hang of turning layers on and off, linking them, adjusting Opacity, trying out blending modes, preserving transparency, making clipping groups and layer masks, and experimenting with Adjustment layers.

1 Making a duplicate. Before you start, copy the **liz** and **elaine** files from the Wow! CD-ROM to a hard disk. Then open both files and open the Layers palette (Window, Show Layers).

2 Reducing palette size. Choosing Palette Options in the Layers palette's pop-out menu lets you choose the size of the thumbnails that appear in the palette, or choose no thumbnails at all. Large thumbnails let you see more detail. But they can also slow down your work, since redrawing them occupies RAM. To fit the entire Liz and Elaine Layers palettes on a small screen, you can turn off their preview thumbnails: Choose Palette Options and click the None button. Yune, who often works with the Layers thumbnails turned off because it can improve Photoshop's speed, has named the layers by their content, so you don't need the icons to know what's what.

3 Hiding layers: Organizing Elaine. Elaine looks like she's prepared for anything, with sweatshirt and sunhat over her evening garb. But to get her ready to go out, click

WATCH THOSE LAYERS!

If you click the name of a layer that isn't currently visible, it will become the active layer and visible. To activate a layer and at the same time hide all other layers, Alt-click the layer's name.

3a

Clicking the eye icons to toggle them off hides the Sunhat, Flowers, Sunglasses, and Sweatshirt layers.

4

Right-clicking on an image element with the move tool brings up a list of all layers under the cursor so you can choose the layer you want.

5

Linking Buster and his bow tie allow them to be moved together. To link a layer to the active layer, simply click in its links column.

6

If you drag and drop layers from one file to another, any linked layers come along. But to move linked layers up or down the stack within a file, they have to be dragged one by one.

to turn off the eye icons for these layers to hide them: Sunhat, Flowers, Sunglasses, and Sweatshirt.

4 Activating a layer: Selecting Buster. You can activate a particular layer in the stack either by clicking its name in the Layers palette or by right-clicking on the image with the move tool to bring up a context-sensitive menu that lists all currently visible layers that have pixels under the cursor; you can then drag through the list to choose a layer. Try selecting Buster by right-clicking on him with the move tool; you can toggle to the move tool from any tool but the pen by holding down the Ctrl key.

5 Linking layers: Putting Buster on the floor. Clicking in the Links column in the Layers palette (next to the "eye" column) will *link* any layer to the *currently active layer*. A chain symbol appears in the links column of any layer that you link. In the Elaine file, activate the Buster layer and then click in the links column of the BowTie layer to link it to Buster; note the chain icons in the palette. Also click the BowTie eye column so you can see the tie. Now activate the Evening Gown layer and link the Heels layer to it; again note the link mark. Now link the Hose to this group also. Then activate the BowTie layer, and notice that the link marks no longer appear for the Heels or Hose — only for the layer (Buster) that's linked to the *currently active layer* (BowTie).

When layers are linked, moving one layer with the move tool also moves any linked layers. With Buster linked to his bow tie, use the move tool to slide him to the floor. (To give Elaine something to do with her hands now that Buster is on his own, click in the eye column of the Notebook layer to make it visible.)

6 Dragging and dropping: Cloning Buster. With more than one Photoshop file open, you can use the move tool to copy a layer from one file into another. It's quick and easy, and it bypasses the clipboard, saving RAM. With both the Liz and Elaine files open, activate the Buster layer of the Elaine file and the Leather Jacket layer in the Liz file, put the move tool on the bear in the Elaine image, and drag him into the Liz window. Buster, with his linked bow tie, will end up approximately where you drop him in the Liz image. Drag him to Liz's shoulder, and then drag the Buster and BowTie names to the top of the Layers palette so he's *on* the shoulder rather than behind it.

> **GOING SOLO**
>
> Dragging a linked layer with the move tool from one image to another brings its linked layers along with it. But to move one of a set of linked layers without moving the others, drag it from its Layers palette instead of from the image itself.

7 Trying out blending modes: Stockings to tights. The blending mode (set by choosing from a pop-out list at the top left of the palette) controls how the pixels of a layer interact with the

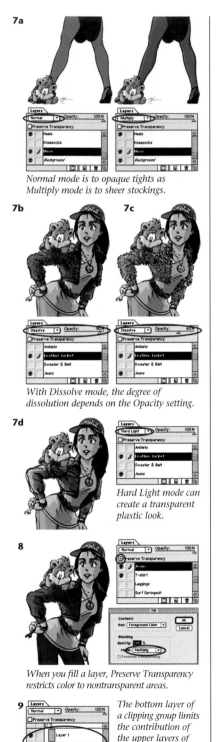

7a

Normal mode is to opaque tights as Multiply mode is to sheer stockings.

7b **7c**

With Dissolve mode, the degree of dissolution depends on the Opacity setting.

7d

Hard Light mode can create a transparent plastic look.

8

When you fill a layer, Preserve Transparency restricts color to nontransparent areas.

9 The bottom layer of a clipping group limits the contribution of the upper layers of the group; the result is shown at the top of page 74.

layers underneath. (A description of the blending modes can be found in the opening section of this chapter.) To see the effect of Multiply mode, in the Elaine file activate the Hose layer. Switch the layer's blending mode from Multiply to Normal and back again; you'll see the change as the muscle contours and skin color of the Background layer disappear and reappear, and the color of the clothed leg goes from a blend of colors with Multiply mode (Background *darkened* by Hose) to a solid gray in Normal mode (Background *hidden* by Hose). In this case, the result of Multiply mode is like putting sheer stockings on a bare leg.

Going for "grunge." In the Liz file activate the Leather Jacket layer. Now change its blending mode to Dissolve. You won't notice much of an effect immediately, but if you move the Opacity slider to the left, Liz's jacket will be headed toward "threadbare" in a hurry.

Going for plastic. For a "plastic" look with exaggerated highlights, restore the Opacity of the Jacket layer to 100% and then choose Hard Light for the mode.

8 Preserving transparency: Expanding a wardrobe. The Preserve Transparency checkbox at the top of the Layers palette keeps color "inside the lines," acting as a sort of built-in mask when you fill a layer. In the Liz file, activate the Jeans layer. Click the checkbox to turn on Preserve Transparency. Then choose a bright color (click the Foreground color square in the toolbox) and choose Edit, Fill, Foreground Color, Normal. The Jeans will change color but the folds of the cloth will be lost. Press Ctrl-Z to Undo, and try the Fill operation again; but this time choose Edit, Fill, Foreground Color, Multiply. Although the layer stays in Normal mode, the color is applied in Multiply mode, allowing the detail of the Jeans to show through.

> **FILLING SHORTCUTS**
>
> A keyboard shortcut for filling only the nontransparent areas of a layer with the Foreground color is Shift-Alt-Backspace; for the Background color it's Shift-Ctrl-Backspace.

9 Using a clipping group: Making patterned stockings. To add a pattern to the Hose, you could use a pattern fill with Preserve Transparency turned on, as in step 8. But if you use a separate pattern layer and make a clipping group so you can use the shape of the stockings from the Hose layer to mask the pattern, you'll be able to move the pattern to adjust its position within the masked area. To help you see how the clipping group works, choose Palette Options from the pop-out menu and choose the smallest thumbnail size.

In the Elaine file turn on visibility for the Flowers layer only by Alt-clicking its eye icon. Use the rectangular marquee with the Shift key to surround a flower; choose Edit, Define Pattern; then click eye icons to turn on visibility for Hose and other layers and turn off visibility for the Flowers layer. Activate the Hose layer and create a new layer above it by clicking the New Layer icon in the center at the

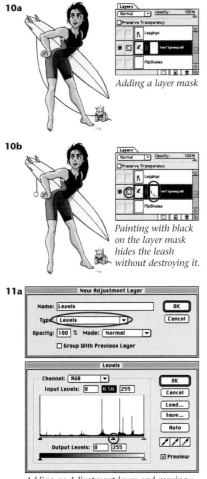

10a

Adding a layer mask

10b

Painting with black on the layer mask hides the leash without destroying it.

11a

Adding an Adjustment layer and moving the gamma slider (gray triangle) darkens the skin tones.

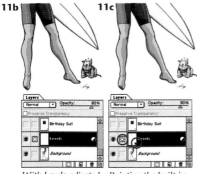

11b **11c**

With Levels adjusted, Liz and her dog sport suntans.

Painting the built-in mask in the Adjustment layer blocks the Levels effect, leaving Liz tanned but the dog pale, as shown here and at the top of page 74.

bottom of the Layers palette. Choose Edit, Fill, Pattern, Normal to fill this new Layer 1 with flowers.

To use the Hose layer to "clip" the pattern-filled layer so the flowers appear on the stockings only, in the Layers palette Alt-click the border between the pattern-filled layer and Hose. The border will become a dotted line, showing that the two layers are "clipped" together, and the Hose name will be underlined, showing that it's the bottom layer of the clipping group. You should now see flower-patterned Hose. To shift the pattern, drag with the move tool.

10 Using a mask: Unleashing the dog. A layer mask lets you remove part of a layer from the image, without necessarily making the removal permanent. The image on the layer stays intact so it can be restored later by turning off or deleting the layer mask. In the Liz file, Alt-click the Surf Springsuit name to activate that layer and hide all others. Click the eye icon for *Background* to turn its visibility back on.

Now you'll make a layer mask for the Surf Springsuit layer that will remove the leash from the picture. Click the Add Layer Mask icon on the left at the bottom of the palette. The mask icon to the left of the Surf Springsuit thumbnail shows that the mask is active, so anything you do now will be done to the layer mask, even though you're looking at the image. Make sure that black is the Foreground color. Then choose the paintbrush tool. Open the Brushes palette (Window, Show Brushes; or the default shortcut is F5). Since you'll want to have good control of the paint when you get to the point where the leash meets the surfboard, choose a fairly small, hard brush tip. Now when you "paint" the leash, the black paint will actually go onto the layer mask, opaquing that part of the mask to make the leash disappear from the composite image.

11 Adding an Adjustment layer: Cultivating a tan. An Adjustment layer adds no pixels to the image. Instead it contains instructions for performing one of the modifications available in the Image, Adjust submenu. To make an Adjustment layer to "tan" Liz, activate the *Background* layer and then Ctrl-click the New Layer icon. In the New Adjustment Layer dialog box, choose Levels from the Type list. In the Levels dialog box, move the gamma slider (the gray triangle in the Input Levels controls) to the right. Click OK to close the dialog box. In the Layers palette, note that the new layer has a black-and-white circle to the right of its name, indicating that it's an Adjustment layer. Like any other layer, an Adjustment layer's contribution to the image can be reduced: To lighten the tan, reduce the Opacity for the layer.

The thumbnail for the Adjustment layer represents a mask (note the mask icon next to it) that controls where the Adjustment layer's effects are applied. Adding black to the mask restricts the effect of the Adjustment layer. For instance, to prevent canine sunburn, with the Adjustment layer active, airbrush with black over the dog.

Putting Text over an Image

Overview *Select the area you want to lighten; make an Adjustment layer to lighten it; add a masked drop shadow.*

The **"Text Panel"** *Actions on the Wow! CD-ROM automate the process of making a lightened area for text with a drop shadow.*

More than 3000 new prescription drugs appear on the shelves of U.S. pharmacies each year. Add to that the multiplicity of brand names and generics and the drug interactions that can occur when more than one prescription — or even prescriptions and over-the-counter medicines are taken together — and it's no wonder drug store customers are confused.

The potential for problems with adverse drug interactions is a problem especially for older patients, who are often treated by more than one physician specialist, who tend to take more prescription medicines than younger patients, and who may not have any one doctor overseeing their drug regime.

Apothecary Confusion

1

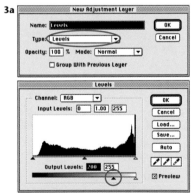

Original image

2

Guidelines established and selection made for the text pad; layout layer deleted

3a

Setting up a Levels Adjustment layer and moving the Output Levels black point

THERE ARE DOZENS OF WAYS to lighten a selected area of an image in Photoshop, with different amounts of detail and contrast preserved in the lightened area. The best method for a particular job will vary, depending on what the original image is and what kind of effect you want to achieve. For example, if you want to put text over an image as in this mock magazine layout, you'll want to reduce contrast so the image won't "fight" with the type.

1 Sizing the image. The first step is to scale the image to the size you need for the layout. Here's one way to do it: Open the page layout file, with real or dummy body copy, in the program that created it and make a screen-capture. You can use a capture utility program, or use the built-in Windows Alt-PrntScrn keyboard command. To trim to the page area, open the resulting image file in Photoshop, select the page area, leaving out any window frame and desktop area but including the edge area for any bleed, and choose Image, Crop. Then open the Image Size dialog box (Image, Image Size), deselect Constrain Proportions (in case your screen grab is a few pixels off the true proportions of the page), and select Resample Image so you can change the resolution as well as the dimensions. Set the Height and Width to exactly the page size you need. For instance, for an 8.5 x 11-inch page with an eighth-inch bleed on all sides, the document would be 8.75 x 11.25 inches. Set the Resolution by clicking the Auto button and entering the halftone screen you'll use for printing.

Display the rulers (Ctrl-R) and drag guidelines onto the image to help visualize where you want the type pad and display type in relationship to the elements in the screen-grab. Now open your photo and drag and drop it into the file with the screen capture and guidelines. Use Ctrl-T to scale this image up or down. But keep in mind that you can't scale it up more than about 10% and still have it look good. If scaling makes the image look slightly fuzzy, choose Filter, Sharpen, Unsharp mask and experiment with settings until it looks sharp (see "Sharpen" at the beginning of Chapter 5 for tips on settings).

3b

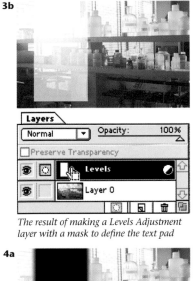

The result of making a Levels Adjustment layer with a mask to define the text pad

4a

A blurred shadow layer was added, using a Gaussian Blur of 10 pixels for this 1160-pixel-wide image.

2 Selecting an area for the type pad. Turn on Snap To Guides (Ctrl-Shift-;) and drag with the rectangular marquee tool to shape the text pad. (If the type is set already in your page layout screen-grab, size the pad to fit.)

3 Lightening the text area. Now add an Adjustment layer to lighten the selected area: Open the Layers palette (Window, Show Layers) and Ctrl-click the New Layer icon next to the trash can at the bottom of the palette.

When the New Adjustment Layer dialog box opens, choose Levels from the Type list and click OK. In the Levels dialog box that opens automatically, adjust the Output slider to lighten the selected area and reduce contrast while maintaining image detail so that when you put text over this area later, the type will be readable.

4 Adding a shadow. The next step is to build a shadow that makes it look like the text pad is floating above the image but that doesn't darken the pad itself. Since the pad as we've built it is really just a lightened area of the image and not a separate layer, there's no way to layer a shadow between the two. Instead, the shadow can be constructed on top and masked to show up only at the edges of the pad.

Load the shape of the text pad as a selection by Ctrl-clicking on the thumbnail of the Adjustment layer in the Layers palette — click the thumbnail itself rather than the layer's name. Create a new layer by Alt-clicking the New Layer icon, and name it "Shadow." With black as the Foreground color (press "D" to reset the colors to the default), press Alt-Backspace to fill the selection with black. Then deselect (Ctrl-D) and choose Filter, Blur, Gaussian Blur to soften the shadow's edges.

To mask the shadow so it shows only at the edges, load the selection from the Adjustment layer again: Ctrl-click the Adjustment layer's thumbnail. With the "Shadow" layer active, Alt-click the Add Layer Mask icon on the left at the bottom of the Layers palette.

5 Changing the shadow. Constructing the shadow as described in step 4 makes several kinds of adjustments possible:

- By default a layer mask is linked to the image in that layer, as shown by the chain icon that appears between the two. But if you click the chain (to unlink), then click the image icon (to make the shadow active), and drag in the image window with the move tool, you can adjust the shadow's position, moving it up or down and to one side or the other.

4b

Loading the mask from the Adjustment layer as a selection in the Shadow layer

4c

Alt-clicking the Add Layer Mask icon to add a mask that will block the shadow except at the edges

5a

The shadow, its mask, and the Adjustment layer were linked and the text pad was moved. Then the shadow and its mask were unlinked so the shadow could be offset.

5b

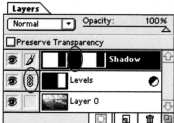

A second copy darkens the shadow.

- You can lighten the shadow by lowering the layer's Opacity.

- Or to increase the darkness of the shadow, duplicate the Shadow layer by dragging its name to the New Layer icon. Now you can adjust the Opacity of this Shadow Copy layer until the shadow is as dark as you like, and then press Ctrl-E to merge it with the original Shadow layer below it.

- You can even change the position of the text pad, moving the shadow along with it: With the Adjustment layer active, click in the linking column (to the right of the "eye," or visibility, column) for the Shadow layer. If you've delinked the Shadow and its mask, click between these two icons to relink. Now, with the Shadow linked to its mask and the Shadow layer linked to the Adjustment layer, you can activate either of the two layers and drag with the move tool to reposition the pad and the shadow.

6 Setting headline type. You could lighten the image to make headline type by using essentially the same method you used for the text pad: Set type with the type selection tool and then add an Adjustment layer and shadow as you did in steps 3 through 5.

Or try this: Set the type with the regular type tool and fill this new layer with white (press "D" for the default colors and press Ctrl-Backspace). Because any layer created by the type tool automatically has Preserve Transparency turned on, only the letters will fill, not the surrounding transparent area.

Another way to get white type is to set it in Adobe Illustrator or CorelDraw, for example, save it in EPS format (in CorelDraw use the "AI" or ".ai" format), and then use Photoshop's File, Place command to bring it in on its own layer. With white as the Background color, press Shift-Ctrl-Backspace.

Make a masked, linked shadow the same way you did in step 4. Again, you can move the type and shadow independently or together. To control how much the image shows in the headline type, use the Opacity slider for the type layer.

6

The headline can be set as white type, with its Opacity reduced. A masked shadow, which can be on a layer above or below the headline, is linked to the headline layer.

FILLING SHORTCUTS

Alt-click to fill a layer or selection with the Foreground color. **Ctrl-click** to fill with the Background color. Add the **Shift** key to either shortcut to limit the fill to non-transparent areas of the layer, as if Preserve Transparency were on.

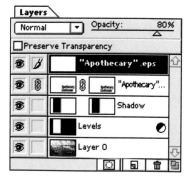

Making Type Stand Out

Overview *Set or import display type; apply an Adjustment layer to darken the type area; duplicate, blur, and mask the type to make a drop shadow.*

 *The **"Graphic Stand Out"** Actions on the Wow! CD-ROM automate the process of making image-filled type with a drop shadow.*

1a

Original image

1b

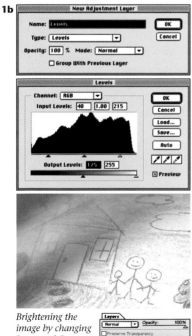

Brightening the image by changing Input and Output Levels in an Adjustment layer

JHD / PHOTODISC, CULTURAL ARTS

PHOTO: CULTURAL ARTS, PHOTODISC

TO "PULL" DISPLAY TYPE OUT OF A PHOTO, you can lighten it against a dark background, or darken it on a light background (as shown here), or leave the type area unadjusted and lighten or darken the background instead. In Photoshop 4 a relatively "economical" and flexible way to make image-filled type that contrasts with the background is to use an Adjustment layer, making a mask of the type.

1 Preparing the image. Open a color image. Open the Layers palette (by choosing Window, Show Layers, or by using the Actions palette or a keyboard shortcut; you can assign a shortcut via the Actions palette, as described in "The Recording Process" in "Automating with Actions" in Chapter 1, or use F7, which is Photoshop's default shortcut for opening the Layers palette).

If necessary, adjust the color in the image with an Adjustment layer, added by Ctrl-clicking the New Layer icon. We adjusted the Output Levels to lighten the shadow areas and then increased contrast by moving the Input Levels black and white points in, so the color wouldn't be too flat.

2 Setting the type. You can set the type in Photoshop or, for more control and flexibility, set it in a PostScript drawing program such as Adobe Illustrator, Macromedia FreeHand, or CorelDraw, and import it into Photoshop, as we did here. We used the font Good Dog Cool.

To set type in Photoshop, set black as the Foreground color (press "D" for "default colors"), choose the type tool, click on the image where you want the type to start, choose a font and size in the Type Tool dialog box, make sure the Anti-aliased box is checked, and type your display heading.

If you set the type in a PostScript program, set it in black and without a background behind it. If you copy the file and convert the type to outlines in the copy, you'll have a set of curves (the copy) that you can reliably import into Photoshop (see "No Surprises" on the next page), as well as "live" text (the original), in case you later find that you need to make changes. Using crop marks around the type and any associated graphics that you may also want to import

2a

Type set and converted to outlines in Illustrator

2b

Type placed as a layer in Photoshop

3a

Visibility for the type layer was turned off and the type was loaded as a selection.

into Photoshop will ensure that you can align all your elements perfectly when you import them. (For more about preparing art for import, see Chapter 7, "Combining Photoshop and PostScript.")

Use Photoshop's File, Place command to import the Illustrator file into your image file. The type outlines will come in as a layer of their own, and you can Shift-drag to scale them before double-clicking inside the bounding box to accept placement.

3 Brightening the type. Turn off the type layer's visibility by clicking in the "eye" column of the Layers palette. You'll use the type again in step 4 to make a shadow. In the meantime, you'll use the layer's transparency mask to make an Adjustment layer for pulling type out of the image: Ctrl-click the type layer's thumbnail in the Layers palette. With the selection active, Ctrl-click the New Layer icon to make an Adjustment layer, choosing Levels as the Type of layer and adjusting the Input Levels to darken the type and maintain contrast and readability.

4 Adding a shadow. To develop a shadow, start by turning on the visibility of the type layer again by clicking in its "eye" column. If you set the type in Photoshop at step 2, at this point you'll need to turn off Preserve Transparency (in the top left corner of the Layers palette). Choose the move tool (press "V") and use the arrow keys to offset the shadow. Blur the type (Filter, Blur, Gaussian Blur). To mask out the shadow except at the edges of the type, load the type as a selection by Ctrl-

JHD / EDGE TREATMENT: AUTO F/X, PHOTO/GRAPHIC EDGES

3b

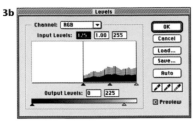

Brightening the type by changing Input and Output Levels in an Adjustment layer

3c

The result of applying the Levels Adjustment layer, with the type layer invisible

4a

Turning on visibility for the type layer to start the shadow

4b

The type layer was blurred and the mask from the top Adjustment layer was loaded as a selection.

clicking the thumbnail in the top Adjustment layer (the one you added in step 3), and then Alt-click the Add Layer Mask icon at the bottom left of the palette to make a layer mask with the selected area black (opaque) and the rest of the mask white (clear).

Variations. Once you have your image and type and their Adjustment layers set up, here are some alternatives you can try for making display type stand out:

- Reverse the effects of the two Adjustment layers, replacing the top Levels Adjustment layer with one that lightens the type, and leaving the background image "as is" by removing its Adjustment layer. (To remove a layer, drag its thumbnail to the trash can at the bottom of the palette.) Or you can even darken the background image by replacing its Adjustment layer with a new one.

- Make light type on a light background by replacing the top Adjustment layer. In the new Levels Adjustment layer, move the white point of the Input Levels to lighten the type.

- Turn off visibility for both Adjustment layers and fill the type with a Foreground To Background gradient of colors sampled from the image. (To choose a Foreground color, use the eyedropper tool to click a color in the image; to set the Background color Alt-click a second image color. Then turn on Preserve Transparency for the type layer. Double-click the gradient tool in the tool palette to choose it and open its Options palette, where you can choose Foreground To Background from the Gradient list and choose Linear for the Type. Then drag the gradient tool across the type.

Lightening the type on a darker background

Lightening the type on a lightened background

4c

A mask created in the type layer hides the shadow except at the edges.

Filling the type with a color gradient

Using Images To Make Selections

Overview *Copy a photo and graphics into two separate alpha channels of an RGB image; invert the channels to negatives; modify channels if needed; load each channel into the main RGB channel as a selection; colorize the selection.*

Grayscale image to be used to make the photo channel (#4)

Scanned map

Channel #4 with image map inverted

STEPHEN KING

THE GRAYSCALE INFORMATION in a photo can be a very effective tool for "pulling" an image out of a background texture. For this T-shirt design, Stephen King started with an RGB scan of kraft paper and then selected, colorized, and darkened parts of this background, using a modified photo, a map, and graphics created in Adobe Illustrator. After the colorizing had been done, he pasted in additional photos.

1 Making masks from the photo and graphics. Open an RGB file to serve as the background for the image; King opened his kraft paper scan. Then open the photo and graphics files you want to use as selections. If these are color files, convert them to grayscale.

If you want to use only part of a particular photo in your composition, eliminate the other parts by selecting and filling with white as King did for the sky of his surfing photo (Edit, Fill, White). When your photo is the way you like it, select all of it (Ctrl-A) and copy (Ctrl-C). Add a new alpha channel to the RGB background file (choose Window, Show Channels; click the New Channel icon at the bottom of the palette). This new channel will be active and visible. Paste the clipboard contents (the copied grayscale photo) into the new channel (Ctrl-V). You can use the move tool to reposition the imported photo or graphic. While the channel is active, invert the tones (Ctrl-I) so the channel now contains a negative with a black background. Repeat the copy, new channel, paste, and invert processes for each photo or graphic you want to import.

King added type and PostScript graphics by placing (File, Place) EPS files saved in Adobe Illustrator format into the channel with the

1d

Setting up alpha channels to load as selections

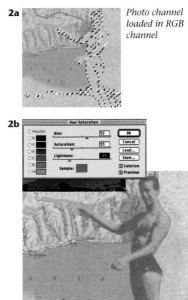

1e

"Modified map" channel, produced by subtracting "photo copy" from "map/ graphics."

2a *Photo channel loaded in RGB channel*

2b

Colorizing the selection

map (the process of importing an EPS file is described in Chapter 7) before inverting the tones to turn the channel into a negative.

King wanted to remove part of his map/graphics from its alpha channel so the photo wouldn't overlap it. To trim one channel with another, first make a copy of the channel that contains the shape you want to use as the "cutter" (King's surfer photo channel) by dragging its name in the Channels palette to the New Channel icon at the bottom of the palette. In this case the new channel (#6) was named "photo copy." Then adjust Levels to turn the grays in this new channel white (Image, Adjust, Levels, moving the white point Input Levels slider). Now, working in any channel, load as a selection the contents of the channel you want to cut into. In this case King wanted to cut away part of the map/graphics channel, so he Ctrl-clicked its name in the Channels palette to load it as a selection. (Ctrl-clicking a channel's name is equivalent to choosing Select, Load Selection and then choosing New Selection as the Operation option in the Load Selection dialog box.) To do the cutting, King held down the Alt key and Ctrl-clicked on the photo copy channel. This subtracted the second selection from the first. (Ctrl-Alt-clicking a name in the Channels palette is equivalent to choosing Select, Load Selection and then choosing Subtract From Selection as the Operation option.)

When you've done the subtraction, save the resulting modified selection by clicking the Save Selection icon, second from the left at the bottom of the Channels palette; a new alpha channel will be formed to hold the modified selection; in this case it was "modified map." At this point King had a stored selection that he could load and use for coloring the photo (#4) and a separate, nonoverlapping one for the modified map/graphics (#7).

2 Colorizing. With the RGB channel active, load each alpha channel (Ctrl-click its icon in the Channels palette) and choose Image, Adjust, Hue/Saturation to colorize the selected area. Checking the Colorize box applies a fully saturated, bright hue to the selection, but by moving the Brightness and Saturation sliders to the left you can tone it down to get a more subtle color. King colorized the modified map/graphics using channel #7. Then he loaded the photo channel (#4) as a selection and colorized that selection with different settings in the Hue/Saturation dialog box.

Completing the image. Next King loaded channel #7 again several times, using the Alt key and selection marquee to remove parts of the selection so he could fill other parts separately.

Other photos were then added from separate files: The two color photos at the top were selected with irregular borders drawn with a slightly feathered lasso and were dragged and dropped into the file. The large middle image was turned into a black and brown duotone (Image, Mode, Duotone, and set the colors and curves) and then converted to RGB mode before dragging and dropping.

Distressing Type

Overview *Set type on a layer in Dissolve mode and adjust Opacity; merge the type layer with a white-filled layer; blur the result; adjust contrast and brightness; load the RGB channel as a selection in a new layer; fill the selection with color; adjust the Opacity and the Layer Options composite controls.*

*The **"Distressed Type"** Actions on the Wow! CD-ROM automate the process of simulating weathered and otherwise distressed type.*

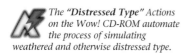

1a

Original background photo

1b

Setting type on a transparent layer

THE SMOOTH TYPE OUTLINES produced by PostScript illustration programs like Adobe Illustrator, CorelDraw, and Macromedia FreeHand, or even by Photoshop with Adobe Type Manager, are just too polished for some uses. Photoshop's layers and Dissolve blending mode make it possible to "distress" type to simulate a photocopy, a poorly inked rubber stamp, a quickly applied stencil, or weathered paint.

1 Setting the type. Open the background photo to which you want to apply the type. We started with a photo of a brick wall at 750 x 450 pixels.

With black as the Foreground color (pressing "D" restores the default colors), set your type: Activate the type tool (press "T"), and click it on your image to open the Type Tool dialog box. (We clicked where we wanted the center of the word "PARKING.") Choose a typeface, size, and alignment, and click the Show Font and Size boxes at the bottom of the dialog box so you'll be able to see how the type will look in your file. Turning on the Anti-aliased function is usually a good idea when you set type — it makes the edges of the letters look as smooth as possible. But in this case you can turn it off, since you're going to erode the edge of the type anyway.

We chose the Steamer font, set the Size at 50 points, left Anti-aliased off, and typed the word "PARKING." **Note:** If you want to set type in more than one size in Photoshop, you'll have to set it in two or more separate type blocks; although it allows you to set more than one *line* of type (by pressing Enter to start a new line), Photoshop's type tool can handle only one type *size and style* at a time. Or you can use a plug-in like the PhotoText component of Extensis PhotoTools (see "Better Control of Type" on page 82).

If the spacing of the type looks generally too loose (spread out) or too tight, you can enter a negative or positive number for Spacing, although the preview won't show the spacing. Then click OK.

The spacing of our type looked generally good; the space between the "P" and the "A" was too wide, but tightening it with a

2a

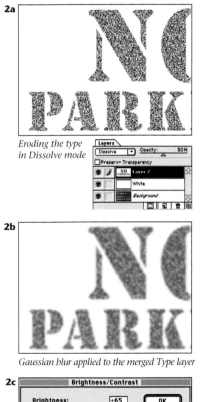

Eroding the type in Dissolve mode

2b

Gaussian blur applied to the merged Type layer

2c

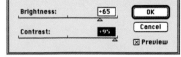

Adjusting Brightness and Contrast to sharpen up the type edge again

negative Spacing setting would also tighten the rest of the letters, so we left it to be done later, after all the type was set.)

When you click OK to close the Type Tool dialog box, the type will appear in your file as a new layer. (Open the Layers palette [Window, Show Layers] to see the layers.) Use the move tool (you can toggle to the move tool temporarily by holding down the Ctrl key) to drag the entire block of type into position.

Set any additional type you need by clicking with the type tool again to start a new type block. Press Ctrl-E (for Merge Down) to combine the layers for the two blocks of type.

Adjusting the spaces between letters is easy with type on a transparent layer. Double-click the magic wand tool to open its Options palette, make sure Sample Merged is deselected, and set the Tolerance at 255, which is the highest possible setting. With the Tolerance set high like this, clicking the wand on a letter will select every pixel of that letter, including any antialiased edges. Shift-click to add more letters to the selection. You can slide the letters around by dragging with the move tool; to keep the type from moving off its baseline, press the Shift key after you start to drag. We clicked on the straight upright part of the "P" and then Shift-clicked on the rounded part and used the right-pointing arrow key to move the letter a little closer to the "A." When the type is aligned as you like it, press Ctrl-D to drop all selections back onto their layer.

2 Eroding the type. To develop the type, you'll need to combine the transparent layer that holds the type itself with a white-filled layer. To make the white layer, click the New Layer icon in the center at the bottom of the palette and press Ctrl-Backspace to fill the layer with the Background color, white. In the Layers palette, drag the white layer's name between the type and the background photo.

Activate the type layer by clicking on its name in the palette. To begin the process of distressing the type, set the blending mode for the type layer to Dissolve. Then adjust the Opacity slider to control the degree of deterioration. Dissolve the type to a point where it's about half black dots and half white background showing through. We used an Opacity setting of 50%.

To build the texture, you can use the Gaussian Blur filter. But for the filter to work, the type layer has to be black-and-white, not black-and-transparent. To merge the type layer with the white layer, press Ctrl-E. Next choose Filter, Blur, Gaussian Blur. We used a 2-pixel Radius setting for the blur.

Now boost the contrast to blacken the type and define the kind of edges you want, and then adjust the brightness to bring out "holes." We chose Image, Adjust, Brightness/Contrast, pushed the Contrast to +95, and increased the Brightness to +65.

3 Coloring the paint. Now you need to put the distressed type back onto a transparent layer so you can overlay it on the

2d

Blackened type after Brightness and Contrast adjustments

3 Channels

- NO PARKING RGB ⌘~
- NO PARKING Red ⌘1
- NO PARKING Green ⌘2
- NO PARKING Blue ⌘3

Loading the RGB channel as a selection, to be inverted and used for creating color-filled type on a transparent layer

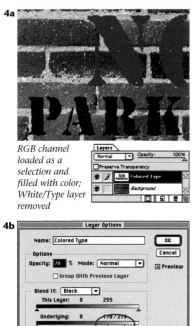

4a

RGB channel loaded as a selection and filled with color; White/Type layer removed

Layers

Normal — Opacity: 100%

Preserve Transparency

- Colored Type
- Background

4b Layer Options

Name: Colored Type — OK

Options
Opacity: 70 % Mode: Normal — Cancel
Group With Previous Layer — ⊠ Preview

Blend If: Black
This Layer: 0   255

Underlying: 0   178/219

Opacity and compositing controls adjusted; the result is shown at the top of page 86.

photographic background. You can do that by using the black-and-white type to make a selection on a new transparent layer, and then fill that selection with color. Start by Ctrl-clicking on the RGB channel's name in the Channels palette to load it as a selection. Then invert the selection (Ctrl-Shift-I) to make the type area the active selection.

Next create a new transparent layer by clicking the New Layer icon. Choose a Foreground color by clicking the Foreground square in the toolbox and designating a color in the Color Picker. Now you can fill the type selection in the new layer with the Foreground color by pressing Alt-Backspace. Then deselect (Ctrl-D).

To make part of the type a different color, select the part you want to refill (you can surround it with the rectangular marquee, for example), choose a new Foreground color, and Shift-Alt-Backspace to fill only the non-transparent pixels with color. We filled all the type with black, then selected "NO" and filled it with red.

AVOIDING A CRUDDY EDGE

If you fill an antialiased or feathered selection with color (Edit, Fill or Alt-Backspace), then repeat the process to fill with another color, the partially transparent edges will only partially fill with the new color, leaving a remnant of the old fill. But on a transparent layer you can avoid this by using a different method for the second fill: After you deselect, set up your new Foreground color and use the keyboard shortcut for filling all the nontransparent pixels: Shift-Alt-Backspace.

4 Applying the type to the image. At this point you can get rid of the black-and-white type layer so you can see your colored type on the photo background: click on its name in the Layers palette and Alt-click the trash can icon at the bottom right corner of the palette. (You don't need the original type any more because you have the type outlines preserved in the transparency mask of the top layer, and removing the type layer will cut down on the amount of RAM used.)

With the intermediate layer removed, you'll see your painted type on the photo background. Now you can use the Opacity slider for the type layer to "fade" the type. We set the Opacity at 70%.

You can also eliminate parts of the type if you want to. In our photo of the brick wall, the mortar was recessed between the bricks. So if paint had actually been applied to the wall with a stencil, it might have colored the bricks but missed the mortar. We used Layer Options (chosen from the pop-out Layers palette menu) to partially eliminate the lettering from the mortar: We split the white point of the Underlying Layer by holding down the Alt key as we moved half of the small triangle, and then the other half, to the left; this kept the type from appearing on the white and near-white areas of the brick image. Splitting the white point made a gradual transition, rather than a sharp break, between the painted and unpainted areas.

LANCE HIDY · ART DIRECTORS CLUB OF TULSA · THE UNIVERSITY OF
TULSA SCHOOL OF ART · ALEXANDRE HOGUE GALLERY · MARCH 16, 1995

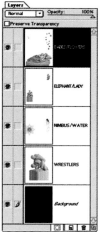

For this *Poster* for a show of his work, **Lance Hidy** assembled a variety of images. The dancing lady was scanned from a Victorian postcard. The flowers were placed directly on the scanner. The statuary (wrestlers and babies) and a detail from a sarcophagus (elephant) were scanned from black-and-white photos. All of these elements were selected with the pen tool and removed from their original backgrounds. To construct the streaked bases for the wrestlers and elephant sculptures, Hidy made a noise-filled area, chose Single Row for the Shape in the Marquee Options palette, made the selection, and stretched the single row of "noise" verti-

cally (Layer, Transform, Scale) to get the streaks. He pasted these rectangular base elements behind the selected statue elements, so they seemed to be part of the sculpture. The color of all scanned elements was adjusted with Image, Adjust, Hue/Saturation; for the sculpture and dancer, Hidy used the Colorize option.

The waterfall element used with the dancer and flowers on the right side of the poster was selected from a photo with the magic wand tool. By scaling down a duplicate of this element and then copying, pasting, and rotating it, Hidy created half of the nimbus behind the figure riding the elephant; he then copied and flipped this half to complete

the circular element (Layer, Transform, Flip Horizontal). With the nimbus on a transparent layer of its own, he turned on Preserve Transparency for the layer and applied a radial gradient fill to the layer; Preserve Transparency restricted the fill to the nimbus only.

The elements were dragged and dropped onto transparent layers above a black background. Hidy paired nonoverlapping parts to cut down on the number of layers needed. The file was flattened and saved in EPS format and brought into an Adobe Illustrator document, where type had been set in Penumbra, a font designed by Hidy as an Adobe Multiple Masters font.

To assemble his portrait of *Katrin Eismann*, **Russell Sparkman** started with two photographs he had taken with a digital camera. He combined negative and positive versions of these two images, using a different combination in each of the three color channels of the RGB image, in which separate gradations of light and dark had already been created. The bevel was made with pen paths that were created with the Shift key held down to make vertical, horizontal, and 45° diagonal paths. The paths were converted to selections so the sides could be individually lightened or darkened with Image, Adjust, Levels to increase the feeling of depth. Noise was applied to the frame, and feathered selections were darkened to create shadows at the top and at the left.

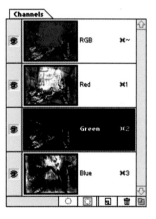

Rather than piling up layers in Photoshop, **Katrin Eismann** built her *Paint* collage on the bed of her desktop scanner She brushed and squeezed paint onto a sheet of clear acetate, set the tubes of paint on top, and then scanned this assemblage with an old three-pass scanner, which actually made the scan three times, each time recording data for one of the color channels — Red, Green, or Blue. Between passes, Eismann moved the paint tubes, added paint strokes to the acetate, and removed a large paintbrush.

Eismann adjusted Levels and Curves for the individual channels until she got the extremely bright colors she wanted, with some elements in full color, and other elements — like the red paint tube and the blue paintbrush, which appeared in only one color channel — as monochrome "ghosts." ▶*You can work in a single color channel while viewing the effect on the full-color image by clicking on one channel's name to make it active and visible, and then clicking in the eye column of the other channels to make them visible also, but not active.*

Though most desktop scanners no longer make three passes to record an image, you can accomplish the same thing — a slightly different image in each of the color channels — by making three scans and then using one color channel from each: In Photoshop open one of the RGB files to use as the composite image. Open one of the other files, choose the color channel to retain from this image, activate the channel by clicking its name in the Channels palette, select all and copy. In the composite image, activate the same color channel and paste, replacing the image in the channel with the image you copied from the other file. Repeat the copying and pasting process for the third channel, using the third scan as the source.

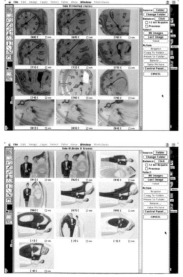

To take the pictures for *Bride & Groom,* **Katrin Eismann** used a Kodak Professional DCS 420 digital camera, building in the distortion by shooting through a standing lens about the size of a coffee saucer, borrowed from an enlarger. The digital camera stored the images on a PCMCIA card. In Photoshop Eismann chose File, Import and used the camera's plug-in (supplied on the Adobe Photoshop 4.0 Deluxe CD-ROM) to acquire and view digital "contact sheets" so she could pick the images to use for the montage. The plug-in allows you to open more than one image at once (by Shift-selecting them) and to automatically adjust color balance (using a tool similar to the gray eyedropper in Photoshop's Levels dialog box).

Eismann assembled the montage by layering the clock (in Difference mode) over the bride and groom (in Normal mode). This turned the skin tones purple, however. So she created a new, empty "repair" layer (in Normal mode) above the clock layer, activated the bride and groom layer, chose the rubber stamp tool, and set it to Clone (Aligned) mode in its Options palette. ▶ *To open the Options palette for the tool that's active, press Enter.*

Eismann loaded up the rubber stamp with the bride and groom image by holding down the Alt key and clicking to sample their layer. Then she activated and painted on the new "repair" layer to restore the skin tones of the faces and hands. Since these features were now on a layer above the Difference layer (and therefore not affected by the Difference setting), they retained their normal color. ▶ *Using a separate layer for "repairs" to an image lets you split the image material from one layer into two parts, so that some of it can be above and some below an intermediate layer in the stack. It also isolates the repairs; if you need to erase or change all or part of your "correction," you can do so without disturbing the image itself.*

3

ENHANCING
PHOTOS

THIS CHAPTER DESCRIBES SEVERAL TECHNIQUES for enhancing photos — from emulating traditional camera and darkroom techniques such as mezzotinting, soft focus, and solarization, to hand-tinting, to retouching. But much of the day-to-day production work done with Photoshop involves simply trying to get the best possible print reproduction of an unretouched photo — a crisp and clear print with its full range of gray or color values.

The Photoshop functions most often used for improving a photo are chosen mainly from the Image, Adjust and the Filter, Sharpen submenus. The dialog boxes for two of the choices from Image, Adjust — **Levels** and **Curves** — look very "techy," and one — **Variations** — looks quite friendly. It's precisely these characteristics that make them so useful. Levels and Curves provide a lot of information about the image and a great deal of control. But Variations lets you see in advance what will happen to the image with each of your choices (pages 116 through 118 show examples).

Another choice in the Image, Adjust submenu — Brightness/Contrast — is easy to understand and relate to, unlike Levels and Curves. But the Brightness/Contrast control has a restricted set of functions that can compromise the color or tonal range of an image if they're applied alone. If using Levels and Curves on an image is analogous to tuning up all the sections of an orchestra so it can play harmoniously, then using Brightness/Contrast is more like the brass playing loud to cover up problems in the woodwinds section.

When you make tone and color changes to an entire layer or a selected area, you can apply the commands of the Image, Adjust submenu either directly to the image or indirectly, by means of an **Adjustment layer.** Direct application is quick and intuitive. But Adjustment layers provide so much flexibility that it's almost always worthwhile to use them:

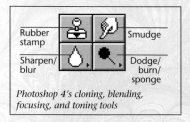

When you use more than one Adjustment layer to correct the dynamic range, exposure, and color in an image, it's as if you had applied the corrections in order: The lower the Adjustment layer is in the stack, the earlier in the process its correction was applied.

Photoshop 4's cloning, blending, focusing, and toning tools

- It's easy to reopen the dialog boxes and change the settings later to fine-tune the image — for instance, after you've produced a test print.

- You can target the corrections with each Adjustment layer's built-in mask, which can be edited like any layer mask, and modified later if you like.

- An Adjustment layer applies to all nontransparent areas below it in the Layers stack. But you can restrict the effect to certain

continued on page 94

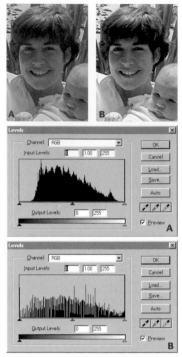

Choosing Image, Adjust, Levels, Auto to adjust tonal range; before (A) and after (B)

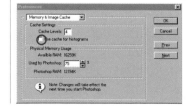

layers. Either move the Adjustment layer below any layers you don't want it to affect, or if that isn't possible, make it part of a clipping group: Alt-click between the Adjustment layer and the layer below it to restrict the adjustment to that layer only. (See "Clipping Groups" on page 72 for more about clipping groups.)

The **sharpen/blur, dodge/burn/sponge, smudge,** and **rubber stamp** tools can play an important role in correcting local flaws in an image. Sharpen/blur applies the same functions as some of the Sharpen and Blur filters (described in Chapter 5), but with hand-held precision.

Dodge/burn can be thought of as Image, Adjust, Levels in a wand, varying contrast, brightness, and detail, with independent control in the highlights, midtones, and shadows through the Options palette. The third phase of the tool — sponge — gives pin-point control of the Saturation function from Image, Adjust, Hue/Saturation, again in highlights, midtones, and shadows.

IMAGE CORRECTION

Is there a standard approach to evaluating a photo and preparing it for reproduction in print? Color correction is a skill that's refined through long and broad experience. If you ask a color expert where to start in correcting a black-and-white or color photo, you're almost certain to hear, "It depends on the photo." That's certainly true. But here are some tips that may be generally helpful, whether you apply them directly or through Adjustment layers. (Remember that for your printed image to match your screen display, your monitor and output system need to be calibrated and matched, as described in "Calibration and Color Matching" in Chapter 1.)

Extending dynamic range. In a typical image — not a close-up portrait of a black Angus bull or a photo of lace appliquéd on white satin — you'll want to get the broadest range of tones (and thus the largest amount of detail possible) by making the lightest area in the image pure white and the darkest pure black. (For printing the images, you may need to restrict the tonal range so it doesn't exceed what the printing process can produce. But an effective approach is to *first* get the image looking the way you want it, and *then* correct for the inadequacies of the printing process.)

To see whether an image uses the full brightness range, you can choose Image, Adjust, Levels and inspect the *histogram*, the graph that shows what proportion of the pixels (the vertical measure) are in each of 256 tones (spread along the horizontal axis, from black on the left to white on the right). The darkest pixels in the image are where the leftmost vertical bar of the histogram shows up; the lightest pixels are represented by the bar at the right end. If the histogram doesn't extend all the way across the horizontal axis, it means the full range of tones is not being used in the image — the blacks are not really as black as they could be and the whites are not pure white.

Adjusting Levels and Curves overall and using the dodge/burn tool on selected local areas can restore information that seems to be lost, as shown in this image restored by Jim Belderes of Digital Design, Inc. Where damage is severe, Belderes uses the rubber stamp to paint missing features.

Adjusting Curves to bring out shadow detail; before (left) and after (right)

Working in the Levels dialog box, you can expand the tonal range (and thus increase the contrast) by simply clicking the Auto button or by moving the white and black sliders of the Input Levels just inside the first bars of the histogram on each end. The goal of moving the sliders like this is to tell the program to make the darkest pixels in the image black, make the lightest ones white, and spread the intermediate ones over the full range of tones in between. (The reason the sliders are moved *just inside* the ends of the range is to make sure the ends are defined by meaningful black and white tones. The whitest white in the image could be due to dust specks, for instance.)

The Auto or manual Levels adjustment works well for images that just need a boost in contrast. Sometimes the Auto button can even correct color, because a color cast can be the result of the way brightness values in the image are distributed among the colors (red, green, and blue, or cyan, magenta, and yellow), and the Auto correction takes into account the histograms for the individual colors. Always worth a try because it's so quick, the Auto correction can easily be undone if it doesn't do what you want: Just press Ctrl-Z and the effect will be reversed, leaving the Levels box open and ready for manual adjustments. (Pressing Ctrl-Z again will redo the Auto correction.)

Correcting "exposure." One of the most common problems with photos is incorrect exposure — the image is too dark overall (underexposed) or too light (overexposed) or the shadows are too dark. If adjusting the black and white Input Levels doesn't solve a photo's color problems, it may be that they can be corrected by fixing the exposure. To increase or decrease the amount of detail you can see in the highlights, midtones, or shadows, choose Image, Adjust, Curves. To change the tonal range, click on the curve to create a point; then drag the point to change its position. The rest of the curve will change shape to make a smooth transition from the black point to the white point through the new point. You can make general corrections by reshaping the curve so it bulges toward the black side to lighten an underexposed image (by default this is to the left and upward for RGB images and to the right and downward for Grayscale or CMYK images, but you can reverse this by clicking on the grayscale bar that runs across the bottom of the dialog box). Conversely, reshape the curve to bulge toward the white side to darken an overexposed photo.

Overall exposure corrections can also be made with the gamma (gray) slider in the Levels dialog box. But in the Curves dialog box you can adjust particular values. If you move the cursor out of the Curves dialog box, it turns into an eyedropper. Click on a particular value in the image to identify its position on the curve. Then you can move that point on the curve to lighten or darken that part of the tonal range (see pages 116 and 121 for examples).

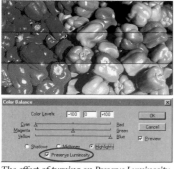

The effect of turning on Preserve Luminosity in the Color Balance dialog box varies with the type of color change you make and with whether the change is made to Highlights, Midtones, or Shadows. In some cases turning on Preserve Luminosity dampens changes in brightness. In other cases (like this one) the effect is exactly the opposite. The original color is shown at the top; the middle part shows changes made with Preserve Luminosity off; the lower part shows the same changes with Preserve Luminosity on.

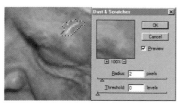

The Dust & Scratches filter (under Noise) can be used on blemished images to eliminate the defects.

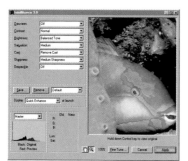

The Intellihance plug-in from Extensis (see Appendix B) analyzes an image and automatically makes corrections, providing a one-button, often successful, try at image correction. Alternatively, you can open the filter's Preferences interface (as shown here) and "tweak" individual settings while viewing both "before" and "after" versions of the Levels histogram.

Removing a color cast. If the image still seems to have color problems after you've expanded the dynamic range and corrected for exposure, try zooming in on some part of the image that should be neutral — that is, without color, and then select the gray eyedropper in Levels or Curves and click it on the neutral spot. Unlike the black and white eyedroppers, the gray one has nothing to do with brightness or contrast. Instead, it adjusts the color balance of the entire image based on the fact that you've told it what neutral should be. If you can't get the image color-cast-free with the Levels or Curves dialog box, try Image, Adjust, Color Balance.

Retouching. Once the general tone and color corrections have been made, individual problems can be addressed. Here are some examples:

- **To correct the color of a particular area,** make a feathered selection and use Image, Adjust, Variations or Color Balance to adjust it. (Chapter 2 has tips on selecting and feathering.)

- **To correct only one particular color or family of colors throughout the image,** you can use the Select, Color Range command (see "Selecting by Color" section of Chapter 2) or use Replace Color or Selective Color from the Image, Adjust submenu. To constrain the color change to one area, make a selection that includes the region you want to change before you apply Color Range or Replace Color or Selective Color. (For an example of using Replace Color, see Katrin Eismann's *Nightmare* image in the "Gallery" section at the end of Chapter 4.)

- **To remove dust and small scratches,** make a slightly feathered selection around the blemish and choose Filter, Noise, Dust & Scratches. The Dust & Scratches filter works by finding a distinct color break, such as you see when film has dust or scratches on it, and blurring the surrounding color into it to hide the blemish. To minimize the blurring of the rest of the selected area, start by setting the Dust & Scratches Threshold high and the Radius low. Lower the Threshold until the blemish begins to disappear, and then raise the Radius until it's gone. The feathered selection limits the area that's blurred when you run the filter, so you want to keep it small; but it also restricts the area from which the "repair" pixels can come, so you don't want to make it too small or the filter won't be able to tell what's the damage and what's the good part.

- **To remove larger blemishes,** use the rubber stamp, especially in Clone (Non-aligned) mode with a soft brush tip, Alt-clicking to pick up neighboring color and texture and clicking to deposit it.

- **To smooth the texture of a spotted area,** make a feathered selection, copy it as a separate layer, and blur it. Then use the Layers palette to set the mode (try Lighten or Darken, depending on the kinds of splotches you're trying to eliminate) and adjust the Opacity to blend it with the original.

Changing the color balance of a selection can lead to harsh color breaks (top right), but feathering the selection before making the adjustment helps the new colors blend in (bottom right).

To begin to rescue a severely overexposed photo (above), copy it into two or more layers and set the mode of each extra layer to Multiply.

Sharpening. Running the Unsharp Mask filter almost always improves a scanned photo. Usually it's the last thing that should be done to an image before it's prepared for the press, because the synthetic effects of sharpening can be magnified in other image-editing processes, such as increasing saturation of the colors. Sharpening is discussed more extensively in Chapter 5, "Using Filters."

SAVE THAT PHOTO!

When you want to reproduce a photo in print, it's nice to have a good image to begin with — it may need a little tweaking of the exposure, or you may have to remove a color cast, but it's basically sound. It isn't too badly focused, it's well-framed or at least croppable, the subjects have their eyes open and aren't grimacing inappropriately, and the background doesn't include anything distracting. But there are times when a particular photo *must* be used in a publication — it's the only picture of an important event, or it's free and the client's budget is limited, or the portrait is damaged but the subject is no longer available — and the photo just can't be redeemed by the normal correction processes. Here are some ideas for handling those kinds of photos:

- **To restore color to a severely overexposed (washed-out) photo,** layer two or more copies of the image, with the blending mode for the extra copies set to Multiply in the Layers palette. The result may not be perfect, but it could improve the image enough so you can proceed to rescue it. (This trick won't work well with an image that's blemished or shows obvious film grain, because these artifacts will also be multiplied.)

"NONDESTRUCTIVE" RETOUCHING

Using the retouching tools — rubber stamp, smudge, focus, and toning tools — involves "hand-painting," which can be tricky, since it's harder to undo a mistake than if you apply a filter or a command from the Image, Adjust submenu. Here are some ways to apply these tools so you don't permanently damage the image if you make a mistake, and so individual corrections can be selected and removed or repaired without affecting other hand-crafted changes:

- Use the rubber stamp, smudge, or sharpen/blur on a transparent layer above the image (to add a transparent layer, open the Layers palette [Window, Show Layers] and click the New Layer icon in the middle at the bottom of the palette), first setting the tool to Sample Merged in its Options palette.

- The dodge and burn tools don't offer a Sample Merged option, but you can use them on a new layer in Overlay mode filled with 50% gray, which is neutral in Overlay mode. (If you Alt-click the New Layer icon to open the New Layer dialog box, you can set the mode and fill when you first make the layer).

- With the sponge tool it's a good idea to make a feathered selection of the area you want to work on and copy it as a new layer (Ctrl-J), before you use the sponge tool. If you make a mistake, you can delete the layer (drag its name to the trash can at the bottom of the Layers palette), select and copy again, and reapply the sponge.

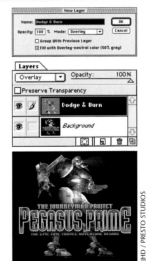

Using a separate layer for dodging and burning

Posterizing an image

Removing unwanted detail

Silhouetting a subject with a clipping path allows it to be exported without its background

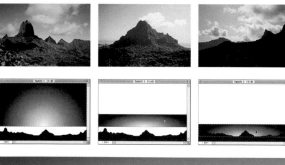

Blurring the background (right) can eliminate detail that competes with the subject.

- **To brighten up a lackluster portrait,** duplicate it to a new layer with blending mode set to Color Dodge and Opacity reduced.

- **To simplify and stylize an image,** choose Image, Map, Posterize and select a number of colors or shades of gray. Or try Filter, Blur, Smart Blur as described on page 156.

- **To show activity or setting but get rid of unwanted detail in the subject,** select the subject and fill it with black to create a silhouette against a bright background.

- **To get rid of unwanted detail in the background,** select the background and blur it, or use the rubber stamp in a Clone mode to paint over some background objects with other background texture.

- **To get rid of a background altogether,** select it and fill it with white or with a color. Or make a clipping path that will silhouette the subject and mask out the background when you export the photo to another program: Press the "P" key to choose the pen tool, and outline the subject. Or make a selection by other means and save it as a path. (Refer to Chapter 2 for the specifics of operating the pen and selection tools). Open the Paths palette (Window, Show Paths), choose Save Path from the palette's pop-out menu, then choose Clipping Path from the same menu, and select your named path in the Clipping Path dialog box. Enter a higher Flatness value if the path is very long and complex. Now you'll be able to save the file in EPS format to be imported into another program and printed. But before you save it, convert it to CMYK mode (choose Mode, CMYK Color) in case the other program can't separate RGB EPS files.

- **To piece together a panorama,** remove and replace the original sky. Blending the part of the scene that continues from one photo to another — often this is the sky — is usually the

Five scanned photos were combined using the rubber stamp to eliminate the seams. Then the sky was selected and filled with blue; the selection was also saved as an alpha channel, which was then duplicated as a grayscale file; Image, Canvas Size was used to make room for a half-circle radial fill, which was started at the lower edge of a rectangular selection, and which could be used to keep the sky from looking flat. Then the entire new sky area was selected and reshaped into a squashed oval (Image, Effects, Scale). This selection was floated, dragged over the silhouette of the mountains, and dropped as a new layer; Darken was selected as the blending mode in the Layers palette. The file was cropped, flattened, copied back into the alpha channel of the panorama document, and loaded as a selection so Levels could be used to lighten the bottom of the sky.

The PhotoVista plug-in filter from Live Picture (see Appendix B) is designed to help you turn still photos into QuickTime VR interactive panoramic "movies" by blending the edges of the photos and correcting for camera angle. Icons at the top of the screen guide you through the process of loading, rotating, and aligning the images, which can be useful not only for making a "movie" — a process controlled by the last icon on the right — but also for making still panoramas.

The original RGB Color image

Converted with Image, Mode, Grayscale

Converted with Image, Mode, Grayscale and then treated with Auto Levels

Converted by choosing Image, Mode, Lab Color and removing the "a" and "b" channels

Converted by removing the Green and Blue channels, leaving only the Red

hardest part of making a panorama sequence into a single image. One solution is to remove the sky, and then replace it with a sky from a different photo, a stretched version of the sky from one of the montaged images, or a synthetic sky.

COLOR TO GRAY

Photoshop provides several ways of converting a color photo to black-and-white. Each method produces a somewhat different result. The method you choose will depend on what you want to do with the image, and you may need to do some experimenting and compare the results. With any of these methods you can try using Image, Adjust, Levels, Auto to optimize the dynamic range.

- The **quickest way** to convert a color file to grayscale is to choose Image, Mode, Grayscale. This may produce the best results if your output will be to a film recorder to make a photo negative or slide.

- Often you get a **crisper grayscale image for print reproduction** by converting from RGB Color to Lab mode (Image, Mode, Lab Color) and then deleting the "a" and "b" channels by opening the Channels palette (Window, Show Channels) and dragging these channels' names to the trash can at the bottom of the palette. Convert the resulting Multichannel file to Grayscale for export.

- For a photo that will be reproduced in black-and-white with a printing method that uses a low halftone screen density, like a **laser print** or a newspaper, you can sometimes get a better result by converting to Bitmap mode as described in step 2 of "Making a Mezzotint" on page 100.

- For **special photographic effects,** such as simulating an infrared photo, you can create a grayscale image by deleting one or more of the color channels: Open the Channels palette (Window, Show Channels) and click the eye icons on and off so you can view the channels one at a time and in pairs. When you've chosen the combination or individual channel you want to preserve, drag the name(s) of the other color channels to the trash can at the bottom of the palette.

- For **special artistic effects,** most of the filters found in the Filter, Sketch submenu produce black-and-white results, although they don't actually make the mode change (you can do that afterwards with Image, Mode, Grayscale).

- If you'll need **to add color back to selected parts** of the image once you've removed it, use the Image, Adjust, Desaturate command, and then apply Image, Adjust, Variations (as in "Hand-Tinting an Image" on page 116) or Image, Adjust, Hue/Saturation with the Colorize box checked.

Making a Mezzotint

Overview *Experiment with the Mezzotint filter, Bitmap mode, and the Andromeda Series 3 filter.*

PHOTO: PHOTODISC, BEYOND RETRO

Filter, Pixelate, Mezzotint, Medium Dots

Mode, Bitmap, Diffusion Dither

Mode, Bitmap, Pattern Dither, Mezzotint-shape (from the PostScript Patterns folder)

Filter, Andromeda, Standard Mezzo, 85 lpi

A TRADITIONAL MEZZOTINT is produced with a halftone screen made up of custom dot shapes. (Halftone screens convert photos into patterns of tiny dots for printing.) Before experimenting with several ways to create a mezzotint from a grayscale image, choose Image, Image Size and set the Print Dimensions of your file. If you don't want to be able to see pixels, use a Resolution above 300 dpi. The exception is for the Diffusion Dither method (see step 2), where the Resolution should be set at 300 dpi or less.

1 Using Photoshop's Mezzotint filter. Choose Filter, Pixelate, Mezzotint; pick a dot, line, or stroke pattern in the Mezzotint dialog box's pop-out menu. (Unlike the other native Photoshop methods in steps 2 and 3, this treatment can also be applied to a color photo.)

2 Using a diffusion dither. Convert the image by choosing Image, Mode, Bitmap and choosing Diffusion Dither as the Method.

3 Using a pattern dither. Choose a pattern from the Patterns subdirectory that comes with Photoshop 4 and open the pattern document. Or paint with black on white to create your own pattern (see Chapter 6 for tips on making seamlessly wrapping non-uniform patterns). If you make your own pattern, keep the balance between black and white fairly even, and then blur the file slightly to get a full range of grays.

When the pattern tile is ready, Select All (Ctrl-A) and choose Edit, Define Pattern. Now in your grayscale photo file choose Mode, Bitmap. Enter an Output resolution, click the Custom Pattern button, and click OK. (The higher the resolution, the smaller the mezzotint "grain" will be and the less visible the pixels. But be careful you don't create a dot pattern too fine to print well.)

4 Using Andromeda Software's Screens filter. For a variety of well-crafted mezzotint effects, you may want to buy the Andromeda Series 3 filter (see "Filter Demos" in Chapter 5). Install it in your Plug-ins folder and choose Filter, Andromeda, Screens. Select from the Preset menu, or enter your own settings. We used a Mezzotint for the image at the left and a Mezzogram for the image above. *Wow!*

Using an Image as a Halftone Dot

Overview *Use a grayscale image to make a custom "halftone dot" pattern; apply it to a photo.*

1a

1b

Image to be "halftoned" (834 x 995 pixels) *Image to be used as the halftone dot*

2a

"Dot" image scaled down to 75 x 88 pixels

2b

Edit	
Undo All	⌘Z
Cut	⌘H
Copy	⌘C
Copy Merged	⇧⌘C
Paste	⌘U
Paste Into	⇧⌘U
Clear	
Fill...	
Stroke...	
Create Publisher...	
Publisher Options...	
Define Pattern	
Take Snapshot	
Take Merged Snapshot	

Defining the scaled and selected photo as a pattern

3a

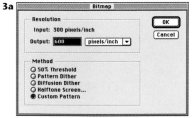

Converting the grayscale photo to Bitmap

3b

Close-up of the Bitmap image

WORKING WITH A RECOGNIZABLE IMAGE as a "halftone dot" rather than a random, seamlessly tiling pattern can produce an interesting mezzotint effect.

1 Choosing images. Choose the photo file that you want to "halftone" with your custom dot pattern. Also choose a grayscale image, or a selection from an image, with a broad range of tones — black, white, and a full range of grays — to use as your halftone dot.

2 Defining the pattern. Reduce the "dot" image or selection to the relative size you want it to appear when it's used as a custom halftone dot. For instance, if you will use 600 pixels/inch for the final image (as described in step 3) and you want to see about 8 of your dots per inch (as we did), you should reduce the dot image to about 75 pixels wide (600 dpi ÷ 75 pixels = 8 "halftone dots"). You can do this by using Layer, Transform, Numeric on a selection or by choosing Image, Image Size. Then surround this small version with the rectangular selection marquee and choose Edit, Define Pattern.

3 Applying the pattern. "Halftone" your large photo by choosing Image, Mode, Bitmap (if the photo is in color, choose Image, Mode, Grayscale first and then Image, Mode, Bitmap). To convert the 256 tones of your grayscale photo to the black-and-white-only Bitmap, click the Custom Pattern button, enter an Output Resolution value (we used 600 pixels/inch). The value you enter here will determine how small your "halftone dots" will be relative to the image (the higher the number, the more dots) and whether you'll be able to see the pixels (lower resolutions) or not (higher resolutions).

"Artistic" Noise

Overview *Apply a Noise filter in Monochromatic mode; Despeckle.*

 *The **"Artistic Noise"** Actions on the Wow! CD-ROM automate Adding Noise and Despeckling.*

1a

PHOTODISC, VINTAGE VIGNETTES

Original image

1b

Setting up the Preview options and choosing Monochromatic Noise

2a

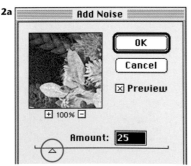

Experimenting with the Amount setting for Monochromatic Noise

AN EXAGGERATED FILM GRAIN EFFECT for a color image can be achieved quickly and simply with the Add Noise filter, applied so that it causes a random brightness pattern at the pixel level without introducing the color speckles of random hue variation.

1 Choosing hue-protected Noise. Open a color image in RGB mode. Choose Filter, Noise, Add Noise and choose Uniform. Click to select the Monochromatic option to produce *hue-protected noise.* Within the dialog box, set the preview size (the line with the + and – boxes) at 100% for the most accurate view of the effect. If you want to see the effect on the image overall, not just in the preview box within the Add Noise dialog box, make sure Preview is selected.

2 Experimenting with the amount and kind of Noise. Use the pointer (which turns into the scrolling hand) to move the image around in the Preview box until you see an area that will give you a

2b

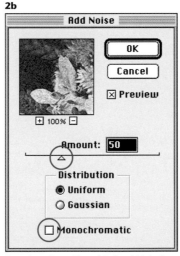

Experimenting with multicolored Noise by turning off Monochromatic

good view of the changes, especially the lights and darks.

Adjust the Amount slider until you see the effect you want in the preview window. When the preview looks good, move the Add Noise dialog box out of the way so you can see the effect on the image overall. Finally, click OK in the dialog box to accept the Noise settings and close the dialog box. We tried settings of 100, 50, and 25 for this 900-pixel-wide image, and also tried turning off Monochromatic.

3a

3b

The Despeckle filter softens the grain, as shown here applied to the image after filtering with Uniform Monochromatic Noise at a setting of 100.

FADING THE EFFECT

Photoshop 4's Filter, Fade command provides a way to "soften" the effect of a filter immediately after applying it, without completely undoing it and starting over. The Fade command isn't necessarily equivalent to using a lower filter setting. Instead, it's as if you had run the filter on a copy in a layer above the original and you were now reducing the Opacity of this top layer, varying the contribution of the filtered and nonfiltered images to the final effect. The Fade command can also be used with the commands of the Image, Adjust submenu and with painting in versions 4.0.1 and later.

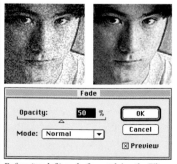

Before (top left) and after applying the Filter, Fade command after Noise, Add Noise

3 Trying more variations. For a larger but softer and more "painterly" grain, apply the Despeckle filter (Filter, Noise, Despeckle) to the image after applying the Monochromatic Noise. The result shown at the top of page 102 was developed by running the Despeckle filter on an image filtered with a Uniform Monochromatic Noise setting of 50.

FILTER SETTINGS AND IMAGE SIZES

When you apply a filter or other special effect that operates at the pixel level of an image, the setting to use will depend on the degree of effect you want *and on the resolution* of the image you're working on. The larger the absolute size of the image — indicated by the dimensions of the image in pixels or the size of the file (in K or MB) — the higher the setting will need to be to produce the effect. In the examples shown below, note that a low setting has a much stronger effect on a smaller image than on a larger one. For the larger version, the setting has to be increased quite a bit to get a similar-looking result. So if you see a filtered image and want to create that particular effect on an image of your own, you need to know not only the filter settings that were used, but also the size of the image.

Image size: 250 pixels wide (157 K); Uniform Monochromatic Noise, Amount setting: 20

Image size: 500 pixels wide (625 K); Uniform Monochromatic Noise, Amount setting: 20

Image size: 250 pixels wide (157 K); Uniform Monochromatic Noise, Amount setting: 40

Image size: 500 pixels wide (625 K); Uniform Monochromatic Noise, Amount setting: 40

Image size: 250 pixels wide (157 K); Uniform Monochromatic Noise, Amount setting: 40, Despeckle

Image size: 500 pixels wide (625 K); Uniform Monochromatic Noise, Amount setting: 40, Despeckle

ORIGINAL PHOTO: RUBBER/BALL, FACES 1

Dithering

Overview *Convert the image to Bitmap mode with a low-resolution Diffusion Dither; convert the Bitmap image to RGB color; select and copy the black pixels only to a separate transparent layer; replace black with a color gradient; replace the color in the Background layer with another gradient.*

The "Dithering" Actions on the Wow! CD-ROM automate the process of creating mezzotint-like effects using Diffusion Dither.

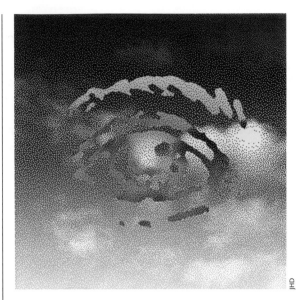

1a

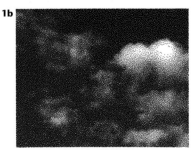

Converting a Grayscale photo to Bitmap

1b

The Bitmap image converted to RGB

CONVERTING IMAGES TO BITMAP MODE with Photoshop's Diffusion Dither pattern can be useful for making the plates used for silkscreen printing or for adding a distinctive texture to a color illustration. If you start out by putting the black and the white elements of the dithered image on two separate layers of an RGB file, it's easy to experiment with color until you have exactly the result you want.

1 Converting a photo. Start with a color or grayscale image. Convert it to Bitmap through the Mode submenu: If the image is in Grayscale mode to start with, choose Image, Mode, Bitmap. If it's in color, you'll have to choose Image, Mode, Grayscale first, because you can't convert directly from a color mode to Bitmap or vice versa. When you make the conversion, specify a low resolution in the Bitmap dialog box. We used 123 dpi, but you can use any resolution low enough to show a pleasing pattern. The resolution that looks best to you may vary, depending on how large you want to print the image and what its particular content is.

2 Making a layer for the black pixels. To convert the dithered image to RGB mode so you can add color, choose Image, Mode, Grayscale and then Image, Mode, RGB.

Now you'll select all the black pixels: Double-click the magic wand in the toolbox to open the Magic Wand Options palette. Turn off Anti-aliased. Since there are only black and white pixels in the image — no intermediate colors — the wand's Tolerance can be set to anything but 255 and still pick out only black pixels when you click on a single black pixel. (To get a closer view so you can pick out a pixel, hold down the Ctrl-spacebar key combination to turn the magic wand into the magnifier temporarily.) Once you've clicked on a black pixel, choose Select, Similar to add all the rest of the black

2

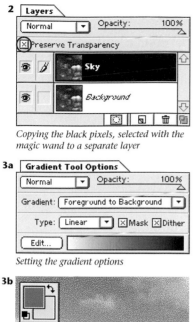

Copying the black pixels, selected with the magic wand to a separate layer

3a

Setting the gradient options

3b

Black pixels filled with gradient

4

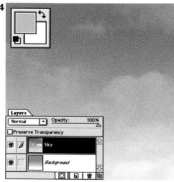

Background layer filled with a gradient

5

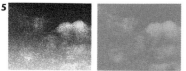

Gradients replaced with other gradients (left) and with two solid colors (right)

pixels to the selection. Copy the selection (Ctrl-C) and choose Edit, Paste to make a layer that includes the black pixels only; we named our layer "Sky."

3 Coloring the black pixels. With the new layer active, turn on Preserve Transparency (click the check box at the top of the Layers palette) to ensure that when you color the layer, the existing pixels will be colored but the transparent areas will remain transparent.

Double-click on the gradient tool to open its Options palette; set it for a Linear fill, for Normal mode, for Foreground To Background style, and for 100% Opacity. Then, in the toolbox, click on the Foreground and Background color icons in turn and choose colors for the extremes of the color gradient you'll use to replace the black pixels; we used a blue for the Foreground color and a lighter blue for the Background color. In the image, drag the gradient tool from where you want the color to start to change to where you want the transition to end (we dragged from top to bottom). The black pixels will fill with the color gradient.

4 Adding the second color gradient. Activate the Background layer by clicking on its name in the Layers palette. You can now apply your second gradient — the one that will color the white pixels — to the entire Background layer. Set the Foreground and Background squares in the toolbox to new colors (we used a pink and white), and use the gradient tool again to apply the color (we again applied the gradient vertically, this time dragging from about a third of the way from the top to about a third of the way to the bottom). Although this operation will color both the black and the white pixels in the Background layer, the layer above (Sky in our example) will allow only the pixels that used to be white (the clouds in our example) to show through its transparent areas.

5 Experimenting with other color schemes. Now you can try new color gradients by repeating the coloring instructions in steps 3 and 4 with different colors. Or you can use a solid color rather than a gradient for either or both of the layers. Set one of the colors as the Foreground color and the second as the Background color. Instead of using the gradient tool in steps 3 and 4, use the Edit, Fill command (or Alt-Backspace and Ctrl-Backspace) to refill the pixels in the two layers. Whichever method you use, be sure to keep Preserve Transparency turned on when you fill the top layer.

Combining resolutions. To combine a low-resolution dither with a higher-resolution element as we did for the eye-in-the-sky image, you can use Image, Image Size, Resample Image: Nearest Neighbor, increasing the Resolution to an even multiple (2, 4, 6, or 8 times) the current resolution to reach print resolution. Then drag and drop your high-resolution element into the file. *Wow!*

Coloring a Black & White Photo

Overview *Convert the grayscale image to RGB; add color with an Adjustment layer for Color Balance or Hue/Saturation, or by layering color over the image.*

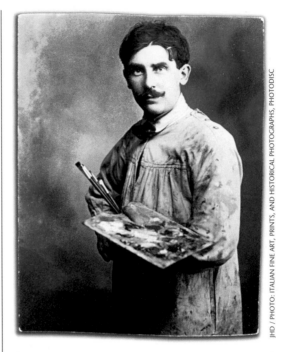

JHD / PHOTO: ITALIAN FINE ART, PRINTS, AND HISTORICAL PHOTOGRAPHS, PHOTODISC

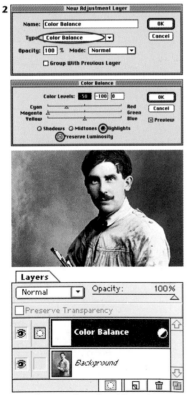

Original grayscale image converted to RGB

An Adjustment layer for adding color

ADDING COLOR TO A GRAYSCALE IMAGE can produce from subtle to spectacular results. There are many ways to do it, and you'll see examples throughout the book. But here are three fairly quick and easy approaches, based on using Image, Adjust, Color Balance; using Image, Adjust, Hue/Saturation; and applying a new layer of color imagery in Color mode.

1 Preparing the grayscale image. Convert the grayscale image to color by choosing Image, Mode, RGB Color.

2 Changing the color balance. Open the Layers palette (Window, Show Layers) and Ctrl-click the New Layer icon in the center at the bottom of the palette to add an Adjustment layer. From the pop-out Type list in the New Adjustment Layer dialog box choose Color Balance. In turn, click and adjust the Highlights and Shadows. For a dramatic effect, use opposite settings that produce colors that are opposite on the color wheel (complementary colors). We used yellow for the shadows and pushed the highlights toward purple by increasing magenta and cyan. If changing the Color Balance settings drastically changes the tonality of the image, turn Preserve Luminosity on or off to preserve the original brightness levels.

3 Changing the hue. If step 2 doesn't give you exactly the color you want, modify the image further: Add another Adjustment layer, this one for Hue/Saturation and move the Hue slider left or right to shift the colors around the color wheel until you find the option you like best. When you're sure you have what you like, you can choose Flatten Image from the Layers palette's pop-out menu.

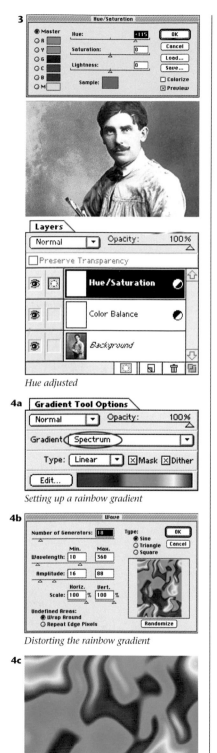

3

Hue adjusted

4a

Setting up a rainbow gradient

4b

Distorting the rainbow gradient

4c

Gaussian Blur applied to distorted gradient

4 Adding a layer of color. Try adding a layer of color over the flattened image: Choose Window, Show Layers to open the Layers palette (or use a keyboard shortcut; the default is F7). Add a layer by clicking the New Layer icon at the bottom of the Layers palette. We named our new layer "Color Overlay."

To fill your color layer, you can hand-paint some areas or use a color photo, a pattern, or an abstract color gradient, as we did here. To put color into our new layer, we used one of the preset gradients: We double-clicked the gradient tool in the toolbox to open the Gradient Tool Options palette, and chose Spectrum from the Gradient list and Linear for the Type. After dragging with the gradient tool to fill the layer with the rainbow gradient, we applied the Distort, Wave filter several times. Finally, we chose Filter, Blur, Gaussian Blur and applied a 10-pixel blur to blend the colors in this 618-pixel-wide spectrum image.

When your Color Overlay layer is complete, you can experiment with its mode and Opacity settings. We changed the mode to Color, so that only the color (hue and saturation but not luminosity) was composited with the image in the Background layer, and we adjusted the Opacity to 25%.

5 Adding finishing touches. After you finish experimenting with color, you can combine effects if you like. We liked the overall effect we had produced in step 4, but we wanted to tone down the color in the upper left corner. So we used a softly feathered lasso to select this area of the image, and then turned the selection into a layer mask that would partially block the effect of the Color Overlay layer: With the selection made and the Color Overlay layer active, we Alt-clicked the Add Layer Mask icon at the left on the bottom of the Layers palette. This created a layer mask with the selection as the darkened part, and we could airbrush the edges of the mask to get the result we wanted. With this new mask still active (as indicated by the mask icon next to the eye icon for this layer), Image, Adjust, Levels was used to lighten the mask overall, resulting in the final color blend you see at the top of the previous page.

4d

Applying the color layer in Color mode with Opacity adjusted over the flattened image from step 3

5

Adding a layer mask to tone down the color in the upper left corner

"Sketching" a Portrait

Overview *Convert a grayscale image to RGB, or desaturate a color image; apply a filter or special effect on the Red, Green, and Blue channels separately; experiment with removing the color from different channels.*

KATRIN EISMANN / PHOTO: DOUGLAS KIRKLAND

1

Grayscale converted to RGB and Levels adjusted

2

Setting up to work on one channel while viewing all

3a

Setting parameters for the Graphic Pen filter

WORKING IN THE INDIVIDUAL RGB CHANNELS can produce some interesting treatments of color photos or of grayscale images converted to color. Katrin Eismann explored this technique in a portrait that began as a black-and-white photo. While there may be a number of different methods for accomplishing this effect in Photoshop, we reproduced it as shown in these steps. Looking at the steps that built the effect provides a good demonstration of how the positive and negative values in the individual channels can interact in the overall image. Try the Graphic Pen filter used here, or experiment with the individual-channels technique using one of the other Photoshop filters that produce random variations, such as Noise, Pointillize, or Mezzotint and then applying other effects, such as a Stylize filter, to the individual channels.

1 Converting the photo to RGB. If you start with a Grayscale file, convert the image to RGB by selecting from the Image, Mode submenu. If you start with a color photo, choose Image, Adjust, Desaturate. The conversion will put the same grayscale information in each of the color channels. For this photo, after the conversion to RGB, the gamma (gray) slider in the Image, Adjust, Levels dialog box was moved a little to the left to lighten the image overall.

2 Setting up to work on individual channels. Set black as the Foreground color and white as the Background color. (A quick way to do this is to press the "D" key for "default

---

COLOR CHANNELS IN COLOR

To view individual color channels in color rather than in grayscale, choose File, Preferences, Display & Cursors, Color Channels In Color.

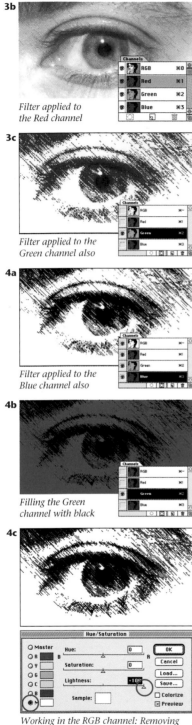

3b

Filter applied to the Red channel

3c

Filter applied to the Green channel also

4a

Filter applied to the Blue channel also

4b

Filling the Green channel with black

4c

Working in the RGB channel: Removing the magenta

colors.") Select the first color channel you want to work on by clicking on that channel's icon in the Channels palette (opened by choosing Window, Show Channels). You can view the effect on the entire image by clicking in the eye icon column next to the RGB channel name.

3 Operating on the channels.

Now make changes to the individual channels. For this image, the Graphic Pen (Filter, Sketch, Graphic Pen) was applied with the maximum Length setting (15), a Stroke Direction setting of Left Diag., and a Light/Dark Balance setting of around 30. The setting was the same for all channels, but because the filter operates with a degree of random variation, a slightly different effect was produced each time it was run. The filter was run first on the Red channel, then on the Green, and then on the Blue, although the order of operations is not important. Shown here are the progressive results as seen by viewing all the channels together as each step was added.

4 Eliminating one color.

Now you can eliminate the color effect contributed by one of the channels. To produce the red, blue, and black composition seen in the opening image, the Green channel was selected by clicking on it again in the Channels palette. Pressing Alt-Backspace filled the channel with black. This effectively removed the green lines from the RGB image, but it also removed the green component of the white background, leaving a strong magenta component, since magenta is the complement (opposite, or negative) of green. To remove the magenta, leaving a white background, the RGB channel was activated by clicking on its icon in the Channels palette. Image, Adjust, Hue/Saturation was chosen, and the M (for magenta) button was selected; this would make the color adjustments apply only to that particular color. The Lightness slider was moved all the way to the right, to a value of +100. This turned the magenta white without affecting other colors.

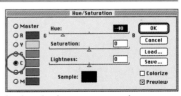

Popping Color

Overview *Open a color file; copy the subject to a new layer; adjust the hue and saturation of the Background layer.*

A popular effect in both print and video is to isolate the subject of an image by "graying out" the background. This effect can be used to emphasize the subject, to simplify the background for overprinting type, or to tie an image to others in a publication.

1 Isolating the subject. Choose the appropriate selection tool or command, and select the subject (see the beginning of Chapter 2 for tips on choosing the right selection method). We used the pen tool (activate it by pressing the "P" key) to outline the runner because the shape consisted largely of smooth curves. Once a path is drawn, you can adjust it, if necessary, by using the pen tool with the Ctrl key held down as you drag the curve points or their control handles to make the curve better fit the subject. With a path you can fine-tune the outline without accidentally dropping and losing the selection.

When the path is finished, save it by double-clicking the Work Path name in the Paths palette. Then convert it to a selection (by pressing the Enter key), and turn the selection into a new layer (Ctrl-J).

2 Desaturating the background. Activate the Background layer by clicking on its name in the Layers palette. Then choose Image, Adjust, Desaturate.

3 Trying another variation. For the image at the top of the page we used a variation of the desaturation process. We chose Image, Adjust, Hue/Saturation. The Colorize box was selected, the Hue slider was adjusted to the desired color, and then the color was desaturated to 25%. (When Colorize is off, the Saturation scale goes from –100 to +100; when it's on, the range is 0 to 100.) Finally we added type to the image.

1a

Outlining the subject with the pen tool

1b

Adjusting the path

1c

Isolating the subject on a layer of its own

2

Desaturating the Background layer

3

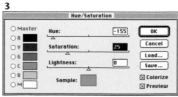

Settings for colorizing and desaturating

Softening the Focus

Overview *Copy an image, or part of an image, to an independent layer; blur this layer; recombine it with the original.*

The *"Soft Focus" Actions* on the *Wow! CD-ROM automate several haze and fog effects.*

1a

Original image

1b

Image copied into a new layer

2a

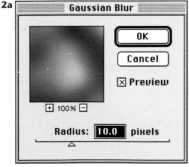

Blurring the image

SINCE THE END OF THE 19TH CENTURY, photographers have used haze and fog effects to impart a soft quality to an image, hiding the detail in the highlights, or in both highlights and midtones, or in the image overall. With a camera, the effect can be achieved by smearing petroleum jelly on a filter in front of the lens, by breathing on the filter, or by placing fine nylon mesh over the enlarging lens in the darkroom. This technique is often used to hide small skin blemishes, to make hair look softer, or to add a romantic air. In Photoshop you can get a similar effect with Gaussian Blur and layers.

1 Making a duplicate of the image on a new layer. Open an image and open the Layers palette (Window, Show Layers). Drag the *Background* layer's name to the New Layer icon in the center at the bottom of the Layers palette to make a copy of the image.

2 Blurring Layer 1. Choose Filter, Blur, Gaussian Blur to make the new layer look hazy. We used a setting of 10 pixels for this 760-pixel-wide image.

3 Adjusting mode, Opacity, and Layer Options to make haze. Now make one of the following changes to the palette settings for the top layer:

- To reduce the haze effect but still apply it to all the tonal values in the selected area, choose Normal and change the Opacity.
- To refine the haze effect to soften the highlights only, choose Lighten and adjust the Opacity to control the strength of the haze effect. (We used this technique for the opening image.)
- To create a painted look, reducing the number of colors and softening them, choose Darken and reduce the Opacity.

2b

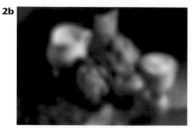

Layer 1, blurred

Other haze effects can be achieved by using the This Layer and Underlying sliders in Layer Options, chosen from the Layers palette's pop-out menu. To soften the image only within a particular tonal range, hold down the Alt key and drag the Underlying black and white sliders. Holding down the Alt key as you drag will allow you to split each slider triangle, so you can smooth the transition by defining a range of colors that are to be only partially composited. Experiment with the slider positions, moving the two parts of each triangle apart slightly to avoid harsh color breaks. The settings that work best will depend on the colors in the image and the effect you're trying to achieve. (For tips on using the Layer Options sliders, see "Floating and Underlying Sliders at the beginning of Chapter 4.)

Saving the file. When you have an effect you like, click OK to close the Layer Options dialog box. If you think you may want to experiment with the image some more in the future, save it in Photoshop format to preserve the layers. If not, you can make the haze effect permanent by combining the file's layers into a single Background layer (choose Flatten Image from the Layers palette's pop-out menu). Flattening saves file space and also lets you save the file in a format — EPS or TIFF, for example — that can be imported into a page layout program. Another alternative is to use File, Save A Copy to save a renamed copy in any file format Photoshop supports, leaving the current Photoshop version of the file intact and open.

3a

Reducing the opacity of the blurred layer

IN THE PINK

To add a "healthy glow" to a portrait or still life, you can use the color channels of an RGB file rather than a blurred layer: Activate only the Red channel but turn on the eye icons so you can view all three channels together; apply the Gaussian Blur filter. The image is softened and a small amount of the red component is blurred outward, creating a glow. The unblurred Green channel maintains the detail so that the blurring effect is not too strong.

3b

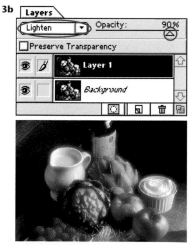

Softening the highlights with Lighten

3c

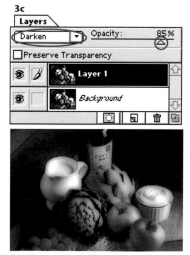

Creating a painted effect with Darken

3d

Softening only part of the tonal range

Fixing a Problem Photo

Overview *Make selections for dark and light areas; use these as masks in Curves Adjustment layers; touch up dust, scratches, and other flaws.*

1a

Original photo

1b

Two Curves settings — one for the sky (left) and one for the rest of the image — were applied with Adjustment layers with masks based on a Color Range selection.

2a

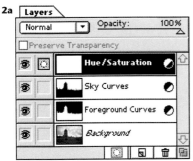

A Hue/Saturation layer was applied, without a mask but targeted to affect green hues only.

2b

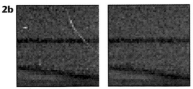

Blemishes on the photo (left) were selected and removed with the Dust & Scratches filter.

FOR MANY OUTDOOR PHOTOS the camera can't meter both the subject and the sky, and the subject is too far away for a flash to do any good. Ideally, a photo like the one above would have been snapped twice — exposed once for the light sky and once for the dark subject. Or the single photo could have been scanned twice at different settings. Either way, the two versions of the image could then have been masked and merged to make a good-looking composite. But in this case the image came as a single scan, so the goal was to select and mask the subject and sky separately and then apply tonal corrections to each part through these masks. The same process can be applied to other photos with exposure problems.

1 Making masks and adjustments. Start by opening the Layers palette (Window, Show Layers), and select either the dark or light areas. For this image we could use the Select, Color Range command, Shift-dragging its default eyedropper over the dark foreground. With the selection active, Ctrl-click on the New Layer icon (in the center at the bottom of the Layers palette) to make an Adjustment layer with a mask, and choose Curves as the Type. Click the Auto button to make a good start at correcting tones and color casts. Make further Curves adjustments (see page 121 for tips on adjusting Curves) and click OK. To make an Adjustment layer for the other part of the photo, drag the Adjustment layer's name to the New Layer icon. In the new duplicate layer invert the tonality of the mask (Ctrl-I) and double-click the black-and-white circle next to the layer's name in the Layers palette to open the Curves dialog box. Click the Auto button and make other changes as necessary.

2 Making final fixes. Make any further color corrections, and fix flaws — the rubber stamp tool and Dust & Scratches filter can often help. We added a Hue/Saturation Adjustment layer to make the grass greener. We also lassoed some marks in the lawn area and removed them with Filter, Noise, Dust & Scratches with a Radius setting of 1 and a Threshold of 40.

Simulating Motion

Overview *Isolate the subject of an action photo on a layer of its own; copy the original photo to another layer; motion-blur the copy; adjust the blurring of the image by masking the subject or changing the opacity of the blurred layer.*

1a

Original image

1b

Subject isolated on a new layer made from a feathered selection

2a

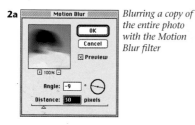 *Blurring a copy of the entire photo with the Motion Blur filter*

2b

Motion-blurred copy of the original image

JHD / PHOTODISC, SPORTS & RECREATION

ADDING A SENSE OF MOTION to a photo can draw the viewer into the excitement of the scene and give a good static image the added drama to make it great. Using blurring techniques in Photoshop, you can simulate the effect of a camera panning to follow the subject (as shown above) or of a stationary camera with the subject in motion. With layers, layer masks, and the Motion Blur or Radial Blur filter, you have an amazing amount of flexibility in localizing the motion effect to a particular area of the image if you like — a waving hand, for example. And the Opacity control in the Layers palette lets you interactively reduce the blur until you see exactly the effect you want.

1 Isolating a sharp copy of the subject. You'll need a way to keep the moving subject in focus when you blur the background. First open your image file, and then open the Layers palette (Window, Palettes, Show Layers). Now select the subject: We made a rough selection, using a feathered lasso (we set a 10-pixel feather for this 900-pixel-wide image). We kept the selection border just far enough away from the subject so the feathering didn't encroach on its outline. A rough, feathered selection can be used if the background image lacks detail, as this one does. But if the background is busy, you'll need a tighter, less feathered selection.

Turn the selection into a layer of its own (Ctrl-J).

2 Blurring the picture. To give yourself more options later (as described in step 3), make a duplicate copy of the full image in a new layer by dragging the Background label in the Layers palette to the New Layer icon in the middle at the bottom of the palette. Then apply a blur to this layer. We used Blur, Motion Blur at an angle of –9° and a distance of 30 pixels.

At this point, the blurred image in the "Background Copy" layer entirely hides the original in the Background layer underneath it. But the sharp copy of the subject (in the top layer) keeps the subject in focus; and the feathered edge of the sharp subject blends seamlessly into the blurred image below it.

2c

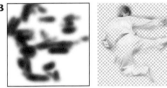

The result of layering the sharp subject and blurred Background Copy

3

The dark parts of a painted layer mask (left) hide the corresponding parts of the subject. This will allow the blurred layer below to show through.

4

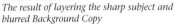

Layers palette for the image shown at the top of page 114, with the top layer and its mask offset to produce a strobe effect

An alternate approach: To simulate a photo taken with a stationary camera, the subject is isolated and blurred over the sharp background image.

3 Tailoring the blur effect. Now you can add a little "blur detail" to the subject by masking out some areas of the top layer. With the top layer active, click the Add Layer Mask icon on the left at the bottom of the Layers palette. Now the mask will be active but the subject itself — not the mask — will be visible, so you can see the blur start to show through as you use a soft airbrush to apply black paint where you want to see more of the blur — for instance, at the trailing edge of the moving subject. The dark areas of the mask will prevent the sharp layer from contributing to the composite. If you "erase" too much of the sharp image, just paint the mask with white to bring back detail. Also, if the blur effect on the background seems too strong, you can sharpen the entire image by adjusting the Opacity slider of the blurred Background Copy layer to let the sharp original show through.

4 Simulating a strobe. To get the effect of a panning camera with a strobe (a flash that freezes part of the subject in focus while the slower shutter speed records the motion), you can offset the sharp copy of the subject. Working in the top layer, use the move tool to slide the subject a short distance in the direction of motion. Because by default the layer mask is linked to the image, as shown by the chain icon between them, the mask will move with the subject.

Trying a variation. To simulate a stationary camera photographing a moving subject, you can blur the subject and keep the background in focus: Select and copy the subject to its own layer as in step 1, and then apply a blur filter to this layer only.

More variations. Here are some other ways to tailor the blur to the image: You can show more motion in some parts of the subject than others by copying the subject onto two layers, blurring one more than the other, and then painting masks to allow more or less blur to show in different areas. And you can use a Radial Blur to show swinging or zooming motion.

A radial blur with a spin setting was used to show the motion of the swing. Extra height was added with the Image, Canvas Size command so the blur center could be defined outside the image — above, where the chain is fastened to a tree limb. Then the final image was cropped. For the photo of the runner, the Background Copy layer was treated with a Radial blur in Zoom mode, centered in the lower right corner of the image, to bring the runner forward.

"Hand-Tinting" a Portrait

Overview *Convert the black-and-white image to RGB mode; select areas and adjust color, primarily in the midtones; desaturate light areas; add color details.*

JHD / PHOTO: PHOTODISC, RETRO AMERICANA

Original grayscale image

Converted to RGB

INCREASED CURVES PRECISION

Alt-click the grid in the Curves dialog box to get a finer scale (10% increments) so you can see more precisely where to place points when you adjust the curve.

THE COLORING OF BLACK-AND-WHITE PHOTOS with paints and pigments began very early in the history of photography, and its popularity persisted until color photography became widespread. Today the look is popular again — not a technicolor imitation of a color photo, but a subtle coloring reminiscent of the early hand-tinting process.

1 Correcting the tonality of the image. Whether you start with a color or a grayscale scan of the black-and-white image, you can use Photoshop's Levels (Ctrl-L) and Curves (Ctrl-M) adjustments to spread the tones in the image over the full range of possibilities and to bring out the shadow and highlight detail. For this image, which seemed a little dark to begin with, we used Image, Adjust, Curves to lighten the three-quarter tones, increasing the shadow detail. To find where to adjust the curve, move the cursor out of the Curves dialog box and onto the image. The cursor will turn into an eyedropper. Click to pinpoint a tone that you want to adjust. A small circle will appear on the diagonal line in the Curves dialog box to show which part of the curve corresponds to the tone currently under the eyedropper. If you drag the eyedropper, the circle will move to reflect the current tone. When you've seen where to adjust the curve, release the mouse button, move the cursor back into the dialog box, and click on the diagonal line at the point where you saw the circle.

We identified a dark area of the image with the eyedropper, clicking on the original curve at an Input value of about 15. Clicking on the diagonal line established a point, and then dragging the point upward raised the entire curve. Clicking to form another point at an Input value of about 128 (halfway in the 0 to 255 range of the curve) and dragging downward closer to the center of the

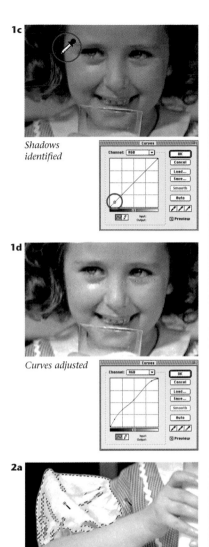

1c

Shadows identified

1d

Curves adjusted

2a

Magic wand selection

2b

Selection enlarged by Shift-clicking

grid returned the midtones, quarter tones, and highlights to values close to their original settings.

When making these kinds of Curves adjustments, it's important to maintain a smooth curve shape, without drastic changes in direction. Otherwise you can flatten the color or produce a sort of solarization effect with harsh tonal breaks.

LOCAL TONE ADJUSTMENTS

If you want to lighten or darken the three-quarter tones in only certain parts of an image, use the dodge and burn aspects of the dodge/burn/sponge tool instead of Image, Adjust, Curves. In the Brushes palette choose a soft brush tip of an appropriate size. In the Toning Tools Options palette choose a tonal range (Highlights, Midtones, or Shadows) and choose Dodge or Burn, depending on whether you want to lighten or darken.

Hold down the left mouse button and keep it down as you drag the tool back and forth over the area you want to change, watching until you've achieved the effect you want; then release the mouse button. Holding the mouse button down the entire time you're working makes it possible to undo (Ctrl-Z) the entire operation if you don't like the effect.

To reduce the intensity of the dodge/burn tool's effect, lower the Exposure setting before you start using the tool. If you want to reduce the effect even more, choose Midtones or Highlights to work on the shadow tones. At any of the three settings, these tools work on the entire range of tones but they have a more pronounced effect on the part of the range that matches the setting you choose.

2 Making selections. Now select various parts of the image so you can make color adjustments. Select one area, change it by the method in step 3, then select another, and so on. For this image the dress was selected by clicking on it with the magic wand tool with a Tolerance setting of 32 (double-click the magic wand in the toolbox to open the Magic Wand Options palette to change the setting). Additions to the selection were made by Shift-clicking on other parts of the dress. When the selection was complete, it was assigned a 5-pixel feather for this 1155-pixel-wide image. (To open the Feather Selection dialog box so you can set the feather radius, choose Select, Feather.)

The skin was selected with the lasso, feathered 5 pixels (double-click the lasso to open Lasso Options to set the feather radius). This selection was drawn loosely to imitate the old hand-tinting process, which often involved soft overlapping of colors.

ADDING COMMANDS

You can add any of Photoshop's commands to any Actions palette by choosing New Action from the palette's pop-out menu, then choosing Insert Menu Item, choosing your command from its menu, clicking OK, and pressing the round button at the bottom of the Actions palette to stop recording.

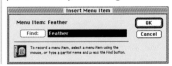

3

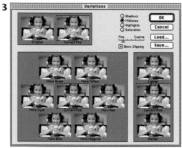

Adjusting color balance in the midtones

4

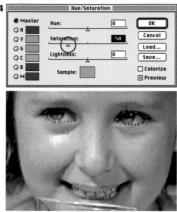

Desaturating white areas

5

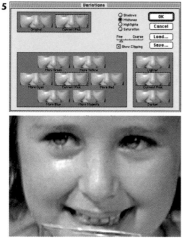

Adding color details

3 Coloring the selections.

Once selections have been made, open the Variations dialog box (Image, Adjust, Variations). The hue adjustment in the Variations box is especially good for skin tones — it's an electronic cosmetologist's dream that lets you see the tinting possibilities at a glance. Starting with fairly coarse adjustments (set with the slider near the top right corner of the dialog box), you can clearly see what color changes you're selecting. As you zero in on the changes you want, move the slider left to make finer adjustments.

4 Desaturating white areas. Areas that have been colored too much can be desaturated or recolored by selecting them with a very slightly feathered lasso (we used a 1-pixel feather) and choosing Image, Adjust, Hue/Saturation. For example, selecting the eyes and teeth and moving the Saturation slider to the left tends to take away most of the tint, while still maintaining the overall warm color cast that makes these features "at home" in this tinted image.

5 Adding color details. After hard-edged areas (such as the chair, butter, bread crust, and wrapper in this image) have been selected with a 1-pixel-feathered lasso and colored by using the Hue slider in the Hue/Saturation dialog box, subtle color variations can be added to the face. For instance, the cheeks in this image were selected with the lasso feathered to 5 pixels, and the Variations dialog box was used again to apply a little color by selecting the More Red version of the Midtones in the selected region.

AVOIDING HARSH BREAKS

For the most part, when you colorize parts of an image, change only the *hue* of the *midtones*. Changing the highlights or shadows or the brightness or saturation of selected areas tends to make selections look unnaturally distinct from their surroundings.

SAVING TIME ON IMAGE ADJUSTMENTS

If you hold down the Alt key as you choose any of the Image, Adjust submenu's multistep functions from the menu or with a keyboard shortcut, the dialog box will open with the last settings used, rather than with the built-in defaults. (Threshold and Posterize do this even without the Alt key.) If you're working through a series of images, layers, or channels that all need the same kind of adjustment, holding down the Alt key to choose the Image, Adjust functions and then clicking OK can be quite a bit faster than using the dialog box's Save and Load buttons.

Better yet, the first time you make the change, record an Action, and then play it on a batch of files (see "The Recording Process" In "Automating with Actions" in Chapter 1). Or make an Adjustment layer and drag-and-drop it from one file's Layers palette into your other files.

✓Levels...	⌘L
Auto Levels	⇧⌘L
✓Curves...	⌘M
✓Color Balance...	⌘B
✓Brightness/Contrast...	
✓Hue/Saturation...	⌘U
Desaturate	⇧⌘U
✓Replace Color...	
✓Selective Color...	
Invert	⌘I
Equalize	
Threshold...	
Posterize...	
✓Variations...	

"Antiquing" a Color Photo

Overview *Reduce the color to a hand-tinted look by partially desaturating the image, or by combining a filtered top layer in Color mode with a completely desaturated bottom layer.*

 *The **"Antiquing"** Actions on the Wow! CD-ROM automate the process of producing a hand-tinted look for a color photo.*

1a

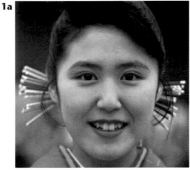

Original image

1b

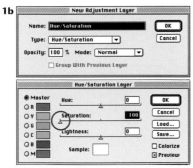

We added an Adjustment layer (top) and reduced Saturation until there was no color left in the image.

ORIGINAL PHOTO: PHOTODISC, WORLD COMMERCE & TRAVEL

IF YOU'RE STARTING WITH A COLOR PHOTO and aiming for an old-fashioned hand-tinted look, you can take the color out (by choosing Image, Desaturate, for instance) and then recolor the photo as described in "Hand-Tinting a Portrait" on page 116. Or, instead of tackling all that hand work, you can try one of these methods.

1 The quickest way: partially desaturating. So that your original image will remain untouched, add an Adjustment Layer by Ctrl-clicking the New Layer icon in the center at the bottom of the Layers palette. In the New Adjustment Layer dialog box, choose Hue/Saturation from the list of Types and click OK. Then adjust the Saturation slider in the Hue/Saturation dialog box, desaturating the image completely. Now you can experiment with increasing the color by reducing the opacity of the Adjustment layer, moving the Opacity slider in the Layers palette.

2 Flattening the tints. The second method produces an image that looks more like a real hand-painted photo. Duplicate your bottom-layer image from step 1 to a new layer by dragging its thumbnail to the New Layer icon. Drag the new layer's thumbnail up above the Adjustment layer in the palette. Working in this new layer, choose Filter, Noise, Median and

INTERACTIVE ADJUSTMENT

When you use an Adjustment layer to change Saturation, make the setting in the Hue/Saturation dialog box as extreme as you can — move the Saturation slider all the way left to desaturate completely (or right to boost saturation as high as it will go). Then, with the adjustment layer in Normal mode, you'll have complete interactive control over the effect by moving the adjustment layer's Opacity slider to add color back (or remove color).

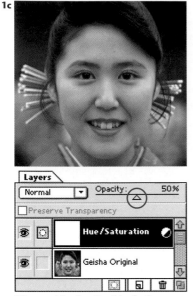

1c

We moved the Opacity slider for the Adjustment layer to restore color until we had the effect we wanted.

choose a setting that turns the image into blobs of color. For this 900-pixel-wide image, we used a Radius of 10 in the Median filter's dialog box. In the Layers palette, choose Color from the pop-out blending mode list, and adjust the Opacity slider to reduce the color.

If the detail in the photo looks too sharp for a convincing old-fashioned effect, click the bottom layer's thumbnail in the Layers palette. Then open the Channels palette and click the Red, Green, and Blue thumbnails one by one, to view the channels separately, choosing the one with the most image detail (we chose Red). Leave that channel alone, but run the Median filter on each of the other two color channels (press Ctrl-F to run the last filter you applied).

3 Coloring outside the lines. A third approach adds to the hand-worked look by blurring the color beyond the edges of the "painted" areas. Activate the top layer from step 2; choose Filter, Blur, Gaussian Blur and choose a Radius; we used 10. Set the blending mode to Normal, and adjust Opacity.

2a

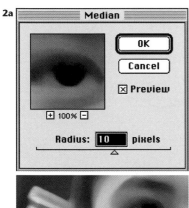

The Median filter "averages" the brightness of similarly colored adjacent pixels but leaves sharp color breaks unchanged. This makes the color look more like hand-tinting, as if only a few colors were applied to the image.

2b

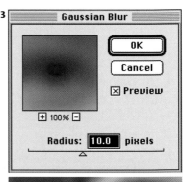

In this version of the image, the top layer, in Color mode with Opacity reduced, contributes the tints, and the bottom layer, desaturated by the Adjustment layer above it, provides the image detail.

3

Adding a Gaussian Blur makes the Color layer "bleed," (top), while the bottom layer keeps the image sharp (see the final result at the top of the previous page).

Retouching a Photo

Overview *Scan the image; use Curves to adjust shadow and highlight density, if necessary; roughly select any large, mostly uniform area that contains details that need to be removed; clean up the selection; save the selection as a mask; replace the selected area; make repairs to other parts of the image using duplicated portions and cloning.*

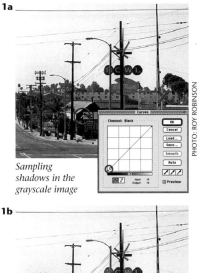

Sampling shadows in the grayscale image

PHOTO: ROY ROBINSON

1b

Shadow tones adjusted

NOT ALL PHOTO-RETOUCHING JOBS are glamorous, but the technique can be practical and profitable. The San Diego Gas & Electric Company wanted to show the City Council of Oceanside, California how their streets would look if power lines were buried. The goal was to produce "before" and "after" photos the officials could hold in their hands for comparison.

1 Adjusting "exposure." Before retouching begins, the tonality of the original image may need correcting. We had scanned the original black-and-white photo as an RGB file to gain more information than a grayscale scan would have provided. After the scan was converted to grayscale (Image, Mode, Grayscale), we applied Image, Adjust, Curves to bring out shadow detail without changing midtones and highlights.

The Curves function provides a way to isolate contrast and brightness changes to specific tonal ranges, such as quarter tones or three-quarter tones. Move the cursor out of the Curves box and onto the image (it becomes an eyedropper) and click to sample a tone you want to change. A small circle on the Curve shows the location of that tone. Note the position of the circle and click there on the Curve to establish a point; drag to adjust its position. Then move other parts of the Curve back toward their original positions.

2 Selecting the background. It can be very hard to seamlessly remove elements like power lines from a background texture like the sky, which can extend over a large area with subtle color

2

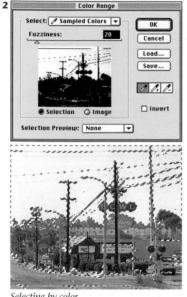

Selecting by color

3a

Selection turned into a Quick Mask

3b

Adding to the Quick Mask

3c

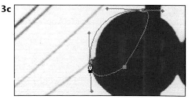

Repairing the mask

changes. Sometimes it's easier to select the background, turn the selection into a mask, edit the mask to remove the extraneous elements, and then replace the entire background with a new one. For instance, instead of trying to remove the power lines by using the rubber stamp to paint sky over them, we decided to select the sky by color, add the power lines to the sky selection, and replace the entire selected area.

To select the sky by tone, we chose Select, Color Range. We wanted to make a selection that included all the grays in the sky. With Selection chosen for the display in the Color Range dialog box and starting with a Fuzziness of 20, we began by clicking with the Color Range eyedropper tool on a light part of the sky. To extend the range of selected tones, we held down the Shift key and clicked on what seemed to be the darkest part of the sky. We continued to Shift-click, widening the range of selected tones, until the entire sky showed up as white in the preview box. Our selection included some light spots among the buildings, and it had missed the poles and wires. But now that the selection by Color Range had done most of the work, we could correct these omissions in the mask.

CHOOSING THE RIGHT FUZZINESS SETTING

When you select by Color Range it's a good idea to set the Fuzziness no lower than 16, to provide antialiasing. With a lower Fuzziness setting you get a very hard-edged selection and risk abrupt color breaks at the edges of the selected area. As the Fuzziness setting gets higher, though, you tend to get a feathered effect, making the selected area partly transparent. To select an area by color with a smooth, antialiased (but not feathered) edge, Shift-click with the Color Range eyedropper to expand the selection until it includes the area you want, and try to keep the Fuzziness setting between 16 and about 32 or higher.

3 Using Quick Mask. When the selection is as complete as you can get it with the eyedropper and Fuzziness slider, click OK and then click on the Quick Mask icon in the toolbox. Then use the selection tools, eraser, and paintbrush to edit the mask.

The goal was to create a mask to protect everything but the sky and power lines. With black and white set as the Foreground and Background colors, respectively, we started by selecting a large rectangular area at the bottom of the mask, pressing Alt-Backspace to fill it with mask material, and deselecting (Ctrl-D). To repair the few remaining white spots that were outside the sky, we painted with a paintbrush. We used the eraser to remove parts of the mask that covered the power lines.

Still in Quick Mask mode, we clicked and drew with the pen tool (press "P" to select the pen) to surround geometric areas that had been only partially included in the selection by color, such as parts of the "BOWL" sign. Opening the Paths palette (Window, Show Paths), we converted each path to mask material as soon as we built it by clicking the Fill Path icon (at the bottom left of the Paths palette) to make it part of the protective mask.

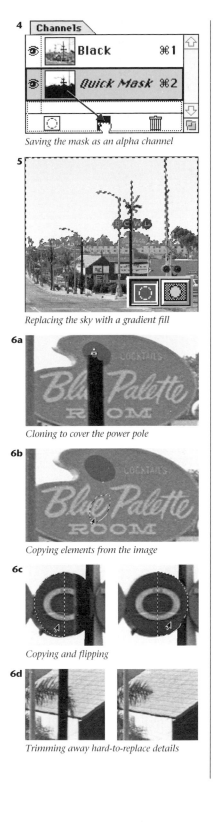

4

Saving the mask as an alpha channel

5

Replacing the sky with a gradient fill

6a

Cloning to cover the power pole

6b

Copying elements from the image

6c

Copying and flipping

6d

Trimming away hard-to-replace details

4 Saving the selection. Since your mask will probably be a complex one, store it in an alpha channel for safekeeping: Open the Channels palette (Window, Show Channels) and drag the Quick Mask channel icon to the New Channel button at the bottom of the palette.

5 Replacing the background. Next make the Quick Mask selection active by clicking the Standard Selection icon (next to the Quick Mask icon in the toolbox). You can now replace the background. We used a gradient fill between two shades of gray from the existing sky: With the main Black channel active (clicked in the Channels palette) and the sky selection loaded (in the Channels palette, Ctrl-click its thumbnail), we started by clicking the eyedropper tool on the top of the sky to set the Foreground color; then we held down the Alt key and clicked near the skyline to set the Background color. Next we double-clicked the gradient tool in the tool palette to open the Gradient Tool Options dialog box and set the tool to Normal, Foreground To Background, and Linear, with the Dither checkbox turned on. We dragged the tool from the top of the sky selection to the bottom. To simulate the grain of the original photo, we added Noise (Filter, Noise, Add Noise) at a very low Gaussian setting.

6 Completing retouching tasks. Use the rubber stamp, lasso, and other tools and functions to retouch smaller areas of the image. We used the rubber stamp in Clone (Non-aligned) mode to grab (Alt-click) textures to paint over the power pole. We also lassoed and copied (Ctrl-Alt-dragged) parts that could be reused, such as the "e" in the "Blue Palette" sign.

For the "O" in "BOWL," we flipped a selection to mirror the intact half of the letter (press Ctrl-T for Free Transform, then right-click to bring up a context-sensitive menu and choose Flip Horizontal.

Knowing what elements *not* to restore completely can save you a lot of time. For example, rather than trying to paint the missing part of a palm frond, we shortened the frond by rubber-stamping the roof texture over it.

Printing the picture. So that city officials could compare "before" and "after," the original and retouched scans were output to negative film at a halftone screen of 200 lines per inch, and contact prints were made.

Solarizing an Image

Overview *Prepare the image; add Adjustment layers, trying dramatic Curves settings.*

The *"Solarizing"* Actions on the Wow! CD-ROM automate the solarizing process, giving you several Curves settings to mix and match.

JHD

Original image

PHOTO: PHOTODISC, EVERYDAY PEOPLE

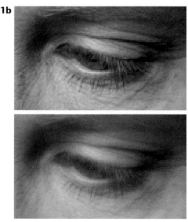

Blurring a duplicate of the image (bottom) softened the fine lines in the face.

2a

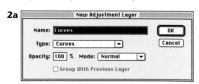

Adding a Curves Adjustment layer

SOLARIZATION, FIRST OBSERVED BY SABBATIER in 1860 and later discovered accidentally by Lee Miller and Man Ray in 1929, is the partial reversal of negative to positive, caused by a brief exposure to light during development, often with dramatic effect. Today's photographic materials are much faster, which makes it difficult to solarize a photo in the darkroom. But you can get similar effects by manipulating Photoshop's Curves.

1 Preparing the scan. Both color and black-and-white (grayscale) images can be solarized. Open a scanned photo; if necessary, eliminate fine detail that might be undesirably exaggerated by the solarization process. The portrait shown here was duplicated (choose Window, Show Layers to open the Layers palette and drag the Background layer to the New Layer icon in the center at the bottom of the palette), and the copy was blurred slightly. We used Filter, Blur, Gaussian Blur with a Radius of 2 pixels for this 675-pixel-wide image to soften the image more than we needed and then reduced the Opacity of the blurred layer to about 50% for a more subtle effect.

2 Making Curves Adjustment layers. To experiment with solarization without permanently changing your image, add an Adjustment layer: With the top layer active Ctrl-click the New Layer icon in the middle at the bottom of the palette. In the New Adjustment Layer dialog box, choose Curves for the Type. When the Curves dialog box opens, select the pencil icon. Experiment by Shift-clicking with the pencil at the end points of the straight line segments you want to draw. At this point you can tell whether your combi-

2b

Before adjusting Curves

2c

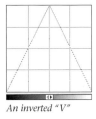

Drawing this "V" produces the same effect as the Solarize filter.

2d

An inverted "V"

2e

Leaving midtones intact and pushing the lightest highlights to white

2f

Using a four-point curve

2g

The image at the top of page 124 was made by stacking two Curves layers (2e and 2f above) with a small masking stroke of black over the nose in the 2e layer.

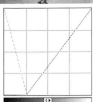

Solarizing a grayscale version of the file

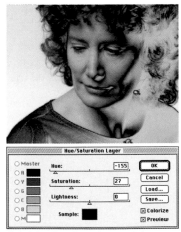

Colorizing the solarized grayscale image with a Hue/Saturation Adjustment layer.

nation of blurred and original image works well for solarizing. If not, you can adjust the Opacity of the blurred layer or delete it by dragging its name to the trash can icon at the bottom of the Layers palette and start over by making a new duplicate layer for blurring at a different setting. When you have the result you like, merge the two layers (activate the top layer and press Ctrl-E to Merge Down).

Try new Curves settings by duplicating the Adjustment layer and then double-clicking the black-and-white circle icon on the duplicate layer and resetting the curve. View alternate settings by clicking the eye icons to turn your various Curves layers on and off. Try mixing and matching the Curves layers with different blending modes and Opacity settings. You can also apply black paint to a Curves layer to mask out the solarizing effect in particular areas. When we had the effect we wanted, we flattened the file (choose Flatten Image from the Layers palette's pop-out menu) and applied Filter, Blur, Smart Blur to tone down pixel artifacts in the color without interfering with edge detail.

Trying other approaches. Convert a copy of your image to grayscale (Image, Mode, Grayscale) and apply solarizing curves. To colorize, add an Adjustment layer for Hue/Saturation, click the Colorize check box, and adjust Hue and Saturation.

Customizing Spot Color

Overview *Copy a grayscale image to two of the color channels of a new CMYK file; display the color channels in color and change the Printing Inks Setup to show custom ink colors; customize the two color channels; make film for printing plates by outputting only the two color channels you used in the CMYK file.*

Original image, converted to grayscale

Opposites on the standard artist's color wheel form a dark brown when mixed.

For the Duotone; we chose custom colors Pantone 032 CV (red) and 368 CV (green).

Noting the RGB composition of one of the custom colors

HERE'S AN APPROACH TO TRY when you've got expensive ideas but a two-color budget. Most color printing is done with four color plates — cyan, magenta, yellow, and black. But you can also get a broad range of colors — with brights, neutrals, highlights, and shadows — and direct these colors exactly where you want them, using only two complementary colors of ink. (Read this section all the way through before beginning on a custom two-color project, because some of the printing and proofing considerations discussed in the later steps may affect your choice of ink colors.)

1 Setting up the file. Open a grayscale image, or convert a color (RGB) image to grayscale (see "Color to Gray" on page 99 for tips on converting).

2 Testing Duotone mode. Preparing a Photoshop image for printing in two colors almost automatically suggests the Duotone mode, which can either add an obvious color accent to a photo or subtly but effectively extend the range of tones the printing press can produce. Just in case a standard Duotone might produce the results you want, you can start out by choosing Image, Mode, Duotone. In the Duotone Options dialog box, select Duotone from the pop-out Type menu, click the Load button, and select one of the Duotone curve sets supplied in the Duotone Presets folder inside the Goodies folder. (You can find printed samples of a few of the preset Duotones in Chapter 14 of the *User Guide* that comes with Photoshop.) Or make your own set of curves: Click the color squares for Ink 1 and Ink 2 in turn and choose a color from the color sets offered when you click the Custom button in the Color Picker dialog box. If you want to get as full a range of colors as possible, choose complements (colors opposite each other on the classic color wheel), and make sure the colors you choose are vivid rather than pastel tones or tints. As you choose each color, click the Picker button and write down the RGB composition — you'll need these values in step 4 if you don't get the effect you want in this step.

2d

Experimenting in Duotone mode

3a

Setting up to show color channels in color

3b

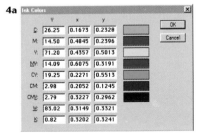

With color channels displayed in color, a copy of the grayscale image was pasted into the Cyan and Magenta channels of a new CMYK file.

4a

The default Ink Colors

Once the colors are chosen, if you click the curve box next to each color square in the Duotone Options dialog box, you can change the curves to modify the color treatment.

You'll find that the Duotone mode has limitations. First of all, you're working blind — you can't see how the image is shaping up until you close the Duotone Options dialog box. And second, no matter how you fiddle with the curves, it's virtually impossible to direct the colors to specific places in the image, independently of the overall curve settings for highlights, midtones, and shadows.

3 Making a two-color file. Sometimes the only way to put the color exactly where you want it in your two-color image is by "hand-painting" with your two colors. But how can you pinpoint where the two colors go, view the results interactively on-screen, and still be able to separate the file into two spot colors so you can make the plates for printing the two custom inks?

The first step is to copy your grayscale image to two channels of a CMYK file: In your grayscale file, select all (Ctrl-A) and copy (Ctrl-C). Then choose File, New; in the New File dialog box change the Mode to CMYK Color; and accept the size and resolution settings, since they will exactly fit the image you've copied to the clipboard. Click OK.

In the new image file, open the Channels palette, click on the name of the color channel most similar to one of your two ink colors; we chose Cyan as the closest to our green ink. With only that channel activated (black in the Channels palette), paste your image into it (Ctrl-V). Repeat this activating-and-pasting process to put your image into the channel that most closely matches your second color; we chose Magenta for our red. Press Ctrl-D to drop the floating selection. You should now have a single-layer (*Background*) file with your image in two of the color channels and nothing in the other two.

4 Setting up your two colors. So that you'll be able to see the interaction of your two custom colors, first choose File, Preferences, Display & Cursors, Color Channels In Color. Then choose File, Color Settings, Printing Inks Setup. This next step will make drastic changes to the Printing Inks Setup, so if you've already customized the settings in this dialog box, click the Save button now, before you begin, to save your settings so you'll be able to load them again to return to your normal setup after you've finished your two-color work.

Now switch the default channel colors to the custom colors you chose in step 2, as follows: In the Printing Inks Setup dialog box choose Custom from the pop-out list of ink setups. Then in the Ink Colors dialog box click on the color swatch that most closely matches one of your ink colors (we clicked C for our green). When the Color Picker opens, enter the R, G, and B values that you noted for that custom color. Repeat the process for the second color swatch (we used M for our red), using the values you noted for your second color.

4b

Entering the RGB value for Pantone 032 CV red (from step 2) as the Ink Color for the Magenta channel

4c

To approximate the color for both inks printed at full strength (for the CM swatch in the Ink Colors dialog box), color-filled shapes were stacked in layers, with the top layer in Multiply mode

4d

	Y	x	y	
C:	55.48	0.3291	0.5701	
M:	18.80	0.5869	0.3252	
Y:	71.20	0.4357	0.5013	
MY:	14.09	0.6075	0.3191	
CY:	19.25	0.2271	0.5513	
CM:	6.04	0.4991	0.3177	
CMY:	2.79	0.3227	0.2962	
W:	83.02	0.3149	0.3321	
K:	0.82	0.3202	0.3241	

Clicking on the CM swatch and then clicking on the stacked colors (see 4c, above) assigned the dark brown to represent the mixture of the two colors.

5a

After pasting the grayscale image into the Cyan and Magenta channels and changing the Printing Inks setup, the on-screen image looked like this.

ADDING BLACK

Black ink adds a crispness to dark colors that you can't get by simply mixing two complements. It also gives you more freedom in choosing the other two colors — you don't have to use vivid colors if you can darken with black. But before you add black to a budget-limited two-color project, check to see how much it will increase your printing costs. Three-color custom printing may be as expensive as four-color process.

Finally, you'll need to set a color for the appropriate two-color combination swatch. To do this you'll need a sample of how your two colors will look when printed over each other at full strength. Request a printed sample from your printer, or use a book of samples published by the ink manufacturer, or "cheat" as we did, although there's no guarantee this will exactly match the printed color: Click OK to close the Printing Inks Setup temporarily. In a new file make overlapping swatches of your two colors, each in its own layer, choosing Multiply from the pop-out blending mode list in the Layers palette for the top layer. Reopen the Printing Inks Setup (File, Color Settings, Printing Inks Setup, Custom) and click the appropriate two-color swatch in the Ink Colors dialog box (we clicked CM); then click on your overlapped colors in the file you just made to pick up a Foreground color. Or if you're using a printed sample, click in the Color Picker on a color that matches. Now close the Printing Inks Setup.

5 Working in color. To see the color develop in your two-color image, you can work on an individual color channel (click its name in the Channels palette to activate it) while viewing both channels (click to turn on the eye icons for both channels). Here are some of the kinds of changes you can make, working on one channel at a time:

- Adjust Curves as you would for a duotone (press Ctrl-M to open the Curves dialog box), but now, unlike in Duotone mode, you can watch the combined color change as you adjust each curve.

- Make a selection and adjust Curves in one or both channels.

- Apply white paint in Screen mode (or black paint in Multiply mode) with a soft airbrush at a low Pressure setting to reduce (or intensify) color in the channel you're working on (with the airbrush selected, press the Enter key to open the Airbrush Options palette to set the Pressure). You can also use feathered or unfeathered selections to restrict the paint.

- Set type with the type selection tool and fill or stroke the selection (Edit, Fill or Edit, Stroke) with black, white, or gray in one or both channels (click both channel names to make both active at once).

- Add an alpha channel (click the New Channel icon next to the trash can at the bottom of the Channels palette), and paste type or graphics via the clipboard. Then load the channel as a selection and fill with black, white, or gray in one or both channels.

We created alpha channels by selecting with the pen tool and saving the selections (see "Selecting with Curves: The Pen Tool" on page 55) so we could modify color. For instance, we clicked the Magenta channel's name in the Channels palette to activate it, loaded the selection stored in channel #4 (Ctrl-Alt-4), opened the Levels dialog box (Ctrl-L), and moved the gamma (gray triangle) to the right on the Input Levels slider to intensify the red tones. In the Cyan channel we also used Levels, this time moving the Output Levels black point slider inward to "wash out" the green.

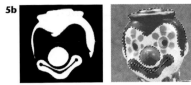

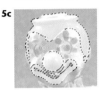

5b

Channel #5 (left) was used for selecting the face in the M channel; a Levels adjustment boosted the red in the selected areas.

5c

The same channel was used in the C channel as shown here, so a Levels adjustment could lighten the green.

5d

Adjusted M and C channels viewed together after whitening the face and darkening the background

5e

Channels

Red Head	Ctrl+4
Face	Ctrl+5
Eyes	Ctrl+6
Box Red	Ctrl+7
Box Green	Ctrl+8
Jack Outline	Ctrl+9

Some of the alpha channels used for coloring the image

5f

White-filled type (top); with highlight and shadow, and airbrushing added in the two channels (bottom)

5g

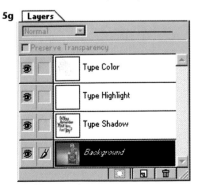

Final Layers palette

We made and loaded an alpha channel to select the background area and darkened the top of the background by applying levels through a gradient Quick Mask made by pressing "Q" to switch to Quick Mask mode, making a Foreground To Background (black-to-white) gradient from bottom to top, pressing "Q" again to turn the Quick Mask into an active selection, and applying Levels.

We imported white type (set in Adobe Illustrator) by choosing File, Place; the imported type became a layer of its own. To start a highlight and a shadow for the type, the type layer was duplicated twice (by dragging its name to the new layer icon at the bottom of the palette). The shadow layer was filled with black (press "D" for the Default colors and then Shift-Alt-Backspace to fill only the pixels, not the transparent areas) and blurred (Filter, Blur, Gaussian Blur) to soften the shadow. Shadow and highlight layers were offset in opposite directions by activating each layer in turn, holding down the Ctrl key to get the move tool, and pressing arrow keys to move the layer. We applied black paint at the tops of the letters in the Cyan channel only and at the bottoms of the letters in the Magenta channel, using a soft airbrush and a low Pressure setting.

Printing a comp. Very few desktop or other digital printers are set up to print with custom inks. So if you want to make a color composite print — to show a client as a comp, for example — you'll need to make a special copy of your file: Choose Image, Duplicate and then Image, Mode, RGB Color. Then print this copy. Remember that digital prints always look somewhat different than pages from a printing press. And because custom inks will be used on press, your digital print may be even more different than usual.

Making the printing plates. For imagesetting, use your original two-color CMYK file (not the RGB file you made for composite printing). Tell the imagesetting service to output only the two plates you used, at the halftone screen angles your printer recommends for your two ink colors. When you give the film to the printer, identify which plate to use to print each of the custom colors. You may be able to have photomechanical transfers (PMTs) made from the film so you can see in advance what the printed image will look like. Your imagesetting service can tell you which custom ink colors are available for PMTs.

Returning to normal. When you've finished with your two-color job, save your custom Printing Inks Setup so you can use it again later: Choose File, Color Settings, Printing Inks Setup and press the Save button. Then restore your normal ink setup: Choose the default SWOP (Coated) or some other setup from the Ink Colors list, or click Load to retrieve a custom setting.

Authors' note: We got the idea of using the Printing Inks Setup for controlling the color display in the CMYK channels from designer/printmaker Rob Day, author of Designer Photoshop (Random House).

Even with a strobe, **Eric Hanauer's** photo of the *Cormoran,* a World War I German merchant ship scuttled in Guam's Apra Harbor over 75 years ago, lacked contrast and impact (above). But Photoshop's Auto Levels brought out colors that hadn't been detectable in the murky water and brought to life a flat image. Hanauer also used Curves, working in the Green channel to reduce the cast in the water. ▶*Photoshop 4's Adjustment layers, added by Ctrl-clicking the New Layer icon at the bottom of the Layers palette, make it possible to experiment with several changes to Levels and Curves, without permanently modifying the pixels of the image until you have exactly the result you want.*

Hanauer used the Unsharp Mask filter to sharpen the image. He sometimes runs the Despeckle filter on the Green or Blue channel of an underwater photo before sharpening, to reduce the film grain so it won't be exaggerated by the sharpening process. But in this case the image detail he wanted to sharpen would have been blurred along with the grain of the high-speed film, and the graininess didn't really detract from the image, so he didn't use Despeckle.

This *Clown Triggerfish,* photographed in Borneo by **Eric Hanauer,** seemed lost against a bright, sharp background (lower left). In addition, there was too much backscatter — lit, out-of-focus particles in the water column that look like snow, a common problem in underwater photography (lower right). Hanauer sometimes uses the Dust & Scratches filter to remove backscatter from uniform blue-water backgrounds, but in this case the color variation in the ocean floor made it necessary to clone out the backscatter using the rubber stamp. He then selected the fish, starting the selection with the magic wand, switching to Quick Mask mode, and painting with black and white to complete the mask. Switching back to normal mode, Hanauer used the selection to cut the fish to a new layer. ▶*Ctrl-Shift-J cuts to a new layer.*

He adjusted Input Levels (Image, Adjust, Levels) to brighten exposure of the fish layer and used Output Levels to darken and reduce contrast in the background layer. Finally, he used Filter, Blur, Gaussian Blur to soften the background so the fish would stand out.

Jeff Burke and Lorraine Triolo of **Burke/ Triolo Productions** combined traditional food styling and camera tricks with Photoshop techniques to put together this promotional image for their stock picture agency, *FoodPix.* After they worked up a layout sketch, stylist Triolo mounted the tray on a large studio stand in front of the camera and assembled its contents: The orange juice was actually juice and gelatin solidified into the "almost spilling" position; the "steam" was produced with Calcium Turnings from the local science store mixed with water; pancakes were skewered into position with thin wooden sticks; and studio manager Cheryl Anderson donned rented waiter's garb and positioned her hand as

if she were holding the tray up, just as the 4 x 5-inch transparency was shot.

The background image was chosen from a dozen rolls of film shot by Burke at the *S.S. Queen Mary* in Long Beach, California. All of the "selects" from that shoot were transferred to PhotoCD, which provided an inexpensive way to try out a few rough composites before committing to drum scanning the final selected image. The shot that was chosen was taken with a 20mm lens, a slow shutter speed, and a panning motion to simulate movement.

Burke began compositing in Photoshop by cleaning up the tray shot, retouching out the grip stand and smoothing out the paper reflections in the bottom of the tray with the airbrush tool. He made the

background vignette with a feathered oval selection. ▶ *To make a soft vignette, select the area you want to keep; choose Select, Feather to create the soft edge; invert the selection (Ctrl-Shift-I); and, with white as the Background color, press Backspace.*

Burke made a mask to silhouette the tray and copied and pasted the tray into the background file, where it became a new layer. Using black paint on a layer mask, he made the steam translucent. To finish blending the photos into a convincing image, Burke used Photoshop's airbrush with nearly pure white paint and a pressure-sensitive drawing tablet, very gently spraying a glowing white "light bleed" around the edge of the tray where there was strong light in the background.

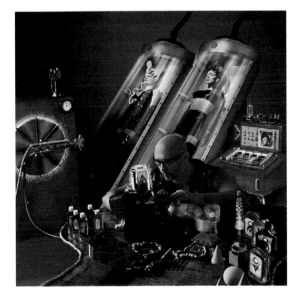

Richard Ransier produced this image for the International Hair Show to illustrate the theme *"What's New in the Year 2000?"* Aiming for a sci-fi look, Ransier and others designed and built an elaborate set, designed hairdos to match, and photographed live models in place.

In Photoshop Ransier added highlights and reflections to the glass enclosures by selecting feathered triangles with the polygon lasso and airbrushing within those triangles on a separate layer with white paint to give the glass a more convincing appearance. With his triangles of white on several layers, he could adjust the opacity of individual layers until he got just the effect he wanted.

Ransier used the burn and sponge tools to increase color in the bottles on the table. He also made a mask for the table and the man so he could isolate this foreground area, soften it with a mild blur, and adjust its color balance to orange to shift the viewer's attention to the coiffed women in the background. The image in the computer monitor was made by selecting, copying, and scaling the face of one of the women in the enclosures.

MONTAGE AND COLLAGE

If you want to mask a copied and pasted element inside or behind part of an existing image, you can select that part of the image and then choose Paste Into from the Edit menu. The pasted element will come in as a new layer, complete with a layer mask that lets it show only within the area you selected.

If you hold down the Alt key as you choose Paste Into, the effect will be to Paste Behind instead. Keyboard shortcuts are Ctrl-Shift-V for Paste Into and Ctrl-Shift-Alt-V for Paste Behind.

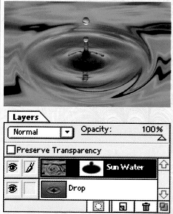

Typically, when you add a layer mask, the image and mask are linked, so moving the image moves the mask too. But when you use Paste Into or Paste Behind (above), the mask and image are unlinked by default. That way you can move the image around and still keep it "inside" or "behind" the area that was selected when it was pasted.

IN TRADITIONAL PHOTOGRAPHY and photo-illustration, *montage* is a method of making a single photographic print by superimposing several negatives. *Collage* is the assembly of separate photos mounted together, sometimes with other nonphotographic elements, to form another picture. With Photoshop, since photos, illustrations, and original painting can be combined in a single image, and since the "print" is likely to be output as part of a complete page layout, the distinction between montage and collage breaks down. But whatever you call it, the process becomes much easier, with no need for darkroom or glue.

Some of Photoshop's most useful compositing techniques involve feathered selections, gradient selections applied in layer masks, blending modes, alpha channels, the rubber stamp tool, Paste Into (and Paste Behind) from the Edit menu, Apply Image, and the composite controls provided in the Layer Options dialog box, available through the pop-out menu in the Layers palette. In addition to reading about the montage/collage projects described in this chapter, check Chapter 2 for more about the selecting, layering, and masking techniques that are so important for combining images.

CHOOSING AND PREPARING COMPONENTS

One essential element of making a successful "seamless" photo montage, when that's your goal, is choosing the right kind of selection and compositing techniques — like using a feathered lasso or marquee to create a soft, blending edge for the selection, or getting rid of background pixels at the edge of an image to get a clean silhouette, or using Gaussian Blur on the Background layer to create a realistic depth of field. But another requirement for a seamless blend is making sure that the component images match in several respects. For example, the light should be coming from the same direction, the color and amount of detail in the shadows and highlights should be the same, and the "graininess" of the images should match.

Highlight and shadow detail can be manipulated by using Image, Adjust, Curves and Image, Adjust, Levels. A color cast can be identified with the RGB or CMYK readings in the Info window (you can choose Window, Show Info to open it, or use the F8 default keyboard shortcut); then the color cast can be adjusted — with Image, Adjust, Curves or Levels or Color Balance, for instance.

continued on page 134

The hand, silhouetted on a transparent layer above the sky Background, before masking

("Correcting a Batch of Scans" on page 47 includes tips for detecting and correcting a color cast.) And the Add Noise filter can be used to simulate film grain.

Changing the direction of the light, on the other hand, can be much more difficult than managing shadow detail or color cast. If the elements you want to blend are fairly flat (like pictures on a wall), the Lighting Effects filter may be helpful. For example, if the final effect you're looking for will tolerate it, you may be able to "overpower" the varied "native" lighting of the elements of a composite image by applying the same lighting effect to all the parts; you can see an example of this in "Combining with Light" on page 160 in Chapter 5. You can also use the dodge and burn tools to create highlights and shadows for flat subjects. But if Lighting Effects or dodging and burning won't work, you'll generally get better results if you continue your search for photos whose lighting matches, rather than trying to make further adjustments to correct the lighting.

MAKING SEAMLESS TRANSITIONS

Photoshop's Layers palette makes it easy to combine images:

- Elements on different layers can be moved around as separate objects with the **move tool** until you're happy with the arrangement. Photoshop 4's **"Big Data"** feature even preserves the parts that extend outside the margins of the canvas. So if you change your mind, the entire element will still exist and you can move it back into the image frame.

- The **blending mode** for each layer can be set to control how that layer is composited with the image beneath — by color, saturation, or brightness values, independently or in combination.

- The **Opacity** of a layer can be adjusted to give an entire element an "only partly there" or "ghosted" look.

- To make an element fade into the rest of the image gradually, you can create a

Using a gradient layer mask

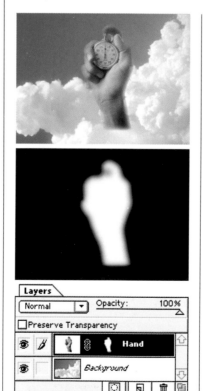

Using a mask with a blurred edge

Adding a gradient to a blurred-edge layer mask

Hand-painting a mask to "ghost" the hand

gradient layer mask, as follows: With the layer active, click the mask icon at the bottom of the Layers palette. The new layer mask will be active. Use the gradient fill tool to make a black-to-white transition, using white where you want the image on that layer to show through at full strength and black where you want it to be completely absent from the composite.

- You can make a **custom-fitted blurred mask** for the object you want to composite: With the object's layer active Ctrl-click its name in the Layers palette to load its transparency mask as a selection. Then click the Add Layer Mask icon at the bottom of the Layers palette. This will add a layer mask with the selected area clear and the surrounding area opaque, so the mask just fits the object. Drop the selection (Ctrl-D) and blur the edges: Choose Filter, Blur, Gaussian Blur, and view the composite image as you experiment with settings for blurring the mask until you get the amount of edge softness you want.

- A **gradient** can also be **combined with another kind of mask** — for instance, a mask that blurs the object at its edges. Make the edge mask first and then add a black-to-white gradient to the mask by opening the Gradient Tool Options palette and setting the blending mode for the gradient to Multiply, and then dragging the tool to make the gradient.

- With a **hand-painted layer mask** you can control exactly which parts of the active layer are composited with the image below and which parts are "ghosted" out of the picture. If you use black paint and the airbrush with Pressure set low in the Airbrush Options palette, you can paint and repaint, viewing only the image as you paint on the mask, until you get exactly the degree of ghosting you want.

- With the sliders in the **Layer Options** dialog box, you can control how the pixels of the active layer (called "This Layer" in the dialog box) and the image underneath (called "Underlying") will combine in the composite. The sliders of the **Underlying** bar define the range of colors in the underlying image that are made available to be affected by the active layer. So if you wanted to protect light or dark pixels, you would move the Underlying sliders inward to eliminate these tones from the available range.

The sliders of the **This Layer** bar determine what range of colors in the active layer will be allowed to contribute pixels to the composite image by *replacing* the corresponding underlying pixels if the active layer is in Normal mode, or by blending with them if the active layer is in a different blending mode. So if you want to use only the dark pixels, move the This Layer white slider inward to exclude light pixels from the range of contributing colors.

Together, the two sliders set up a sort of "If . . . then" proposition for each pixel in the underlying image: "If the pixel falls within

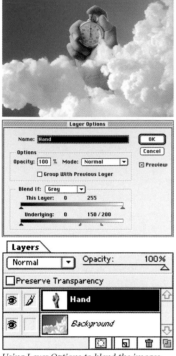

the range established in the Underlying slider bar *and* the corresponding active-layer pixel falls within the range established in the This Layer slider bar, then replace (or blend) the underlying pixel with the active one; otherwise, leave the underlying pixel as it is, ignoring the active one." Holding down the Alt key allows you to split each slider for a softer transition.

- To blend images, you can rubber-stamp from one part of the composite into another, or make feathered selections and paste. *Wow!*

Using Layer Options to blend the images

QUICK & EASY EXPERIMENTS

The Layer Options dialog box can help you arrive at a layout for elements you want to composite. Although you'll often have to go back and do a more sophisticated masking job later, the Layer Options sliders can help eliminate backgrounds so you can quickly see how the parts will go together.

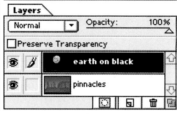

For this comp used to plan a montage, the Blue channel was chosen in the Blend If section of the Layer Options dialog box. The This Layer slider was set to mask out the black background of the earth-from-space image, and the Underlying slider was used to limit composition to the blue sky, protecting the reddish-brown pinnacles from compositing.

USING A SKETCHPAD FILE

When you're making a montage, an efficient way to "borrow" textures from a large image so you can apply them to another image with the rubber stamp tool or by some other means, is to collect the material you need in a third, smaller "sketchpad" file. Start a file for your sketchpad. In the large file, select the parts you need, and then drag and drop them into the sketchpad file. Then you can close the large image and work from the smaller one. Using the smaller sketchpad file doesn't require as much RAM, and you can modify the collected textures (rotating, flipping or scaling them with the Layer, Free Transform command, for example) without changing the original image.

To integrate the vodka bottle into the waterfall image, Jack Cliggett made a sketchpad file, much smaller than the original waterfall image, of textures he wanted to apply to the bottle. Then he used the rubber stamp tool in Clone, Aligned mode to copy image material from the sketchpad onto the bottle. When the bottle was complete, he copied and pasted it into the original waterfall image.

Making Montages

Overview *Open a background image file; add collage elements by selecting, dragging, dropping, and creating layer masks.*

1

Background image after applying Variations and inverting the color of the right half

2a

Original Couple image

2b

Layer mask for Couple: feathered selections filled and adjusted with Levels

2c

Masked Couple image over background

THERE ARE PROBABLY ALMOST AS MANY WAYS to merge photos as there are Photoshop artists. The montage shown here was put together using several different methods of blending images. It began with a number of black-and-white photos that were composited in RGB mode so both warm and cool grays could be used. The elements were layered, mostly in Normal mode and at full Opacity.

Second only to choosing the right composition to communicate your idea, the most important factor in making a successful photo montage is what happens at the edges where the parts blend. A smooth but dynamic merging of images can make the difference between a unified, effective collage and an awkward "cut and pasted" look.

1 Making a background. Open the image you want to use as a background. This collage began with two group photos — one of women and one of men. Most of this side-by-side image composite would be hidden, but it would act as a "texture" that conveyed the idea of human relationships. We reduced the contrast with Image, Adjust, Levels, moving the black point slider of the Output Levels to the right. The color change — a shift toward the cool (blue-violet) end of the spectrum — was accomplished with adjustments to the midtones via Image, Adjust, Variations, as were all the other changes used in making this collage. The right half of the composite image was selected with the rectangular marquee in its default (Normal) Style and turned into a negative (Ctrl-I) for contrast with the other images in the collage.

2 Using a feathered, freeform layer mask. The first blending method we used involves making a layer mask that will hide part of an overlaid image. Open the second image of the collage and use the move tool to drag and drop it into the background image.

Add a layer mask by clicking the Add Layer Mask icon, on the left at the bottom of the Layers palette. The mask will be active (indicated by the mask icon in the column to the left of the layer's

3a

Diver masked with airbrushed layer mask

3b

Layers palette after adding the couple, the divers, and the people running on the beach

4a

Selection made with the elliptical marquee with a Feather

4b

Selection dragged into the montage file

5a

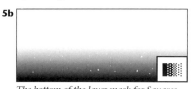

Square images added

5b

The bottom of the layer mask for Squares

5c

The Squares layer, masked into the montage

thumbnail in the Layers palette) but you'll be looking at the image itself. Use a feathered lasso to surround the parts of the image you want to mask out. We used a feather of 75 pixels for this 1100-pixel-wide image to get a very soft blending edge. Hold down the Shift key to add new lassoed areas to the selection. To completely mask out certain areas, make sure the Foreground color is set to black and press Alt-Backspace. Once the mask is made you can reselect and lighten some areas to let the image show partially. We selected the area to the left of the couple, again with a feathered lasso, chose Image, Adjust, Levels (or press Ctrl-L), and moved the black Output slider to lighten this area of the mask to dark gray.

3 Softening the edge of the mask. We used a method similar to step 2 to import and mask the two diving board images and the couple running on the beach. But to further soften the edges of each layer mask, we used a fairly large, soft airbrush with white paint to paint the edge of the mask so these images would fade into the background image more gradually.

4 Making a traditional vignette. Framing an image by selecting it with a rectangular or round shape is another collage technique. To create a "world of their own" effect for the boy and girl running on the beach, a feathered elliptical marquee was used to select them, along with part of their background. (To select the elliptical marquee, you can double-click the marquee in the toolbox to open the Marquee Tool Options palette and choose a Shape. Set the Feather in this palette also.) With the move tool, the selection was dragged and dropped into the collage file, where it became a new layer.

5 Using a graduated mask. Another way to blend collaged images is to build a gradient layer mask, going from black to white in a vertical, horizontal, or diagonal direction. This was the method used to add the square images at the bottom of our collage and also to add the type. To make the square selections, the Shift key was held down while dragging with the rectangular marquee. The selection was dragged and dropped into the collage file with the move tool. Then each of the other squares was selected, dragged into the file, and merged with the Squares layer below it (Ctrl-E).

To make a black-to-white gradient, add a layer mask (click the Add Layer Mask icon), double-click the gradient tool in the tool palette to open its Options palette, and choose Foreground To Background for the Style. With the layer mask active, drag the gradient tool from where you want the image in that layer to be completely masked to

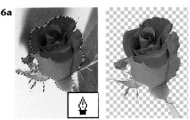
5d
Layers palette after Squares and Type layers have been added

6a
Rose selected from its background (left) and imported into its own layer and desaturated

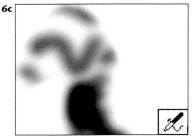
6b
Rose in place; all layers visible

6c
Close-up of hand-painted mask for Rose layer

6d
Rose "ghosted" through its layer mask

where you want it to show fully. Remember — images show through the white parts of the layer mask and are blocked by the black parts. We used a gradient mask for the Squares layer and also for the Type layer; we adjusted Output Levels (Ctrl-L) on the Type layer mask so the lightest part of the mask was gray instead of white and all the type would be partially transparent. The mode for the layer was set to Multiply so the type would darken the image underneath, rather than cover it up.

6 Silhouetting with the pen tool. Choose the pen tool (press the "P" key). Clicking to place points and dragging curve-shaping handles, outline an element you want to add to the collage. Save the path: Open the Paths palette (Window, Show Paths) and double-click the Work Path name. Then convert the path to a selection (Ctrl-click the path name), and drag the selected area into the collage with the move tool. After selecting and dragging the rose into the collage, we used Image, Adjust, Desaturate to turn it gray, and then used Variations to warm up the gray.

7 Painting a "ghosting" mask. A hand-painted mask can make it look like a collage element is partly in front of another element and partly behind it. On the Rose layer we used the airbrush with black paint and various Pressure settings in the Airbrush Options palette to paint a mask to "ghost" the rose in front of and behind the type.

We used a similar technique to bring the couple's faces to the front: We copied the original Couple layer by dragging its name in the Layers palette to the New Layer icon at the bottom of the palette and then dragging the new "Couple copy" name up to the top of the palette. We used Image, Adjust, Variations to give this layer a warm brown tone, added a layer mask filled with black (Alt-click the Add Layer Mask icon), and airbrushed with white and black to add parts of

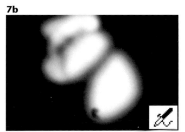
7a
Sepia-toned Couple copy layer

7b

the brown image to the collage. Opacity was adjusted to 90%, the image was flattened (choose Flatten Image from the palette's pop-out menu), and Levels was used to make final adjustments to the tonal range.

7c
Layers palette for the completed montage

Mask for the Couple copy layer

Blending with Layer Masks

Overview *Silhouette, color-correct, and enhance the individual components of the montage; bring each element into the compositing file, position it, and create a layer mask to composite it with a softened edge.*

DESIGN: HAROLD SWEET DESIGN / PHOTOS: DONAL PHILBY / ILLUSTRATION: JHD

1a

Monitor image silhouetted by removing the background

1b

Screen color adjusted with Color Balance and Levels

1c   *Highlights mask*

1d   *Highlights enhanced and glow added*

PHOTOSHOP'S LAYER MASKS provide an excellent way to fade the layered elements of a montage into one another. This cover illustration for the packaging of TurboTax and MacInTax software started with a comprehensive sketch from Harold Sweet Design. Four separate photographs were scanned on a drum scanner and saved in CMYK color. Starting with the back element (the monitor), each piece was color-corrected and enhanced in its own file to keep RAM requirements low and working speed high. Then the pieces were layered into the final composite. For all but the back element, layer masks were created, and the edges of the masks were softened to accomplish the transitions as the fingers typed, the keyboard faded into the monitor, and the finished tax form emerged. The blending of images could have been done by deleting feathered selections from the elements on the individual layers. But using layer masks instead left these elements intact so that when the client wanted a minor change in the position of some element, the change could be made easily.

1 Preparing the back element. It's a good idea to do as much of the color correction and enhancement of the separate pieces as you can before you begin to put them together, because once they're combined, the process of selecting parts and making changes becomes more complicated and also slower because of the ballooning file size.

We began with the photo of the monitor. Opening the Layers palette (Window, Show Layers), we double-clicked the *Background* label in the palette to open the Make Layer dialog box, and renamed the layer "Monitor." We used the pen tool (press "P" to choose the pen) to draw a path around the monitor, and opened the Paths palette (Window, Show Paths). The path was saved (double-click the Work Path label in the palette) and then converted to an antialiased, unfeathered selection (Ctrl-click the path name). Inverting the selection (Ctrl-Shift-I) and pressing the Backspace key removed the background.

2

Tax form/arm dragged and dropped

3a

Graduated layer mask created

3b

Monitor and tax form blended by means of the graduated layer mask

4a

Keyboard added, distorted, and scaled

4b

Layer mask with edge softened

4c

Keyboard blended into the montage by means of its layer mask

Another path — to isolate the monitor's screen — was drawn, saved, and turned into a selection. With this selection active, Color Balance and Levels adjustments were used to "colorize" the screen.

The still-selected screen interior was then copied (Ctrl-C) and saved in an alpha channel to make a grayscale mask that would select the highlights (open the Channels palette and click the New Channel icon at the bottom of the palette; then paste — Ctrl-V). In this highlights alpha channel (#4) Image, Adjust, Levels was chosen and the Input Levels sliders were adjusted to increase the contrast. This mask was then used to select the highlights on the screen (click the RGB channel's name in the Channels palette and then Ctrl-click the alpha channel's name) so they could be brightened by adjusting Levels. A glow was added at the edge of the screen (methods for creating glows are described in Chapters 8 and 9).

More space was added around the monitor with Image, Canvas Size. The result was a 1700-pixel-wide file.

2 Starting to build the montage. Now start isolating the other elements from their backgrounds and assembling them into the montage. The next element that was added was a hand holding a tax form. To get the stretched and skewed shape needed for the illustration, the rectangular form had been distorted using Corel-Draw's Envelope function and printed out on paper. The photographer then positioned this prop so that it was curving away from the hand, and the curve and distortion worked together to create the exaggerated perspective needed for the photo. The element (arm and tax form) was outlined with the path tool like the monitor in step 1. To blur the left edge of the form, the edge was selected by clicking with the polygon lasso with a 50-pixel feather, and a motion blur was applied (Filter, Blur, Motion Blur). Softly feathered selections were made and Image, Adjust, Levels was used to exaggerate the shadows and highlights on the form. The path was loaded as a selection (Ctrl-click the path name), and the selected object was dragged and dropped with the move tool to make a new layer in the monitor file (press "V" to choose the move tool).

3 Making a layer mask. To make a gradual transition from one element to another, you can create an "instant" layer mask and apply a gradient to it: Open the Layers palette (Window, Show Layers), and with the upper layer active (the tax form and arm in this case), Ctrl-click the thumbnail in the palette to load the transparency mask for the layer as a selection. With this selection active, click the Add Layer Mask icon on the left at the bottom of the palette to make a mask that exactly fits the layer's content; then deselect (Ctrl-D). The mask icon in the column to the left of the layer's thumbnail in the palette shows that the mask is active, even though the layer's content, rather than the mask itself, appears in the working window.

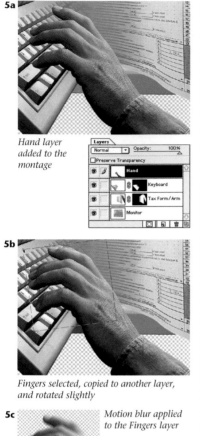

5a

Hand layer added to the montage

5b

Fingers selected, copied to another layer, and rotated slightly

5c

Motion blur applied to the Fingers layer

5d

Layer mask for the Hand layer (left) and Fingers layer in place over masked Hand (right)

5e

Final layers palette before flattening

Use the gradient tool in Multiply mode to make a gradient from black to white in the mask. The gradient mask makes the tax form seem as if it's emerging from the monitor. (You could get the same blending effect by making a layer mask that's a simple black-to-white gradient, without making a white shape from the transparency mask. But having the shape there helps you to see exactly how the mask is working.)

4 Making a layer mask with an irregular soft edge. Isolate and adjust the other components of the image, drag and drop each one into the composite file, and create a layer mask for it.

The keyboard photo was the next piece to be added. Again, the element was selected with a path, isolated, color-corrected, and dragged into the composite file as described for the arm and tax form in step 2. Because the keyboard had been photographed in a more "straight-on" view, it had to be rotated and scaled to match its position in the original comprehensive sketch. (Press Ctrl-T for Free Transform; then drag a handle inward or outward to scale, or move the cursor outside the handles and drag around to rotate. Double-click inside the selected area to accept and finalize the transformation.)

A layer mask was created as in step 3, except that this time the transition edge was made with a feathered lasso selection filled with black (Alt-Backspace) and then with the airbrush tool with a large soft tip and black paint applied at a low Pressure setting.

5 Creating the illusion of motion. To simulate the motion that can be caught on film with a strobe, you need more than a simple application of Photoshop's Motion Blur filter. The goal is to show both the starting and ending positions, with a blur in between.

The first step in making the fingers of the left hand appear to be typing, was to isolate the hand, correct its color, drag it into the composite file, and position it over the keyboard. A slightly feathered lasso was then used to select the four fingers and copy them to a new layer.

With all the layers visible and the Fingers layer active, the Fingers layer was rotated to create a basis for the motion blur. Then Blur, Motion Blur was applied in the direction of the movement between the two positions of the fingers and with a Distance setting of 10 pixels for this 1700-pixel-wide image.

The Opacity of the separate Fingers layer was set at 50%. Then a hand-painted layer mask was added to the original Hand layer to make its fingertips partially transparent to add to the illusion of motion.

Saving a flattened copy of the file. When the montage is complete, choose File, Save A Copy; choose a Format, and turn on Flatten Image. This creates a single-layer nontransparent copy of the file. In flattening, Photoshop can retain alpha channels or not (at your option); all layer masks are applied and discarded, and any remaining transparent areas are filled with the Background color. *wow!*

Casting Shadows & Reflections

Overview *Draw a mask for the objects; make "luminance" masks for reflections and shadows; use these masks to add reflections and shadows to a new background.*

1a

Opening the part of the product shot that includes products, reflections, and shadows

1b

Selecting the products with the pen tool

1c

Double-clicking the Work Path opened the Save Path dialog box, where we named and saved the path.

2a

Copying a color channel to an alpha channel

SUCCESSFULLY INTEGRATING A FOREGROUND OBJECT from one photo into a new background image involves more than just cutting out the object and sticking it on top of the background. Adding a shadow cast onto the new background can help make the object part of the scene, but adding a reflection does an even better job. To put together this collage illustration for promotional materials for Pioneer, Japan, we borrowed the reflections and shadows present in the original studio shot of the products and used them as alpha channels to selectively lighten and darken a new, more colorful background that was part of a larger poster.

1 Making a mask for the object. From a scanned image, you'll select the objects you want to transplant. We began with a product shot — a 4 x 5-inch transparency, scanned and saved as a CMYK TIFF. To make the file smaller and easier to work with, we used the crop tool to eliminate parts of the image above and below the products.

To make our selections we used the pen tool because the objects we wanted to select were streamlined, hard-edged, and smooth. To use the pen to outline the object you want to transplant, choose the tool (press "P"), click to make anchor points, and drag to adjust the curves, as described in Chapter 2. When you've completed the path and closed it by clicking again on the first point, save the path: Open the Paths palette (Window, Show Paths) and double-click the Work Path name. We named the path "Products."

(Although we've used the pen tool to draw the selection border for this example and saved the selection as a path, your object may be better suited for selection with the lasso or by some other

Black channel duplicated as Reflections channel (#5 in our CMYK file)

Reflections channel with Levels adjusted and Motion Blur applied

Products path loaded in the Reflections channel and filled with black

Black channel duplicated as Shadows channel (#6), with Levels adjusted, Motion Blur applied, and color inverted

selection method (see the beginning of Chapter 2 for tips on choosing a selection method). If you select by a method other than making a path, store the selection in an alpha channel: With the selection active, choose Select, Save Selection, or open the Channels palette (Window, Show Channels) and click the mask icon (second from the left at the bottom of the palette).

2 Starting a mask for the reflections. To start a reflections mask, you'll first choose the color channel in your image that shows the reflection most distinctly. To do this, open the Channels palette, and activate the color channels one by one so you can see which one shows the most contrast between the reflections and the rest of the image (for our image, Black was the best). In the Channels palette Alt-drag the thumbnail for this channel to the New Channel icon at the bottom of the palette to make an alpha channel. In the Duplicate Channel dialog box, enter the name "Reflections," and click OK. With the "Reflections" channel active, choose Image, Adjust, Levels and move the white point of the Input Levels slider inward to emphasize the highlight areas.

3 Creating a surface texture. If you want to "texturize" the background of your image — the surface on which the objects will rest — you can set it up at this point by adding the texture to the Reflections alpha channel. We used Filter, Blur, Motion Blur with a setting of 20 pixels for this 1615-pixel-wide image to create the feeling of a "brushed" surface consistent with the high-tech nature of the products. The rubber stamp tool in Clone Aligned mode was used to touch up areas of the mask where the products had blurred into the background area.

4 Completing the Reflections channel. Now use your object path to develop the Reflections channel: With the Reflections channel active, we clicked on the name of our Products path in the Paths palette and filled the path with black by making black the Foreground color and then clicking the Fill Path icon (at the left at the bottom of the palette). Use this process to isolate the reflections alone in this channel. With black as the Foreground color, clean up the mask, blacking out any light areas other than the reflections by using the lasso and Alt-Backspace or by painting with a paintbrush.

5 Making the Shadows mask. Once again, as you did in step 2 to make the Reflections channel, choose the best color channel: This time pick the one that shows the most contrast between the shadows and the rest of the image (we used Black again). Alt-drag the thumbnail for this channel to the New Channel icon to make another alpha channel. Name it "Shadows" and choose Image, Adjust, Invert to make a negative of the channel, turning the shadows into light areas that can act as selections. Again, as you did for the Reflections channel, adjust the Levels, add texture, fill the

5b

Products path loaded into Shadows channel and filled with black

6a

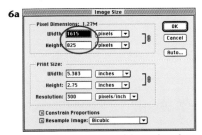

Finding the dimensions of the product shot

6b

Setting the dimensions of the marquee

6c

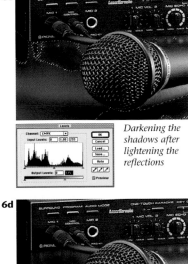

Darkening the shadows after lightening the reflections

6d

Reflections and shadows in place on the new background

Products path with black, and do any necessary touch-up, leaving a mask that represents the object's cast shadow.

6 Making reflections and shadows. The last step is to put the objects, reflections, and shadows into the new background. You can do this by copying part of the new background image into your object photo and layering it behind the object, loading your Reflections and Shadows channels as selections so you can pull reflections and shadows out of this new background by adjusting Levels, and then bringing this altered composite back into the larger new background file. Here's how we did it:

We started by checking the exact dimensions of the product image in pixels. One way to do this is to choose Image, Image Size and read the Pixel Dimensions at the top of the Image Size dialog box.

Next we double-clicked the rectangular selection marquee and set its size at the dimensions we had noted in the Image Size dialog box. Switching to the new background image file, we clicked on the image to open the marquee; then we dragged the marquee around until it surrounded the part of the new background image where we wanted the products to end up. We copied this selection to the clipboard (Ctrl-C), leaving the selection border active.

Working in the composite CMYK channel of the product shot, we loaded the Products path as a selection (with the path active, click the Make Selection icon, third from the left at the bottom of the Paths palette). Then we held down the Alt key and chose Edit, Paste Into. This created a new layer containing the clipboard contents (the new background) and a ready-made layer mask that allowed the product to show through. (Window, Show Layers opens the Layers palette.)

Working in this new layer, we loaded the Reflections and Shadows channels in turn (Ctrl-Alt-5 and Ctrl-Alt-6) and used Image, Adjust, Levels to lighten and darken each of the selected areas. Finally, we made a new layer with a merged copy of the products on their new background (Ctrl-A for Select, All; then Ctrl-Shift-C for Edit, Copy Merged; and then Ctrl-V to Paste as a new layer). We selected all, copied, and pasted the enhanced copy back into the larger background image file. *Wow!*

HOLDING A PLACE

If you need to select and copy or temporarily remove part of an image so you can work on it outside the original file, leave the selection border active in the original file. That way, when you paste the part back into the larger image (Ctrl-V), it will settle back into exactly the right spot. Better yet, when you make the selection, save it as an alpha channel (Select, Save Selection) that you can load later if your original active selection is lost — for instance, if you don't have enough RAM to keep the original file open as you work on other elements.

PASTING BEHIND

Paste Behind does not appear in Photoshop's Edit menu. But holding down the Alt key and choosing Paste Into activates the Paste Behind function.

When Neil Kopping, art director for Structo Design in San Francisco, commissioned **Jeff Brice** to Illustrate the *Adobe FrameMaker package*, he envisioned a technical 3D look combined with Brice's layered collage style (see the facing page). Brice began by photographing a thick manual in the perspective he wanted and scanning the photo. In Photoshop he isolated the book from its background by outlining it with the pen tool, converting the outline to a selection, inverting the selection, and deleting the surroundings. ►*Photoshop 4 now has a shortcut (Ctrl-Shift-I) for Select, Inverse.*

Using pages from the FrameMaker tutorial supplied by the client as PICT files, Brice dragged each page into his composite image as a separate layer. He used the move tool to offset each layer to create the illusion of a floating stack. To make very soft drop shadows for the book and pages, he duplicated each layer, filling the duplicate with black; then he blurred the shadow and reduced the layer's Opacity.

►*In Photoshop 4, pressing Alt-Shift-Backspace fills the pixels in a layer with the Foreground color while maintaining the layer's transparency. This means it isn't necessary to turn on Preserve Transparency in the Layers palette to do the color fill and then turn it off again in order to blur the shadow.*

Brice rotated, skewed, and scaled all the page and shadow layers to the same angle. To repair small artifacts caused by the skewing, he used the airbrush with a tiny tip, as well as the rubber stamp. ►*In Photoshop 4 several layers can be transformed at once by linking the layers together and using the Layer, Free Transform command.*

To build the floating chart, graph, and text elements, Brice created some of the black-and-white artwork in Macromedia FreeHand 5.5, exported it in Macintosh EPS format, and dragged and dropped each piece of art into the Photoshop composite file as a separate layer. He rotated and skewed each layer into position with Free Transform and filled each layer with color (Alt-Shift-Backspace). Other graphic elements were selected from his collection

of scanned antique technical drawings. He dragged and dropped them into the file as separate layers, and dropped out the background to leave only the line work.
►*The This Layer slider in Layer Options, selected from the Layers palette's pop-out menu, makes it easy to eliminate a white background by moving the right triangle leftward; holding down the Alt key separates the triangle into two independently operated parts to make the transition more gradual and help smooth the border of the remaining art.*

To change the color of the scanned line work, and also to make color changes to the FreeHand graphs as requested by the client, Brice used Photoshop's Image, Adjust, Replace Color command: In each layer he clicked the colored line work to select it and sample its color; then he moved the Hue, Saturation, and Value sliders in the Replace Color dialog box, working interactively until he achieved the new color he wanted.

The final illustration was delivered as a Photoshop file with layers intact, so the client could make slight alterations needed for different applications of the image.

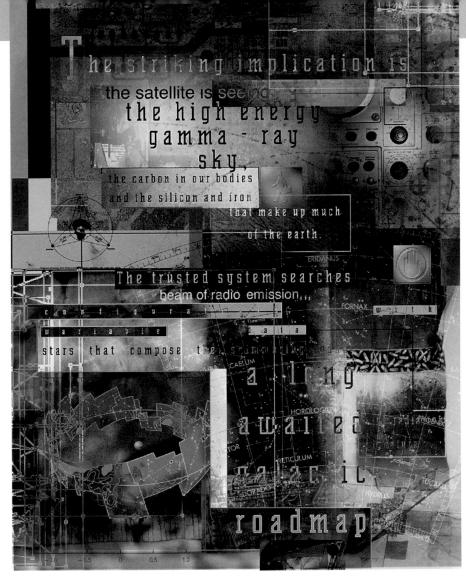

The striking implication is
the satellite is seeing
the high energy
gamma - ray
sky,
the carbon in our bodies
and the silicon and iron
that make up much
of the earth.

ERIDANUS

The trusted system searches
beam of radio emission...

configura
FORNAX with
variable data

stars that compose the shimmering

CAELUM

a long

HOROLOGIUM

awaited

PICTOR

galactic

RETICULUM

roadmap

For **High Energy Gamma**, one of a series of collage poems, **Jeff Brice** began by setting type in Macromedia FreeHand, inspired by his collection of found text elements. He experimented with different fonts and sizes until he was satisfied with the page of type, and saved it in Macintosh EPS format.

Brice used the File, Open command to rasterize the EPS file in Photoshop in RGB mode at 300 pixels per inch, with Anti-aliased turned on to smooth the edges of the type. The file opened with a single transparent layer holding the type.

Brice built the background file as a composite of many small images, each on its own layer. He experimented by repositioning layers with the move tool and scaling them. ▶*A quick way to get to*

the Scale command is to press Ctrl-T for Layer, Free Transform, and then press the right mouse button to pop out the context-sensitive menu that includes Scale.

To finalize the composition, Brice started with the lowest layer above *Background,* activating each layer in turn and merging down. ▶*Pressing Ctrl-E merges the active layer with the layer just below it; both layers must be visible for this to work.*

He dragged the type file into the background file and worked to set up a "push-pull" tension between the type and the composite image. ▶*By using Ctrl-Shift-J to cut a selection to a new layer, it's possible to separate individual words and phrases from a page of text so they can be moved independently and the Opacity and blending mode of each piece can be controlled separately.*

Brice used several techniques to make the type more readable: Some of the type was selected with the rectangular marquee and the box was outlined. ▶*Choose Edit, Stroke to stroke an active selection outline.*

For other words the type itself was outlined. ▶*Ctrl-click a layer's thumbnail in the Layers palette to load its transparency mask as a selection; then choose Edit, Stroke.*

Brice added to the depth of the collage by lightening or darkening areas of the image behind the type, creating a new layer between the type and background and painting with the airbrush in Normal mode at a low Pressure setting, using a large, soft brush tip and black and very light colors sampled from the background.

Moments, by **Katrin Eismann,** started with a snapshot taken with a panoramic camera held over the shower. After the film was processed, Eismann picked a shot from a contact sheet and sent the film to be digitized using the Kodak Photo CD process. She got the photo back in two image files, which she put back together by using Image, Canvas Size to add empty space to the left-side image so she could drag and drop the right-side image into the file, aligning this new layer, then merging the two layers into one. ▶*Pressing Ctrl-Shift-E merges all visible layers.*

To enhance the steamy look, she duplicated the image to a new layer, ran the Dry Brush filter on this layer, reduced its Opacity to a low value, lightened it with Levels, and added a layer mask so she could paint the mask to limit the streaky effect to particular areas of the photo.

Eismann used a water image to replace the urban view in the window. ▶*In Photoshop 4 if you make a selection, such as the window, and then activate a layer, such as the water, and click the mask icon at the bottom of the Layers palette, a layer mask is automatically added to the active layer with the selected area white to let the image show through, and the rest of the mask black; so in this case the water would appear in the window area.*

To compose *Cathedral Light with French Horn,* **Katrin Eismann** layered a background photo of the floor of an abandoned cathedral outside Arles, France with a 4 x 5-inch studio shot of a French horn. She silhouetted the horn by tracing its smooth curves with the pen tool, turning the path into a selection, inverting the selection, and deleting the background.

To make the horn seem at home in its new environment, Eismann duplicated the cathedral floor layer, moved the copy above the horn layer, and combined it with the horn in a clipping group. ▶*To use the shape in one layer to trim layers above it, activate the layer you want to use as the masking shape and Alt-click on the border between that layer's name and the one above; you can continue Alt-clicking up*

the stack of layers, masking as many as you like.

Eismann reduced the Opacity of the top layer so the horn's metallic surface would show again and used the move tool to drag the top layer so the image "reflected" in the horn didn't line up exactly with the image underneath.

Eric Hanauer assembled *Annular Eclipse* from a series of photos he had shot and filed away, at the time unaware of a way to combine them. When he later started working with Photoshop, he began with a wide-angle shot overlooking Scripps pier in La Jolla, California, and lasso-selected and added three more phases of the setting sun and the sky around it. The sun images were enlarged, with the total eclipse scaled to twice the size of the others. ▶*You can scale a selection by pressing Ctrl-T and Shift-dragging a corner handle to keep the selection in proportion; double-clicking inside the selection completes the resizing.*

Hanauer used the smudge tool to blend the background sky with the sky of the collaged sun images.

Katrin Eismann's *Nightmare* is a montage of two photos: a winter scene reflected in a puddle, and a fountain at Caesar's Palace in Las Vegas with boutiques behind it. Both were shot with panoramic cameras, which caused the images to curve. Eismann layered the Pegasus on top and the trees underneath. She added a layer mask to the top layer and used the airbrush tool with brush tips of varying sizes to paint the mask so only the horse and some of the clouds and "ghosted" buildings showed through. ▶*To add a clear layer mask to the active layer, click the mask icon at the bottom of the layers palette. Then you can paint with black to mask out the parts of the layer you don't want in the image.*

Eismann used Image, Adjust, Replace Color once to change the hue and increase the saturation of the golden light on the statue and again to reduce saturation on the rest of the animal. ▶*When you use Replace Color, you can make a mask by selecting by color with the eyedropper and then adjust the color of the selected area, all in one interactive step, using the Fuzziness slider to control the way the recolored areas blend with the surroundings. But if you're not happy with the color change and want to undo it, you can't undo just the color — you lose the selection as well. So that you won't need to remask if you decide to undo the color change, try a different method: Instead of Replace Color, you can use Select, Color Range, save the selection as an alpha channel, and then use Image, Adjust, Hue/Saturation. The trade-off in doing it this way is that you won't be able to adjust Fuzziness and color at the same time.*

Rainwater Ritual by **Burke / Triolo Productions** consists of just two elements composed together. The primary illustration of bottle, cloth, soap, and foam was a 4 x 5-inch photo shot with strobe lighting and a "hosemaster" fiber optic light painting device. The second element, a set of glass bubbles, was shot on the same stone background as the first photo, as shown at the right.

Jeff Burke began with a drum scan of the primary image and enlarged the canvas size (with default white as the Background color), which gave him some image area to clone bubbles onto. Then he selected a single glass bubble, outlined it with the pen tool and saved the path. He converted the path to a selection, copied the bubble onto a layer above the image (Ctrl-J), selected it (Ctrl-click the layer's name in the Layers palette), then Alt-dragged with the move tool several times to create copies of the bubble, sometimes resizing a bubble to make it smaller. ▶*With a selection active, pressing Ctrl-T sets up the Free Transform box; Shift-dragging a corner handle resizes the selection proportionally.*

Burke adjusted the opacity of the layer using Layer Options (from the Layers palette's pop-out menu). By moving the Underlying white slider inward, he was able to lighten the opacity of the dark bubble copies where they appeared over the white background, while maintaining their full intensity over the dark picture area. ▶*Holding down the Alt key while moving a slider in the Layer Options dialog box splits the slider, which allows smooth rather than abrupt transitions at the composited edges.*

Soap foam from the bottom half of the image was extended onto the white background by painting with the rubber stamp tool in Clone (Non-aligned) mode at a low Opacity setting.

J eff Burke of **Burke / Triolo Productions** composited *Utensils* from two photo elements: the pitcher of utensils on a table and a sheet of diamond-patterned metal. Working in RGB mode, he selected the background of the utensils photo by color. ▶*Select, Color Range is often the most efficient way to select several isolated areas of the same color.*

The selection was saved as an alpha channel (#4), and Burke added to and subtracted from the channel by making more selections by hand to make a channel that could be used to select all the background of the utensils photo so it could be deleted. ▶*To add to or subtract from an existing alpha channel mask, you can work on the channel as you view it along with the RGB composite: Activate the alpha channel by clicking its name in the Channels palette, then click also on the eye icon for the RGB composite. Paint with black (to add to the mask) or white (to subtract),*

or make a selection and fill it with black (to add) or select and press Delete to subtract.

Burke adjusted Color Balance separately for the utensils and the metal, warming the color of the utensils with a shift toward red and cooling the background metal with a shift toward blue. ▶*The effect of an Adjustment layer can be restricted to a particular target layer by making a clipping group that includes only the target layer and the Adjustment layer, stacked just above it. To make the clipping group, Alt-click on the border between them in the Layers palette.*

To give the image more texture, Burke first painted with white in a scratchy motion onto the edges of the diamond metal background to produce a worn-away effect. Then he texturized the area outside the edges of the pitcher and utensils without compromising the integrity of the utensils themselves. ▶*To put a textured edge around a subject, start by selecting the subject (in this case that*

could be done by loading channel #4 as a selection by pressing Ctrl-Alt-4 and inverting the selection (Ctrl-Shift-I). Feather the selection to make a soft edge. Activate the layer to be texturized (the metal background in this case), and Ctrl-click the New Layer icon in the Layers palette to make an Adjustment layer above it, choosing Levels as the type. Adjust Levels to darken the edge area, choose Dissolve from the Layers palette's blending mode list, and adjust the Opacity slider until the texture looks right.

Burke flattened the image and imported it into Painter to do some additional edge work using Chalk brushes.

USING
FILTERS

PHOTOSHOP'S FILTERS — SMALL SUBPROGRAMS that are grouped under the Filter menu — can be run on an entire image or a selection. A spectacular addition to Photoshop 4 are 48 filters designed for special effects and painterly treatments (described later in this chapter and in Chapter 8), plug-ins that used to be sold separately as the three volumes of Gallery Effects filters. In addition to these and other artistic, special effects, and special-purpose plug-ins, Photoshop supplies three kinds of filters that can do a lot to improve the quality of scanned photographs, and can even improve painted images. You'll find these "workhorse" filters in the Sharpen, Blur, and Noise submenus. In addition, Lighting Effects and other filters of the Render submenu can add drama to photos. They have great potential for synthesizing entire environments and creating special effects.

SHARPEN

Photoshop provides four sharpening filters. Sharpen and Sharpen More accentuate the color differences between adjacent pixels of different colors. **Sharpen Edges** and **Unsharp Mask** find "edges," areas where a continuous run of pixels of one color comes up against other colors, and then they increase the contrast between that run of pixels and the pixels nearby. Areas that aren't edges, like very slight or gradual color transitions, are left pretty much unchanged, so they still look smooth, or "soft." The use of sharpening filters comes up again and again throughout the book, but here's a quick list of sharpening tips:

Use only Unsharp Mask. In general, forget the other sharpening filters and use Unsharp Mask. Unlike Sharpen and Sharpen More, which can accentuate blemishes, film grain, and any artifacts you may have created by editing an image, Unsharp Mask accentuates the differences only at "edges," where you want the differences to be distinct. And unlike Sharpen Edges, it gives you precise control. With Unsharp Mask you can set:

• The **Amount** (the strength of the application, or how much the difference at an edge is enhanced by the filter).

• The **Radius** (how many pixels in from the color edge will have their contrast increased). Increase the Radius with increasing resolution, because at higher resolutions the individual pixels are smaller relative to the image components.

continued on page 154

Original scan

Sharpen

Sharpen Edges

Sharpen More

Unsharp Mask default: 50, 1, 0

Unsharp Mask: 100, 1, 0

Unsharp Mask: 100, 3, 2

Unsharp Mask, 4 times: 25, 3, 2

Photo delivered at 100 dpi

Resolution increased to 200 dpi

Unsharp Mask applied: 200, 1, 0

Original scan

Unsharp mask: 500, 50, 50; oversharpened for a special effect

PHOTO: DIGITAL STOCK CORP., BUILDINGS & STRUCTURES

- The **Threshold** (how different the colors on the two sides of an edge have to be before the filter will sharpen it). Use higher settings for images that are "grainy" or have subtle color shifts, such as skin tones, so the filter won't sharpen the "noise."

Use it on scanned images. As a rule, run the Unsharp Mask filter to see if it improves a scanned photo by getting rid of blurriness from a poor original or from the scanning process.

Use it on resized or reoriented images. Whenever you use Image, Image Size with Resample Image turned on, or when you use the Image, Rotate Canvas, Arbitrary command, or if you use any of the Scale, Rotate, Skew, Distort, Perspective, or Numeric functions from Layer, Transform or Layer, Free Transform, use Unsharp Mask afterwards. Any such change involves *interpolation* — that is, creating or recoloring pixels based on calculations — and is bound to "soften" the image (see the flag image at the left).

Use it more than once. Running Unsharp Mask more than once at a lower Amount will sharpen more smoothly than if you run it once at a setting twice as high. (Note that Sharpen More and Sharpen shouldn't be run twice, since they multiply the artifacts they create if you apply them more than once.)

Use it last. Because it can generate artifacts that can be magnified by other image-editing operations, Unsharp Mask should generally be applied after you've finished editing the image.

Use the sharpen tool for pinpoint precision. For handheld control of the Sharpen filter, use the sharpen (triangle) tool. If the tool isn't visible in the tool

palette, select it by Alt-clicking the blur (water drop) tool, or press "R" to cycle through the focus tools. You can change the settings in the Brushes and Focus Tools Options palette to control the area (brush size) and intensity (Exposure) of sharpening. You can set the blur tool to Sample Merged so that it blurs as if all the visible layers were merged, even though the blur effect is recorded only on the active layer.

BLUR

Photoshop's blurring filters can be used to soften all or part of an image. **Blur** and **Blur More** (which is three or four times as strong as Blur) smooth an image by reducing the contrast between adjacent pixels. With the **Gaussian Blur** filter, the transition between the contrasting colors occurs at a particular mathematical rate, so that most of the pixels in a black-to-white blur, for example, are in the middle gray range, with fairly few pixels in the very dark or light shades. And you can increase the amount of blurring that occurs by raising the Radius value.

Photoshop 4's new **Smart Blur** filter is designed to leave edges sharp but blur the other parts of an image. The result is a kind of posterization of the non-edge areas — the number of colors is reduced, detail is lost, and the image is presented as blobs of flat colors.

- The higher the **Threshold** setting for Smart Blur, the less "smart" the filter is about recognizing edges — that is, the more different the color and tone of adjacent areas have to be in order for the difference to be recognized as an edge. And since the filter blurs everything that isn't an edge, the higher the Threshold setting, the more blurring occurs.

- At a given threshold setting, the higher the **Radius,** the farther away from the edge the original color is preserved. A low setting preserves very little, resulting in a lot of blurring. (The exception to this is at the very bottom of the Radius scale, below 0.5 pixels, where the filter seems to be inactive.) A higher Radius setting preserves more of the edges, maintaining more of the image detail. (But once all possible edges are preserved given the Threshold setting, increasing the Radius has no effect.)

- For a particular combination of Radius and Threshold, changing the **Quality** changes the degree of posterization, with Low producing the most colors and High producing the least.

- The Edge Only and Edge Overlay **Mode** settings were designed mainly for use in the preview window of the dialog box, to help you see where the filter is identifying edges with your current Radius and Threshold settings.

Use Smart Blur as an interactive posterization tool, with better control of the effect than with Image, Adjust, Posterize. Experiment with the Threshold and Radius sliders and the Quality setting to get the degree of posterization you want.

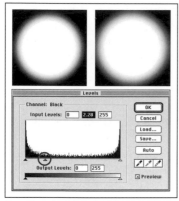

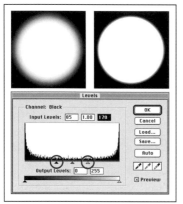

On a Gaussian Blurred mask, move the Input Levels gray point slider to enlarge (here) or shrink the mask.

On a Gaussian Blurred mask, move the Input Levels black and white point sliders inward to "harden" the edges.

The Smart Blur filter can be used to make an image (left) "cartoonlike" (right).

To turn an image into a drawing, Smart Blur was used in Edge Only mode (left). Then the image was inverted, the Jag II program smoothed the lines, and the file was converted to grayscale.

Use Smart Blur at "mild" settings for "cosmetic" purposes — to subdue wrinkles in a portrait, for instance, or hide the freckling of a ripe banana.

Use Smart Blur, Gaussian Blur, and Image, Adjust, Levels to produce a drawing from an image: Run the Smart Blur filter in Edge Only mode to generate a white-on-black line drawing. Invert to black-on-white (Ctrl-I). Then smooth the jaggy lines by running the Gaussian Blur filter at a low Radius setting and using the Input Levels slider (Ctrl-L) as described at the left. Or do the smoothing with MetaCreations' Jag II program.

Use Blur to make the background recede. One of the most common errors in Photoshop montage is combining a sharply focused subject with an equally sharply focused image used as background. You can fix the problem by blurring the background slightly to simulate the depth of field a real camera lens would capture. You can also apply this background-blurring technique to a single photo to reduce the perceived depth of field and focus attention on the foreground subject.

Use Gaussian Blur to smooth out flaws in a photo. You may be able to do some photo repair work (such as eliminating water spotting) by using Gaussian Blur on one or all of the color channels.

Use Gaussian Blur to control edge characteristics in alpha channels or layer masks. Once a selection is stored in an alpha channel or layer mask, the Gaussian Blur filter can be run to soften or smooth out the transition between black and white. Then the Image, Adjust, Levels function can be run on the channel to fatten, shrink, or harden the edge of the selection area.

Use the blur tool for precision. This tool (the counterpart of the sharpen tool) gives you pinpoint control of the blur.

The other three Blur filters fall into the special effects category: **Motion Blur,** which lets you set a direction and an amount for the

USING DISTORTION FILTERS

When you apply a distortion filter, you can often get smoother (though not as crisp) results by running the filter at a lower setting several times than by running it at a higher setting once, especially if the image includes straight lines. For this example we started with a screen dump of a color palette.

Original palette

Twirl applied 10 times at an Angle setting of 50

Twirl applied once at an Angle setting of 500

Blur the background to reduce the apparent depth of field and to focus attention on the foreground.

HUE-PROTECTED NOISE

In a color image, Photoshop's Noise filter draws from the whole spectrum to change pixel colors; this can produce an artificial "electronic rainbow" look. But you can introduce noise without color change by checking the Monochromatic box in the Add Noise dialog box. A similar effect can be achieved with three filters from Kai's Power Tools (see page 188). The KPT hue-protected noise filter has the advantage of not applying noise in the lightest highlights and darkest shadows.

Original gradient, no noise   *Noise, Add Noise, Gaussian, 40*

Noise, Add Noise, Gaussian, 40, Monochromatic   *Noise, KPT H-P Noise Maximum*

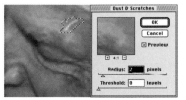

Dust & Scratches (under Noise) can be used on blemished images to eliminate the defects.

blur, produces an effect like taking a picture of a moving object. **Radial Blur** provides two options: With **Spin** you can simulate the effect of photographing an object spinning around a center that you specify in a Blur Center box; **Zoom** simulates the effect of zooming the camera toward or away from the center you define.

NOISE

Under Noise in the Filter menu, **Add Noise** creates either random or Gaussian variation in pixel color or tone. **Despeckle** and **Median** detect edges and then leave these alone while smoothing out less abrupt changes in color. Median averages the brightness of pixels within an image or selection after you determine the Radius used to select the pixels to be averaged. High Radius settings produce a posterized effect. The **Dust & Scratches** filter looks for "defects" (areas that are markedly different from their surroundings) and blurs the surrounding pixels into the defects to eliminate them. The Threshold setting determines how different from the surrounding pixels something has to be in order to be detected as a defect; a setting between 70 and 128 often works well. The Radius setting determines how far from the edge of the defect the filter goes to get the pixels used in the blur. Dust & Scratches works best if you select a fairly small feathered area around the defect and run the filter only on that area, also keeping the Radius setting as low as possible. Using a bigger selection or a higher Radius setting can noticeably blur the image.

Add Noise to improve a color gradient. Color gradients created in PostScript-based graphics programs like Illustrator or Free-Hand can be too "slick"-looking or can show unwanted color banding. Adding Noise with an Amount setting of just 3 to 5 for a 300 dpi image and with Monochromatic checked can make the gradient look much more natural. For an especially subtle effect, you can run the filter on one or two of the RGB channels, or run it separately on the individual C, M, Y, and K channels.

Add Noise as the basis for generating a texture. Add Noise used with other filters such as Gaussian Blur, Difference Clouds, and Lighting Effects can generate some interesting textures. Examples appear on pages 159 and 174.

Use Despeckle or Median to reduce scan artifacts. The "ridges" that can appear in desktop-scanned images can be reduced or eliminated by applying the Despeckle or Median filter. (Despeckle is a one-click operation but Median offers more control.) These filters can also help eliminate *moiré,* an interference pattern that happens when the halftone screen in the printed image you're scanning interacts with the scanner's sampling pattern. After these scanner artifacts are eliminated, use Unsharp Mask to sharpen the image.

BUILDINGS & STRUCTURES, DIGITAL STOCK CORP.

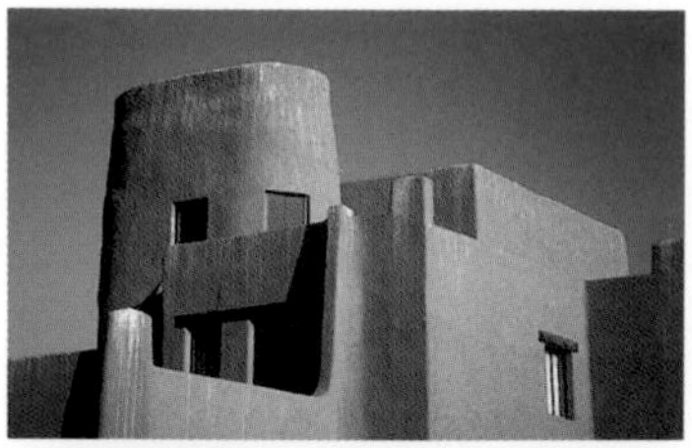

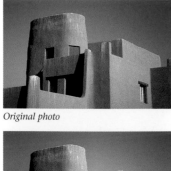

Original photo

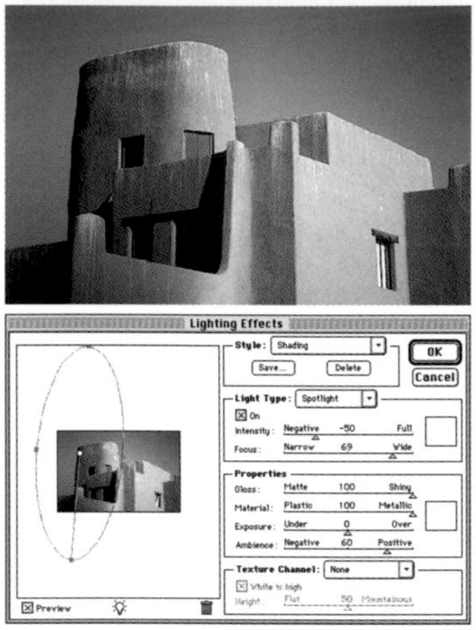

A Spotlight with negative Intensity can be used to shade part of an image.

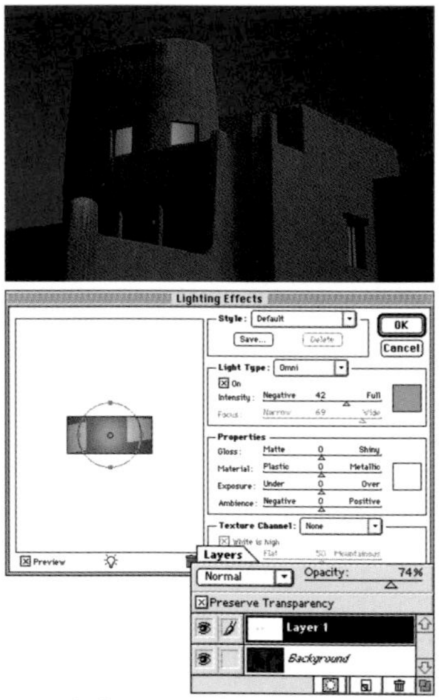

Two windows were selected with the polygon lasso, and copied to a new layer (Ctrl-J). Negative ambient light was applied to the Background layer. The windows layer was filled with White with Preserve Transparency turned on and an orange Omni light was applied to this layer. Opacity was adjusted.

RENDER

The filters of Photoshop's Render menu are some of the most powerful in the program.

The **Clouds** filter creates a cloudlike pattern using the Background and Foreground colors. If you use sky-blue and white, the effect tends to look like high, diffuse clouds. To make bulkier-looking clouds on a darker sky, hold down the Alt key when you select the filter.

Difference Clouds works the same way, except that the cloud effect interacts with the image as if the clouds were being applied in Difference mode. In Difference mode black is the neutral color — that is, black pixels don't cause any change in the target image — so you can use Difference Clouds with the Foreground and Background colors set to black and white to apply a cloudlike pattern of color inversion. Repeated application of Difference Clouds starting with a blank layer in a grayscale image generates a veined effect like marble (see page 174); in a color file you get marble with an "oil slick" rainbow.

The **Lens Flare** filter simulates the photographic effect you get when a bright light shines into the lens of a camera. Immediately after you apply the Lens Flare, you can use the Filter, Fade command to experiment by adjusting the Opacity.

The **Lighting Effects** filter's dialog box can be used to set up both **ambient** lighting and **individual light sources.** Ambient light is diffuse, nondirectional light that's uniform throughout the image, so it casts no shadows, like daylight on an overcast day. And it may have a color, like daylight underwater. Ambient light affects the density and color of shadows cast by any individual light sources you set up. There are three varieties of light sources: **omnidirectional** lights (sending a glow in all directions, like a light bulb in a table lamp), **spotlights** (directional and focused, to make a pool of light like their counterparts in the real world), and **directional** light sources (too far away to be focused, like bright sunlight or moonlight on the earth), which are ideal for creating textured surfaces and embossed effects.

- **To set the strength of ambient light,** use the Ambience slider in the Properties section of the Lighting Effects dialog box. The more positive the setting, the stronger the ambient light relative to the Directional, Omni, and Spotlight sources you add, and so the less pronounced the shadows produced by these lights. Other settings in the Properties section also affect the overall environment, rather than any individual light source.
- **To add a light source,** drag the light bulb icon at the bottom of the palette into the Preview area.
- **To color the ambient light,** click on the color box in the Properties section of the dialog box to open the Color Picker.
- **To color a light source**, click on the color box under Light Type.
- **To select one of several light sources** so that you can adjust

Try these methods as a start for experimenting to make natural-looking textured surfaces:

• Make a stone surface by running the Difference Clouds filter repeatedly on a grayscale file and then colorizing it to make "marble." Then Add Noise at a low setting, Gaussian Blur at a low setting, and run the Lighting Effects filter with a Directional light source, using one of the color channels (R, G, or B) as the Texture Channel.

• Make brushed metal or the start of wood grain by filling a layer with Add Noise, using a Motion Blur to create streaks, and finishing with a subtle application of Lighting Effects.

• Make rough paper textures for painting by running the Add Noise filter at a low setting, then Blur or Blur More (used here), and then Emboss (from the Stylize submenu). Or try using Facet (from the Pixelate submenu) between the blurring and embossing steps. Use Image, Adjust, Levels to whiten the paper and reduce the contrast.

its settings, click on the little circle that represents it in the Preview area, or use the Tab key to cycle through the lights.

• **To move a light source,** drag the central light spot.

• **To control the direction, size, and shape of a Spotlight,** drag the handles on the ellipse. **To control the angle** without changing the shape, Ctrl-drag a handle. **To change the shape** without affecting the angle, Shift-drag a handle.

• **To duplicate an existing light source,** Alt-drag it.

• **To turn off a light source temporarily,** so you can see the effect of removing it without actually disrupting its position, click to deselect the On box in the Light Type area of the dialog box.

• **To turn off a light source permanently** (that is, to remove it), drag its circle from the Preview area to the trash can icon.

• **To save a lighting scheme** so you can apply it to other layers or files later, click the Save button. Your new Style will be saved with the Styles supplied with Photoshop, and will be added to the dialog box's pop-out Style menu.

Lighting Effects works well to cast light onto an image as if it were mounted on a wall, as shown on page 160. But here are some other ways you can use it to trick the eye:

• To **unify** several fairly different images in a publication or an on-screen presentation, apply the same lighting scheme to all of them. You can do this by naming and saving the lighting style and then loading it to apply to another layer or file.

• To create a **shadowy area** in an image, use a Spotlight set at a negative Intensity with Ambience set to a positive value.

• To make light appear to come from **inside** something (such as a bulb in a lamp), position an Omni light at the source.

• To add a **texture** to the surface of an image, set up a light source and choose a Texture Channel to use as a bump map. A bump map interacts with the light sources for an image or layer, tricking the eye into perceiving bumpiness, or texture. The things that can be used as bump maps for applying Lighting Effects to any layer are the individual color channels (red, green, or blue, for example), any alpha channel in the file, or the transparency mask or layer mask for that layer.

The **Texture Fill** filter gives you a quick way to import grayscale files to use with the Lighting Effects filter. The process is described in "Using Texture Fills with Lighting Effects" on page 175.

If you've set up several light sources in Lighting Effects and you like the overall effect but your image is now too bright, try reducing the Ambience or Exposure in the Properties section of the box. Or use Filter, Fade after the fact. Either method often fixes the problem, and it's much easier than adjusting each light source individually.

Combining with Light

Overview *Layer the elements of your montage, adding drop shadows if you like; treat all but the shadow layers with the Lighting Effects filter.*

1a

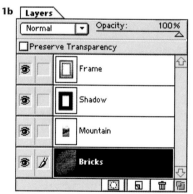

Original montage of three images

IMAGE CLUB GRAPHICS, PHOTOGEAR

1b

The layered, lit images and the unlit drop shadow

2

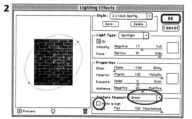

For the bricks layer only, we used a Texture Channel, turning off White Is High to make the white mortar look recessed.

JHD

THE LIGHTING EFFECTS FILTER IS IDEAL for helping the elements of a montage look at home in their surroundings. Here we've combined drop shadows with the filter's ability to light and to "emboss."

1 Assembling the pieces. Open an RGB file to use as the backdrop for your image. Open each of the other component images, select the part you want to use, drag with the move tool, and drop it into the backdrop file to form a new layer. We used a brick background, a frame, and a landscape photo, adding a shadow between the image layers (see steps 3 and 4 of "Casting a Shadow" in Chapter 8).

2 Lighting the image. Now choose Filter, Render, Lighting Effects and apply the filter to each layer except the shadows. Use the same Style setting in each case (we used "2AMSPOT" for the image at the top of the page). If the image in any layer has an inherent texture, as our brick wall did, use one of the color channels of that layer as a Texture Channel for the filter (we used Green).

Experimenting and saving styles. Try other settings from the Style list. For some kinds of lighting, you may want to make the drop shadow layer invisible by clicking to turn off its eye in the Layers palette, or reposition the shadow with the move tool to match the direction of the lighting. When you have the Light Type, Properties, and Texture Channel settings you like, click the Save button in the Lighting Effects dialog box. The style you save will appear in the Style list whenever you use the filter. The styles shown here are included on the Wow! CD ROM in the back of this book. *Wow!*

WOWRGB: Colors for lights are set with the Light Type color square.

WOWSoft: Ambient light (pink here) is set in the Properties section.

WOW3Down: Angles can be set for Spotlights and Directional lights.

Combining Filter Effects

Overview *Duplicate the image into two layers; apply separate filter or color effects to each; combine the effects by adjusting the Opacity of the top layer.*

MICHAEL GILMORE

FILTERS OFFER ENDLESS POSSIBILITIES for combining their potentially spectacular effects. For an illustration for the Japanese edition of *Step-By-Step Electronic Design,* Michael Gilmore was inspired by *Jurassic Park* to use this dinosaur as the centerpiece.

1 Choosing an image. An out-of-the-ordinary original image works well as the subject for the unusual effects that filters can apply. Gilmore started with a photo he took of a toy dinosaur from a local hobby shop. He scanned the photo and began experimenting to make it look a bit more fearsome.

1

Original photo

2

Making two layers for filtering

DUPLICATING FOR SAFEKEEPING

In the rush of inspiration, it can be hard to remember to save a copy of your original so you can start fresh if you want to. Even with the Revert command available, it's a good idea to start a project by duplicating the original image, and then save often during image development. Choose Image, Duplicate to quickly make a copy to work on, or use Save A Copy or Edit, Take Snapshot (to copy a single layer) or Edit, Take Merged Snapshot (to make a single-layer copy of all currently visible layers) so you'll be able to revert to this intermediate version of your file by selecting all or part of the image and choosing Edit, Fill, Snapshot.

2 Setting up layers. To give yourself two layers that you can filter and then blend experimentally, open the Layers palette (Window, Show Layers) and drag the Background icon to the New Layer icon in the middle at the bottom of the palette to copy the image to a new layer. Repeat the process to make another layer.

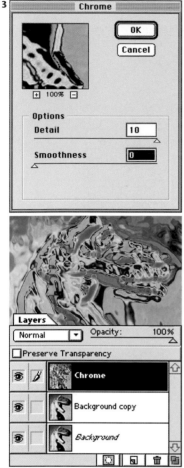

Applying the first filter

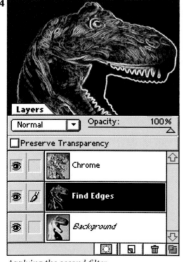

Applying the second filter

3 Applying the first filter. Make the top layer active in the Layers palette and rename it if you like. (Double-clicking a layer in the Layers palette opens the Layer Options dialog box so you can rename the layer.) Choose an effect from the Filter menu and, if necessary, set its parameters. Gilmore chose Filter, Sketch, Chrome and tested various settings on a part of the image in the interactive dialog box. When he was happy with the result, he clicked the OK button.

4 Applying a second filter. Click the eye icon on the already filtered layer to hide this layer from view so you'll be able to see the new filter effect when you apply it to the layer below. Now activate the second layer of the Layers palette and rename it if you like. Apply another filter. Gilmore applied Photoshop's Find Edges and then used Image, Adjust, Invert to get bright lines on a dark background.

5 Blending the two effects. Now you can adjust the way the two images blend. With the top layer active and all layers visible, choose an Opacity setting. Gilmore blended the Chrome layer at 25% Opacity so the Find Edges filter would have a stronger effect than the Chrome. The result is shown at the top of the preceding page. (Try adjusting the opacity of the middle layer to let some of the original image show through, or experiment with the blending modes — Multiply, Difference, and others.)

6 Experimenting with filters. Try out other filter combinations, as well as applying color and tonal changes (to experiment without making permanent changes to your image, Ctrl-click the New Layer icon and choose a Type of Adjustment layer). Shown at the right are two of Gilmore's experiments.

Blending the filter effects

6a

For this effect, Photoshop's Ripple filter (from the Distort submenu) was applied at its default settings to the original photo; color was adjusted through Hue/Saturation; and the Dry Brush filter (from the Artistic submenu) was applied.

6b

To produce the image above, the original was solarized (Filter, Stylize, Solarize), and Image, Adjust, Equalize (not available through an Adjustment layer) was applied to brighten the result.

Rendering a Sunset

Overview *Set up a gradient of sunset colors and apply it to a layer; create the round glow of the setting sun; add clouds in perspective; adjust the color; add graphics or type.*

*Several **Sunset** and **Rainbow** gradients can be found in the **Goodies** directory on the Wow! CD-ROM.*

1

Setting up a new sunset gradient, or loading a stored one

2a

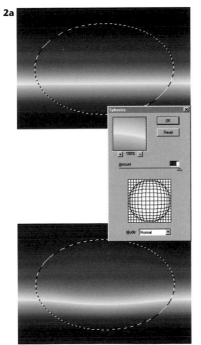

Selecting and spherizing a portion of the sky

STARTING WITH A MULTICOLOR GRADIENT of exaggerated sunset colors, the Clouds, Spherize, Waves, and Motion Blur filters, along with the Free Transform command, can create a dramatic, "larger than life" sky-over-water background. (To render a photorealistic sky, MetaCreations' Bryce does an excellent job; see Appendix B.)

1 Setting up the gradient. To make a custom multicolor gradient for a sunset over water, open a new RGB file (Ctrl-N) and open the Gradient Tool Options palette (choose the tool in the toolbox and press the Enter key) and click the Edit button. When the Gradient Editor dialog box opens, choose New and set up your gradient: With the Color button on, click below the top bar to add each color you want in the gradient, starting with your top sky color at the left end. For each color, click the color sample to the left of the Location box to open the Color Picker so you can choose a color. Or press the default F6 keyboard shortcut to open the Color palette and click the color bar to sample from there.

Between every pair of colors a diamond appears above the bar, to show where the halfway point occurs in the change from one color to the next. By sliding the diamond left or right, you can control the rate of transition between colors. Use the Save button to name the gradient and preserve it for future use. The gradient we used, as well as some other custom sunset and rainbow color blends can be loaded (by pressing the Load button in the Gradient Editor) from the **Goodies** directory on the CD-ROM that comes with this book. For more about using the gradient tool, see Chapter 6.

With the gradient defined, click OK and then choose Linear in the Gradient Tool Options palette. To get perfectly horizontal bands of color, hold down the Shift key as you drag from the top to the bottom of your *Background* layer.

2 Suggesting the setting sun. Open the Layers palette (Window, Show Layers) and duplicate your gradient-filled layer by dragging its name to the New Layer icon in the middle at the bottom of the palette. In this new top layer, make a feathered elliptical

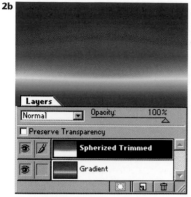

2b

The rounded sunset glow after trimming

3

A layer of high-contrast clouds added with Filter, Render, Clouds and the Alt key

4a

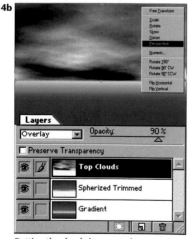

The clouds layer scaled vertically

4b

Putting the clouds in perspective

selection: To set the Feather, choose the elliptical marquee tool (press "M" once or twice), press the Enter key to open the Marquee Options palette, and enter a Feather value; we used 50 pixels for this 1100-pixel-wide file. To make the oval selection from the center, hold down the Alt key as you drag outward.

Now use Filter, Distort, Spherize, working with the Amount slider to bulge the selected area as much as you want. The feathering on the selection makes the bulge gradual.

To trim the lower portion of the spherized sky so the gradient is undistorted below the horizon, use the rectangular marquee tool (pressing "M" selects it) with a Feather setting of 0, to select the area; then press Backspace and deselect (Ctrl-D). If you're sure you're happy with your sky at this point you can Merge Down (Ctrl-E) to condense the two parts into a single layer. (We left ours separate.)

3 Adding clouds. With your top layer active, click the New Layer icon to add another layer above your sunset gradient. With black and white as your Foreground and Background colors (press "D" or click the little default icon to the lower left of the color squares in the toolbox), fill the layer with clouds by holding down the Alt key and choosing Filter, Render, Clouds; using the Alt key produces higher-contrast clouds than without it. If you don't get satisfactory clouds the first time, rerun the filter (Ctrl-Alt-F) repeatedly until you get a pleasing mix of light and dark.

4 Putting the clouds into perspective. Now you can scale the clouds vertically to fit the sky part of the sunset gradient, and then apply a perspective distortion so they appear to be looming forward from the distant horizon: Press Ctrl-T for Layer, Free Transform. Drag the bottom center handle of the Free Transform box upward to the horizon. To accomplish the perspective distortion, with the cursor inside the Free Transform box, press the right mouse button to open a context-sensitive menu. Choose Perspective and drag one of the top corner handles far outside the image. The other top handle will move outward also, creating a symmetrical distortion. To accept the scaling and perspective, double-click inside the Free Transform box. Put the clouds layer in Overlay mode so the clouds lighten and darken the sky underneath rather than hide it, and adjust the Opacity to taste (we used 90%).

5 Reflecting the clouds. Duplicate the clouds layer and use Layer, Free Transform (Ctrl-T) with its context-sensitive menu as in step 4, this time choosing Flip Vertical to reflect the clouds. Drag inside the Free Transform box to move the flipped clouds down so they start at the horizon and extend downward. Then drag the bottom center handle down or up until the clouds layer fills the bottom of the image; double-click inside the Free Transform box. The layer's blending mode should be Overlay. Since these clouds are reflections in the water, set the Opacity for this layer lower than for the sky clouds; we used 60%.

5

Clouds reflected in the water by duplicating and then flipping and scaling the copy

6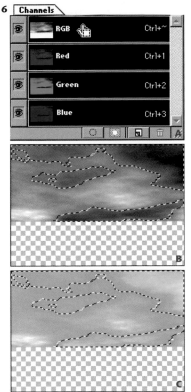

Channels

RGB Ctrl+~
Red Ctrl+1
Green Ctrl+2
Blue Ctrl+3

B

C

Loading the luminosity of the image as a selection (A) and inverting the selection so part of a duplicate sky layer (B) can be filled with color (C)

7a

The finished sunset over water, with saturation adjusted, before adding graphics, type, reflections, and water motion

6 Coloring the clouds. To make the clouds reflect one of the colors of the sunset, start by duplicating the sky cloud layer and flipping it horizontally (press Ctrl-T and then press the right mouse button, choose Flip Horizontal from the context-sensitive menu, and double-click inside the box). Then load the luminosity of this layer as a selection: Alt-click this new layer's eye icon in the Layers palette to turn off visibility for all the other layers. Then open the Channels palette (Window, Show Channels) and Ctrl-click the composite (RGB) channel's name, or press Ctrl-Alt-~. Invert the selection (Ctrl-Shift-I).

Click the Foreground color square at the bottom of the toolbox and choose a color from the Color Picker or Color palette to make it the Foreground color (we used yellow). Fill the selection with the Foreground color by pressing Alt-Backspace. Turn on visibility for the other layers by clicking their eye icons and try some different blending modes — for instance, Screen — for your new color layer. You can further modify the sky by using a feathered lasso to delete parts of the color layer, or intensify the color by duplicating the layer.

7 Adding final touches. To subdue the bright colors, you can add a Hue/Saturation Adjustment layer: With the top layer active, Ctrl-click the New Layer icon. Choose Hue/Saturation for the Type of Adjustment layer and click OK. Experiment with reducing the Saturation and increasing the Lightness setting. With the new Adjustment layer active, you can use a soft airbrush with a low Pressure setting in the Airbrush Options palette with white or black as the Foreground color to paint the layer's mask, so it varies the Hue/Saturation effect on the layers below.

7b

Layers

Normal   Opacity: 100%

☐ Preserve Transparency

G	'G' Wow-afied
G	'G' Dark Halo
GLASS OFF	Type
GLASS OFF	Type Dark Halo
⊗	Type Waved..
	Hue/Saturation
	Top Clouds colored 2
	Top Clouds colored
	Top Clouds
	Reflected Clouds
	Spherized Trimmed
	Gradient

The final layers palette with all layers in place

For our final image, we added type that had been treated with the Wow!-Steel/Brushed/Oiled Action on the CD-ROM that comes with this book. The dark "halo" behind it was made like a drop shadow (see steps 3 and 4 of "Casting a Shadow" in Chapter 8) but without offsetting it. A copy of the graphic was flipped and put into perspective (like the clouds in step 4), and faded with a layer mask (as in step 6 of "Casting a Shadow"). Filter, Distort, Wave and Filter, Blur, Motion Blur were then applied to this "reflected" graphic and to the water area of the bottom layer to make the final image seen at the top of page 163.

Filter Demos

*Overview For any plug-in filter you want to use, first copy it (separately or in a subdirectory with other filters) to **Plugins** in the **Photoshop** directory; start the Photoshop program; open an image; select the area you want to filter (make no selection if you want to filter the entire image); choose Filter and select a filter from the pop-out submenus.*

This 800-pixel-wide image is a layered composite of the original image and a copy treated with Photoshop's native Reticulation filter (Filter, Sketch, Reticulation) in the layer above. The filtered layer was in Overlay mode at 50% Opacity. Above that was a Hue/Saturation Adjustment layer with a mask that allowed the Hue change only at the edges of the image.

IN ADDITION TO PROVIDING PLUG-IN FILTERS with Photoshop, Adobe has made available to other software developers the program code they need to write more filters. The following pages provide a catalog of many of the available filters, showing the effects of applying them to two kinds of images — a photo of a hula doll set off from a natural background by a glow, and a "Wow" graphic with a glow behind it. Some filters are made to work on selections. To show the effect of those plug-ins, we've used a version of the Wow graphic stored in an alpha channel and loaded as a selection in a muted version of a natural background image. Where numerical settings are shown in the captions, they are listed in the order they appear in a filter's dialog box, from upper left to lower right. If the default settings were used, no settings are shown.

Because filter effects require a good deal of calculation, applying a filter can be a time-consuming process. Besides showing you the results of applying the filters themselves, this gallery includes tips for using filters efficiently and effectively.

This is the original image before filters were applied. The image is 408 pixels wide.

For filters that create a special effect on a selected area, this version of the graphic (left) was loaded as a selection on a muted background image (right).

FILTER RERUNS

To reapply the last filter effect you used, press Ctrl-F. To select that filter again but open its dialog box so you can change the settings before you apply the filter, press Ctrl-Alt-F.

REPRODUCING FILTER EFFECTS

The size of an image (in pixels) is important for filters and other transformations whose settings are measured in pixels. That's why image widths are given throughout the book. If you see an effect you want to reproduce, here's how to figure out a setting to try:

[Filter setting we used (in pixels) ÷ Width of our filtered image (in pixels)] x Width of your image (in pixels) = Filter setting you should try (in pixels)

(Unlike filters whose settings are measured in pixels, those filters whose settings are in percentages or degrees will produce similar amounts of change when a setting is used with either a large or a small image.)

Adobe:
Artistic

The Artistic filters are a regrouping of some of the plug-ins from the three volumes of Gallery Effects, formerly sold separately from Photoshop. Most of the other Gallery Effects plug-ins are in the Brush Strokes and Sketch submenus.

A typical Adobe filter interface

Artistic: Colored Pencil

Artistic: Cutout

Artistic: Dry Brush

Artistic: Film Grain

Artistic: Fresco

Artistic: Neon Glow

Artistic: Paint Daubs

Artistic: Palette Knife

Artistic: Plastic Wrap

Artistic: Poster Edges

Artistic: Rough Pastels

Artistic: Smudge Stick

Artistic: Sponge

Artistic: Underpainting

Artistic: Watercolor

NAVIGATING GAUSSIAN BLUR

In the preview window of the Gaussian Blur dialog box (as well as Unsharp Mask and some others), you can scroll by dragging, zoom in by Ctrl-clicking, zoom out by Alt-clicking, or select a particular area of the image by clicking the cursor on the image itself.

Adobe: *Blur*

Two of the Blur filters (Radial Blur and Smart Blur) can produce two or more very different effects.

TESTING A RADIAL BLUR

Use a Quality setting of Draft (quick but rough) to experiment with the Amount and the blur center; then use Good (or on a very large image, Best) for the final effect.

Blur: Blur

Blur: Blur More

Blur: Gaussian Blur (5)

Blur: Motion Blur (45/30)

Blur: Radial Blur (Spin)

Blur: Radial Blur (Zoom)

Blur: Smart Blur

Blur: Smart Blur (Edges Only)

Adobe:
Brush Strokes

The Brush Strokes filters are a regrouping of some of the plug-ins from the three volumes of Gallery Effects, formerly sold separately from Photoshop. The other Gallery Effects plug-ins are in the Artistic and Sketch submenus.

Brush Strokes: Accented Edges

Brush Strokes: Angled Strokes

Brush Strokes: Crosshatch

Brush Strokes: Dark Strokes

Brush Strokes: Ink Outlines

Brush Strokes: Spatter

Brush Strokes: Sprayed Strokes

Brush Strokes: Sumi-e

Adobe: *Distort*

The Distort filters add special effects and textures to an image.

MORE DISPLACEMENT MAPS

When you use Filter, Distort, Displace, you're not limited to the Dispmaps files in **Filters** (inside **Plugins**). Also try out the files in the **textures** subdirectory on the Photoshop 4 CD-ROM.

Distort: Diffuse Glow

Distort: Displace (Honeycomb)

Distort: Displace (Dispmaps: Random)

Distort: Displace (Dispmaps: Streaks)

Distort: Glass (Blocks)

Distort: Glass (Custom texture/lightened)

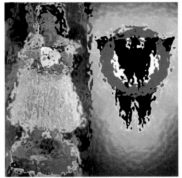

Distort: Ocean Ripple

Distort: Pinch (+100%)

DISPLACEMENT MAPS

Some of the displacement maps Adobe supplies in **Filters** to be used with the Distort, Displace filter produce quite different effects when applied in the Tile mode than when used in Stretch To Fit mode. If you try one of the **Dispmaps** files and get an effect that seems uninteresting, try the other mode — it's likely to be more rewarding.

Distort: Pinch (–100%)

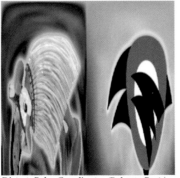

Distort: Polar Coordinates (Polar to Rect.)

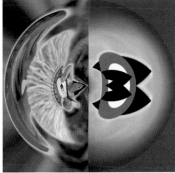

Distort: Polar Coordinates (Rect. to Polar)

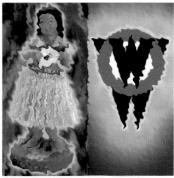

Distort: Ripple

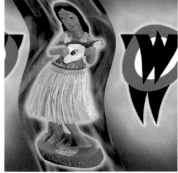

Distort: Shear

Distort: Spherize (+100%)

Distort: Spherize (–100%)

Distort: Twirl

Distort: Wave

FANCY FRAMING

Some of the filters of the Distort submenu, as well as Spatter and Sprayed Strokes from the Brush Strokes submenu, can be used to create a custom edge treatment for an image. Open an image and open the Layers palette (Window, Show Layers). Turn the *Background* layer into a layer with the capacity for transparency by double-clicking its name in the palette and clicking OK. Then double-click the marquee tool in the toolbox to open the Marquee Options palette. Select the Rectangular or Elliptical Shape, and set a Feather amount. Drag to select the part of the image you want to frame. Then click the Add Layer Mask icon at the bottom of the palette to turn the selection into a layer mask. Adding a white-filled layer below the image layer will give you a better look at the frame edges (**A, B**). For a more unusual effect, experiment on the layer mask with filters that will stylize the edge area of the mask, such as Ocean Ripple or Wave from the Distort submenu, or one of the Brush Strokes or Artistic filters, like Underpainting, as shown here (**C, D**).

Distort: Zigzag (Pond Ripples)

Adobe: *Noise*

One of the Noise filters (Add Noise) "roughens" the color in an image, and the other three (Despeckle, Dust & Scratches, and Median) smooth it.

Noise: Add Noise (Gaussian, 50%, Mono)

Noise: Add Noise (Uniform, 50%)

Noise: Despeckle

Noise: Dust & Scratches (4/0)

Noise: Median

Adobe: *Other*

The Other submenu houses an eclectic collection of filters.

REPAINTING THE LINES

Try running the Minimum filter with a low setting to thicken up the lines of scanned, hand-drawn line art, at the same time giving the lines the variable density of painted strokes.

CHER THREINEN-PENDARVIS

Other: High Pass (10)

Other: Maximum (2)

Other: Minimum (2)

Other: Offset

Adobe:
Pixelate

Most of the Pixelate filters turn an image into patterns of spots of flat color. For all but Facet and Fragment, you can control the size of the spots, producing very different effects depending on the size settings.

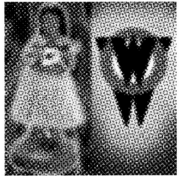

Pixelate: Color Halftone (on CMYK)

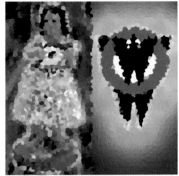

Pixelate: Crystallize

Pixelate: Facet

Pixelate: Fragment

Pixelate: Mezzotint (Coarse Dots)

Pixelate: Mezzotint (Fine Dots)

Pixelate: Mezzotint (Short Lines)

Pixelate: Mezzotint (Short Strokes)

Pixelate: Mosaic

Pixelate: Pointillize (white Background color)

Pixelate: Pointillize (black Background color)

Adobe:
Render

The Render filters create "atmosphere" and surface texture. Two of them, Clouds and Texture Fill, act independently of the color in the image: Clouds creates a sky, and Texture Fill fills a layer or channel with a pattern.

RENDERING A STORM

Holding down the Alt key as you choose Filter, Render, Clouds produces a contrastier, more dramatic cloud pattern.

MAKING MARBLE

The Difference Clouds filter can generate a veined, marble look: In the white-filled Background layer of an RGB file, with black and white as the Foreground and Background colors, choose Filter, Render, Difference Clouds; then press Ctrl-F repeatedly to build the degree of marbling you want. Colorize the marble by adding an Adjustment layer (Ctrl-click the New Layer icon at the bottom of the Layers palette), choose Color Balance as the Type, and adjust the sliders.

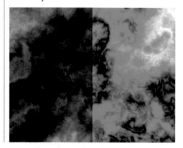

Render: Clouds (with default colors)

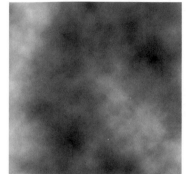

Render: Clouds (with blue Background color)

Render: Difference Clouds

Render: Lens Flare

Render: Lighting Effects

Render: Lighting Effects (Blue Omni)

Render: Lighting Effects (Soft Spotlight)

Render: Lighting Effects (Triple Spotlight)

Render: Lighting Effects (Red channel as Texture)

Render: Lighting Effects (alpha channel as Texture; White Is High on)

Render: Lighting Effects (alpha channel as Texture; White Is High off)

Render: Lighting Effects (Blistered Paint as Texture)

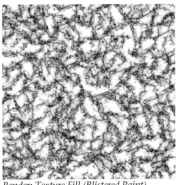

Render: Texture Fill (Blistered Paint)

MULTI-LAYER EFFECTS

There's a way to run a filter, such as Lighting Effects, on several layers of an image without flattening the file or without affecting all layers. Start by making a merged copy of the layers you want to affect: Add a new, empty layer at the top of the stack (click the New Layer icon at the bottom of the Layers palette); turn on the eye icon for this layer and the ones you want to filter; hold down the Alt key and choose Merge Visible from the Layers palette's pop-out menu. Now experiment with filtering this merged copy, noting the filter settings, until you arrive at the filter settings you want. Then turn off visibility for this merged layer and apply the filter to the individual layers using the filter setting you chose. When you're happy with the result, you can discard the merged layer by clicking its name to activate it and Alt-clicking the trash can icon at the bottom of the palette.

USING TEXTURE FILLS WITH LIGHTING EFFECTS

Photoshop's **textures** subdirectory in the **goodies** subdirectory (from the Photoshop CD-ROM) holds files designed to make seamlessly repeating patterns when used with the Texture Fill filter. Here's how to use one of these textures as a "bump map" for creating surface relief for the Lighting Effects filter's light to act on: Open the Channels palette for the image you want to run Lighting Effects on (Window, Show Channels), and click the New Channel icon at the bottom of the palette to make an alpha channel. With this channel active, choose Filter, Render, Texture Fill; choose a texture from the **textures** subdirectory; click the Open button to fill the alpha channel with texture. Then click the RGB channel's name to make it active, and choose Filter, Render, Lighting Effects, picking your texture-filled alpha channel as the Texture Channel in the Lighting Effects dialog box.

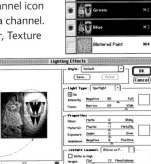

Adobe: Sharpen

Although there are four Sharpen filters, the one you'll use most is Unsharp Mask, because you can control the effect (see the "Sharpen" section at the beginning of this chapter for tips on using Unsharp Mask).

Sharpen: Sharpen

Sharpen: Sharpen Edges

Sharpen: Sharpen More

Sharpen: Unsharp Mask (100/1/0)

Sharpen: Unsharp Mask (500/5/0)

Adobe: Sketch

The Sketch filters are a regrouping of some of the plug-ins from the three volumes of Gallery Effects, formerly sold separately from Photoshop. Most of the other Gallery Effects plug-ins are in the Artistic and Brush Strokes submenus.

Sketch: Bas Relief

Sketch: Chalk & Charcoal

Sketch: Charcoal

Sketch: Chrome

Sketch: Conté Crayon

Sketch: Graphic Pen

Sketch: Halftone Pattern (Dot)

Sketch: Halftone Pattern (Line)

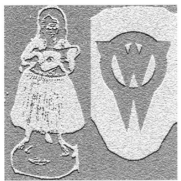

Sketch: Note Paper

Sketch: Photocopy

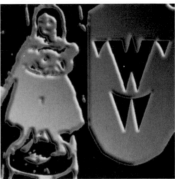

Sketch: Plaster

Sketch: Reticulation

Sketch: Stamp

Sketch: Torn Edges

Sketch: Water Paper

COMPOSITING WITH SKETCH FILTERS

Some of the Sketch filters are ideal for making filtered layers that can then be composited with the original image. Here we've layered an image filtered with Reticulation over the original, reduced its Opacity, and used the Color Dodge blending mode to lighten and brighten the pixels under the white parts of the filtered layer, creating a glowing effect.

Adobe:
Stylize

The Stylize filters are a diverse collection of special effects. Glowing Edges, from the former Gallery Effects 2 collection, complements the original Adobe edging filters, Find Edges and Trace Contour.

Stylize: Diffuse

Stylize: Emboss

Stylize: Extrude (Blocks)

Stylize: Extrude (Pyramids)

Stylize: Find Edges

Stylize: Glowing Edges

Stylize: Solarize

"SOFTENING" A FILTER

If you run a filter and the result seems too strong, you can choose Filter, Fade Filter and use the Opacity slider in the Fade dialog box to "soften" the effect. With Fade you can also control the blending mode of the filtered image. (Since Fade only works immediately after you apply a filter, the change becomes permanent once you do any other work on the image. For more flexibility later, use this approach instead: Copy your original image to a new layer by dragging its name to the New Layer icon at the bottom of the Layers palette. Apply the filter to this layer and use the layer's Opacity and blending mode controls.)

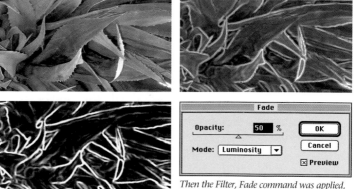

The original photo (top) was filtered with Stylize, Glowing Edges

Then the Filter, Fade command was applied, treating the Glowing Edges version like a top layer, reducing its Opacity and compositing it in Luminosity mode.

Stylize: Tiles

Stylize: Trace Contour

To get the look of hand-painted tiles, start by running the Stylize, Tiles filter on the image. (For a mosaic look with each tile a single color, try the Texture, Stained Glass filter.) Next create an alpha channel (click the New Channel icon at the bottom of the Channels palette), repeat the filter on this channel (Ctrl-F), and blur slightly (Filter, Blur, Gaussian Blur). Working in the RGB composite channel again (Ctrl-~ activates the composite), choose Render, Lighting Effects and set up a Directional light source; if the grout in the alpha channel is white, turn off White Is High.

Filtered and blurred alpha channel   *Tiles and Lighting Effects applied*

Stylize: Wind (Stagger)

Stylize: Wind (Wind)

Adobe: *Texture*

Most of the Texture filters create the illusion that the image has been applied to an uneven surface. But Stained Glass remakes the image into polygons, each filled with a single color.

Texture: Craquelure

Texture: Grain

If you load an image as the Texture in the Texturizer dialog box, the preview box may not show the result. To update the preview, change the Scaling setting.

Texture: Grain (Clumped)

Texture: Grain (Enlarged)

Texture: Grain (Speckle)

Texture: Grain (Vertical)

Texture: Mosaic Tiles

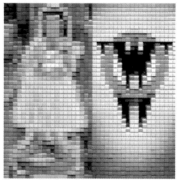
Texture: Patchwork

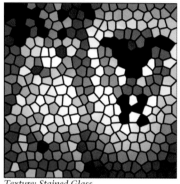
Texture: Stained Glass

Texture: Texturizer (Brick)

Texture: Texturizer (Canvas)

TRYING OUT TEXTURIZER

Choosing Texture, Texturizer brings up the Texturizer dialog box, which is sort of like a mini version of the Lighting Effects filter. Texturizer doesn't have Lighting Effects' flexibility in setting the type of light source; all its lighting is directional. And it doesn't let you add extra lights or define surface characteristics like shininess. But it's easier to operate, it does let you use images in Photoshop file format as the texture pattern for embossing, and it lets you scale the pattern down to 50% or up to 200% so you can control how many times it repeats. To get a smaller pattern with more repetitions, start with a texture file that's smaller in relation to your background image. To get a rounder edge, apply a slight Gaussian Blur to the texture file before you run the Texturizer filter.

For the image at the left the Photoshop file used as a texture was scaled to 100%, so it kept its original size relationship to the background image. For the version in the center, it was scaled to 50%. For the image at the right, the texture file was given a slight Gaussian Blur before the filter was applied, which resulted in smoother embossing.

Texture: Texturizer (Load Texture: **Weave7**)

Andromeda: Series 1

Andromeda Software's Photography Filters provide special effects similar to those you can achieve with specialized lenses for a 35mm camera. The filters are listed in the Andromeda submenu in the Filter menu.

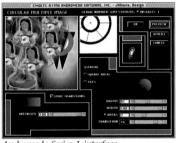

Andromeda Series 1 interface

cMulti

Designs

Diffract

Halo

Prism

Rainbow

Reflection

sMulti

Star

Velocity

Andromeda: Series 2

Andromeda Software's 3D Filter allows three-dimensional surface mapping in Photoshop. The filter appears under the Andromeda submenu in the Filter menu.

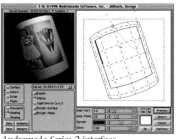

Andromeda Series 2 interface

3-D (Cube, Tile, Wrap Corner)

3-D (Cylinder)

3-D (Plane)

3-D (Sphere, Tile)

Andromeda: Series 3

Andromeda Software's Screens Filter provides preset Mezzotint treatments for screening images, as well as an interface that lets you choose your own settings and preview several settings at once.

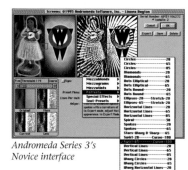

Andromeda Series 3's Novice interface

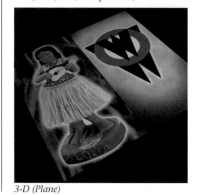

Screens: Patterns (Circles, 65 lpi)

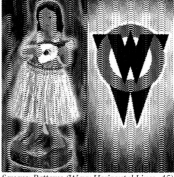

Screens: Patterns (Wavy Horizontal Lines, 45)

Screens: Patterns (Circles) on a Grayscale version of the image

Screens: Mezzoblends (Mezzoblend Lines Wavy Sharp)

Screens: Mezzograms (Mezzogram 45)

Screens: Mezzograms (Mezzogram 65)

Clicking the Expert button while in the Novice mode interface (shown on the previous page) puts the Andromeda Series 3 filter in Expert mode. There you can change any of the parameters for the filter's presets, customize your own Screens settings, or even create new presets, which can then be saved in Novice mode.

Andromeda Series 3's Expert interface

Screens: Special Effects (Intaglio, Woodblock)

Screens: Special Effects (Fabric, Well…,Velvet!)

In addition to Series 1, 2, 3, and 4 filters, Andromeda Software also offers the Velociraptor plug-in, which makes livens up images by creating customizable motion trails. Among the kinds of trails you can add are arcs, bounces, cascades, loops, spirals, springs, and waves.

Screens: Mezzotints (Mezzotint 45)

Screens: Mezzotints (Mezzotint 100)

The Velociraptor interface

Screens: Mezzotints (Mezzotint 65)

Screens: Mezzotints (Mezzotint 65) on a Grayscale version of the image

Andromeda: Series 4

Andromeda Software's Techtures filter comes with a library of 900 hand-rendered textures that can be overlaid on, blended with, or embossed into an image. Also included are Environment patterns and Displacement Maps. Examples shown here are blended, except Polished Stone, which is overlaid.

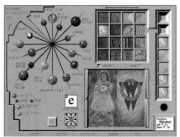

Andromeda Series 4 interface

Techtures: Textures (Bold pattern)

Techtures: Textures (Coarse)

Techtures: Textures (Decay)

Techtures: Textures (Foliage)

Techtures: Textures (Masonry)

Techtures: Textures (Polished stone)

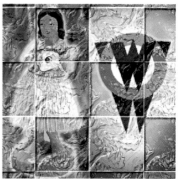

Techtures: Textures (Tiles)

Techtures: Textures (Wood)

Techtures: Environments (Smoke)

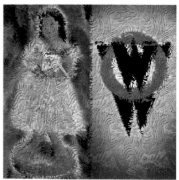

Techtures: Maps (Life)

Auto F/X:
Photo/Graphic & Typo/Graphic Edges

Photo/Graphic Edges consists of three volumes (Traditional, Geometric, and Artistic) of hundreds of edge treatments for rectangular, nontransparent images. The 460 Typo/Graphic Edges effects are designed for type or graphics on transparent layers.

Photo/Graphic Edges interface

Auto F/X: Photo/Graphic Edges (Artistic 22)

Auto F/X: Photo/Graphic Edges (Artistic 243)

Auto F/X: Photo/Graphic Edges (Geometric 98)

Auto F/X: Photo/Graphic Edges (Geometric 152)

Auto F/X: Photo/Graphic Edges (Tradit. 307)

Auto F/X: Photo/Graphic Edges (Tradit. 124)

Typo/Graphic Edges

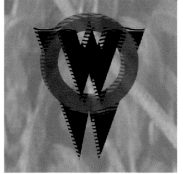

Typo/Graphic Edges

OUTSETS AND INSETS

Each Auto F/X Photo/Graphic Edges package consists of a plug-in and source files. You use the plug-in by picking out an edge treatment from the samples printed in the manual, noting its number, and then choosing Filter, Auto F/X, Photo/Graphic Edges and loading the effect from the CD-ROM. Edges are applied as Outsets (the edge shape acts like a cookie cutter scaled to fit the image) and then can be reapplied as Insets (or a different edge can be Inset) to create a black or colored border whose width can be varied with a slider.

Outset edge applied

Inset edge added

PHOTO: PHOTODISC, EVERYDAY PEOPLE

Alien Skin:
Eye Candy

Many of the special effects filters that make up the Eye Candy 3.0 set have ten or more presets (we've shown only one here). All presets can be customized — for color, lighting angle, opacity, relative strength of highlight or shadow, or other qualities. And you can name and save your own settings. (Eye Candy was formerly known as The Black Box.)

Eye Candy interface

Eye Candy 3.0: Antimatter

Eye Candy 3.0: Carve (Chisel)

Eye Candy 3.0: Carve (Soft light outline)

Eye Candy 3.0: Chrome (Gold)

Eye Candy 3.0: Cutout (Typical)

Eye Candy 3.0: Drop Shadow (Soft)

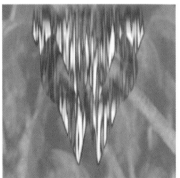

Eye Candy 3.0: Fire (Burning inside)

Eye Candy 3.0: Fur (Well defined strands)

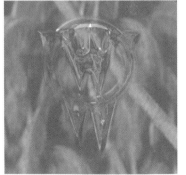

Eye Candy 3.0: Glass (Strong distortion)

Eye Candy 3.0: Glow (Red glow)

Eye Candy 3.0: HSB Noise (Cells)

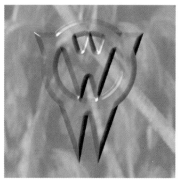

Eye Candy 3.0: Inner Bevel (Button)

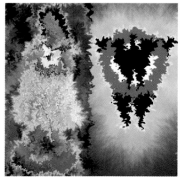

Eye Candy 3.0: Jiggle (Twisty)

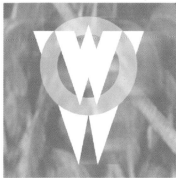

Eye Candy 3.0: Motion Trail (Moving left)

Eye Candy 3.0: Outer Bevel (Dull)

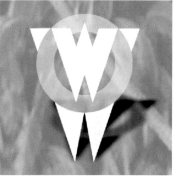

Eye Candy 3.0: Perspective Shadow (Classic)

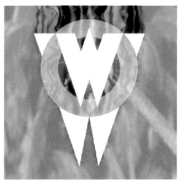

Eye Candy 3.0: Smoke (Typical)

Eye Candy 3.0: Squint (Beer goggles)

Eye Candy 3.0: Star (Sea urchin)

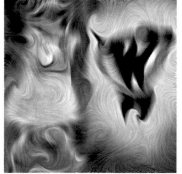

Eye Candy 3.0: Swirl (Typical)

Eye Candy 3.0: Water Drops (Typical)

Eye Candy 3.0: Weave (Typical)

MetaCreations: *Kai's Power Tools*

The 19 filters in Kai's Power Tools (KPT 3.0) provide special effects for print and on-screen images. For the "f/x" filters, intensity of the effect and opacity (like that in Photoshop's Fade command) are set on a curved sliding scale. The interfaces for these and other filters allow real-time interaction. "Help" buttons provide directions.

KPT Lens f/x interface

KPT Gradient Designer interface

KPT Interform interface

KPT 3.0: KPT 3D Stereo Noise

KPT 3.0: KPT Gaussian f/x

KPT 3.0: KPT Gradient Designer

KPT 3.0: KPT Interform

KPT 3.0: KPT Edge f/x

KPT 3.0: KPT Glass Lens

KPT 3.0: KPT Intensify f/x

KPT 3.0: KPT Noise f/x

KPT 3.0: KPT Page Curl

KPT 3.0: KPT Planar Tile

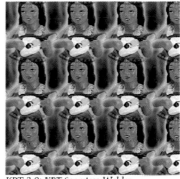

KPT 3.0: KPT Seamless Welder

F/X FUN

Another, separate plug-in from MetaCreations, **KPT Convolver**, offers Explore and Design modes for both random and directed experimentation. Tweak mode offers separate control over all the factors that contribute to a particular effect. The interface is gamelike, with stars for good behavior. Settings can be saved as named presets.

KPT 3.0: KPT Smudge f/x

KPT 3.0: KPT Spheroid Designer

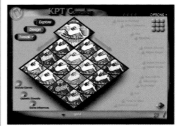

KPT Convolver interface

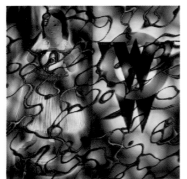

KPT 3.0: KPT Texture Explorer

KPT 3.0: KPT Twirl

KPT 3.0: KPT Video Feedback

KPT 3.0: KPT Vortex Tiling

Frank Vitale used Strata StudioPro in conjunction with Photoshop to create *The Garden* for a promotional poster for Strata, Inc. All of the design and construction of a wasp was done in StudioPro, and the texture maps for coloring it were made in Photoshop. Vitale used screen captures of the model as guides for designing the texture maps to fit the model.

After the texture maps were applied in the 3D program, the wasp was positioned, the lights were placed, and the wasp images were rendered, the bodies separately from the wings. The wings were rendered twice for each body rendering, in two different "strobe-captured" positions in the motion of flight. Then the renderings were opened in Photoshop. Each pair of wings was dragged into the composite Photoshop file on its own layer so that Opacity could be controlled separately for each pair.

With a body layer and two wing layers in place, Vitale went to work with various Blur filters. The wing blurs were accomplished by generating noise (Filter, Noise, Add Noise), selecting and copying two narrow horizontal bands of the noise pattern — one for each wing — onto a transparent layer, deselecting, and spinning the band (Filter, Blur, Radial Blur, Spin). Stacking and merging several layers of this "spun noise" and changing the opacity produced a convincing illusion of motion for the top and bottom parts of the wing blur.

To blur parts of the body, Vitale started by duplicating the wasp as a new layer (drag the layer's name to the New Layer icon at the bottom of the Layers palette) and making feathered selections of various body parts — especially extremities like the ends of the antennas and the legs where the motion would be greatest. He applied a blur in what he saw as the direction of motion for each selected part (Filter, Blur, Motion Blur).

To control the blur even more precisely, he added a mask to the upper (sharp) body layer, which he hand-painted with a soft brush and black paint. He used a Wacom tablet to control the opacity of the paint, selectively "painting away" the areas of the sharp image where he wanted the blur to show through.

To ensure that the wing blurs didn't interfere with the motion blur on the legs, Vitale "knocked out" the wing blur in those areas. He activated the lower wing blur layer, Ctrl-clicked on the blurred body layer's name in the Layers palette to load its transparency mask as a selection, and pressed Backspace to cut away that area of the wing blur.

Vitale saved the motion effects on transparent layers so that he could maintain control of the opacity of the separate components when he dropped the wasps onto any background he chose. In *The Garden,* the Gaussian blur applied to the background photo works with the lighting on the wasps to create the illusion of depth.

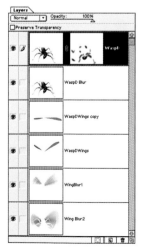

Max Seabaugh drew *Balthus Woman* in Adobe Illustrator, creating the shading on the face and highlights in the hair with blends. To add warmth and texture to the image, he rasterized it (turned it from vector objects into pixels) by opening it in Photoshop. To add texture, he chose Filter, Noise, Add Noise, Gaussian (left). With the artist's permission, we've tried four more choices from the Filter menu on Seabaugh's rasterized artwork (above). Clockwise from top left they are Texture, Texturizer with the Canvas setting; Render, Lighting Effects set for Soft Omnidirectional light; Render, Difference Clouds; and Sketch, Photocopy with Detail set at 8 and Darkness set at 11.

Diane Fenster started with a still-video image to create *Rena Sketch*. She duplicated the image as another layer (drag its name to the New Layer icon at the bottom of the Layers palette). Working on the original image, she chose from the Filter menu (Filter, Stylize, Find Edges). To blend the two versions together, she changed the blending mode of the top layer to Color.

Jack Davis designed *New York Lady* for client Thunder Lizard Productions as a possible cover illustration for a New York Photoshop conference brochure. First he made sketches and Photoshop low-resolution comps, and then he located the three images he wanted to use. Starting with the bottom layer of the montage, he bumped up the sky's saturation. ▶*Using an Adjustment layer (for Hue/Saturation, Levels, Curves, and Color Balance, for instance) allows you to go back later and change image adjustment settings. Ctrl-clicking on the New Layer icon adds an Adjustment layer above the currently active layer.*

Davis next used the pen tool to make a path around the lady of liberty, turning the path into a selection and dragging and dropping the statue image to make a new layer in the sky document. He used the pen tool again to select the statue's face, and he cut that part to a new layer. ▶*Ctrl-Shift-J turns the current selection into a new layer, leaving a hole; Ctrl-J turns a copy of the current selection into a new layer, leaving the original intact.*

To create the illusion of the statue's thickness, Davis added a very simple bevel effect to the edges. On the statue layer he made a rough selection of the left and bottom edges of the opening for the face, copied the selection as a new layer (Ctrl-J), dragged this layer below the original, used the move tool and arrow keys to offset the copy slightly to the right and up, and then used Image, Adjust, Levels to lighten or darken selected areas of the exposed bevel.

The main challenge with the woman's face was finding a photo taken from the right view, from below but with the eyes making contact. Davis cropped, scaled, rotated, and colored the image to fit the final collage, dragged and dropped it into a new layer in the collage file, and moved that layer below the statue layer. The shadows cast on and below her face were made with Levels adjustments to feathered selections.

After roughly selecting the areas of the sky around the statue's crown spikes with a feathered lasso, Davis lightened them with Levels. When he was happy with the result, he flattened all the layers into one by choosing Flatten Image from the Layers palette's pop-out menu. Then he duplicated this single layer by dragging its name to the New Layer icon at the bottom of the palette. He chose Filter, Sketch, Reticulation, which applied a grayscale mezzotintlike effect to the layer. With this layer above and the original color image below, he set the blending mode for the upper layer to Multiply and adjusted its Opacity.

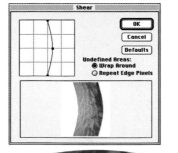

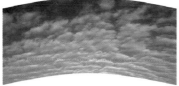

Photoshop's Shear filter played a small but important role in the composition of **Mark Siprut**'s *Tourist Taxi*. After assembling a panoramic background of the city of Istanbul from six photos layered and rotated into a pleasing montage, Siprut wanted to liven up and extend the sky and to make it match the rounded effect he had created in the cityscape. He used the polygon lasso to select the sky so he could delete it.

Next he prepared a new, deeper sky photo with clouds. Since the Shear filter can only bend a selected area of an image sideways — not up or down — Siprut rotated the sky image clockwise to a vertical position (Image, Rotate Canvas, 90° CW). To make room for the bend, he added white space at the sides of the now vertical sky (Image, Canvas Size). He chose Filter, Distort, Shear, dragged on the graph in the Shear box to get the rounding he needed, and clicked OK. Then he rotated the image to a horizontal position again.

After layering the new sky behind the cityscape and flattening the file, Siprut added the silhouetted taxi and ruins images — first the ruins, then the taxi, then a partial copy of the ruins, so the taxi

seemed to be inside the arch. Siprut linked the two layers of the arch together (by activating one of them and clicking in the column next to the eye icon in the other), so that if he needed to move one part of the arch, the other part would move along with it. To help focus attention on the taxi, he reduced saturation in the right side of the top ruins image and in the cityscape.

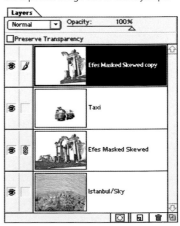

PAINTING

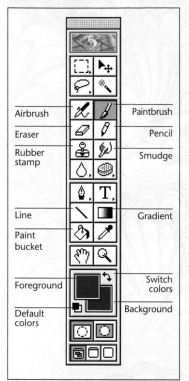

In addition to the tools in the palette, the Fill and Stroke commands from the Edit menu are part of Photoshop's painting kit.

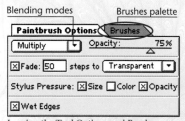

Leaving the Tool Options and Brushes palettes nested together makes it easy to display the current set of brushes by clicking on the Brushes tab.

AS THE ARTWORK IN THIS CHAPTER SHOWS, Photoshop painters have extended their toolkits beyond the brushes and pencil, to use the editing tools, alpha channel "friskets," layers, and many of the program's color controls and layer options. But if we define painting tools as those that can apply Foreground color, Background color, Transparency, or pixels from an image, Photoshop's painting tools include the paint bucket, gradient, line, eraser, pencil, airbrush, paintbrush, rubber stamp, and smudge. All of these tools (except the gradient and line, which must be dragged) can be operated either by selecting the tool and then clicking to make a single "footprint" on the canvas, or by holding down the mouse button or stylus and dragging to make a stroke. Most of these tools can also be constrained to a straight line by holding down the Shift key and clicking from point to point or dragging. (The line and gradient tools, which always paint in a straight line, are constrained to 45° and 90° angles when the Shift key is used.) Each of the tools has its own set of controls, found in a Tool Options palette that appears when you double-click the icon in the toolbox. Tool "footprints" are chosen from the Brushes palette, which by default is nested with the Tool Options palette so you can open it by clicking on the Brushes tab.

PAINTING TOOL OPTIONS

Here's a list of the painting characteristics that can be controlled through the **Tool Options** palette (the options for the rubber stamp and gradient tool, which are more like toolkits than single tools, are covered on pages 199 through 202).

Antialiasing: For the paint bucket and line tool; the airbrush, paintbrush, rubber stamp, and smudge tools are always smooth-edged (antialiased) except in Bitmap or Indexed Color mode; the pencil tool is not; for the gradient tool, antialiasing depends on the selection into which the gradient is applied. Antialiasing cannot be set for the eraser tool. In its Paintbrush and Airbrush modes it's antialiased; in Block and Pencil modes it isn't.

Arrowheads: For the line tool only, you can put a custom arrowhead on the beginning or end of a stroke, or at both ends.

Auto Erase: For the pencil tool, if you start a stroke on an area of the image that is currently the Foreground color, the stroke is made

continued on page 196

Custom arrowheads can be automatically applied to lines drawn with the line tool. Click the Shape button in the Line Tool Options palette and set the Width and Length (as percentages of the line weight) and Concavity. A negative Concavity setting stretches the base of the arrowhead away from the tip, as in the two arrows above on the right. The arrow on the far left was made by clicking with the line tool to place the starting arrowhead and then dragging toward the tip rather than away from it.

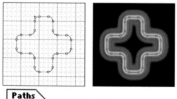

Painting with the paintbrush with Wet Edges, using no Fade setting (top), with Fade To Transparent in 25 steps (center), and with Fade To Background in 25 steps (bottom)

If you choose View, Show Grid and Snap To Grid, you can make the painting tools follow the grid lines as you paint. But you can give yourself more options in your painting if you make a path first, snapping points and handles to the Grid points to draw symmetrical shapes. Then selecting the path in the Paths palette and choosing a painting tool and pressing the Enter key strokes the path. And you can restroke with different tools, brush sizes, and colors to layer the paint, as we did here.

in the Background color; if you start the stroke on a pixel of any other color, the stroke is made in the Foreground color as usual.

Blending Mode: This pop-up list at the upper left of the Tool Options palette controls the interaction of the paint with the current colors of the pixels in the image. All the modes available in the Layers palette (see Chapter 2) and in the Calculations and Apply Image dialog boxes are also available in Tool Options. In addition, in **Behind** mode, only the transparent areas of a layer will accept color; the effect is like painting a background behind any already colored pixels in the layer. **Clear** mode is like painting with paint remover. This mode is available for the paint bucket and line tool (the two painting tools that don't have an equivalent in the eraser tool) and for the Fill and Stroke commands from the Edit menu, and only in layers with transparency.

Erase Image: For the eraser, a one-click way to erase an entire layer.

Erase To Saved: For the eraser, restores the last saved version.

Fade: For the airbrush, paintbrush, eraser, and pencil, strokes fade from the Foreground color to the Background color or to nothing (Transparent); the Steps setting affects the total distance from the beginning of the stroke (at full-strength Foreground color) to the point where the background color is full-strength or the paint is completely transparent. The eraser tool's fade-out (available in Airbrush, Paintbrush, or Pencil mode, but not in Block mode) is always from the Background color (or from Transparency for a transparent layer) to the existing image on that layer.

Finger Painting: For the smudge tool only, which normally just smears existing paint, this option instead applies the Foreground color at the start of the smear.

Opacity: For the paint bucket, gradient tool, line, pencil, paintbrush, and rubber stamp (as well as the eraser in Paintbrush or Pencil mode), opacity of the applied paint can be varied from 1% to 100% by means of the Opacity slider, operated by dragging with the pointer. Or press the number keys on the keyboard to change the Opacity setting in 10% increments; the "1" key sets Opacity at 10%, the "2" key at 20%, and so on, with "0" producing 100%. If your fingers are quick, you can be even more precise, typing in two-digit opacities such as 33% or 75%.

Pattern: For the paint bucket, which can fill an area with the currently defined pattern; and the rubber stamp, which can paint

To make a repeating pattern, you can use the rectangular marquee to select an area of an image or an object, and choose Edit, Define Pattern. Now you can fill all or a selected part of an image file with your pattern. You can stop there or set the pattern up so the elements in alternate rows are offset, like the prints typically used for wrapping paper or fabric: Fill an image file with your pattern, then select one column of the pattern and use Filter, Other, Offset filter (with Undefined Areas set to Wrap Around) to shift it vertically by half the height of your original pattern element. Use the rectangular marquee to select this column and the one next to it, and choose Edit, Define Pattern again.

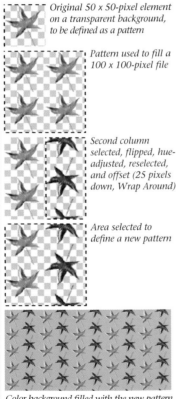

Original 50 x 50-pixel element on a transparent background, to be defined as a pattern

Pattern used to fill a 100 x 100-pixel file

Second column selected, flipped, hue-adjusted, reselected, and offset (25 pixels down, Wrap Around)

Area selected to define a new pattern

Color background filled with the new pattern

(To learn how to make nongeometric patterns to use as textures, see "Creating Textures" on page 159 and "Creating a Canvas Texture" on page 212.)

with the currently defined pattern, either Aligned (painting as if the pattern filled the area behind the image and the rubber stamp was erasing to it) or Non-aligned (starting a new application of the pattern from the same pattern area each time the mouse button is pressed to start a new stroke).

Pressure: For the smudge and airbrush tools (and the eraser in Airbrush mode), this slider, which replaces Opacity in the Tool Options palette, regulates how much paint the airbrush applies in a given time, or how long a smear is produced by the smudge tool, rather than controlling the opacity of entire strokes.

Sample Merged: For the paint bucket, rubber stamp, or smudge tool, the color (to be filled, cloned, or smeared, respectively) is selected as if all visible layers were merged. When Sample Merged is turned off, only the active layer is sampled, cloned, or smeared.

Stylus Pressure: For the airbrush, smudge, paintbrush, pencil, and rubber stamp (as well as the eraser in all its modes except Block), you can set the characteristic that will vary when pressure is applied to the stylus of a pressure-sensitive tablet; characteristics that can be varied, depending on the tool, are Size, Opacity, Color, and Pressure.

Wet Edges: For the paintbrush (and the eraser in Paintbrush mode), color builds up along the edges of the stroke while leaving the center semitransparent as it can with traditional watercolors.

Width: For the line tool, set in terms of the number of pixels. Because line width is set in the Line Tool Options palette, the brush footprint chosen in the Brushes palette has no effect on the line tool.

THE BRUSHES PALETTE

The Brushes palette, which can be opened by choosing Window, Show Brushes or by pressing the default keyboard shortcut F5, makes available all the brushes that come with Photoshop — don't miss the ones in Photoshop's Goodies folder — and also lets you define your own, up to 999 x 999 pixels in size.

- You can **edit one of Photoshop's standard brushes** by double-clicking it in the palette or by clicking it and choosing Brush Options from the pop-out menu.

- If you want to **add a new brush based on one of Photoshop's default brushes** but preserve the existing one as well, click the existing brush to choose it and then click in the

- To fill a selection with the **Foreground** color, press **Alt-Backspace**.

- To fill with the **Background** color, press **Ctrl-Backspace**.

- Pressing the **Backspace** key by itself fills with **transparency on a transparent layer** or with the **Background color on the *Background* layer**.

- To fill with the Foreground or Background color as if **Preserve Transparency** were tuned on, add the Shift key — that is, press **Shift-Alt-Backspace** or **Shift-Ctrl-Backspace**.

To get the look of felt-tip markers, use the paintbrush with Wet Edges chosen in the Paintbrush Options palette. To get the look of a highlighter, use the paintbrush with Wet Edges in Multiply mode.

CYCLING THROUGH BRUSHES

When you're painting, clicking on the Brushes palette to choose a new brush tip can interrupt your work flow. Instead, use the opening bracket key ([ ) to move to the left and up in the palette, and use the closing bracket ( ]) to move down and right. **Shift-[** chooses the first brush in the palette; **Shift-]** chooses the last.

MEDIUM BRUSHES

Half of Photoshop's default brushes have a Hardness of 100%, the other half, 0%. In **goodies\brushes** on the CD-ROM that comes with this book you'll find a set of brushes that includes Photoshop's default set plus six brushes at 50% Hardness. You can substitute this set for the default set by choosing Replace Brushes from the Brushes palette's pop-out menu.

space at the bottom of the Brushes palette after the last brush, or choose New Brush from the palette's pop-out menu. Then specify characteristics in the New Brush dialog box. (Once you've made a new brush based on one of the default set, you can use the new one as a start for others in the same way.)

- To **add a custom brush shape,** construct your brush's foot-print (see "Brush-Making Tips," below, for ideas) or rasterize a shape made in Adobe Illustrator (File, Place) or choose an area of an existing image. Then surround the new footprint with the rectangular marquee and choose Define Brush from the palette's pop-out menu.

- You can also **delete** brushes from the palette one by one by Ctrl-clicking on the ones you want to remove.

- You can name and **save** a particular palette of brushes (choose Save Brushes), **load** a palette you've previously saved instead of the current set of brushes (choose Replace Brushes), or **add** a set of brushes to the current one (choose Append Brushes).

BRUSH-MAKING TIPS

Here are some pointers for making brush tips for Photoshop's painting tools:

- Instead of starting from scratch to design your brush, you can let the Brushes palette do some of the work for you. For example, select a large brush (at least 100-pixel) in the Brushes palette, then click once in the empty area at the bottom of the palette to bring up the New Brush dialog box. Adjust the angle or the roundness if you like, and click OK. Then choose black for the Foreground color, and click the customized brush once in the working win-dow to make a "footprint." Now use a smaller brush to edit the mark's edges. Finally, select the mark with the rectangular marquee and choose Define Brush from the Brushes palette's pop-out menu to add the edited brush to the palette.

- If you notice that a brush you've defined produces a stroke with ragged sides, try decreasing the Spacing setting in the Brush Options dialog box. The tighter you make the spacing, the more slowly the brush will react. But if you experiment with different settings (try the 10–15% range), you can get a smooth, continuous stroke without too much speed loss.

- Once you've defined a custom brush or two, be sure to save them in a cus-tom Brushes palette by choosing Save Brushes from the Brushes Palette's pop-out menu. If you simply add them to the default palette, they'll be lost if you forget and choose Reset Brushes from the pop-out menu.

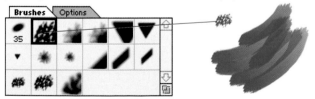

Authors' note: Thanks to Cher Threinen-Pendarvis, author of The Painter 4 Wow! Book *and* The Painter 5 Wow! Book, *for sharing her expertise as the source of this tip. The brushes shown here can be found in* **goodies\brushes** *on the CD-ROM that comes with this book.*

Starting with the original photo (A), the rubber stamp was used in Clone (Aligned) mode to add an alcove (B), then in Clone (Non-aligned) mode to add vegetation (C).

THE RUBBER STAMP

Photoshop's rubber stamp is a combination cloning, restoration, and special effects tool, making it possible to apply existing image information in a brush stroke.

- The tool's two **Clone** options (Aligned and Non-aligned) paint with a portion of a sampled image. The source area is chosen by holding down the Alt key and clicking. Samples can be taken from any open image, from a single layer or from all layers, as if they were merged (see "Sample Merged" on page 197). Once the sample has been collected, you drag the tool to apply the clone of the sampled image. In **Non-aligned** mode, each time you start a stroke, the clone starts over at the sampled point, so you can end up with many copies of the sampled area. In **Aligned** mode, only one version of the clone can be produced, no matter how many stokes are applied; with enough painting, the entire sampled image can be reproduced.

- The **From Saved** option restores the last saved version of the file in the areas you stroke.

- **From Snapshot** restores the version of the file (or a selected part) that was temporarily stored by choosing Edit, Take Snapshot (to store the active layer only) or Edit, Take Merged Snapshot (to store a composite of all visible layers).

- **Impressionist** mode produces an Impressionist (though somewhat smeared) rendition based on the last saved version of the file; Impressionist is a kind of "painterly filter in a brush."

THE GRADIENT TOOL

Double-clicking Photoshop's gradient tool opens a dialog box that lets you accomplish some amazing color-transition effects. The gradient tool in Photoshop 4 is much more powerful than in previous versions. You still have a choice of Linear or Radial gradients, but you can now also regulate the rate at which the color changes. You can make your own multicolor gradients or edit the extensive set that comes with the program, incorporating transparency if you like. (Page 202 shows samples of the gradients included on the Photoshop 4 CD-ROM, as well as a few of the gradients on the Wow! CD-ROM that comes with this book.)

Using the Gradient Editor

Click the Gradient Tool Options palette's Edit button to open the Gradient Editor dialog box, where you can:

- **Modify an existing gradient** by choosing the gradient's name from the scrolling list (the process of making specific changes is described on the next page).

- **Start a new gradient based on an existing one** by choosing a gradient's name, and clicking the Duplicate button. If the

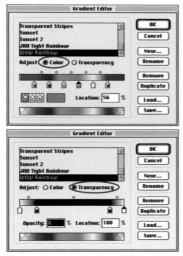

The Gradient Editor set for choosing colors (top) and assigning transparency (bottom). Diamonds indicate the midpoint of a color or transparency transition.

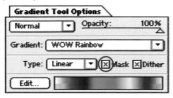
Load, Duplicate, and New buttons are dimmed, it's because the gradient list is full (it holds 75 gradients). To make space you can remove one or more gradients by selecting (or Shift-selecting) from the list and clicking the Remove button.

- **Start a brand-new gradient** by clicking the palette's Edit button and clicking New in the Gradient Color dialog box.

Building a Gradient

Each of the little **house-shaped icons** under the gradient bar represents a color specified in the gradient, with the starting color at the left end and the ending color at the right. The **diamonds** above the gradient bar represent the midpoints in the transition between each pair of colors, the point where the color is an equal mix of the two.

- **Change a color** by clicking its icon and then clicking the "F" or "B" icon to set it to the Foreground or Background color. Or click the color swatch to open the Color Picker so you can choose a color. Or click in the gradient bar, in any open file, or in the Color palette to sample a color.

- **Reposition a color** by dragging it to a new position along the bar or by typing a percentage of the bar length into the Location field.

- **Add a color** by clicking below the gradient bar.

- **Remove a color** by dragging its icon down, away from the bar.

- **Change the rate of color transition** by dragging the midpoint diamond toward one of its two colors.

- **To add transparency** to the gradient, change the Adjust setting in the Gradient Editor dialog box to Transparency. The transparency icons are added, moved, and deleted the same way as the color icons, and the midpoints are set the same way.

- **Change a transparency** by clicking its icon and entering an Opacity setting.

- The Save button lets you name and **save a set of gradients** for loading later.

A Transparent To Foreground gradient can make an image disappear into the mist. Starting with a dawn image (top), we set white as the Foreground color and applied the gradient, dragging the gradient tool from the middle of the picture upward to a point beyond the top edge.

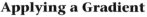
Applying a Gradient

To fill a layer or a selection with a color gradient, double-click the gradient tool in the toolbox to open the Gradient Tool Options palette. Choose a Gradient and a Type (Linear or Radial) and drag the tool from where you want the first color transition (the one on the left in the palette's preview gradient bar) to begin to where you want the last one to end. For a Radial fill the starting point is the center of the gradient. You'll find gradients used in artwork throughout the book. Below and on the facing page are a few examples of applying gradients for special effects.

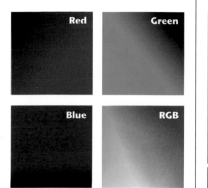

An amorphous multicolor background can be created by applying Black, White gradients (horizontal, vertical, or diagonal) to individual color channels. (The color channels are shown here in color.)

You can offset the "center" of a Radial fill by using the gradient tool inside an elliptical selection. For both balloons white was the Foreground color; the Background color was pink for one balloon and yellow for the other. In each case the gradient tool was dragged from a point off-center within an elliptical selection.

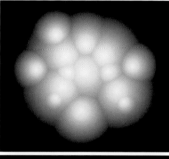
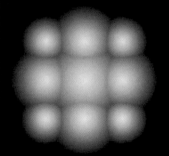

You can get a "molecular" look (top) by setting white and black as the Foreground and Background colors, respectively, and first applying a Foreground To Background Radial gradient in Normal mode (set in the Gradient Tool Options palette) to make the central molecule and black background, then making more of the same kind of gradient around it but with Lighten mode chosen in the Gradient Options palette. Starting the Radial gradients on Grid points can create a symmetrically packed appearance (bottom). After all the "atoms" are built, add color with Image, Adjust, Variations.

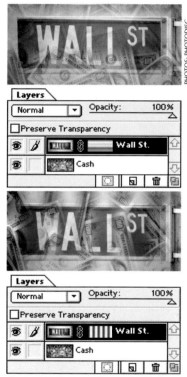

Compositing images using masks filled with two of Photoshop's default gradients: Spectrum (top), which in a mask can only be shades of gray, and Transparent Stripes (bottom, made in Normal mode with black as the Foreground color), which in a mask becomes black-and-white; a Gaussian Blur was applied to the mask to soften the edges of the stripes.

Default Set

Black, White

Blue, Red, Yellow

Blue, Yellow, Blue

Chrome

Copper

Foreground To Background (default colors)

Foreground To Transparent (default colors)

Orange, Yellow, Orange

Red, Green

Spectrum

Transparent Rainbow

Transparent Stripes (default colors)

Transparent To Foreground (default colors)

Violet, Green, Orange

Violet, Orange

Yellow, Violet, Orange, Blue

Color Harmonies

Blue-Violet, Yellow-Orange

Orange, Blue

Orange, Blue, Magenta, Yellow

Red, Blue, Yellow

Red, Violet, YelGreen

Red-Orange, Blue-Green

YelGreen, Red, Orange, Blue

Yellow, Blue, Red, Green

Yellow, Magenta, Teal

Yellow, Violet

Yellow, Violet, Red, Teal

Yellow-Green, Red-Violet

*These swatches (produced with the Linear setting unless otherwise noted) show all the gradients that come with Photoshop 4. The default set is automatically available from the Gradient list in the Gradient Tool Options palette and in the Gradient Editor dialog box. Other sets are provided in **goodies\grdients** on the Photoshop 4 CD-ROM and can be added to the list by clicking the Load button in the Gradient Editor.*

*Also shown (at the right) are a few of the Wow! Gradients from **goodies\wowgrads.grd** on the CD-ROM that comes with this book.*

Metals

Brass

Gold

Silver

Steel Bar

Steel Blue

Special Effects

Gray Value Stripes

Russell's Rainbow (Radial)

Soft Stripes (default colors)

Matte Sphere (Radial)   Shiny Sphere (Radial)

Wow! Samples

Wow Rainbow 1

Wow Sunset 1

Wow Sunset 2

Wow Sunset 3

Reworking a Painting

Overview *Open a painting file and duplicate the artwork into three additional channels; use one channel for experimenting with filters, one for sharpening any line work, and one for running the chosen filter effect.*

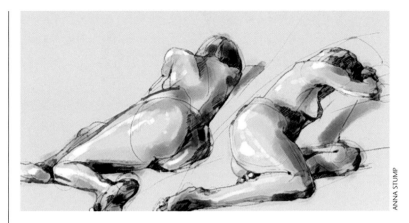

ANNA STUMP

1a

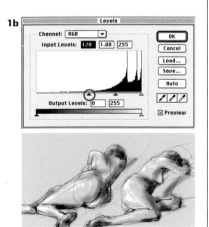

In her original painting, created in Fractal Design Painter, Anna Stump used soft lines and muted colors.

1b

Adjusting the Input Levels black point strengthened the colors.

ONE ADVANTAGE OF PAINTING WITH PIXELS is that the canvas never completely "dries." You can always go back and try out a new approach to your composition — even to art created with traditional media and scanned. Anna Stump found Photoshop's Layers palette the perfect environment for modifying her *Intelligent Woman.*

1 Preparing the art. Open an art file and make any tonal adjustments needed with Image, Adjust, Curves or Levels.

2 Intensifying the line work. Open the Layers palette and copy the Background layer by dragging its name to the New Layer icon, in the middle at the bottom of the palette. Working in the new layer, choose Filter, Sharpen, Unsharp Mask and experiment with settings to darken and sharpen the image.

3 Applying a filter. In the Layers palette, make another copy of the Background layer. Move this layer up to the top of the Layers stack (Ctrl-]). Run a painterly filter on this layer. Opening the Channels palette, Stump clicked on the name of each of the three color channels in turn and ran the Watercolor filter (Filter, Artistic, Watercolor) separately on each, which produced more detailed color variation than running it on the combined channels.

4 Adjusting the mix. Adjust the opacity and blending modes of the layers to mix the sharpening and painterly effects.

2

Darkening the line work in the Sharpen layer

3

The Watercolor filter applied to the individual color channels of the Watercolor layer

4

The Opacity sliders of the Watercolor and Sharpen layers were set at 47% and 50% to produce the result at the top of the page.

Making an Electronic "Woodcut"

Overview *Trace the contours of a photo; convert that sketch to a pattern; convert a copy of the original photo to a bitmap using the pattern; treat the original photo with the Median filter; layer the bitmap back over the filter-treated photo.*

1a

Original photo

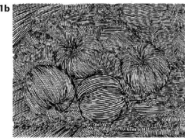
1b

Hand-drawn sketch, scanned

2

Define Pattern

Take Snapshot

Turning the sketch into a pattern

3a

Applying the Median filter to the photo

ARTISTS STRIVE TO TAKE ADVANTAGE of the computer's power and automation without losing the hand-crafted look of traditional artists' methods. Here we've achieved a "woodcut" effect by combining the computer's muscle with the subtleties of drawing by hand.

1 Making and aligning the sketch. Open a color photo in Photoshop. Now you'll trace over the photo to make a sketch that follows the shapes of the objects in the image. One way to trace the photo is to add a new transparent layer (open the Layers palette and click the New Layer icon in the middle at the bottom of the Layers palette) and use a digitizing tablet (with pressure sensitivity turned off) and a paintbrush tool to sketch over the image. Another way is to print out a copy of the photo at full size and hand-trace the contours with a marking pen with strokes of uniform width. In either case keep the line width about the same as the white spaces between the strokes, so that if you squint at the page, the drawn areas look 50% gray overall. If you do your artwork by hand (we used a black marker on white tracing paper), scan it into the computer in grayscale mode at 100% size and the same resolution (pixels per inch) as the color photo. (You can find the resolution of the photo file by choosing Image, Image Size.)

You'll need a fairly full range of gray tones to successfully use the sketch as a pattern in step 3. If the edges of the line work in your sketch file don't have a range of grays, you can experiment with blurring (we used Filter, Blur, Blur More for this 900-pixel-wide scan).

If you're using a scanned sketch, it's time to line it up with the photo. Make the scan file active and use the move tool to drag a copy of the scan into the photo file. Set the opacity of this new layer at about 50% so you can also see the color image. Use the move tool to align the sketch with the photo underneath. If you need to straighten the sketch, use Free Transform (Ctrl-T) to rotate

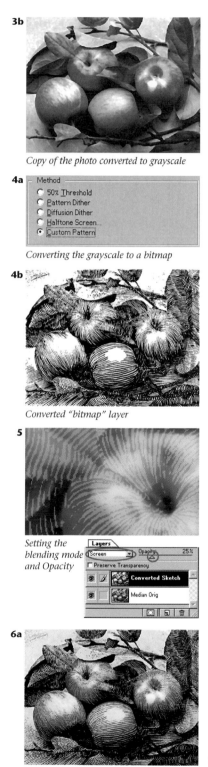

3b

Copy of the photo converted to grayscale

4a

Method
- ○ 50% Threshold
- ○ Pattern Dither
- ○ Diffusion Dither
- ○ Halftone Screen...
- ● Custom Pattern

Converting the grayscale to a bitmap

4b

Converted "bitmap" layer

5

Setting the blending mode and Opacity

Layers
Screen ▾   Opacity   25%
☐ Preserve Transparency
👁 🖌 [thumbnail] **Converted Sketch**
👁   [thumbnail] Median Orig

6a

Soft Light, 100% Opacity over color

the drawing layer: Press Ctrl-Alt-minus to shrink the image without shrinking the window so you can drag with the cursor just outside the Free Transform box. Double-click inside the box to accept the change.

2 Converting the sketch to a pattern. With the sketch layer active, Select All (Ctrl-A) and choose Edit, Define Pattern. (Unless you quit the program or use Define Pattern again, Photoshop will hold the pattern in memory until you need it at step 4.)

3 Preparing the color and grayscale images. In the color photo layer run the Median filter (Filter, Noise, Median) to keep the details of the original photo from fighting with the line work. Median averages the brightness of pixels within the Radius you set, generating a new brightness value for each pixel, but it leaves alone those pixels that are greatly different from their neighbors. The overall effect is to blur the fine details of the image while leaving any edges (the outlines of the apples, stems, and leaves, for example) quite distinct.

After running the Median filter, duplicate the color photo: Activate the color layer and turn off the eye icon in the sketch layer; choose Image, Duplicate, Merged Layers Only to copy the layer to a new file. Convert this file to a grayscale image (Image, Mode, Grayscale).

4 Converting the grayscale to a "woodcut." With the sketch defined as a pattern (at step 2), convert the copy of the photo to Bit-map mode (Image, Mode, Bitmap), choosing the Custom Pattern option for the Method. (Keep the Output resolution the same as the Input.) Convert the file back to grayscale (Image, Mode, Grayscale)

5 Layering the images. With the converted photo from step 4 active, use the move tool with the Shift key held down to drag and drop it back into the color file. Because you made the copy from the color file, it will be exactly the same size as the original, so it will snap into place when dropped. Turn off the eye icon for the original sketch layer so it doesn't contribute to the final image, and turn on the eyes for the newly imported layer and the color layer. Adjust the blending mode and Opacity of the imported layer.

6 Experimenting. We used Screen mode and 75% opacity to get the image at the top of page 206. We also tried applying the custom bitmap layer in Soft Light mode at 100% Opacity. In another experiment, we activated the color layer and added an Adjustment layer (Ctrl-click the New Layer icon), choosing Hue/Saturation and moving the Saturation slider all the way to the left (for more about desaturating with an Adjustment layer, see page 119).

6b

Soft Light, 100% Opacity over desaturated

Coloring Line Art

Overview *Scan a pen-and-ink drawing; clean up the line work, increasing contrast and removing extraneous marks; make selections and fill with flat color; airbrush shades and tones; change colors to taste; add highlights.*

TOMMY YUNE

The scanned line art

Adjusting Levels and duplicating the line art to a transparent layer, here viewed alone

TOMMY YUNE'S *JOURNEYGIRL* IMAGE is a tongue-in-cheek spin-off of *The Journeyman Project 3,* a CD-ROM game developed by Presto Studios, for which Yune served as creative director. Though the line work for *JourneyGirl* was inspired by Japanese character design, Yune took a softer, airbrushed approach to color. He started with scanned and fine-tuned line work, built areas of flat color, developed shades and tones, made special modifications to the color, and added highlights. Because of the way he constructed the color work, the line art completely covered its "seams," trapping the color and leaving no gaps.

1 Drawing and scanning. Start by scanning hand-drawn line art in grayscale mode and opening the file in Photoshop. Yune had inked his illustration on LetraMax bright white marker paper, which provided excellent contrast for scanning. He scanned the art at 400 dpi on a flatbed scanner.

2 Cleaning up the line art. Next you'll use Levels — either by choosing Image, Adjust, Levels or by opening the Layers palette (Window, Show Layers), making an Adjustment layer (Ctrl-click the New Layer icon in the middle at the bottom of the Layers palette), and choosing Levels for the Type.

Make sure that Preview is turned on in the Levels dialog box so you can fine-tune your tonal adjustments by eye. Start by looking at the Levels histogram to see what kind of adjustment is needed to get clean, smooth lines with good contrast. (Before you make changes, read "Turn Off the Cache!" on page 94.)

The histogram for Yune's JourneyGirl scan showed two humps (for the black ink and white paper) with fewer pixels at the intermediate grays — basically, noise from the scanning process. Yune moved the black point and white point Input Levels sliders inward

3

Loading the Black channel as a selection, creating a new layer, inverting the selection, and filling with black made a transparent layer with black "line art."

4a

To select areas for solid color fills, selections were unfeathered and not antialiased.

4b

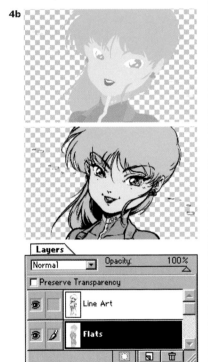

Selected areas were filled with flat colors, shown here with the line art layer invisible (top) and visible.

until they were just inside the two humps. He also moved the gamma slider (the gray one) to 1.2 to make the line work appear finer by brightening the image. (Be careful not to brighten your scan too much or the finest lines will begin to disappear.)

To clean up extraneous marks, make white the Foreground color (you can press "D" for "Default colors" then "X" for "eXchange Foreground and Background colors") and paint over the marks with the paintbrush tool or select them and fill the selection with white (Alt-Backspace). Or Shift-select the individual marks, expand the selection 3 or 4 pixels (Select, Modify, Expand), and use the Dust & Scratches filter to remove them (Filter, Noise, Dust & Scratches; see page 157 for tips on using Dust & Scratches).

FINDING STRAY MARKS

To quickly find black specks on a white background, double-click the magic wand in the toolbox to open its Options palette and set the Tolerance to 0, turn off Anti-aliased, then click on the white background. The flashing selection boundary will appear around the specks, making them easier to see.

3 Making a line art layer. This step makes a transparent layer with black line art. To create a selection based on the scanned line art, open the Channels palette (Window, Show Channels) and Ctrl-click the Black channel's name to load the channel as a selection. Then invert the selection (Ctrl-Shift-I) to change the selection from the white areas to the black line work. In the Layers palette (Window, Show Layers), click the New Layer icon (next to the trash can icon at the bottom of the palette) to create a new layer. Then fill the selection with black (press "D" for default colors and then Alt-Backspace). In the pop-up list of blending modes in the Layers palette, choose Multiply. At this point, save a copy of the file (Ctrl-Alt-S) in Photoshop format to preserve the black-on-transparent line art.

4 Making a flat color layer. Convert the file from Grayscale to RGB (Image, Mode, RGB Color); don't flatten.

So that you'll have a clear view of your cleaned-up line work on its transparent layer, make the *Background* layer active, select all

SAVING RAM AND TIME

When you're coloring line art, especially if your artwork is large — poster-size, for example — you can speed up your work by preserving your cleaned-up Grayscale line art in a separate file (Save A Copy) before you add color, and then converting your working file to RGB (Image, Mode, RGB Color) and reducing its size to 50%, or even 25% (Image, Image Size, Resample Image, Bicubic). After you've completed your coloring, enlarge the file back up to its original size (use Image Size again), delete the existing line art layer, and in its place drag-and-drop the high-resolution copy you saved, holding down the Shift key so the imported line work is perfectly aligned with the color layer. Since all the crisp detail is in the reimported high-res line art layer, resizing the already soft color portions of the file doesn't degrade the image.

5a

Magic Wand Options

Tolerance: 0   ☐ Anti-aliased

Set up with a Tolerance of 0 and no antialiasing, the magic wand tool can be used on the flat color layer to make selections that can then be used to contain airbrushing on a new layer above it.

5b

Layers

Normal ▾   Opacity: 100%

☒ Preserve Transparency

👁 | 🖌 | Line Art

👁 | 🖌 | **Colors**

👁 | | **Flats**

Shading and toning were done on a copy of the flat-color layer using the HSB setting in the Color palette. The line art and shading and toning layers alone constitute the developing artwork. But retaining the flat color layer provides a way to reselect color areas and to start over if a mistake is made in shading or toning one area.

6

Airbrushing in Color mode changes the color but preserves the shading and toning.

(Ctrl-A) and fill with white (Alt-Backspace if white is still the Foreground color). With the *Background* still active, click the New Layer icon to add a layer between the *Background* and the line art layer. Working in this new layer, use the line art layer as a guide as you use the lasso and polygon lasso to select areas to fill with flat color. (Holding down the Alt key while you work with either lasso tool lets you switch back and forth between dragging and clicking to draw the selection boundary.) Fill each selection with color as you make it (click the Foreground color square in the toolbox and choose a color or sample from the Color palette, opened by choosing Window, Show Color; then press Alt-Backspace to fill). Don't worry about shading at this point — just flat color fills.

5 Shading and toning the color. To make a layer for adding shades and tones, duplicate the flat color layer by dragging its name to the New Layer icon at the bottom of the Layers palette. Select regions of color with the magic wand tool, with Tolerance set to 0 and Anti-aliased and Sample Merged turned off in the Magic Wand Options palette. Shift-click with the wand to add noncontiguous areas to the selection. Now use the airbrush tool to add shades and tones of color; the active selection boundaries will keep this additional color "inside the lines."

After toning a region, the expanded color range will make it hard to select the whole region with the magic wand tool again if you want to add more airbrushing. But you can make the selection by clicking the name of the "flats" layer to activate it, clicking the magic wand tool to select a color area in this layer, then activating the modulated color layer again and airbrushing. To fine-tune the shading and toning, Yune used the dodge and burn tools.

USING HSB SLIDERS

The HSB Sliders mode of the Color palette can make it easier to add shades and tones to color-filled areas. Open the Color palette (Window, Show Color), choose HSB Sliders from the palette's pop-out menu, and then choose Color Bars, Current Colors also. Now you can hold down the Alt key with any painting tool chosen and click in the image to sample the color you want to modulate. Then change it to a lighter or darker shade by moving the "B" (for "Brightness") slider, or click in the color bar at the bottom of the palette.

ERASING BRUSH STROKES

With the painting tools and the toning tools (dodge, burn, and sponge), you can choose Filter, Fade if you want to reduce the intensity of your last stroke, or press Ctrl-Z to completely undo it. The ability to fade brush strokes was added in version 4.0.1 of Photoshop.

Filter

Last Filter   ⌘F
Fade Burn Tool...   ⇧⌘F

After the file was converted to CMYK Color mode, highlights were added in a top layer in Screen mode.

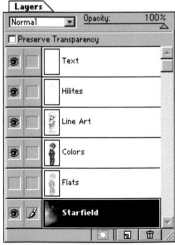

The finished illustration included a background and a top layer with signature and copyright notice.

6 Completing the coloring. Once the primary tonality of the artwork has been established, you can change the color by selecting color regions again using the magic wand on the flat-color layer, and using the airbrush tool in Color mode (from the list of blending modes in the Airbrush Options palette) to paint over the tonal work. Yune used bright, bold colors, fine-tuning the color with Image, Adjust, Color Balance and with the sponge (saturation) tool.

7 Adding highlights. If your artwork is destined for print, now is the time to convert to CMYK (Image, Mode, CMYK Color), so that what you see on-screen as your highlights develop will be a good predictor of what they'll look like in print (see "Blending and Color Modes" at right). Make a new layer at the top of your layers stack and put it in Screen mode. Use any soft-edged painting tool to add highlights to reflective surfaces such as eyes and metal. If you're working in RGB mode, the color you use on this layer will lighten and tint the artwork beneath. In CMYK mode, the artwork will be lightened, but the tint will be less apparent.

8 Adding the background. Yune activated the *Background* layer and dragged-and-dropped a starfield developed for one of the interactive *Journeyman Project* games. He also created another layer at the top of the stack to add his signature and copyright information.

Imitating Paint and Canvas

Overview *Prepare a photo; apply a painterly filter and Lighting Effects; apply canvas texture to a duplicate layer; combine the two layers with Layer Options.*

 The Painting/Canvas Action on the Wow! CD-ROM produces a paint-and-canvas effect similar to this one.

1a

Original digital photo

1b

Rubber-stamping with sky to hide a building

1c

Selecting the dark centers of the flowers

1d

Center lightened with a Levels Adjustment layer

FILTERS FROM PHOTOSHOP'S ARTISTIC and Brush Strokes submenus, as well as the Facet, Crystallize, Median, and Smart Blur filters, can automatically generate some pretty amazing painterly effects. But no one filter provides control over all attributes you might like to include in a painting: the gestural brush strokes, the built-up texture of thickly applied paints, and the texture of the white canvas, showing through in areas where paint is thin or absent. Fractal Design Painter has built-in functions to do this kind of imitation of natural media, and you can also approximate it with Photoshop if you use the right combination of filters. To give this photo of sunflowers, taken with an Olympus digital camera, the "feel" of a painting with Impressionist color, gesture, and play of light, we used the Dry Brush filter and then applied the Lighting Effects filter to create an impasto look.

1 Preparing the image. Start by opening an RGB image, removing unwanted detail, and enhancing the colors or tones if you like. We used the rubber stamp tool to paint sky over the building in the upper left corner of the image. Pressing "S" selects the rubber stamp tool, pressing the Enter key opens its Options palette so you can set it to Clone (Aligned) or Clone (Non-aligned), and Alt-clicking loads the stamp with the image.

We also lightened the centers of the flowers and exaggerated the difference in their brown tones: We made a rough selection of the centers by Shift-clicking with the magic wand and applied Image, Adjust, Levels to the selection. This exaggeration of tones would give the painterly filter something more to work on.

2 Making the paint. So you can experiment without permanently changing your cleaned-up image, choose File, Save A Copy before you begin filtering. Apply a painterly filter to your image, or

2a

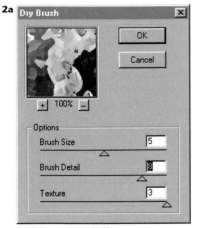

Applying a painterly filter

2b

The filtered image

2c

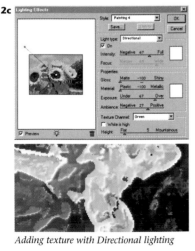

Adding texture with Directional lighting

3a

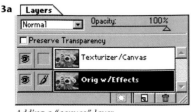

Adding a "canvas" layer

use the smudge tool to create brush strokes by hand. We chose Filter, Artistic, Dry Brush and used high settings for Brush Detail and Texture.

Next you can thicken the paint by applying the Lighting Effects filter. Open the Channels palette (Window, Show Channels) and click on the individual channel names so you can look at each one and choose the channel that best shows the detail of the brush strokes. Then click the RGB composite channel's name to activate the entire image. Choose Filter, Render, Lighting Effects and set up your lighting scheme: Choose Directional for the Light Type to get an overall embossing effect for the paint, without the hot spots a Spotlight would produce. For the Texture Channel, choose the color channel you identified as the one with the best brush stroke detail. Turn off White Is High, adjust the other Lighting Effects settings to taste, and click OK to run the filter. (See pages 158 through 160 for more about using the Lighting Effects filter.)

3 Making canvas. To make the highlights in their paintings, painters sometimes leave the white of the unpainted canvas exposed. To combine this technique with the embossed brush strokes from step 2, you'll need to make a duplicate of the filtered and embossed layer. Drag the name of the filtered layer to the New Layer icon. At this point it might be a good idea to double-click each layer's name in the palette so you can rename it to reflect what's on the layer.

With the new top layer active, choose Filter, Texture, Texturizer. In the Texturizer dialog box, choose Canvas or one of the other textures, or load a texture from the **goodies\textures** folder on the Adobe Photoshop 4.0 CD-ROM, or load one that you've made yourself. (See page 159 for tips on creating textures with filters; and refer to "Creating a Canvas Texture" on page 212 for instructions on making a seamlessly repeating pattern that can be used with the Texturizer filter.)

THE BEST OF BOTH SETTINGS

Often when you're applying a painterly filter, you'll want to vary the size, amount of detail, texture, or direction of the brush strokes from one part of the image to another. To do this, apply the filter to two or more duplicate layers, using different settings for each layer. Then you can add layer masks (for each layer, click the mask icon at the bottom left of the Layers palette) to direct where each kind of stroke appears in the final composite, airbrushing or painting the mask with black paint to hide the filter effect in some areas and white paint to reveal it in other places. When you've got the result you want, choose Merge Visible from the Layers palette's pop-out menu to apply layer masks and reduce the "painting" to a single layer.

3b

Applying the Canvas texture with Texturizer

3c

Adjusting the Layer Options to limit the canvas texture to the lightest areas of the image

Now you'll use the Layer Options dialog box to knock out all but the highlight (white) areas of the canvas layer. Double-click the layer's name in the palette to open Layer Options. You can leave the slider for This Layer as it is. But for Underlying, move the black point triangle far to the right. Then hold down the Alt key to split the black point in two and drag the left half a little to the left so the canvas texture will begin to "fade in" where the colors are light, finally coming in at full strength in the white areas.

Enhancing the color and tone. The Impressionist masters exaggerated light and color to communicate emotion. The same technique can be applied to a digital painting. For instance, add an Adjustment layer: Ctrl-click on the New Layer icon to open the New Adjustment Layer dialog box. Choose Hue/Saturation for the Type. In the Hue/Saturation dialog box, click one of the radio buttons in the column along the left side of the dialog box, and then move the Saturation slider to the right. If you want to saturate another family of colors, click a different radio button and adjust Saturation again.

Also, if the details of the image or the paint have been lost in shadow areas, you can roughly Shift-select these areas with a feathered lasso and then Ctrl-click to add a Levels Adjustment layer so you can move the gamma (gray) triangle on the Input Levels slider to pop them out again. *Wow*

CREATING A CANVAS TEXTURE

To make a canvas texture that you can apply to a digital painting or filtered photo as in "Imitating Paint and Canvas," scan a canvas texture on a flatbed scanner, or create a texture with Noise, Blur, and Emboss (see page 159).

To turn the canvas into a seamlessly wrapping pattern that can fill any size file, you'll first use the Offset filter to reveal the "seams" that would appear between tiles (repetitions of the pattern). Then you'll use the rubber stamp to eliminate them.

Apply the Offset filter (Filter, Other, Offset). Enter Horizontal and Vertical settings that will move the edges of the image into the center. (We offset our 256-pixel-wide scanned canvas image 128 pixels right and 128 pixels down.) Choose Wrap Around for the Undefined Areas (so pixels that are pushed off the right and bottom edges will reappear at the left and top to fill the empty space created there.)

Applying the Offset filer to a scan of canvas

To eliminate the seams, double-click the rubber stamp tool in the tool palette to open its Options palette. Choose one of the Clone options — Aligned might work best for a woven texture, Non-aligned for a random grain. Choose a soft brush tip from the Brushes palette, about twice the size of the "grain" of your canvas. Hold down the Alt key and click the rubber stamp on a part of the image away from any seam to pick up cloning texture. Rubber stamp over the seam, using short strokes if you're working in Non-aligned mode. (In Aligned mode, it doesn't matter whether strokes are long or short because the image is reproduced as a single copy, as described in "The Rubber Stamp" at the beginning of this chapter.) Stay away from the edge of the image so you don't create another "seam." You can see if you've accidentally made a new seam by using the Offset filter again.

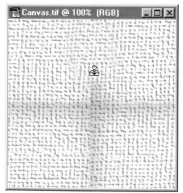

Using the rubber stamp tool to hide the "seams" revealed by the Offset filter

---

Painting with Light

Overview Start with a sketch; rough in the color; build volume; add highlights and detail.

FRANCOIS GUÉRIN

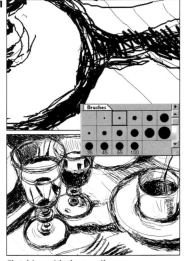

Sketching with the pencil

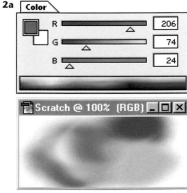

Mixing colors

ACHIEVING A PAINTERLY EFFECT with the computer involves some mental translation from traditional tools to electronic ones. Artist/illustrator Francois Guérin, who also works with oils, pastels, gouache, and Fractal Design Painter, has found several ways to work effectively with Photoshop as a painting program. For *The Meal*, painted from memory, he used primarily the painting tools, the lasso, the Gaussian Blur, and functions from the Image, Adjust submenu. Guérin worked with a Wacom digitizing tablet. He likes the brushlike feel of the stylus but doesn't vary the pressure much.

1 Making a sketch. To start out, click the pencil and begin drawing. Choose pencil tips of different sizes from the Brushes palette. Guérin used a larger tip to darken the shadow areas.

2 Laying down color. You can use the Color palette (Window, Show Color) to mix colors by component percentages. Or make a new small Scratch document (File, New) to mix colors "by hand" that you can then sample with the eyedropper tool. And use the Swatches palette (Window, Show Swatches) to store and recall colors you want to use again. Apply the first strokes of paint with the paintbrush, using brush tips from the top row of the Brushes palette, which provide smooth but hard-edged strokes. Paint in Normal mode so the strokes hide the black-and-white sketch.

3 Building volume. Use your Scratch file to mix the color variations you need to begin painting shapes. At this point, use the paintbrush and airbrush tools, which have softer edges, to achieve color blending in the painting.

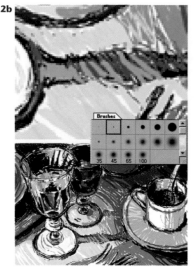
2b

Laying down color with the paintbrush

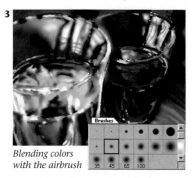
3

Blending colors with the airbrush

4a

Smoothing color with the Gaussian Blur filter

4 Indicating textures. Guérin used the smallest pencil point to add "grain" to the wood of the table, which he later smoothed with the smudge (finger) tool. He also used the Blur filters to add a smooth sheen to some of the surfaces in the image. For instance, he used a feathered lasso to select some areas of the cup and saucer, and applied a Gaussian Blur. (With the lasso chosen in the toolbox, press Enter to open the Lasso Options palette to set the Feather amount.)

SEEING THE BRUSH TIP

To get a cursor that's more useful for painting than the standard paintbrush or eraser icon, choose File, Preferences, Display & Cursors and select Brush Size in the Painting Cursors area of the dialog box. Now the cursor shows the footprint of the current brush tip, so you can see exactly where and how big it is in relation to the image you're working on.

5 Putting the colors in context. To modify the colors to be consistent with the light in the scene, you can use a feathered lasso and commands from the Image Adjust submenu as Guérin did, or use Adjustment layers (choose Window, Show Layers and Ctrl-click the New Layer icon in the middle at the bottom of the palette) for Hue/Saturation, Levels, and Color Balance. You can modify the adjustment overall by changing the Opacity of the Adjustment layer. Or, with black and white as the Foreground and Background colors, you can paint the Adjustment layer's built-in mask: Use a feathered lasso and Alt-Backspace (to fill with black) or Ctrl-Backspace (to fill with white) or paint with a soft airbrush. Guérin used a highly feathered lasso.

6 Adding modeling and highlights. To mold elements in the painting, you can use traditional painting techniques, such as applying strokes to follow the form of an object. Guérin shaped the napkin beneath the fork in this way, for example. The blur tool (water drop) can be used to smooth areas such as the reflections on the glass. (If the water drop isn't showing in the tool palette, press "R" to toggle to it.) The smudge tool (press "U") does a good job of adding texture and making color transitions in areas where light and shadows meet — in the wood of the table, for instance. It can also be used to pull specular highlights out of white paint, as on the tine of the fork.

5

Modifying colors

6

Adding texture and highlights

Sketching with the pencil and filling sketched areas with paint

Smoothing color with Gaussian Blur

Differential blurring to create depth

Developing electronic painting technique. For a painting of his cactus collection, Guérin again started with an electronic pencil sketch. He poured color into the pencil-drawn shapes with the paint bucket tool and added some detail with the paintbrush. Then he used a feathered lasso and the Gaussian Blur filter to blend the colors. He used the smudge tool to blend the edges where colors met, and added more color with paintbrushes. With the paintbrush and airbrush he built volume in the rounded plants, and added spines with the paintbrush and pencil. To capture the lighting on the scene, he played with the color balance, brightness, contrast, hue, and saturation of parts of the image, as he had for *The Meal*. To create the illusion of depth, he used the Blur filter, applying it three times for the round cactus on the right side of the painting, which was farthest in the background, twice for the closer, spiky one in the upper left corner, and once for a still closer one in the center. *wow!*

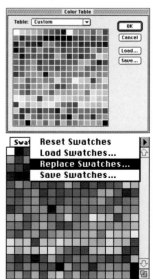

Painting a Rainbow

Overview *Modify Photoshop 4's Russell's Rainbow gradient to include violet and to remove color from the area "under the rainbow"; on a transparent layer above the image, apply the new settings as a Radial gradient, with the center outside and below the picture; add a layer mask to fade the end of the rainbow.*

1

The original photo

2a

Starting with a duplicate of the Russell's Rainbow gradient called "Russell's Rainbow+," we added violet.

2b

We increased the width of the full transparency band at the left end of the gradient.

A RAINBOW FORMS when drops of rain in the air act as prisms to spread the different wavelengths of light in rays of sunshine. Of the seven hues that form the arch of brilliant colors — violet, indigo, blue, green, yellow, orange, and red — usually only four or five are clearly seen, with red on the outside of the arch and violet on the inside. Photoshop's gradient tool now has the multicolor and transparency capabilities needed to produce a rainbow, and Russell Brown of Adobe Systems has used that ability to make Russell's Rainbow, a painless way to put an arch of color across your image.

1 Setting up the file. Open a photo with atmospheric conditions that might produce a rainbow. Since the sun is always behind the viewer when a rainbow is in front, if you're aiming for photorealism you'll want to choose a picture that doesn't show the sun. Open the Layers palette (Window, Show Layers) and add a transparent layer above the image by clicking (or Alt-clicking) the New Layer icon in the middle at the bottom of the palette. (We Alt-clicked the New Layer icon in order to open the New Layer dialog box so we could name the layer "Rainbow.")

2 Modifying a rainbow gradient. Double-click the gradient tool in the toolbox to open the Gradient Tool Options palette. We chose Russell's Rainbow from the Gradient list since we had already loaded the Special Effects gradients from Photoshop's Gradients folder. Whether you see Russell's Rainbow in the list or not, click the Edit button. In the Gradient Editor dialog box, you can choose it from the scrolling list or click the Load button, find and load the Special Effects gradients, and then choose Russell's Rainbow.

Notice that the Russell's Rainbow gradient limits the rainbow colors to a small band near one end. Because of this arrangement, when you use the gradient in Radial form it produces a ring of color around a transparent middle. And if you make the ring large enough to extend beyond the edges of your image, you'll get the arc needed for a rainbow.

Gradient Tool Options

Normal ▼ | Opacity: 50%

Gradient: [Russell's Rainbow+] ▼

Type: [Radial] ▼ ☒ Mask ☒ Dither

[Edit...]

Setting up the gradient for a dithered Radial application at 50% opacity

3b

Dragging the gradient tool from lower left to upper right (top) produced a rainbow arc on the image.

4a

The gradient layer mask applied to make the right end of the rainbow disappear

Use the gradient as it is (skip ahead to step 3) or click the Duplicate button so you can preserve the original as well as develop a new version that adds violet and doesn't include a color cast "under the rainbow." We named our duplicate gradient "Russell's Rainbow+" and changed it by tightening the color band, adding purple at the left end of it, and increasing the transparent area at the left.

To add a color, make sure the Color button is selected in the Adjust line and then click below the gradient band to add a new color control point where you want the color to appear in the gradient. Click the color swatch to the left of the "Location" label to open the Color Picker, choose a color, and click OK.

Then click the Transparency button. To take the color out of the area under the rainbow, adjust the transparency as follows: At the left end of the transparency bar is a white 0%-opacity control point. Move it to the right until it's close to the color band. Slide the light gray 20%-opacity control point a little farther to the right also. Click the Save button to store your new gradient permanently as part of the set of currently loaded gradients.

3 Applying the gradient. Zoom your view out until you see an extensive gray apron around the picture; you can do it as follows: Choose the zoom tool in the toolbox, press the Enter key to open the Zoom Tool Options palette, make sure the Resize Windows To Fit option is deselected, and then hold down the Alt key and click in the image several times.

Choose Radial for the Type and reduce the Opacity in the Gradient Tool Options palette (or you can reduce the rainbow's brightness later with the Opacity control for the Layer); we lowered the gradient's Opacity to 50%. Then drag with the gradient tool from a point near one of the lower corners of the gray apron to a point near the top edge of your image to define the radius of the rainbow arc. If you don't like the result, undo (Ctrl-Z) and try again with a different starting point, direction, or radius. If the rainbow seems too bright, you can dim it by reducing the Opacity of its layer.

4 Hiding the end of the rainbow. To make your rainbow disappear into thin air, you can add a layer mask. With the rainbow layer active, click the Add Layer Mask icon, on the left at the bottom of the Layers palette. In the Gradient Tool Options palette, choose Linear for the Type and choose Black,White from the Gradient list. With the layer mask active, click where you want the rainbow to be completely invisible and drag to where you want it to be completely visible. 𝘮𝘢𝘶𝘪

4b

Layers

Normal ▼ | Opacity: 75%

☐ Preserve Transparency

👁 🖌 | Rainbow

👁 | Background

The final layers palette, with the Rainbow layer's Opacity reduced to further dim the colors, and the layer mask in place, producing the image at the top of the previous page.

Transparent layers and Adjustment layers give painters like **Cher Threinen-Pendarvis** some wonderful opportunities that they don't have with traditional media. The ability to select an area of a painting and continue to work with its color in a new layer, or to protect a foreground subject with a mask while adding brush strokes to the surrounding background, provides a kind of "reworking luxury" that paint can't always provide. For her *Little Wolf* painting, Threinen-Pendarvis began by sketching with a pressure-sensitive tablet using Photoshop's paintbrush with one of the default small, hard brush tips, which felt similar to the Prismacolor pencil she uses for sketching in the field. Because she planned to use warm colors for the painting, she started her sketch with a soft dark brown rather than gray or black, to establish the feel of the palette from the beginning.

She made a temporary copy of the sketch file for use later (Image, Duplicate) and began her color work. She used the lasso tool to select the sky area so she could fill it with a light blue. She also saved the selection as an alpha channel (Select, Save Selection) so she could load it again later if

she wanted to adjust color in the sky as a whole or to restrict brush strokes within that area; or she could invert the selection to keep brush strokes from encroaching. She made a similar alpha channel for the hills in the distance so she could quickly select them to change the saturation (Image, Adjust, Hue/Saturation) to help with depth of field and atmospheric perspective.

She painted the central figure in a file of its own at a larger size, then selected it with a slightly feathered lasso, copied it, and pasted it into the larger painting as a layer. She scaled it to fit with the Free Transform command (Ctrl-T), saved the selection in an alpha channel so she could protect it from paint later, and merged it with the *Background* layer.

By using layers she was able to select parts of the image that needed to have color intensified, duplicate the selected areas as separate layers (Ctrl-J) for further work, and apply them like glazing in watercolor by changing the blending mode to Color, Overlay, Screen, Darken or Lighten and experimenting with Opacity.

When the color work was complete, she dragged the saved duplicate of the line

work into the file to increase line detail, put its layer in Multiply mode, and reduced the layer's Opacity.

Finally, she added canvas texture by making a new layer in Screen mode, filling it with a tiling pattern she had made from a scan of real canvas, and reducing its Opacity. (The process of making a seamlessly repeating canvas texture is detailed in "Creating a Canvas Texture" on page 212.)

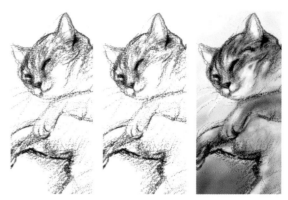

Sharon Steuer started *Puma — Oh, Joy!* as a hand-drawn sketch with pencil on paper. She scanned the sketch to make the *Background* layer of her painting (above left). She added a new layer in Overlay mode to color the ears, nose, and mouth and to lighten some facial markings (center). Most of her work was done in an additional top layer, set up in Multiply mode so the scan would show through. She applied Photoshop's paintbrush tool with a pressure-sensitive stylus that was set to erase as well as paint, so that she could add color and then partially stroke it away.

In this *illustration for* **Computer Gaming** *magazine,* **Philip Howe** layered photos taken by Ed Lowe of the blindfolded man, the computer monitor, and the keyboard, hand, and mouse. The rest of the image was created from scratch in Photoshop. Howe, who has a high-powered computer system, prefers to bypass PostScript drawing programs, even for creating crisp line work and smooth curves, and develop his whole image as a continuous process in Photoshop. He makes his files twice as large as he needs for print, in order to get crisp edges on his lines and geometric shapes. When the image has been completed and saved, he saves (File, Save As) and flattens a copy of the file and reduces it (Image, Image Size) to the appropriate size for output.

The website screens that rise up to meet the man stepping out onto the Internet for the first time were constructed as rectangles, then put into perspective and duplicated several times to build the stacks.

The "zips and dashes" in the foreground were painted with custom brushes, then scaled, distorted, or sheared and then colored. ▶To make a brush that paints a dotted line, click a brush tip in the Brushes palette to choose the dot size, then click in the space beyond the last brush in the palette to open the Brush Options dialog box, and set the Spacing higher than 100%; a setting of

200% makes the spaces the same size as the dots. ▶For a dashed line, make a black-filled rectangle the size of the dash you want, select the mark, and choose Define Brush from the Brushes palette's pop-out menu; then adjust Spacing. ▶One way to make

multicolored dotted or dashed lines is to paint the lines on a transparent layer, then turn on Preserve Transparency and airbrush over the lines or drag over them with the gradient tool.

Combining Photoshop and PostScript

Now that Illustrator paths can be copied to the clipboard and pasted into Photoshop, it's possible to make PostScript-smooth clipping paths for image-filled type: Set type in Illustrator, convert it to outlines, select and copy the resulting paths, and then paste them into a Photoshop file. Save the outlines as a clipping path (choose Save Path and then Clipping Paths from the Paths palette's pop-out menu).

Type converted to outlines in Illustrator

Paths pasted into a Photoshop file and stroked with the paintbrush with Wet Edges

Path saved as a clipping path; file placed in PageMaker

YOU CAN MOVE ARTWORK between Adobe Illustrator 7 and Photoshop 4 almost seamlessly, and you can import both kinds of files into page layout programs such as PageMaker and QuarkXPress. How do you decide when it makes sense to combine Illustrator (or other PostScript object-oriented) artwork with an image created in Photoshop? And when it does, how do you decide whether to import a Photoshop illustration into Illustrator, or an Illustrator drawing into Photoshop, or when to assemble the two in a third program? These pointers can help you make the decision:

- The pen tool in Photoshop can draw smooth Bezier curves, and the other path tools make it easy to modify the curves it draws. The Grid and Guides and the Transform command now allow exact placement and snap-to precision. But object-oriented drawing programs such as Illustrator, FreeHand, and CorelDraw still excel at spacing or transforming several copies of an object through a step-and-repeat operation.

- Photoshop's text tool, working with Adobe Type Manager (ATM), can set smooth-looking antialiased type, and the program can produce some amazing type treatments (see Chapter 2 for more about using type in Photoshop). But for really designing with type or fitting type into a particular shape or along a path, or keeping type "live" (editable as text) as you work with it, PostScript drawing and page layout programs are much easier to use.

- When you want to maintain the PostScript nature of certain elements — for instance, for a brochure cover in which the Photoshop artwork is just one element of an illustration that includes logos, graphics, and typography — incorporate the Photoshop artwork into the PostScript file. That way, you can include the painted or photorealistic Photoshop art and still take advantage of the highest resolution of the output device to produce crisp type and the clean edges of the PostScript elements.

- Bring both the Photoshop files and the PostScript artwork into a page layout program for a multipage document, or to assemble a number of items with precise alignment, and especially if large amounts of text will be typeset. A page layout program also provides a way to assemble Photoshop files of different resolutions.

continued on page 222

Photoshop can successfully import Adobe Illustrator's strokes and solid or patterned fills (A–C), both in live type set in a PostScript Type 1 font and in shapes, including type converted to outlines. Gradient fills in objects or in converted type also translate (D). Raster images masked by live type or by a compound object made from type can also be imported (E), but you have more flexibility if you import plain type and use it as a layer mask for the image in Photoshop.

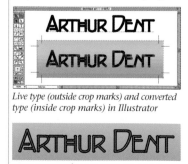
Although PostScript elements play a role in techniques described elsewhere in the book, this chapter presents some how-to examples of using PostScript programs extensively. First, though, here are some tips that will help you move artwork from PostScript drawing programs to Photoshop and vice versa.

ILLUSTRATOR TO PHOTOSHOP

Although it's possible to import encapsulated PostScript (EPS) files from other PostScript illustration programs, Adobe Illustrator shows the greatest compatibility with Photoshop. In fact, any CorelDraw or FreeHand file more complex than black- or white-filled line work may not transfer well when opened or placed. So the best way to make illustrations available for use in Photoshop is to save them in (or convert them to) Illustrator EPS format.

- **FreeHand** files can be saved in Illustrator format, and these files can then usually be opened successfully in Photoshop.

- **CorelDraw** files can be saved directly in Illustrator format by using the program's Export To command.

  (FreeHand and CorelDraw have different ways of dealing with some objects — such as patterned fills, composite paths, and masks — than Illustrator does. So the translation of a complex file from one PostScript drawing program to another may not be completely accurate. If possible, the resulting Illustrator file should be checked in Illustrator before it's imported into Photoshop.)

Illustrator files can be imported in any of the following ways:

- **Open** an Illustrator file to bring the entire file into Photoshop with a transparent background as "Layer 1," unless the graphics fill the canvas.

- **Place** the file to bring all its printable objects in as a layer. To keep the various parts of an illustration in register when they are placed separately in Photoshop, you can define a bounding box for the entire illustration and convert it to crop marks (Object, Cropmarks, Make) before the file is separated into its various parts.

  There are several ways to Place the elements of an Illustrator file into Photoshop separately, so you can control them as independent elements. For instance, while in Illustrator with crop marks at the corners of your artwork, select all objects except the ones you want to place together in a layer, and convert them into Illustrator's guide objects, which aren't imported when a file is opened or placed in Photoshop. By converting back and forth between objects and guide objects and placing the different saved versions of the file into Photoshop as several different layers, you can independently control the imported elements.

  Another way to separate the elements of an Illustrator file so they can be independently imported is to save several copies of

For a high-quality template, a Photoshop file in full color can be placed on an Illustrator layer of its own, and the layer can be locked so the image can't be accidentally nudged. (To reduce the file size of the imported image, you can save it in Indexed Color mode in Photoshop.)

Sometimes you can produce a template with better contrast for tracing if you choose one of the color channels (R, G, or B), select all, copy, paste into a new Grayscale file, and enhance contrast with Image, Adjust, Levels, before importing it into Illustrator. (For more about making a high-contrast image from a single color channel, see the example on page 65.)

The Photoshop file was dragged and dropped into Illustrator, where type was set on a path and converted to outlines. Then the sentence was Ctrl-dragged into the Photoshop file as a layer of its own.

the Illustrator file and then selectively delete elements from each. (This method is described in "Softening the PostScript Line" starting on page 224.)

Or, for each element you want to import, turn off printability for the other layers and Save A Copy.

- Besides using Open or Place, you can also transfer single or multiple Illustrator paths by selecting them, **copying** them to the clipboard, and then **pasting** them into Photoshop.

When you paste an Illustrator object from the clipboard into Photoshop, the Paste dialog box lets you choose to paste it as Bezier paths or rasterized as pixels.

- You can **drag and drop** artwork from an open Illustrator file to an open Photoshop file by selecting the Illustrator objects you want to import and dragging from the Illustrator file to the Photoshop file, where they will come in as a new layer. To import the artwork as **paths** instead of pixels, hold down the Ctrl key as you drag. To **center** the imported art in the Photoshop image, hold down the Shift key while dragging.

PHOTOSHOP TO ILLUSTRATOR

If you want to import a Photoshop image into Illustrator in order to add type or geometric elements, or to trace parts of it to produce PostScript artwork, there are at least three ways to do it:

- One way is to save the Photoshop file as a **TIFF, GIF, JPEG, PICT, PDF, Photoshop** (turn on visibility for all layers you want to include in the imported image), or **EPS** (include a Preview so you can see it on the screen) and use Illustrator's **Open** or **Place** command to import it onto a printing or nonprinting layer. (If you plan to distort [for example, rotate] the Photoshop art in Illustrator and keep it as part of the final Illustrator file, use EPS.)

- If your objective is to fit type to a particular part of your Photoshop image, the simplest way may be to open the file in Illustrator, make a path to fit, set type on it, convert the type to outlines, and then drag the converted type back into the Photoshop file.

Or use Photoshop's pen tool to create a path in the shape you want to fit, then export it (File, Export, Paths To Illustrator), and open the file in Illustrator. It will be invisible in Preview mode, being stroked and filled with None. Use Illustrator's path type tool in Artwork mode to set the type, convert it to outlines, and then copy and paste, Place, or drag and drop the Illustrator art into the Photoshop file. When the Illustrator type on a path is placed back into the Photoshop image, it comes in exactly in register with the original Photoshop path. *rules*

Softening the PostScript Line

Overview *Design artwork in a PostScript drawing program, inside crop marks or a bounding box; separate the drawn elements by making as many copies of the file as needed and deleting elements from each copy; save the files in EPS format and rasterize in Photoshop; combine the files as layers in a single composite; modify to taste.*

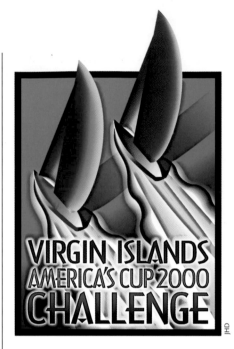

1a

The finished Illustrator artwork, designed in layers to make it easy to delete elements from duplicate files

1b

The duplicate Illustrator files with elements deleted. The border is in two parts; the front one traps the wake but is open so the sails can project above the top edge.

2a

Rasterizing the EPS files into Photoshop

WORKING WITH BOTH Photoshop and an object-oriented drawing program gives you access to both kinds of programs' best features. For this comp for a poster illustration, shape-blending and typesetting were done in the object-oriented (or vector-based) Adobe Illustrator. Then the artwork was opened in the pixel-based environment of Photoshop, where filters and soft-edged selections made it easy to produce the kinds of semitransparent effects that are nearly impossible in an object-oriented program — like the interaction between a soft-edged element like a glow or a shadow and a gradient-filled background.

1 Preparing art in a drawing program. Design a layout, draw objects, and set type in a PostScript drawing program such as Adobe Illustrator, Macromedia FreeHand, or CorelDraw. Start by defining the "canvas" in your object-oriented program by drawing a rectangle and converting it to crop marks, or just retaining it as a no-outline, no-fill object. Inside the crop marks in Illustrator we shaped the sailboats with gradient-filled objects, and formed their wakes with object-to-object blends. The type was set and turned into outlines. All the artwork was done in shades of gray in order to work out values and contrasts.

Next, make separate files to preserve graphic elements that overlap each other. We did this in Illustrator by duplicating the finished artwork file several times (File, Save As) and then deleting unwanted parts from each of the new files. Keep the crop marks or bounding rectangle as part of each file to ensure that all the files have the same overall shape and dimensions. Save the files in EPS format.

2 Importing the files into Photoshop. Rasterize all the EPS files into Photoshop (File, Open), using the same dimensions and

2b

Since our two sailing boats were identical, we rasterized only one boat, one set of sails, and one wake. The elements were then Shift-dragged and dropped into a single composite file.

3

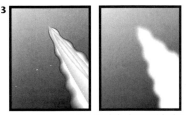

The wake, viewed on the left above with the background and the border, was duplicated and the duplicate was filled with white and blurred to make a glow (shown on the right with visibility for the wake turned off).

4a

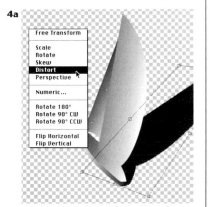

Casting the shadow with Free Transform

resolution for each file. Then open the Layers palette so you'll be able to see the composite building (Window, Show Layers), and Shift-drag each of the elements into a single file to make layers. If you drag the elements into the composite file in back-to-front order, you won't have to rearrange the layers later; we started with the bottom (Border) file and dragged the other elements into it. Because all the files are defined by the same crop marks or bounding rectangle and are exactly the same dimensions, pixel for pixel, Shift-dragging will pin-register all the elements precisely.

3 Building the background and glow. To make a gradient filled-background, start by adding a new layer (click the New Layer icon) and dragging its name to the bottom of the stack in the Layers palette. Next we dragged with the rectangular marquee to select a rectangle the size of the border element. We double-clicked the gradient tool in the toolbox to open the Gradient Tool Options palette, and set up a Foreground To Background Linear gradient with black as the Foreground color and white as the Background color (pressing "D" restores these defaults) and with the Dither option selected to keep the gradient from banding. We dragged from a point beyond the bottom right corner of the selection to a point beyond the top left corner to produce a dark-to-light-gray fill.

To make a glow around one of the sailboat wakes, we first duplicated its layer (open the Layers palette and drag the name of the layer you want to copy to the New Layer icon, in the middle at the bottom of the palette). Next we filled the wake shape in the lower of the two identical layers with white by pressing Ctrl-Shift-Backspace (with white as the Background color, Ctrl-Backspace fills a layer with the Background color, and adding the Shift key restricts the fill to the nontransparent pixels, like turning on Preserve Transparency temporarily). Choosing Filter, Blur, Gaussian Blur softened the edge of the white shape, which was then offset down and to the right with the move tool ("V" is the keyboard shortcut) and the arrow keys. The result was a partially transparent glow over a gradient background that would have been very difficult to produce in Illustrator.

4 Shadowing a multilayer element. You can make a shadow for any element by duplicating its layer, filling the lower of the two elements with black, and blurring (this process is described in more detail in "Casting a Shadow" in Chapter 8). But if you want to make a single shadow for several elements that occupy more than one layer, you can do it as we did for the shadow of the boat and its sails: We created a new layer below the boat by activating the wake layer and clicking the New Layer icon to add a layer just above it. Next we Ctrl-clicked the thumbnail for the boat to load its transparency mask as a selection, and then Ctrl-Shift-clicked the thumbnail for the sails to add its transparency mask to the existing selection. Pressing Alt-Backspace filled the selected area of the new layer with black.

4b

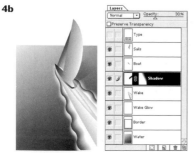

The shadow, with Opacity reduced and a layer mask added

5

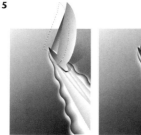

Making a selection that paralleled the curve of the sail, trimming and feathering it, and darkening the selected area adds needed volume and dimension.

6   **7**

Sails, boat, and wake duplicated   *White glow added behind the type*

8a   **8b**

Treating a merged copy with the Photocopy filter

The final Layers palette

With the shadow layer active (though unseen behind the boat and sails), Ctrl-T (for Layer, Free Transform) opened a Transform bounding box around the shadow. Clicking the right mouse button brought up the context-sensitive Transform menu, where we could choose Distort. Then dragging on the top corner handles stretched out the shadow beside the boat. The context-sensitive menu was used again to Skew and Scale the shadow; double-clicking inside the Transform box completed the transformation. The Opacity of the layer was reduced to 30%, and a layer mask was added (click the Add Layer Mask icon) and given a gradient fill to fade the shadow.

5 Adding dimensionality. Feathered selections can be filled to create soft, realistically rounded surfaces like the large sail. Working on the sails layer we loaded the transparency mask for the sail by Ctrl-clicking on the layer's name in the Layers palette. We feathered the selection, offset it with the move tool and the arrow keys, and then trimmed it by deselecting everything to the left of the original large sail. (To subtract from a selection, hold down the Alt key while using a selection tool or loading an alpha channel, layer mask, or transparency mask as a selection. The Image, Adjust, Levels command was used to darken the selected area.

6 Duplicating composite elements. Next we wanted to duplicate the finished boat, its shadow, and its wake and glow. We clicked eye icons in the Layers palette to make all these layers visible and the others (gradient background, border, and type) invisible. We selected all (Ctrl-A); then copied (Edit, Copy Merged, or Ctrl-Shift-C); and pasted (Ctrl-V) to add a layer with these elements combined. We dragged with the move tool to offset the new boat.

7 Treating the type. The type layer was made visible and was given a glow using the same process used for the wake in step 3.

8 Adding dramatic edges. The Photocopy filter can be used to generate soft, thick-and-thin line work. With all layers visible and the top layer active, select all, Copy Merged, and Paste a new layer at the top of the stack. Then choose Filter, Sketch, Photocopy and adjust Detail and Darkness to taste. Putting this layer in Multiply mode overlays the dark edges on the composite image below.

Coloring. To get the result shown at the top of page 224, the Grayscale file was converted to RGB (Image, Mode, RGB Color) and color was added to the image: The individual lines of black type were selected with the rectangular marquee and filled with solid color or gradients. The artwork was colored by applying Image, Adjust, Color Balance to individual layers. For example, for the boat on the right the Shadows and Midtones were pushed toward Red, and the Highlights toward Yellow (this technique is described in step 2 of "Coloring a Black & White Photo" in Chapter 3).

Taking a 3D View

Overview *Prepare artwork in a PostScript illustration program; put it into perspective in a 3D drawing program; import it into Photoshop; create shading; incorporate other elements; create reflections and shadows.*

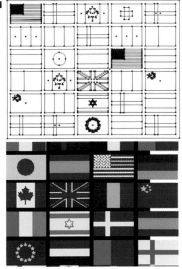

One set of flags created in Illustrator; Artwork mode (top) and Preview mode

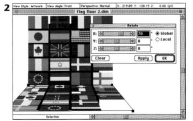

Flags file distorted in Adobe Dimensions

SMOOTHING DIAGONALS

To smooth a jagged diagonal line created with Layer, Transform, Perspective, choose the blur tool (the water drop) with a small brush tip, set Pressure at 100%, hold down the Shift key, and click on the beginning and end of the diagonal.

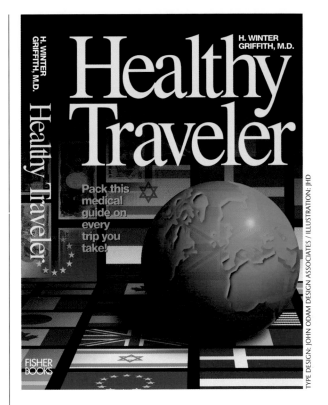

TYPE DESIGN: JOHN ODAM DESIGN ASSOCIATES / ILLUSTRATION: JHD

PHOTOSHOP'S PERSPECTIVE FUNCTION is quick and easy, but a pixel-based program just can't give you the same perfectly smooth results you can get with a vector-based application. The illustration for the cover of this book about health issues in foreign traveling includes a horizontal surface in perspective, made from an assemblage of flags, and a backdrop that blends the original vertical version of the flags into a scanned image of international currency. Adobe Illustrator provided the precise, crisp shapes needed to trace the flags from a scan. Then one set of flags was "laid flat" in Adobe Dimensions to make the horizontal surface. The result was imported into Photoshop and the clip art globe was added.

1 Drawing the artwork in Illustrator. Create two pieces of artwork in an Adobe Illustrator file, one for the vertical part of the backdrop and another for the horizontal surface. We started with two rectangular assemblages of flags and grouped each set. Save the file in EPS format.

2 Putting it into perspective. Open the Illustrator EPS file in the Adobe Dimensions program. (If you don't have Dimensions or another 3D program, you can use Layer, Transform, Perspective after you import the artwork into Photoshop in step 3; the Andromeda Series 2 filter, described on page 182, is another option.) In Dimensions use the trackball tool and the Rotate dialog

Flags imported into Photoshop

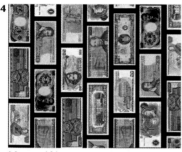

Money grid image

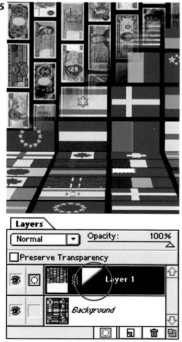

Currency dragged into flags image and montaged with a graduated layer mask

box to tilt the image. One group of flags was rotated 70 degrees around the horizontal (*X*) axis. Either of the two pieces of grouped artwork can be scaled so the two are the same length at the "seam." Since no special coloring or lighting effects were being used here, the rotation completed the Dimensions work; the file was saved in EPS format.

3 Placing the perspective file. In Photoshop set up a new background file (Ctrl-N) at the size and resolution you need. In this case the file (a medium-resolution comp version) was 7½ by 9¼ inches at 200 dpi, making it 1500 pixels wide altogether. Open the Layers palette (Window, Show Layers).

Now use File, Place to import the EPS (the flags in this case). The placed art will come in on a new layer. Shift-Alt-drag on a corner of the placed image to scale it to fit your file. After double-clicking inside the bounding box to accept the size, press Ctrl-E to merge the new artwork layer with the background layer below it.

4 Preparing the second image. In another Photoshop file paint or import the second image you want to combine. In this case we scanned an assemblage of bills on a desktop flatbed scanner, color-corrected and retouched it to create a "money grid," and used Image, Image Size to make it 1500 pixels wide. We used Filter, Sharpen, Unsharp Mask to get rid of any blurriness caused by scanning and resizing.

Next drag and drop the artwork onto the background file (the flags in this case) with the move tool. The dragged artwork will come in as a new layer above the background.

5 Making a mask to blend the two images. With the new layer active, click the Add Layer Mask icon, on the left at the bottom of the Layers palette. Then, with the mask active (indicated by the mask icon next to the Layer's thumbnail), double-click the gradient tool in the toolbox to open the Gradient Tool Options palette. In this case we used a Black, White gradient in Normal mode with a Linear setting; the gradient tool was dragged diagonally over a short distance near the middle of the window; this produced a narrow gray band between black and white, which made a fairly quick transition from currency to flags.

6 Shading. You can darken or lighten areas of the image for adding type or to enhance the 3D illusion you created with the perspective effect. We used a Levels Adjustment layer to darken an area at the top of the illustration to make a background for the title type and to create some "atmosphere" between the front of the image and the "back wall." First we Ctrl-clicked the New Layer icon to add the Adjustment layer, and then chose Levels as the Type. We adjusted Levels (moving the Input Levels black point slider to the right) to darken the two layers below. Then we used the gradient tool

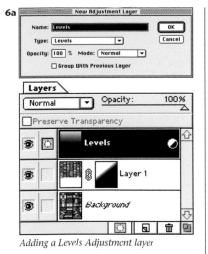

6a

Adding a Levels Adjustment layer

6b

The gradient-filled Levels Adjustment layer applied to darken the top of the illustration

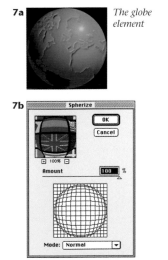

7a

The globe element

7b

Spherizing to make a "decal" for the globe

to make a Black, White bottom-to-top gradient in the Levels Adjustment layer, limiting the darkening effect to the top of the image.

7 Adding a 3D object. Now create or import a 3D foreground object. We imported the globe.

A pseudo-reflection was created by selecting a square part of the original flags image with the rectangular marquee, copying and pasting it as a new layer in the globe file, rounding it (Filter, Distort, Spherize), and then reducing its Opacity in the Layers palette; the effect was like applying it to the globe image as a decal. The globe and reflection layers were merged (Ctrl-E). Then the merged layer was dragged and dropped into the main file with the move tool, creating a new layer, and then moved into place in the composition.

8 Adding shadows. Finally, we needed a shadow in the corner of the scene and a drop shadow for the globe. We made a rectangular selection of the "floor" area and saved it in an alpha channel by opening the Channels palette (Window, Show Channels) and clicking the Save Selection icon (second from the left at the bottom of the palette). We activated the new channel by clicking its name in the Channels palette and also clicked the eye icon for the RGB (composite) channel in the Channels palette so we could see both the mask (a semitransparent red "film") and the image. We used the gradient tool to create a Black, White gradient at an angle inside the still selected rectangle. This would make possible a graduated selection that would shade the corner (as shown in the opening illustration on page 227).

Next we made a feathered selection with the elliptical marquee (set the Feather in the Marquee Options palette). This ellipse would be used to make a drop shadow for the globe. Pressing Backspace cleared the ellipse in the alpha channel mask. To soften the transition of the shadow into the background, we started by clicking off

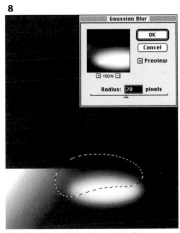

8

Blurring the trailing edge of the drop shadow mask in channel #4

the eye icon for the RGB channel so we could see the alpha channel clearly in black-and-white. A lasso with a 50-pixel feather was used to select the trailing edge of the ellipse, and a Gaussian blur was applied (Filter, Blur, Gaussian Blur, 20 pixels).

With the merged money-and-flags layer active, we Ctrl-clicked channel #4 in the Channels palette, which loaded the channel as a selection. Adjusting Levels created the shadows in the corner and under the globe.

Lance Hidy's 20 x 30-inch five-color *poster for the Gelman Library* of the George Washington University was an exercise in planning and file size economy. He created the components in Photoshop, Adobe Illustrator, and Adobe Streamline, and layered them together in QuarkXPress. Hidy knew he couldn't get the depth of color he wanted for the green-to-aqua sky from process colors alone, so he added a fifth printing ink to his design, Reflex Blue from the Pantone Matching System.

The trees were developed from a scan of a color slide. What seem to be trunks stretching upward in the poster image, in the original photo were actually branches extending outward, since the photo was taken under a tree with the camera pointing straight up. Hidy used Levels to increase the contrast between branches and sky in the 10.5 MB color scan, and then applied Threshold to produce a strictly black-and-white image. The file was converted to Bitmap mode (Image, Mode, Grayscale, and then Image, Mode Bitmap) and saved in EPS format with Transparent Whites selected so the trees could be layered over the background in QuarkXPress. Slightly more than 20 inches wide, the 136 dpi bitmap file was 450K.

The Washington Monument was drawn in Illustrator and filled with a rich gray that included all four process colors (C, M, Y, and K).

Some of the type characters are from Adobe fonts, set in Illustrator and converted to outlines. Others were from printed type, scanned on a desktop flatbed scanner and traced with Adobe Streamline. Characters with counters emerged from the tracing as black-filled type bodies with white-filled counters stacked on top, and each counter-and-body pair had to be converted to a compound object in Illustrator to turn the

counter shapes into holes. To color the characters, Hidy selected them all and set up a pink-to-orange gradient in the Paint Style dialog box, which filled each letter with the entire gradient. Then dragging the gradient tool from top to bottom of the whole assemblage spread the gradient over all the characters. Hidy then sampled the gradient to check color composition at three different heights, and used these three colors to make trapping strokes for the type.

The background was created as two files in Photoshop, each with a gradient. Hidy made an aqua-to-green gradient in a

CMYK file. He added a small amount of noise (Filter, Noise, Add Noise) to keep the gradient from banding over the span of the poster's height. Rob Anderson at Progress Printing in Lynchburg, Virginia made the Reflex Blue gradient in a grayscale file sized to match Hidy's background file.

The files were layered into QuarkXPress, where title and text were added in Penumbra, designed by Hidy as an Adobe Multiple Masters font. Anderson defined a new printing color for his gradient, and the page was separated into C, M, Y, K and a fifth printing plate.

To "paint" *Cedar,* **Bert Monroy** began as he often does, referring to a photograph and using Adobe Illustrator's drawing tools to construct the building and its details. Still in Illustrator he assigned color fills to the elements he had built, saved them in EPS format and imported them into Photoshop, where he added highlights, shadows, and textures.

Monroy painted the tree on its own layer in Photoshop, using a large, round brush for the trunk and decreasing brush sizes for the branches. He added Noise and then applied the Craquelure filter (from Filter, Texture) to make the bark texture.

To paint the leaves on the tree and shrubs, Monroy created a set of custom brushes. For the tree's leaves, about a dozen different shapes were drawn in Illustrator and imported into Photoshop, where each was selected and made into a brush by choosing Define Brush from the Brushes palette. Copies of the leaf shapes

were also skewed, rotated, and distorted to make more brushes, thus creating enough variety to fill the tree with individual-looking leaves. Using the Paintbrush tool and various shades of green, Monroy added the leaves by clicking the paintbrush all over the branches, starting with the dark, shadowed ones in the back. He added dappled light to the forward leaves, trunk, and branches with the dodge and burn tools.

The tree's late afternoon shadow was added by duplicating the tree layer and filling the copy with black. ▶*Pressing Shift-Alt-Backspace fills nontransparent areas of the active layer with the Foreground color.*

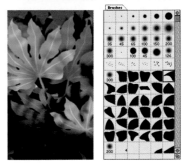

The shadow layer was scaled, skewed, faded, and blurred using methods like those described in "Casting a Shadow" in Chapter 8, except that the blurring of the shadow was done with the Motion Blur filter.

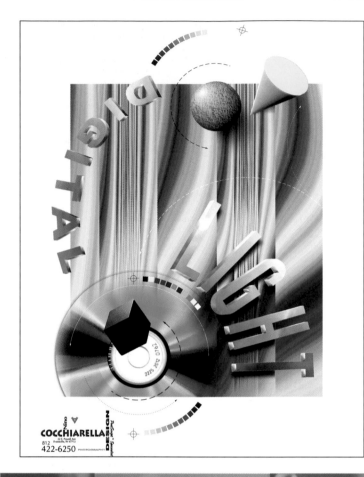

To make his *Digital Light* self-promo poster, **Nino Cocchiarella** started out in CorelDraw, producing the fractal background and fractal-filled 3D type, which he exported as a TIFF and opened in Photoshop. There he added a scan of a compact disc, making it partially transparent by reducing the Opacity of its layer. He also added the cone, sphere, and cube, imported from a 3D program. He Saved As to make an additional low-resolution version of the image, which he imported into Corel-Draw as a template for adding the line work and type fitted to curves. The line work and type assemblage was exported in EPS format, and final assembly of the Photoshop and PostScript components was done in QuarkXPress.

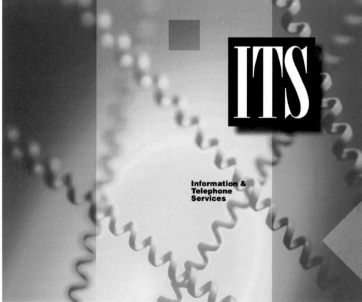

For the combined front and back covers of this *ITS Brochure* about telephone services, **Nino Cocchiarella** began with a dramatically lit photo of telephone cords, shot with a shallow depth of field and with green filters on the light. The rectangles and diamond were drawn in CorelDraw and exported in EPS format so they could be placed in an alpha channel in the photo file. To color the background, he loaded the mask into the main image channel as a selection, adjusted Hue/Saturation to produce the yellow color, and then inverted the mask and repeated the adjustment process to refine

the green. The black rectangle and its drop shadow were added (see "Casting a Shadow" in Chapter 8 for a method). Type was added in QuarkXPress. The printed cover was folded in half to enclose the booklet.

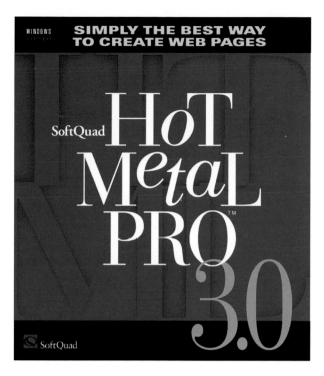

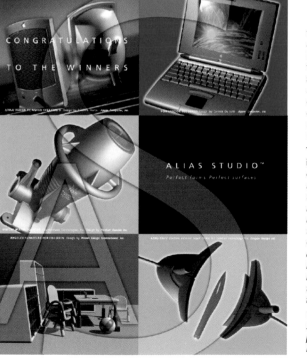

To design the *packaging for SoftQuad's HotMetal Pro* HTML-editing software, **Louis Fishauf** started in Adobe Illustrator. After setting the large red "H," "T," "M," and "L" and converting the type to outlines, he dragged each letter into Photoshop as a separate layer. He applied a gradient fill to each letter. ▶*You can restrict a gradient fill to the non-transparent areas of a layer, keeping the transparent areas clear, by turning on Preserve Transparency for that layer at the top of the Layers palette.*

Fishauf added a drop shadow by duplicating the type layer, moving the duplicate layer below the original, filling with black, and blurring.

To create texture and lighting in the red background layer behind the letters, Fishauf added noise and adjusted Levels. ▶*To "roughen" a smooth background without adding unrelated colors, use Filter, Noise, Add Noise and choose Monochromatic.*

The finished image was taken back into Illustrator. There Fishauf added the white and gold type.

Louis Fishauf created this *ad for the Alias Studio* industrial design package (now Alias|Wavefront Studio) for the annual awards issue of *ID* magazine. The images shown in the ad had been drawn and rendered with the Alias software and were provided to Fishauf in TIFF format. He opened them in Photoshop and used the lasso and pen tools to make selections to silhouette them, and then composited them as layers in a single Photoshop file, where he added white glows. ▶*You can make a glow around a silhouetted object on a transparent layer by duplicating the layer, pressing "D" to ensure that the Background color is set to white, and then pressing Shift-Ctrl-Backspace to fill the object in the new layer. Blurring the white with Filter, Blur, Gaussian Blur completes the glow.*

The large "A" and "S" were set in Adobe Illustrator and brought into Photoshop to create a translucent effect. ▶*One way to create translucent-looking type is by setting or importing black type into its own layer and then using it as a "cookie cutter": Load the transparency mask for the type by Ctrl-clicking the type layer's name in the Layers palette; then activate the image layer underneath and press Ctrl-J to make a new layer of type filled with the image. Choose Image, Adjust, Levels and move the black Output Levels slider to lighten the image and reduce contrast. Make a drop shadow by dragging the original black type layer below the image-filled type, clicking off the Preserve Transparency box, and blurring (Filter, Blur, Gaussian Blur), lowering the Opacity to lighten the shadow. The image-filled type looks translucent but is really fully opaque, so the shadow shows only at the edges.*

Work shown in the ad was submitted by (clockwise from upper left): Susanne Pierce, Apple Computer, Inc.; Daniele De Iuliis, Apple Computer, Inc.; Gingko Design, Inc.; Nissan Design International, Inc.; Product Genesis, Inc.

GRAPHICS SPECIAL EFFECTS

MOST OF THE SPECIAL EFFECTS in this chapter are designed to simulate what happens when light and materials interact — from a simple drop shadow to the complex reflections and refraction of chrome, brushed metal, or crystal. The next six pages present an overview of using Photoshop's alpha channels, filters, layers, and layer masks to start a wide range of dramatic dimensional treatments. The step-by-step special effects techniques later in the chapter give you all the details you need for creating objects and textures where none existed before. And you can find many special effects, with more variations, recorded as Actions on the Wow! CD-ROM, so you can load them into Photoshop's Actions palette and "automate" many photorealistic and superrealistic looks.

- The **Lighting Effects filter** is key. Supplied with the right raw materials in the form of RGB images to be carved, stamped, or otherwise dimensioned, and grayscale channels to shape the dimensioning, Lighting Effects can produce a wide variety of effects. The number and Styles of lights you set up and the overall Properties settings can make the difference between subtle and startling results. For special purposes, other filters — like Emboss or Texturizer — can also do the dimensioning. And filters like Glass, Chrome, and Plastic Wrap can play an important role in modelling the play of light on dull, shiny, transparent, or translucent surfaces.

- **Layers, layer masks,** and **Adjustment layers** make it easy to control embossed objects, their shadows, highlights, and colors independently. They also let you apply several effects to different layers and then customize the way they mix by changing the blending modes and opacity of the layers.

- **Alpha channels** store grayscale images so they can be loaded as textures or duplicated and applied as masks in precisely determined, exactly repeatable positions.

- **Levels, Curves, Color Balance,** and **Variations** can be applied, either directly or through Adjustment layers, to provide subtle changes in color or brightness.

DIGITAL "EMBOSSING"

Each special effect in this chapter showcases some variation of raising a shape from the surface, which we can call *embossing,* or the

continued on page 236

One way to produce the original white-on-black graphic to be used for embossing is to build it in Adobe Illustrator, copy it, and paste it into a Photoshop alpha channel. Another way is to make it directly in Photoshop.

Blurring a copy of the graphic produces "gray matter" at the edges, which will give a smoother emboss or deboss.

The third of the "basic" embossing channels is a "thin" version of the original, to be used for "trimming" the top edge of a copy of the blurred graphic.

A copy of the blurred alpha channel (#5) can be trimmed with the original (#4) and thin (#6) alpha channels, making a specialized channel (#7), shown above.

opposite — sinking it into the surface, called ***debossing.*** Before you tackle the special effects techniques themselves, here's a "primer" that provides the foundation for most of them. If you understand the fundamentals described in this "Digital Embossing" section, it will be easier to carry out the techniques in the rest of the chapter, where instructions are provided at the click-and-drag level of detail.

1 Starting with a graphic. Photoshop's Lighting Effects filter uses the grayscale information of a black-and-white graphic as the basis for creating dimensionality in an RGB file. So a good first step in creating a dimensional effect is to store a black-and-white graphic in an alpha channel. By default the white in the channel will raise the surface when the channel is used with Lighting Effects' default settings, and black will leave the surface flat. If the graphic is only black and white, with no more gray than you find in an antialiased edge, sharp vertical sides are created at the edge of the graphic.

2 Generating "gray matter." For a smooth, realistic, embossed or debossed appearance, you need a range of gray tones between black and white, to make a gradual transition between the raised or sunken graphic and the surrounding surface. So the next step in creating a dimensional effect is often to store a blurred copy of the graphic in a second alpha channel. Blurring a black-and-white graphic spreads gray tones both inward and outward from where the black and white meet, making a soft "shoulder" instead of a "cliff." By using the Gaussian Blur filter, you can control the character of the edge: The larger the Radius setting for the Gaussian Blur, the more the edge softens up, and the more gradual the transition will be between the low and high surfaces of the emboss.

3 Making "cookie cutters." Once you have a grayscale channel with the original graphic and another with a blurred ("gray matter") copy of it, there's another basic stored selection you need: a slimmed-down (less bold) version of the original. Then both the original and this thin version can be used to create sharper top and bottom edges for the embossing graphic, while keeping some rounding and "slope" in the shoulder itself. This thin graphic can be produced by creating a new black-filled alpha channel, loading the original graphic as a selection in it, shrinking the selection a little (Select, Modify, Contract), and filling the selection with white.

4 Shaping the gray matter with the original graphic and the thin graphic. With the three alpha channels described in steps 1 through 3 you can create specialized alpha channels for producing a variety of dimensional effects. For instance, loading the thin version as a selection in a copy of the blurred channel and filling the selection with white removes the blurring that had encroached into the graphic. The sides and outside edges of the graphic are still gray. So when the graphic is used for embossing,

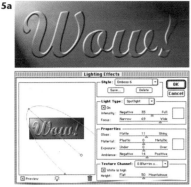

Lighting Effects can be applied to an RGB image, with an alpha channel (#7 is shown here) used as the Texture Channel.

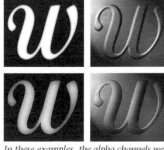
the sides will still rise gradually from a softly curved bottom edge, but the top surface will be flat and its edges will be sharp.

On the other hand, if you load the original (fatter) graphic as a selection in a copy of the blurred channel, then reverse the selection to select the black background instead of the white graphic, and fill this new selection with black, you effectively trim away the blurring that had extended into the background. So when you emboss, the top edge will be rounded, but the edge where the graphic meets the surrounding surface will be sharp.

5 Embossing and debossing with Lighting Effects. The Lighting Effects filter embosses or debosses a surface image using an

The alpha channel that holds the original graphic (#4) was used as the Texture Channel when the Lighting Effects filter was applied to a gold-colored surface for embossing (center) and debossing (right). It produced the look of a thin cut-out laid on top of a background.

When the blurred alpha channel (#5) was used as the Texture Channel for the Lighting Effects filter, both the inner (top surface) and outer (bottom) edges of the "W" were rounded.

The surface of the embossed/debossed "W" was flattened by "trimming" a duplicate of the blurred channel (#5) with the "thin" channel (#6) and using the result as the Texture Channel.

The outer edge of the "W" was sharpened by trimming a copy of the blurred channel (#5) with a reversed selection made from the "original" (#4); the result was used as the Texture Channel.

To make a beveled edge like the one used to emboss the "Wow!" graphic at the left, both the inner and outer edges of the blurred "W" channel (#5) were trimmed, as described for the two versions above, and the result was used as the Texture Channel.

5g

To make a Texture Channel for "quilted" embossing, the "original" channel (#4) was loaded as a selection in a duplicate of the blurred channel, the tonality of the selected area was inverted (Ctrl-I), and the result was used as the Texture Channel.

5h

The best way we've found to create a raised or sunken chiseled look with a sharp central ridge is to load the "original" channel (#4) as a selection in a new black-filled alpha channel and run the KPT Gradient Designer, which is part of Kai's Power Tools, on this channel. Then use the alpha channel as the Texture Channel for the Lighting Effects filter. Though it means buying a set of plug-ins, it's worth the expense if you want to get results like these. (Step-by-step directions are given in "Chiseling," starting on page 251.)

MATCHING BLUR AND TRIM

When you use a "thin" version of a graphic to trim a blurred version, the setting you choose for Select, Modify, Contract is related to the Radius setting you used for the Gaussian Blur. Using the same or a slightly smaller setting for Contract often does a good job.

6a

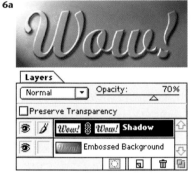

Here's one way to create a **cast shadow** to add to the illusion of depth in an **embossed** image: With the embossed layer active, load the "original" alpha channel as a selection, make a new layer, fill the selection in this new layer with black, deselect, blur the layer, and offset the shadow. To mask the shadow so it appears to be cast onto the background by the embossing, use a layer mask made from the original graphic. Step-by-step directions for this technique are provided in step 4 of "Chiseling" on page 254.

6b

The **cast shadow** and layer mask for a **debossed graphic** are created the same way as for the embossed example in figure 6a, except that the tonality of the Shadow layer and its mask are the opposite — the graphic is white in both shadow and mask, and the surrounding area is black. This method is described in step 4 of "Carving" on page 249.

alpha channel as the Texture Channel. The White Is High option raises the surface where the graphic is light. In contrast, turning off White Is High raises the surface where the graphic is dark.

6 Enhancing embossed images. Adjusting the Gloss and Material settings to simulate a shiny or matte surface, which can be done in the Lighting Effects dialog box, helps make dimensional images look more realistic. Adding cast or drop shadows also adds to the photorealism.

The **"Embossing Sampler"** Action on the Wow! CD-ROM starts with an RGB file and a graphic in the first alpha channel and generates five of the additional kinds of alpha channels shown in step 5 on pages 237–238. It then brings up the Lighting Effects dialog box so you can choose one of these alpha channels as the Texture Channel for embossing or debossing.

CHOOSING THE RIGHT METHOD

The addition of layers to Photoshop 3 greatly increased the number of ways to create special effects such as drop shadows and rounded and beveled edges. And when Adjustment layers were added in

6c

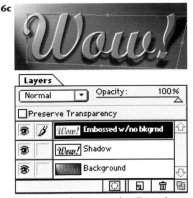

In this example we wanted to distort the shadow alone, without distorting the type. One way to do it was to put the type and the background on two separate layers, with the shadow in between. To accomplish this, the type was embossed on a Background and the embossed type alone was selected and copied to a new layer (Ctrl-J). Then this layer with embossed type and no background was duplicated to make the Shadow layer. The Shadow was dragged below the original in the Layers palette, filled with black, blurred, and offset, using a method described in step 4 of "Coloring and Embossing" on page 244. Using the Free Transform command's context-specific menu made it possible to Distort the shadow.

THE CLEAN-UP DETAIL

The embossing you do in Photoshop with blurred and trimmed alpha channels can sometimes cause unwanted artifacts at the edges. If your embossing is on a transparent layer, you can trim away the unwanted pixels by loading the original graphic as a selection in the embossed layer, shrinking the selection by 1 pixel (Select, Modify, Contract), reversing the selection (Ctrl-Shift-I), and deleting.

Embossed graphic with "raw" (left) and cleaned-up edges

Photoshop 4, the range of possibilities got even broader. The techniques in this chapter introduce a wide range of approaches to creating special effects. For example:

- A **drop shadow** can be sandwiched in between the subject and the background (as shown in figure 6c at the left and in "Coloring and Embossing") or layered from above if you use a mask (as shown in 6a and 6b on page 238, as well as in "Carving" and "Chiseling").

- A **dimensional effect** can be achieved by using channels and the **Lighting Effects filter** to achieve dramatic lighting (as in "Chiseling") or a more subtle raised effect (as in the embossing done in "Casting a Shadow").

- Using the **Emboss filter** gives you less control over the lighting and surface character of a dimensional effect, but it takes less RAM than Lighting Effects. So methods like that used in "Coloring and Embossing" or "Carving" may sometimes be a more workable option.

- The **reflected and refracted light** and images that make chrome, brushed metal, crystal, and glass sparkle and shine can be manufactured by setting up multiple spotlights in the Lighting Effects dialog box as in "Forging Steel," or with a combination of a photo, Lighting Effects, and a special-effects filter — Glass, Plastic Wrap, or Chrome — as in "Creating Chrome."

With all these possibilities, here are some things to consider when choosing a method for implementing a special effect:

- **Is the illusion convincing?** Sometimes a method that makes a nice-looking embossed, highlighted edge works fine on a rounded object or letterform but looks like a "white shadow" when you apply it to something with sharp corners.

- **Does it give you the control you need?** Some methods that lighten or darken an edge using only layers and blending modes don't let you change the color balance of a highlight or shadow individually. But with alpha channels, layer masks, or Adjustment layers you can target the fine-tuning of color and tonality.

- **Does it produce a clean edge?** Some methods leave a residue around edges. You can fix some problems after the fact as described in "The Clean-up Detail" on this page, but it's usually cleaner and quicker if you can avoid producing the messy edge in the first place.

- **Is it flexible?** You may want to house your special effect in transparent layers that are completely independent of the background image, instead of applying them directly to the image. That way you can drag and drop any new background image into the file, instantly applying the effect to the new photo.

Casting a Shadow

Overview *Import a graphic element; "emboss" it with Lighting Effects; add a shadow; scale and skew it; to fade it, apply a blur in stages and add a layer mask.*

The **"Cast Shadow"** *Action on the Wow! CD-ROM automates the process of throwing a fading shadow, slightly different than the one shown here, behind a foreground element.*

1

The original clip art

2a

Alpha channels added: Graphic (#4) and Blurred Graphic (#5)

2b

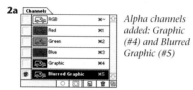

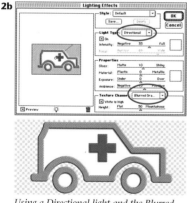

Using a Directional light and the Blurred Graphic alpha channel to "emboss" the graphic with Lighting Effects

3

Adding a shadow layer

ONE WAY TO HELP A GRAPHIC look at home in an environment you've created is to make it cast a shadow onto the background so it appears to stand up. We started with clip art, "embossed" it for dimensionality, and built a shadow.

1 Setting up the graphic. Start with a graphic element on a transparent layer in an RGB file. We opened an EPS file and used Image, Adjust, Levels (Ctrl-L) to lighten the line work to a medium-dark gray, so that when we embossed it (at step 2) the highlights and shadows would show well. Also, the lighter tone would set it off from the dark shadow we planned to add. (You could also set up the file with the File, New command, then turn the bottom layer from *Background* to transparent by double-clicking the *Background* name in the Layers palette, and create a graphic on that layer. Or drag and drop a graphic from Adobe Illustrator and choose Merge Down from the Layers palette's pop-out menu.)

2 Embossing the graphic. The next step will be to make an alpha channel to use with the Lighting Effects filter to "emboss" the graphic. We Ctrl-clicked the name of the composite (RGB) channel in the Channels palette to load the luminosity of the ambulance graphic as a selection. We inverted this selection (Ctrl-Shift-I) to select the lines of the ambulance rather than the lighter area inside and outside the lines). Then we turned the inverted selection into a new alpha channel by clicking the mask icon (second from the left) at the bottom of the Channels palette. We double-clicked the "#4" name in the Channels palette to open the Channel Options dialog box so we could rename the channel "Graphic."

To make the "gray matter" needed for a rounded edge on your graphic, duplicate the new alpha channel by dragging its name to the New Channel icon (next to the trash can) at the bottom of the Channels palette, press Ctrl-D to deselect, and choose Filter, Blur, Gaussian Blur. We used a Radius of 2 pixels for this 1100-pixel-wide file.

Now emboss your graphic layer by activating it and applying Filter, Render, Lighting Effects, using the blurred alpha channel as the Texture Channel. (For more about embossing with Lighting Effects, see pages 234–239 and "Coloring and Embossing" on page 242.)

4

Offsetting the blurred shadow layer to make a drop shadow

5

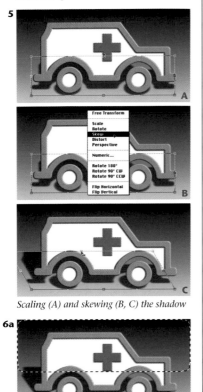

Scaling (A) and skewing (B, C) the shadow

6a

Using a feathered rectangular marquee to blur the shadow repeatedly

6b

Adding a layer mask to fade the shadow

3 Starting the shadow. Duplicate the embossed graphic layer by dragging its name to the New Layer icon at the bottom of the Layers palette. Now you can use the lower of the two identical layers to make the shadow.

With the shadow layer active and with black as the Foreground color, fill with black by pressing Shift-Alt-Backspace. The Shift key will keep the transparent area of the layer from filling, as if Preserve Transparency were turned on for the layer. (The shadow will be hidden beneath the graphic layer, but you can see it if you click the graphic layer's eye icon to toggle its visibility off.) Soften the shadow by applying Filter, Blur, Gaussian Blur. We used a Radius of 5 pixels.

Now continue with step 4 to make a drop shadow, or to make a cast shadow instead, skip step 4 and go on to step 5.

4 Making a drop shadow. To make a drop shadow, offset the shadow layer by choosing the move tool (press "V") and using the keyboard arrow keys. Then experiment with Opacity settings.

5 Making the cast shadow. First add a background. We used the gradient tool to make a Linear Foreground To Background color ramp, with black as the Foreground color and blue as the Background color. (For more about the gradient tool, see the beginning of Chapter 6.)

To tilt the cast shadow into position, you can use the Layer, Free Transform command to both "squash" it and skew it to one side: Starting with the blur-edged shadow at the end of step 3, press Ctrl-T (Layer, Free Transform). Grab the top center handle of the Transform box that appears around the graphic and drag downward to reduce the shadow's height. Put the cursor inside the Transform box and press the right mouse button to open a context-sensitive menu from which you can choose Skew. Then drag the top center handle sideways in the direction you want the shadow to fall. If you need to shorten the shadow more, use the right mouse button to bring up the menu again and choose Scale. When the shadow is the size and angle you want, double-click inside the Transform box to accept the changes.

6 Fading the shadow. For added realism you can gradually blur and lighten the shadow as it fades into the distance. Choose the rectangular marquee, press Enter to open its Options palette, and enter a large Feather setting; we used 20 pixels. Drag out a marquee slightly taller than the shadow, and move it to select the top of the shadow layer, just down to where the top 20% or so of the shadow is included in the selection. Apply a Gaussian Blur; we used a radius of 5 pixels. Then slide the marquee down to include another 20% or so of the shadow and repeat the blur (Ctrl-F). Continue moving and blurring until you get to the bottom of the shadow. To lighten the shadow, add a layer mask to the shadow layer (click the Add Layer Mask icon at the bottom of the Layers palette) and apply a Linear Foreground To Background (black-to-white) gradient. 🖌

Coloring and Embossing

Overview *Use tone-inverted line art in an alpha channel to create a line art layer; on a separate color layer add color inside the lines; emboss the line work; add a shadow.*

The *"Graphic Emboss"* Actions on the Wow! CD-ROM automates an embossing technique similar to this one. Coloring the spaces is not included, since paint bucket fills can't be automated.

1a

The original clip art, placed in channel #4 of a Photoshop file 1100-pixels wide

1b

Layers		
Normal ▼	Opacity:	100%
☐ Preserve Transparency		
👁 ✏	Original Graphic	⇧
👁	*Background*	⇩

The black-on-transparent graphic created in a layer above the Background

2a

Paint Bucket Options		
Normal ▼	Opacity:	100%
Tolerance: (254)	☐ Anti-aliased	
Contents: Foreground ▼		
☒ Sample Merged		

Setting up the paint bucket for filling the spaces

2b

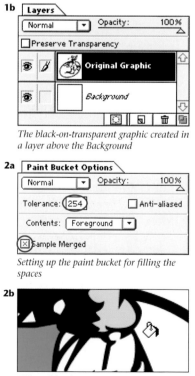

Filling with color

SOMETIMES A LITTLE CLIP ART can go a long way — especially if you're willing to customize it. Two easy-to-accomplish Photoshop enhancements to PostScript clip art are adding color and creating dimension by embossing.

1 Setting up the graphic. You'll start with an RGB file with a white-filled *Background* layer. You'll also need a white-on-black graphic in an alpha channel. Open the Channels palette (Window, Show Channels) and add a black-filled alpha channel to the file by clicking the New Channel icon, next to the trash can icon at the bottom of the palette. Create a white-on-black graphic in the channel, or import an EPS from Adobe Illustrator or another PostScript program (File, Place). Shift-drag the corner handles to size the import, double-click to accept the sizing, invert the tones if needed (Ctrl-I), and deselect (Ctrl-D).

Click the RGB (top) name in the Channels palette so you'll be working in the main image next, not in the alpha channel (#4) that you just created. Open the Layers palette (Window, Show Layers) and add a new layer by Alt-clicking the New Layer icon, in the middle at the bottom of the palette; name the layer "Original Graphic." To construct your graphic in this new layer, load alpha channel #4 as a selection (by pressing Ctrl-Alt-4). Fill the selection in the new layer with black (you can press "D" to restore default Foreground and Background colors and then Alt-Backspace to fill the selection with black). Deselect (Ctrl-D).

2 Adding color. Next you'll add another transparent layer. In the Layers palette click the name of the *Background* layer to activate it,

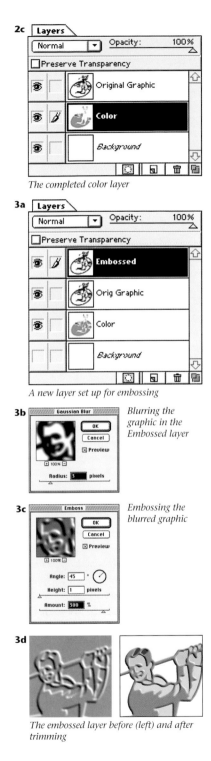

2c Layers

Normal ▼ | Opacity: | 100%

☐ Preserve Transparency

👁 | | 🖼 Original Graphic

👁 | ✏ | **Color**

👁 | | *Background*

The completed color layer

3a Layers

Normal ▼ | Opacity: | 100%

☐ Preserve Transparency

👁 | ✏ | 🖼 **Embossed**

👁 | | 🖼 Orig Graphic

👁 | | 🖼 Color

| | *Background*

A new layer set up for embossing

3b Gaussian Blur

OK | Cancel | ☒ Preview

⊕ 100% ⊟

Radius: 3 pixels

Blurring the graphic in the Embossed layer

3c Emboss

OK | Cancel | ☒ Preview

⊕ 100% ⊟

Angle: 45 °

Height: 1 pixels

Amount: 500 %

Embossing the blurred graphic

3d

The embossed layer before (left) and after trimming

and then Alt-click the New Layer icon to add a layer between the *Background* and the Original Graphic layer; name the new layer "Color."

Now you'll use the paint bucket's ability to define its fill areas using some layers but apply paint in another. With the new Color layer active, double-click the paint bucket in the toolbox to choose it and to open the Paint Bucket Options palette. Set the Tolerance to 254, leave the blending mode as Normal, turn Anti-aliased off, and turn on Sample Merged. Choose colors from the Color palette (opened by choosing Window, Show Color) and click with the paint bucket to fill the spaces defined by the Original Graphic and *Background* layers. The paint bucket defines the areas to fill by "looking at" all the currently visible layers as if they were a single image.

3 Embossing the graphic. To emboss, you'll need a layer with the black graphic on a white background. Click the name of the Original Graphic layer in the Layers palette and then Alt-click the New Layer icon to add a layer above it, naming it "Embossed." With white as the Background color (pressing "D" restores the default colors), press Ctrl-Backspace to fill the layer with white. Then load the graphic as a selection again (Ctrl-Alt-4) and fill with black (Alt-Backspace). Deselect (Ctrl-D).

To round the edge of the embossing that will come next, you'll need some "gray matter," which can be created by choosing Filter, Blur, Gaussian Blur; we used a setting of 3 pixels. Then choose Filter, Stylize, Emboss and set the embossing parameters in the Emboss dialog box. After running the filter, trim the embossed layer by loading the graphic as a selection again (Ctrl-Alt-4), inverting the selection (Ctrl-Shift-I), and pressing Backspace. Deselect. Delete the Original Graphic layer, which would otherwise show at the edges of the emboss, by dragging its name to the trash can at the bottom of the Layers palette.

To darken the embossed graphic, activate that layer and Ctrl-click the New Layer icon to add an Adjustment layer above it. So

3e

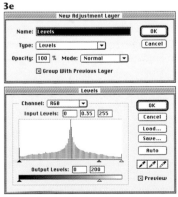

New Adjustment Layer

Name: Levels | OK

Type: Levels ▼ | Cancel

Opacity: 100 % Mode: Normal ▼

☒ Group With Previous Layer

Levels

Channel: RGB ▼

Input Levels: 0 | 0.35 | 255

OK | Cancel | Load... | Save... | Auto

Output Levels: 0 | 200

☒ Preview

Using a Levels Adjustment layer to darken the raised graphic

that it will affect only the embossed layer and not the Color or Background layer, turn on Group With Previous Layer in the New Adjustment Layer dialog box. Choose Levels for the Type of Adjustment layer and click OK. In the Levels dialog box, darken the grays by moving the Input gamma (gray) slider to the right; darken the highlights by moving the Output white point slider to the left.

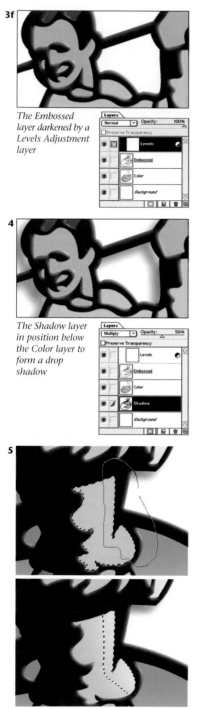

3f

The Embossed layer darkened by a Levels Adjustment layer

4

The Shadow layer in position below the Color layer to form a drop shadow

5

Making an intersecting selection (left) and using it to lighten part of the shirt with Levels

4 Adding a drop shadow. To make a shadow, Ctrl-click on the Embossed layer to load its transparency mask as a selection. Alt-click the New Layer icon to add a layer, naming it "Shadow" and putting it in Multiply mode. Then fill the selection with black (Alt-Backspace). Deselect (Ctrl-D) and blur the shadow (Filter, Blur, Gaussian Blur). To put the shadow behind the artwork, drag the Shadow layer's name below the Color layer in the Layers palette. Offset the shadow to taste with the move tool and arrow keys.

5 Enhancing the color. Now you can introduce a little more sophistication to the color scheme. Double-click the magic wand in the toolbox to choose it and open its Options palette. Make sure Sample Merged is turned off and Tolerance is set to 0. Now click in the Color layer to select an area (Shift-click to add more areas to the selection) and fill with a gradient, as we did for the sky. (Try applying the gradient in Screen, Multiply, or Overlay mode; for other tips on using the gradient tool, see pages 199–202.)

Or you can apply the Levels command to darken or lighten the color of the intersection of a colored area and a soft (feathered) selection, this way: Click with the magic wand to select the colored shape. Double-click the lasso in the toolbox to choose it and open its Options palette; set the Feather Radius to make a soft edge. With the Shift and Alt keys held down, drag the lasso to make a selection that intersects with the magic wand selection. When you release the mouse button to complete the lasso selection, the result will be a selection with sharp outer edges created by the magic wand and soft inner edges created by the feathered lasso; the soft edges will become apparent when you choose Image, Adjust, Levels and move the Input Levels (gray) gamma slider to lighten or darken the selected area.

6

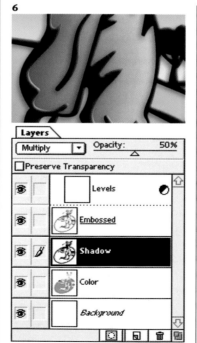

The finished file with a reduced-opacity cast shadow in place

6 Turning the drop shadow into a shadow cast by the embossed edge. To exaggerate the dimensionality of the raised graphic, you can make it cast the shadow. Drag the Shadow layer's name up in the Layers palette until it's just above the Color layer.

Edges Aglow

Overview *Prepare a background image; add a graphic layer; load the graphic's outline as a selection in a new layer in Screen mode; feather the selection; fill with red; build yellow- and white-filled Screen layers; put the graphic layer in Color Burn mode and colorize.*

*The **"Glow"** Actions on the Wow! CD-ROM automate the process of making several different glows.*

1

Background photo, copied and flipped

2

A biohazard graphic imported as a layer

3a

Corners darkened through a mask in an Adjustment layer

3b

Blurring the mask in the Adjustment layer

3c

The effect of blurring the Levels layer's mask

4a

Feathering the graphic selection for the red part of the glow

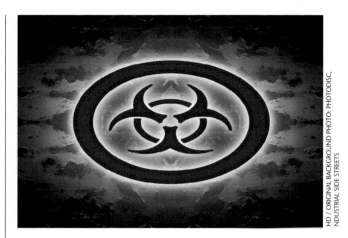

A GLOW EFFECT applied to type or graphics can light up the page. Here are directions for adding a glow that extends both inward and outward from the edges. The technique can be applied to lettering or shapes created in Photoshop, or to an imported graphic element.

1 Making a background. Open an image or a new file (Ctrl-N) and create a background. We started with a stock photo, selected part of it, dragged with the move tool with the Alt key held down to copy it, flipped the copy (Layer, Transform, Flip Horizontal or Flip Vertical), and repeated the process two more times to make a "Rorschach"-like background that would emphasize the symmetry of our glowing symbol.

2 Adding the graphic. Create or import a graphic element. We dragged and dropped a black graphic from Adobe Illustrator.

3 Preparing the background. To emphasize the glow that we would build in the center of the image, we darkened the edges of our background. One way to accomplish this is by activating the *Background* layer and choosing Filter, Render, Lighting Effects, with an Omni lighting Style.

Another way — the way we did it here — is to activate the *Background* layer and then make an unfeathered selection with the elliptical marquee (Alt-drag with the marquee tool to draw the selection from the center), invert the selection (Ctrl-Shift-I), and turn the inverted selection into the mask of a Levels Adjustment layer: With the inverted selection active, Ctrl-click on the New Layer icon in the middle at the bottom of the Layers palette to make an Adjustment layer. In the New Adjustment Layer dialog box, choose Levels as the Type, and click OK. Move the Input Levels black point and gamma (gray) sliders to the right to darken the corners of the *Background*.

Now soften the edges of the oval of light by choosing Filter, Blur, Gaussian Blur and trying different Radius settings. Instead of blurring, you could have made the soft edge by feathering the original selection, but you'd have had to guess at the Feather setting, trying

4b

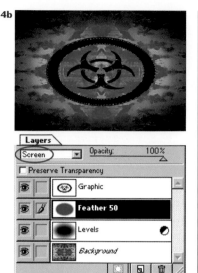

The red glow layer, in Screen mode after Alt-Backspacing 10 times

4c

Yellow (left) and white glow layers added

4d

With the graphic layer in Color Burn mode at 90% Opacity

4e

The finished "hot" interior/exterior glow

5

Colorizing through an Adjustment layer

again until you worked it out. If you blur the Adjustment layer's mask instead, though, you can work interactively, watching the lighting change in your artwork until the edge is as soft as you want it.

4 Building the glow. Add a new layer by clicking the New Layer icon, and drag its name in the Layers palette, if necessary, so it's just below the graphic layer. In the blending mode list at the top left on the Layers palette, change the mode to Screen. Load the graphic's outline as a selection by Ctrl-clicking the graphic layer's name in the Layers palette. Choose Select, Feather and enter a large Feather Radius value in the Feather Selection dialog box. We used a setting of 50 pixels for this 1000-pixel-wide image. (Don't worry if you don't see "marching ants" around this highly feathered selection.)

Now click the Foreground square to open the Color Picker, choose a red, and click OK. Press Alt-Backspace to fill the selection with red. To build the intensity of the red glow, repeat the Alt-Backspace several more times; the glow gets brighter as the feathering and filling are compounded. We Alt-Backspaced 10 times in all.

For the concentric yellow and white parts of the glow, you'll repeat the process of creating a new layer, loading the graphic's selection, feathering it slightly less for each color, and filling multiple times. We used a 25-pixel feather for the yellow, filled twice in Screen mode, and a 10-pixel feather, also filled twice, for the white. Filling too heavily with the final color (in this case white) will affect the graphic "halo" effect, so don't refill too many times. You can always intensify the effect later by duplicating a particular glow layer (by dragging its name to the New Layer icon).

Set the top (graphic) layer to Color Burn mode and reduce the Opacity to about 90%. (If the Opacity is too high, the color transitions in the glow will be posterized rather than smooth.)

If you like the "hot" look of the glow at this point, you can stop. Or go on to step 5 to limit the glow to the outside of the graphic.

5 Coloring the graphic. Ctrl-click the graphic layer's name to load its outline as a selection. Then Ctrl-click the New Layer icon to make an Adjustment layer with a built-in mask. Choose Hue/Saturation for the Type, choose Colorize in the Hue/Saturation dialog box, and adjust the color to your liking.

Carving

Overview *In a layer above the background, emboss a black-on-transparent graphic; put the embossed layer in Overlay mode to turn the embossing into "edges" for the carving; darken the "recessed" area of the carving; make a shadow layer and mask it so the shadow shows only in the recessed area.*

*The **"Recessed"** Actions on the Wow! CD-ROM automate similar processes for creating a carved look.*

1a

1b

PHOTO: VIVID DETAILS, RUSTIC WOOD

Background image, 1000 pixels wide

Original graphic, stored in channel #4

2a

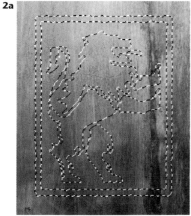

Channel #4 loaded as a selection in a transparent layer above the background

2b

Feather Selection	
Feather Radius: 1 pixels	OK
	Cancel

Feathering the selection to create "gray matter" for rounding the edge that will be created by embossing

SOMETIMES ALL YOU NEED to create the illusion of the third dimension is an edge, defined by a subtle highlight and shadow that add thickness to a two-dimensional item by making it look carved or cut out. The technique that produced the carving above uses Photoshop's Emboss filter to add that dimensionality. Though not capable of creating results as sophisticated as Lighting Effects, this filter nevertheless has the advantage of not requiring every bit of RAM you have — or more — in order to get the job done. And if you create the dimensionality on a layer *above* the background, instead of doing it *to* the background, you can change materials instantly, just by dragging and dropping a new background image.

1 Setting up the file. In a PostScript drawing or in Photoshop, copy to the clipboard the white-on-black graphic you want to use for carving the background. Then open the RGB image you want to "carve"; we chose a photo of wood. Into an alpha channel in this file, paste the clipboard contents as follows: Open the Channels palette (Window, Show Channels) and click the New Channel icon to the left of the trash can icon at the bottom of the palette. With the new channel active, paste the copied graphic (Ctrl-V).

   If necessary, use the move tool to center the graphic in the channel or use Free Transform (Ctrl-T) to scale the graphic or the

CARVING **247**

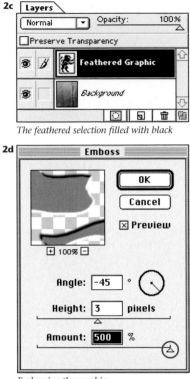

2c

The feathered selection filled with black

Embossing the graphic

2e

Viewing both layers of the file with the embossed layer in Normal mode

background image by Alt-Shift-dragging on a corner handle to resize the graphic proportionally from the center.

When your background and channel are sized and positioned the way you like, trim away any parts that extend beyond the frame of the image — that is, any "big data" — by selecting all (press Ctrl-A, which selects everything within the image frame but not beyond it) and choosing Image, Crop.

2 Embossing the graphic. Make a new layer above the *Background* this way: Open the Layers palette (Window, Show Layers) and click the New Layer icon, to the left of the trash can icon at the bottom of the palette. Click on the new layer's name to activate it. To load the graphic you've stored in channel #4 as a selection, Ctrl-click its name in the Channels palette. So that the edge of the carving will be rounded slightly, feather the resulting selection (Select, Feather; we used a setting of 1 pixel).

Now fill the selection with black (press "D" for "default colors" and press Alt-Backspace to fill the selection). Then deselect (Ctrl-D). To emboss the graphic, choose Filter, Stylize, Emboss and set the direction of the light and the amount of the relief. We positioned the light at the lower right. Adjusting the Height setting determined the depth of the carving. We moved the Amount slider all the way to the right to maximize the contrast of highlights and shadows.

The result of your embossing will be a 50% gray graphic with lighter highlighted edges and darker shadowed edges that make it look like the gray graphic is recessed into the background image.

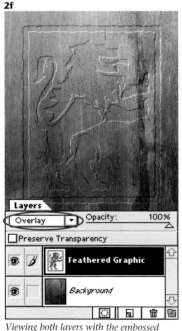

2f

Viewing both layers with the embossed layer in Overlay mode

From the pop-out list of blending modes in the Layers palette, choose Overlay. Since 50% gray is neutral in Overlay mode, the gray disappears and only the highlights and shadows are composited with the image underneath.

3 Darkening the carved-out area. To increase the contrast between the carved and uncarved surfaces, you can darken the carved-out area with an Adjustment layer: Again, load the graphic as a selection (Ctrl-click its name in the Channels palette) and then Ctrl-click the New Layer icon on the Layers palette to add an Adjustment layer with a built-in mask that will restrict the

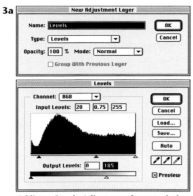

3a

Adding a Levels Adjustment layer to darken the "recessed" area of the carved image

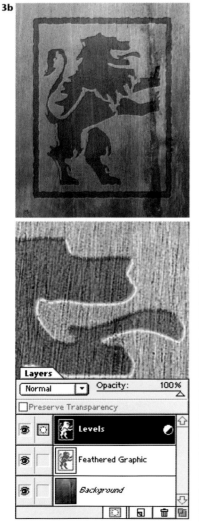

3b

Layers

Normal | Opacity: | 100%

☐ Preserve Transparency

👁 ▢ 🦁 **Levels** ⬤

👁 ▢ 🦁 Feathered Graphic

👁 ▢ ▧ *Background*

The recessed area darkened by the Adjustment layer

adjustment to the shape of the graphic. In the New Adjustment Layer dialog box, choose Levels for the Type. Move the Input Levels sliders to adjust the overall tonal range if you like, and then move the white Output Levels slider to the left to darken and reduce contrast.

4 Adding a shadow. A shadow cast by the carved surface can add depth, either by making the surface look thicker or by making the carved surface appear to float above the background. To start the shadow add a new layer above the Levels Adjustment layer. Load channel #4 as a selection once again, but this time invert the selection (Ctrl-Shift-I) before you fill with black. Deselect (Ctrl-D) and blur the edges of the shadow (Filter, Blur, Gaussian Blur; we used a Radius of 5 pixels). Offset the shadow to taste by dragging with the move tool (or using the arrow keys) in a direction that matches the lighting created by the embossing at step 2. (Remember that holding down the Ctrl key turns any tool but the pen into the move tool temporarily.) To lighten the shadow, move the Opacity slider in the Layers palette.

To trim the shadow, make a mask for the shadow layer: Ctrl-click the Levels Adjustment layer's thumbnail (the *thumbnail*, not the name) in the Layers palette to load its mask as a selection. Then, with the shadow layer active, click the Add Layer Mask icon, on the left at the bottom of the palette. This will add a layer mask to the shadow layer that allows the shadow to show only inside the graphic, as though the carved surface were casting the shadow. By default the mask is linked to the shadow — if you move one, the other moves along with it. But if you want to change the offset of the shadow after you add the mask, you can unlink the two by clicking the chain icon. Then click the shadow's thumbnail to make it active, and use the move tool to change the offset.

4a

The graphic selection inverted in preparation for making a shadow in a new transparent layer

4b

The result of filling the selection in the shadow layer with black

CARVING **249**

4c

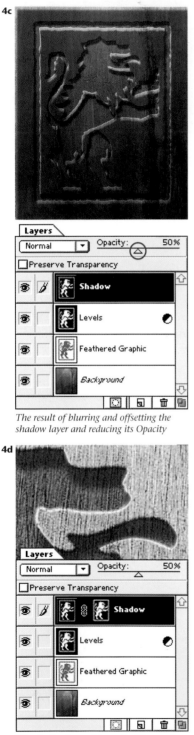

The result of blurring and offsetting the shadow layer and reducing its Opacity

4d

The shadow layer, trimmed with a mask to produce the result shown at the top of page 247

Switching surfaces. Because of the way the file has been layered, it's easy to change the carved material. Simply click on the *Background* layer's name to activate it and drag and drop a new surface image into the file so it comes in as a layer just above the *Background*. You can add as many alternate surfaces as you like this way, clicking in the eye icon column at the far left of the Layers palette to turn each surface layer's visibility on or off as needed.

Using two surface materials. To make a cut-out in one surface that lets an underneath surface material show through, simply add the second (recessed) surface *above* the other (carved) surface. With this new layer active, Ctrl-click the thumbnail — not the name — of the Levels Adjustment layer to load its mask as a selection, then click the Add Layer Mask icon to mask the recessed surface. ⚡

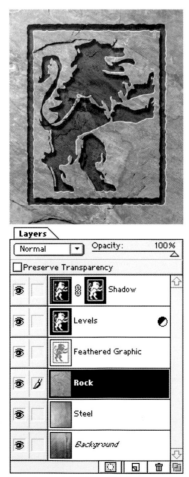

Dragging and dropping other backgrounds produces instant carved images.

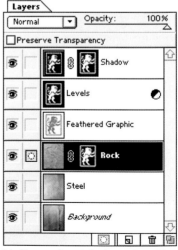

Masking an alternate background provides a carving with two surface textures, one for the recessed areas and one for the top surface.

Chiseling

Overview *Import or set type; adjust spacing; store the type in an alpha channel; run the KPT Gradient Designer plug-in on a duplicate of the channel to create a gradient fill in the type; use the channel to apply Lighting Effects to an imported background image; add a masked shadow.*

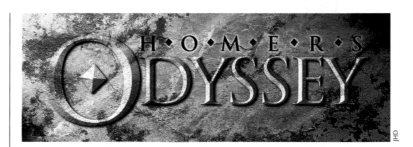

A KEY CHARACTERISTIC OF CHISELED TYPE — like you see on the marble entrances of banks and public offices — is the sharp, "V"-shaped cross-section of the carved strokes of the letters. Whether you raise the lettering or cut it in, the key to creating chiseled type in Photoshop is the KPT Gradient Designer filter, which is part of Kai's Power Tools (see page 188 for examples of this filter set's effects). **Note:** The KPT Gradient Designer plug-in is *not* included on the CD-ROM that comes with this book. If you want to use it, you'll have to buy the Kai's Power Tools filter set (version 3.0.1 or later) from MetaCreations (see Appendix B).

Using the KPT Gradient Designer filter in Circular Shapeburst mode with a black-to-white gradation gives you the raw material needed to create the smooth, raised center ridge and corners characteristic of raised chiseled lettering or the sharp-sided channel of recessed carving using the Lighting Effects filter. It even produces the gouge marks of the chisel. Added visual effects help to define the lettering as raised or cut in. (If your computer is short on memory, you can use the Emboss filter instead of Lighting Effects; see "Low-RAM Chiseling" on page 253.)

1 Setting and kerning type. Set type by choosing Photoshop's type tool from the toolbox, clicking it where you want the type to begin, setting type specifications, then clicking in the bottom part of the Type Tool dialog box, typing the characters you want to set, and clicking OK. (Check "The Type Tools" on page 57 for more about setting type in Photoshop.) Or you can do as we did: Set type in Adobe Illustrator, convert it to outlines, fill with black, and drag and drop it into Photoshop.

Once the type had been imported, we decided to letterspace the word "HOMER'S" using Photoshop's built-in Grid. To use the Grid, first turn on the rulers (Ctrl-R) and drag the 0 point over to align with the middle of the first letter. We aligned it with the "H."

Double-click on one of the rulers to open the Preferences dialog box (or choose File, Preferences, Units & Rulers), and for the Rulers, Units setting choose a convenient unit of measure; we chose pixels. Before closing the Preferences dialog box, set up a grid for letterspacing as follows: Choose Guides & Grid from the pop-out menu in the upper left corner of the dialog box (or click the "Next" button) and choose a Color and Style for the grid. Then use the ruler

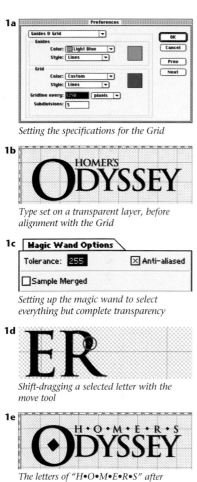

1a

Setting the specifications for the Grid

1b

Type set on a transparent layer, before alignment with the Grid

1c

Setting up the magic wand to select everything but complete transparency

1d

Shift-dragging a selected letter with the move tool

1e

The letters of "H•O•M•E•R•S" after dragging to align them with the Grid

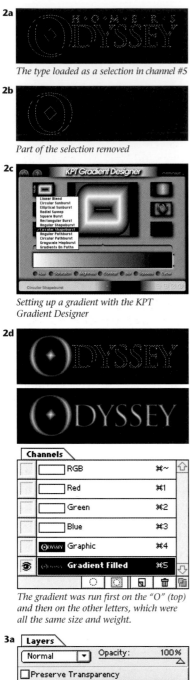

2a

The type loaded as a selection in channel #5

2b

Part of the selection removed

2c

Setting up a gradient with the KPT Gradient Designer

2d

The gradient was run first on the "O" (top) and then on the other letters, which were all the same size and weight.

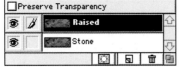

3a

A background surface image was imported and duplicated, and the original type layer and Background layer were deleted.

to measure the distance from your 0 point to where you want the last letter to be. For us the distance was 1250 pixels, so we used that measurement for the Guides Every setting. We needed to spread five letters over that distance ("O," "M," "E," "R," and "S"; the "H" was already set at the 0 point and we would eliminate the apostrophe, substituting one of the bullets we would add). So we entered "5" for the Subdivisions setting. In the View menu, make sure Show Grid is turned on. Since we wanted to visually center the letters on the grid lines and wanted some leeway in positioning them, we turned off Snap To Grid.

To letterspace the type, you can use the method illustrated on page 57, like this: To move the individual letters, double-click the magic wand in the toolbox to choose it and open its Options palette. Set the Tolerance at 255. Now if you click the wand on a letter, it will be entirely selected, including its antialiased edges. Shift-clicking will select additional letters. By holding down the Ctrl key to turn the wand into the move tool, you can drag the letter sideways (or use the arrow keys to move it), and if you hold down the Shift key as well, movement will be constrained to horizontal so the letter will stay on its baseline. When you've finished moving letters, press Ctrl-D to drop the floating selection.

Choosing the type tool again, we clicked it between the "H" and "O" and set a single bullet by typing Alt-8. This character appeared on a layer of its own. We held down the Ctrl key and dragged the bullet into position. Then we made the other bullets we needed by clicking the bullet with the magic wand, holding down the Ctrl and Alt keys (Ctrl to turn the wand into the move tool and Alt to duplicate the selected item) and dragged a copy of the bullet between the "O" and "M," holding down the Shift key as well to keep the copy aligned with the original. We used the same copying-and-moving method to make and position the other three bullets we needed. We pressed Ctrl-E (for Merge Down) to combine the bullet layer with the layer below, which held the type.

2 Making a channel for chiseling. Once you've set and spaced the type using the convenience of a transparent layer in step 1, you can store it permanently in an alpha channel this way: Open the Layers palette and Ctrl-click the type layer's name to load its transparency mask as a selection. Then open the Channels palette and make an alpha channel by Alt-clicking the mask icon, second from the left at the bottom of the palette. Using the Alt key lets you name the channel as you create it; we called ours "Graphic." Don't deselect.

With the selection still active, Alt-click the New Channel icon next to the trash can icon at the bottom of the Channels palette; we named our new channel "Gradient Filled." You should now see a black-filled channel with the type loaded as a selection, as in figure 2a.

If your type varies in size, as ours did, you'll need to apply the KPT Gradient Designer separately to the different sizes. To select

3b

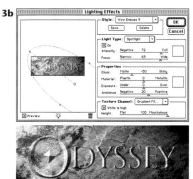

Running Lighting Effects produced the raised chiseled look.

4a

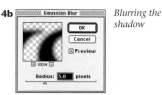

Starting a shadow

4b

Blurring the shadow

only the "O" and its enclosed diamond, we chose the marquee tool (press "M" for marquee, or press "L" if you'd rather use the lasso) and held down the Option key as we dragged to surround all the other selected letters, thus deselecting them, and leaving only the "O" and its diamond selected.

With the KPT Gradient Designer installed, choose Filter, KPT 3.0, KPT Gradient Designer, and choose Circular Shapeburst from the Mode pop-up menu. Position the cursor at the left end of the gradient band (below the curved bracket that extends across the middle of the Gradient Designer interface) and press and hold the mouse button. The cursor will turn into an eyedropper; a spectrum gradient band will appear, and above it a thinner black-to-white gradient; drag the eyedropper over to the white end of this thin gradient and release the mouse button. Then repeat this color-sampling procedure, but this time drag the eyedropper from the right end of the gradient to the left (black) end of the thin gradient band. When you finish, the interface should look pretty much like the one in figure 2c, with a shapeburst in the center box that's white in the middle and black at the edges. (If it's black in the center instead, pop out the menu from the gradient icon and switch from Sawtooth B->A to Sawtooth A->B, or vice versa, so your Gradient Designer setup matches figure 2c.) Click OK.

If you have different-size letters, as we did, repeat the process of loading channel #4 as a selection in channel #5, deleting parts of the selection, and running the KPT Gradient Designer on the remaining letters (you can rerun the filter by pressing Ctrl-F). We ran the Gradient Designer once more — on "DYSSEY," since all these letters are the same weight. We decided to use a different treatment on "H•O•M•E•R•S," as described in step 5.

3 Chiseling a surface. Copy and paste or use the move tool to drag and drop a background surface image into your developing chiseling file. (You can delete the original type layer since you have the type stored in channel #4, and you can also delete the file's original *Background* layer.) Duplicate the new layer by dragging its name to the New Layer icon next to the trash can icon at the bottom of the Layers palette. This lets you preserve the original background surface image while you treat the top layer with the Lighting Effects filter, using your Gradient Filled alpha channel (#5) as the Texture Channel.

With the top layer active, choose Filter, Render, Lighting Effects. Make sure White Is High is turned on. The other settings you use in the Lighting Effects dialog box will vary, depending on the pixel dimensions of your file, the darkness of your background, and the amount of contrast you want between background and chiseled letters. Using a Spotlight for the Light Type will add drama; it's also the best option for helping the viewer's eye know where the light is coming from, providing a visual clue to whether the chiseled graphic is raised or recessed. For a more traditional, less dramatic emboss, try a Directional light, but keep in mind that it won't be as easy for the viewer to tell

4c

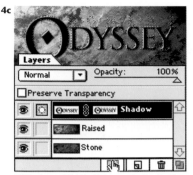

With channel #4 loaded as a selection in the Shadow layer (top), Alt-clicking the Add Layer Mask icon made a "hiding" mask.

4d

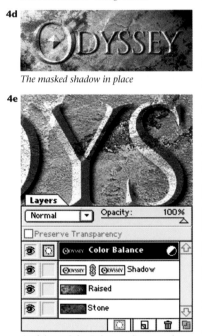

The masked shadow in place

4e

Applying a Color Balance Adjustment layer to further differentiate the raised lettering from the background

5

The final Layers palette, with "haloed" type

whether the carved type or graphic is projecting from the surface or receding. The Properties settings and the Height setting for the Texture Channel affect the shadow density and contrast of the chiseled ridge.

4 Making a shadow. A shadow helps to make the chiseled letters look raised. You can create the shadow in a layer above the chiseled layer and mask it so that it doesn't fall on the letters themselves, but instead seems to be cast by the letters onto the surrounding surface. With this arrangement of layers you can economize, keeping both the chiseled type and the surrounding surface on a single layer.

Start by creating a new blank layer (click the New Layer icon), and load channel #4, which holds the original graphic or type, as a selection (Ctrl-Alt-4 is the keyboard shortcut). (At this point we subtracted "H•O•M•E•R•S" from the selection.) Fill with black. Drop the selection (Ctrl-D) and choose Filter, Blur, Gaussian Blur to soften the shadow. Offset the shadow in the direction that corresponds to the lighting scheme you used with Lighting Effects. To mask the shadow so it appears to be cast on the background by the chiseled type, load channel #4 as a selection again and Alt-click the Add Layer Mask icon at the bottom of the palette (using the Alt key makes the selected area black in the mask and the unselected area white, thus hiding the selected area, which is the opposite of the default mask-making operation).

To darken the shadow, you can duplicate the layer and then adjust the Opacity of one of the shadow layers.

5 Applying another type treatment. For the "H•O•M•E•R•S" type we loaded channel #4 as a selection in a new layer, deselected the other type by Alt-dragging around it, and filled with black. Then we duplicated the layer and filled the type in the lower layer with white. (If white is the Background color, you can do this by pressing Shift-Ctrl-Backspace; Ctrl-Backspace fills with the Background color; adding the Shift key limits the fill to nontransparent areas.) Applying a Gaussian Blur made the white type into a light glow.

CHISELING IN

To make chiseled type look carved in instead of raised, turn off White Is High when you run the Lighting Effects filter. By experience we expect light on a wall to shine from the top down, whether it's sunlight outdoors or a ceiling light indoors. So position the light source to shine from somewhere above the image. We tend to view images and pages from the upper left, so positioning your light source there takes advantage of viewers' expectations and helps them see the chiseling as recessed. (If you use the chiseling method described in "Low-RAM Chiseling" on page 253, use an angle of about 140°.) Make sure

the lighting you establish is dramatic, so the viewer will have no doubt where the light source is. Don't add a shadow, since there's nothing sticking up above the surface to cast one.

Creating Crystal

Overview *Use a blurred and trimmed graphic in an alpha channel as a displacement map for running the Glass filter on a copy of a background image and as a Texture Channel for embossing a white-filled layer in Overlay mode; use the original graphic (unblurred and untrimmed) as the bottom layer of a clipping group.*

*The **"Crystal"** Actions on the Wow! CD-ROM automate a crystal-generating process similar to this one.*

PHOTO: PHOTODISC, PANORAMIC LANDSCAPES

1a

Original photo

1b

White-on-black graphic in channel #4

2a

Channel #4 loaded as a selection in channel #5

2b

Feathering the loaded selection

SEVERAL OF PHOTOSHOP'S FILTERS use the lights and darks of a *displacement map* file to distort an image. If you use a recognizable shape as a displacement map, you can get some very interesting results, such as the look of water, crystal, or carving.

Besides the subtle highlights and shadows it uses to simulate the reflections and refractions of glass, Photoshop's Glass filter works like other displacement filters, by moving the pixels of the layer it's applied to. The distance each pixel moves depends on the luminance (or brightness) of the corresponding pixel in the displacement map. Any image in Photoshop format except a bitmap can serve as a displacement map. White pixels move their corresponding pixels in the filtered image the maximum positive (up or right) distance, black pixels produce the maximum negative (down or left) displacement, and 50% brightness produces no displacement at all. Displacement maps can be wrapping patterns (like the Widgets on the Wow! CD-ROM) or graphics, like the "H_2O" type used for this crystal effect. (Note: This process uses the Lighting Effects filter, which is RAM-hungry and can be work-intensive as you set up several lights. For a crystal-making method that doesn't involve Lighting Effects, check the "Crystal Light" Action on the Wow! CD-ROM that comes with this book.)

1 Setting up the file. Open the RGB image you want to use as the background for the crystal. If necessary, adapt it to the layout of the graphic you want to turn into crystal. We selected all and used Layer, Free Transform (Ctrl-T) to distort our background image, dragging side and corner handles to scale it. After scaling we double-clicked inside the box to accept the change. Then we used the rectangular marquee tool to surround the part of the image we wanted to keep and chose Image, Crop to trim the file.

Open the Channels palette (Window, Show Channels) and add a black-filled alpha channel to the file by clicking the New Channel icon, next to the trash can icon at the bottom of the palette; this will be channel #4. Create a white-on-black graphic in the channel, or import an EPS from Adobe Illustrator or another PostScript program (File, Place). Shift-drag the corner handles to size the import, double-click to accept the sizing, and deselect (Ctrl-D).

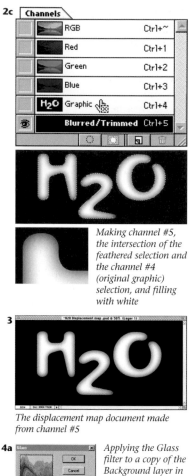

2c

The displacement map document made from channel #5

Making channel #5, the intersection of the feathered selection and the channel #4 (original graphic) selection, and filling with white

The displacement map document made from channel #5

Applying the Glass filter to a copy of the Background layer in the RGB image

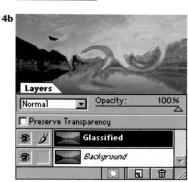

The file after the Glass filter was applied

You have to be sure to crop away "big data" on a layer before subjecting the layer to a displacement-based Photoshop filter. For instance, when you run the Glass, Displace, or Texturizer filter, all of which cause displacement of part of the image by an external file, the displacement is done by aligning the upper left corner of the displacement map with the upper left corner of the layer to be filtered. If the layer happens to include pixels beyond what you see in the frame of the image — for instance, if Photoshop 4's new "big data" has preserved the outlying pixels of a large image that has been dragged and dropped into a layer — the "upper left corner" of the layer may be "off stage." In that case the embossing that you expected the filter and its displacement map to produce in the center of your image will be shifted to the left and up.

This problem doesn't occur with the Lighting Effects filter, since the texture map for Lighting Effects comes from a channel in the file itself, and the filter is smart enough to keep track of the current "boundaries" of the document, ignoring any big data that may extend beyond them.

2 Making a "blurred and trimmed" version of the graphic.
To make the "gray matter" needed in a displacement map for distorting the background image as if light were being refracted by crystal, you'll create a blurred and trimmed version of the graphic. Try the following (or you can produce the same result by following the blurring and trimming procedure in step 2 of "Creating Chrome" on page 259): Load channel #4 as a selection (Ctrl-click its name in the Channels palette). Then make another new alpha channel, and feather the selection (choose Select, Feather and choose a Feather Radius). The bigger the Feather Radius, the more gradual the rounding of the edges of your crystal graphic will be. Then sharpen the outer edge of this soft selection by selecting the intersection of it and the original graphic as follows: In the Channels palette, Ctrl-Alt-Shift-click on channel #4; then, with white as the Foreground color, Alt-Backspace to fill the selection with white.

3 Making a displacement map. To copy the blurred and trimmed channel (#5) as a displacement map, select all (Ctrl-A), copy (Ctrl-C), start a new file (Ctrl-N), and paste (Ctrl-V). Save the new file in Photoshop format (File, Save As).

4 Creating refractions. The next step is to bend the background image as if it were being viewed through a crystal version of your graphic: In your developing crystal file — not the displacement map file you just made — open the Layers palette (Window, Show Layers) and duplicate the *Background* layer by dragging its name to the New Layer icon in the middle at the bottom of the palette (Alt-drag if you want a chance to name the new layer). Click the new layer's name in the Layers palette and drop any active selection (Ctrl-D). Apply the Glass filter to this new layer by choosing Filter, Distort, Glass; select Load Texture as the Texture setting and load your displacement map file. Experiment with the Distortion and Smoothness settings until you get the amount and kind of refraction effect you want.

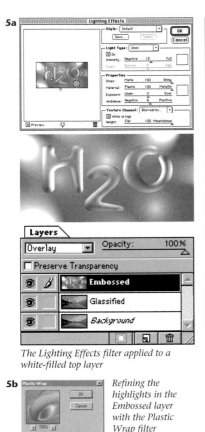

The Lighting Effects filter applied to a white-filled top layer

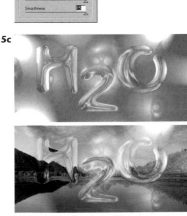

Refining the highlights in the Embossed layer with the Plastic Wrap filter

A view of the file after adding the Embossed layer, in Normal mode (top) and Overlay mode (bottom)

5 Embossing. With your "glassified" top layer active, make a new layer above it by Alt-clicking the New Layer icon and naming the layer "Embossed." Fill the new layer with white (press "D" for the default Foreground and Background colors; then press Ctrl-Backspace). Choose Filter, Render, Lighting Effects, and use channel #5 as the Texture Channel, setting up a number of small Omni lights to imitate the multiple reflections seen in a shiny surface.

To create reflection highlights that follow the form of the embossed graphic, apply the Plastic Wrap filter to the Embossed layer (Filter, Artistic, Plastic Wrap).

Now change the mode of the Embossed layer to Overlay to reveal the magic! You can increase the effect of the Embossed layer's lighting by duplicating the layer and then adjusting the Opacity of the top layer. When the overall lighting is as you like it, merge the two copies (Ctrl-E). You can also control the intensity of highlights and shadows with Layer Options: Double-click the Embossed layer's name in the Layers palette to open the Layer Options dialog box and experiment with the This Layer and Underlying sliders; for smooth transitions, you can split the black and white point sliders by holding down the Alt key as you move them.

6 Trimming the crystal. To trim away the exterior of the Glassified and Embossed layers, make a clipping group as follows: Activate the *Background* layer and click the New Layer icon to create a transparent layer immediately above it (or Alt-click if you want the opportunity to name the new layer). Load your original graphic as a selection in this layer (Ctrl-click on channel #4's name in the Channels palette). Fill this selection in the new layer with the Foreground color (black) by pressing Alt-Backspace, and then deselect. Next, Alt-click in the Layers palette on the border between this new layer and the Glassified layer above it, and on the border between the Glassified and Embossed layers. All the layers whose borders have been Alt-clicked become members of a *clipping group;* the bottom layer of the group — the graphic in this case — acts like a mask, effectively "trimming" the other layers, so that only pixels that fall within the masking shape will show.

At this point your crystal effect is complete. Depending on your image, you may want to customize the effect further, as we did.

7 Embellishing the crystal. You can add a rainbow color cast to the crystal by applying an Adjustment layer: With the top layer of your file active (click its name in the Layers palette), Ctrl-click the New Layer icon to make an Adjustment layer. Choose Curves for the Type and click the check box for Group With Previous Layer to make it part of the existing clipping group so the Curves adjustment will apply only to the crystal graphic, not to the surrounding background. Click OK, and in the Curves dialog box, click with the curve tool to create a wildly (but smoothly) oscillating curve.

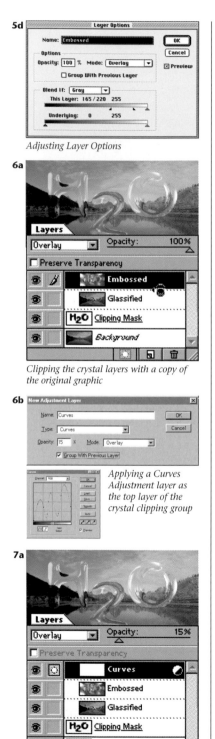

5d

Adjusting Layer Options

6a

Clipping the crystal layers with a copy of the original graphic

6b

Applying a Curves Adjustment layer as the top layer of the crystal clipping group

7a

The "rainbow" crystal effect

You may want to add a shadow or "dark halo" effect to emphasize the separation of the crystal graphic from its original background: Add another new layer at the top of the file. Then load the original graphic as a selection (Ctrl-click channel #4's name in the Channels palette) and expand and soften the edges of the selection by choosing Select, Feather; we used a Feather Radius of 10. Fill the selection with black (Alt-Backspace). To limit the darkening to the area *around* the graphic, load the original graphic as a selection again (Ctrl-click channel #4) and press Backspace; deselect.

To add a reflection to our water image, first we made a merged copy of the layers that comprised the crystal graphic (Curves, Embossed, Glassified, and the clipping graphic) as follows: We clicked to turn on the eye icons for these layers and turn off the eyes for the others; then we activated the Curves layer and added a new layer above it; with this new layer active, we pressed Alt-Ctrl-E, the shortcut for making a merged copy of the visible layers. Then we flipped the new merged layer vertically to make an upside down graphic by applying Free Transform (Ctrl-T), moving the cursor inside the Free Transform box, and pressing the right mouse button to bring up a context-sensitive menu where the Flip Vertical command could be chosen. With Free Transform still active, we dragged with the cursor inside the box to align the base of the upside-down "2" with the base of the upright "2." Pressing the right mouse button again and choosing Perspective from the context-sensitive menu allowed us to expand the upside-down graphic forward by dragging out on a bottom corner handle of the Free Transform box. (To see the handles we had to press Ctrl-Alt-minus several times.) When the perspective was right, we double-clicked inside the Free Transform box. We added a layer mask filled with a black-to-white bottom-to-top Linear gradient to fade the reflection (see step 6 of "Casting a Shadow" on page 241).

To add to the water illusion, we made a series of feathered selections with the elliptical marquee, making ripples in the selected areas with Filter, Distort, Zigzag.

7b

A "dark halo" helps the crystal stand out from the background (see page 255).

7c

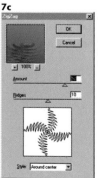

Applying the "Around Center" Style of the Zigzag filter to a feathered oval selection

Creating Chrome

Overview *Apply the Glass filter to a Background image, using a blurred and trimmed graphic as the Texture; apply Lighting Effects to a white-filled layer in Overlay mode; trim away the area outside the graphic; add a shadow and a recessed area for the chrome.*

The **"Chrome"** *Actions on the Wow! CD-ROM automate the process of simulating chrome, using several methods to produce different chrome effects.*

Image for reflection map

Original graphic in channel #4

Blurred graphic in channel #5

Blurred and trimmed graphic in channel #6

POLISHED CHROME IS UNIQUELY SHINY and reflective. But in terms of how it's made, this chrome is really a special case of "Creating Crystal" on page 255, with the chrome "Radio" graphic isolated on a contrasting background. (Note: The method for "Creating Chrome" relies on hand-tuning the Glass, Plastic Wrap, and Lighting Effects filters, which can be both RAM-hungry and work-intensive as you adjust them to suit your particular graphics file. For a method that doesn't rely on these filters, try the "Mercury" Action on the Wow! CD-ROM that comes with this book.)

1 Setting up your file. Create a new RGB Photoshop document (File, New) with a white background. For this example, our file was 1000 x 500 pixels; the blur and Lighting Effects settings were chosen to fit the horizontal-format "Radio" graphic at this size. If your file is larger or smaller or if it has a different aspect ratio, your settings may need to be different.

For photorealistic chrome, the choice of an image to use as a *reflection map* — the surroundings reflected back from the shiny, curved surfaces of the chrome — is all-important. Usually, you'll want good contrast, a color scheme that matches your design concept, and limited detail (you can blur the image or reduce saturation to reduce detail). Open the image you want to use for the reflection map, and use the move tool to drag and drop it into your chrome document so it becomes a separate layer above the white *Background*. If needed, scale it with Free Transform (press Ctrl-T and drag inward or outward on a corner handle, or Shift-drag for proportional scaling). Double-click inside the Transform box to finish the transformation. Then select all (Ctrl-A) and choose Image, Crop to trim the layer ("Bye-Bye Big Data" on page 256 tells why this cropping is critical to many filter operations).

Create an alpha channel (#4) in your chrome file: Open the Channels palette (Window, Show Channels) and click the New Channel icon, second from the right at the bottom of the palette. With this channel active, either create a white-on-black graphic or import one from Adobe Illustrator or another PostScript drawing program (File, Place). When you finish, if you have an active selection, deselect (Ctrl-D).

PHOTO: PHOTODISC, PANORAMIC LANDSCAPES

JHD

1a

1b

2a

2b

2c

Close-up of the blurred and trimmed graphic in channel #6

2d

Channels

RGB	⌘~
Red	⌘1
Green	⌘2
Blue	⌘3
Graphic	⌘4
Blurred	⌘5
Trimmed	⌘6

The Channels palette, showing the blurred and trimmed channel active and ready to be copied to make a displacement map for the Glass filter

3a

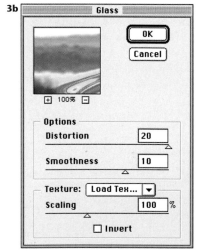

The displacement map file, made by pasting a copy of channel #6 into a new file

3b

Glass

OK
Cancel

⊞ 100% ⊟

Options

Distortion   20

Smoothness   10

Texture: [Load Tex... ▼]

Scaling   100 %

☐ Invert

Running the Glass filter

2 Making the other alpha channels you need. Now you'll develop a blurred and a trimmed version of the graphic in two additional alpha channels: Duplicate your alpha channel by dragging its name to the New Channel icon (the new one will be #5). Then choose Filter, Blur, Gaussian Blur; we used a Radius setting of 7 pixels.

For the "trimmed" channel (#6), duplicate the blurred channel. Then with channel #6 active, load the original (#4) as a selection by Ctrl-clicking its name in the Channels palette. With #6 still active, trim away the outside edge of the blur by inverting the selection (Ctrl-Shift-I) and filling with black: If black is the Foreground color, press Alt-Backspace; if black is the Background color, press Ctrl-Backspace.

3 Making and applying a displacement map. Besides using the trimmed channel as a Texture for Lighting Effects (in step 4 below), you'll need to save it as a separate file to use as a displacement map with the Glass filter. To make the displacement map file, To copy the blurred and trimmed channel (#6) as a displacement map, select all (Ctrl-A), copy (Ctrl-C), start a new file (Ctrl-N), and paste (Ctrl-V). Save the new file in Photoshop format (File, Save As).

Back in the developing chrome file, in the Channels palette click the name of the RGB composite channel to activate it. Then choose Filter, Distort, Glass, loading as the custom Texture the displacement map you just made.

4 Adding dimensionality with Lighting Effects. Next make a white-filled layer above the "glassified" image by clicking the New Layer icon in the middle at the bottom of the Layers palette and filling with white. Then run the Lighting Effects filter on this layer: Choose Filter, Render, Lighting Effects; select your "trimmed" channel (#6) as the Texture Channel; and turn on White Is High. We used five Omni lights, positioned to produce an overall edge highlight with an emphasis on lighting from below. Clicking to select the individual lights in turn, we clicked the color box in the Light

3c

The reflection map layer after running the Glass filter

4a

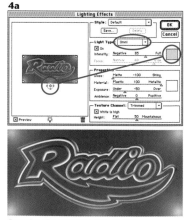

Running the Lighting Effects filter on a new white-filled layer to create chrome highlights

4b

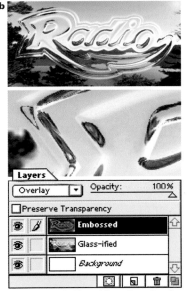

The combined effect of the embossed and "glassified" layers

4c

Plastic Wrap

OK

Cancel

⊞ 100% ⊟

Options

Highlight Strength   20

Detail   15

Smoothness   15

Running the Plastic Wrap filter on the embossed layer

4d

The result of applying Plastic Wrap

Type section and assigned pale colors to the lights — yellow for the upper ones to tint the highlights on the top edges, and blue for the bottom ones.

When you have the overall lighting effect you want, click OK. Choose Overlay from the blending mode list in the Layers palette to combine the highlights and shadows of this "embossed" layer with the glassified effect. For added specular highlights, try running the Plastic Wrap filter on the embossed layer: Choose Filter, Artistic, Plastic Wrap.

5 Trimming the chrome. Trim both layers of the chrome: Working in the top layer, load the original graphic as a selection (Ctrl-click on channel #4's name in the Channels palette), invert the selection (Ctrl-Shift-I), and press Backspace. Then click the name of the glassified layer and, with the selection still active, press Backspace to trim this layer also. Deselect (Ctrl-D).

6 Making a base for the chrome. Activate the white *Background* layer by clicking its name in the Layers palette and apply Lighting Effects, using the blurred alpha channel (#5) as the Texture Channel with White Is High turned off to make a slight depression for the chrome to sit in. We used a single Spotlight light source.

7 Adding a shadow. To pop the chrome off the background more, duplicate the glassified layer, and drag the copy below the original in the Layers palette. We double-clicked to open the Layer Options dialog box so we could rename the new layer "Shadow."

To fill the shadow with black, make black the Foreground color (press "D") and then press Shift-Alt-Backspace, which acts like a temporary "Preserve Transparency" setting, to fill only the nontransparent area with black. Choose Filter, Blur, Gaussian Blur and soften the shadow to taste. Use the move tool to offset the shadow if you like. *Wow!*

5

The result of trimming the two layers of the chrome with a selection made from channel #4

6

The chrome file after "debossing" the white Background layer

7

Layers

Normal   Opacity: 100%

☐ Preserve Transparency

👁   Embossed/PW

👁   Glass-ified

👁 ✎   **Shadow**

👁   Background

The chrome file with a shadow between the two-layer chrome and the debossed Background

Forging Steel

Overview *Make two alpha channels, one with a white-on-black graphic and one with a blurred and trimmed version; "emboss" a 3D version of the graphic on a transparent layer with the Lighting Effects filter; add more highlights with the Plastic Wrap filter; color with Adjustment layers; trim the "metal" with a clipping group; add a brushed texture and a dark "halo."*

 *The **"Brushed Steel"** Actions on the Wow! CD-ROM automate several ways to make "metal."*

JHD

1

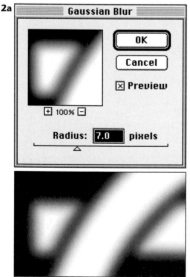

Original graphic in channel #4

2a

Blurring a duplicate graphic in channel #5

STEEL CAN HAVE A HIGHLY POLISHED, mirrorlike surface, or it can be dull, burnished, or brushed. Starting with a white *Background* layer and a white-on-black graphic in an alpha channel, you can use Photoshop to manufacture the steel, heat it to the point where it shows a rainbow sheen, brush the surface, and cut out a 3D version of the graphic, with perfectly beveled polished edges. (Step 3 of this technique uses the Lighting Effects filter. If your computer doesn't have enough memory to run this RAM-hungry filter, you can create the form and metallic highlights using the "Mercury" Action on the CD-ROM that comes with this book.

1 Setting up the file. Start a new RGB file (File, New) with a white-filled *Background*. The file we used was 1000 pixels wide. Open the Channels palette (Window, Show Channels) and add an alpha channel by clicking the New Channel icon next to the trash can icon at the bottom of the palette. You can either create a graphic in this channel by making a selection and filling with white, or import one as we did. Our logo was created in black in Adobe Illustrator, placed in the Photoshop file with the alpha channel (#4) active (File, Place), stretched to fit the file, turned into a selection by double-clicking inside the placement box, and filled with white.

(The pixel settings used for commands that come later in this technique were chosen based on our 1000-pixel-wide file size, on the relative width of the graphic shapes that made up our logo, and on how wide we wanted the bevels to be. If your file is a different size, or if the thicknesses of your graphic elements or the desired bevel are very different from ours, you'll need to adjust accordingly for any command that requires a setting in pixels.)

2 Making the alpha channel to use with Lighting Effects. In addition to the original graphic in channel #4, you'll need a modified version of the graphic to produce the bevel when you apply

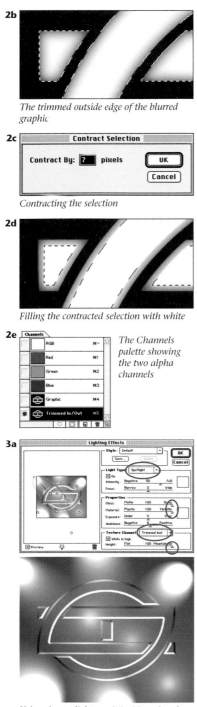

2b

The trimmed outside edge of the blurred graphic

2c

Contract Selection

Contract By: 7 pixels

OK

Cancel

Contracting the selection

2d

Filling the contracted selection with white

2e

Channels

RGB ⌘~

Red ⌘1

Green ⌘2

Blue ⌘3

Graphic ⌘4

Trimmed In/Out ⌘5

The Channels palette showing the two alpha channels

3a

Lighting Effects

Using six spotlights and the blurred and trimmed alpha channel to add dimensions and specular highlights on the embossed layer

the Lighting Effects filter in step 3. The channel will need to be white where you want it to create the top surface of the metal logo, black outside the logo shape, and shades of gray where you want to create the bevel. The edge between the bevel and the top surface should be sharp, so you'll want a sharp transition between the gray ramp that defines the bevel and the white area that forms the top surface. You can produce this alpha channel from a copy of the original graphic as follows: In the Channels palette, duplicate channel #4 by dragging its name to the New Channel icon next to the trash can at the bottom of the palette. If you have a selection active, deselect (Ctrl-D). To create the "gray matter" for the bevel, blur the graphic by choosing Filter, Blur, Gaussian Blur; we used a Radius of 7 pixels.

Next trim the outside and inside edges: For the outside trim, load the original graphic as a selection by Ctrl-clicking Channel #4's name in the Channels palette; then invert the selection (Ctrl-Shift-I) and fill with black (if black is the Foreground color, press Alt-Backspace; if black is the background color, press Backspace). For the inside edge, load the original graphic as a selection (either re-invert the selection you just filled with black by pressing Ctrl-Shift-I or Ctrl-click channel #4's name again). Then make the selection smaller by choosing Select, Modify, Contract. For the Contract By setting, use the same number of pixels you used for the blur, or a few pixels less for a narrower bevel. Fill the selection with white and deselect (Ctrl-D).

Finally, soften the edges of the alpha channel slightly as follows to cut down on the artifacts that the Lighting Effects filter can produce: With channel #5 active and nothing selected, choose Filter, Blur, Gaussian Blur and set the Radius at 0.5 pixels.

3 Creating the 3D graphic. Next you'll use the Lighting Effects filter to create a 3D beveled metal version of the graphic. Open the Layers palette (Window, Show Layers) and click on the name of the *Background* layer. Choose Filter, Render, Lighting Effects. Choose channel #5 from the Texture Channel pop-out list, and set up several spotlights to create the multiple specular highlighting associated with shiny metal; you can duplicate a light by Alt-dragging. You can get radically different results in the "personality" of the metal, depending on how you design the play of lights on the embossed object. In the Properties area of the dialog box, move the Gloss setting all the way to Shiny and the Material setting to Metallic. When the preview shows a result you like, click OK to accept it.

At this point we gave our *Background* layer the option for transparency just by double-clicking its name in the Layers palette to open the Layer Options dialog box. We also renamed it, typing in the new name (we called ours "Embossed"), and clicked OK.

4 Adding more highlights. To make a layer whose highlights and color you can adjust, Alt-drag the Embossed layer's name to the

3b

Close-up of the Embossed layer

3c

A duplicate layer for adding color and more highlights

4a

Running the Plastic Wrap filter on a duplicate of the Embossed layer

4b

The result of applying Plastic Wrap

New Layer icon in the middle at the bottom of the Layers palette. Running the Plastic Wrap filter (Filter, Artistic, Plastic Wrap) will make highlights and shadows that conform to the curves of the graphic. From the pop-out list of blending modes in the Layers palette, choose Overlay to blend these new highlights and shadows with the layer below.

5 Coloring the steel. With the new layer active, Ctrl-click the New Layer icon to make an Adjustment layer that will store information for coloring the steel. In the New Adjustment Layer dialog box choose Color Balance for the type. In the Color Balance dialog box adjust the color sliders for the Midtones; we made adjustments that would give our steel a blue tone.

To get the multicolored sheen of heated or oiled steel, add another Adjustment layer, this time choosing Curves as the Type. In the Curves dialog box use the curve tool to place points that produce the dramatically alternating colors.

6 Trimming away the excess. To cut the three-dimensional graphic from its background, make a clipping group: Make a new layer, load the original graphic as a selection by pressing Ctrl-Alt-4, and fill with the Foreground color (Alt-Backspace). Deselect (Ctrl-D). Drag the layer's name to the bottom of the list in the Layers palette. To make the nontransparent part of this layer (the graphic) serve as a mask for all the layers above, hold down the Alt key and click on the border between the new layer's name and the one above it; continue Alt-clicking up the Layers palette until all the layers are clipped by the graphic layer at the bottom.

5a
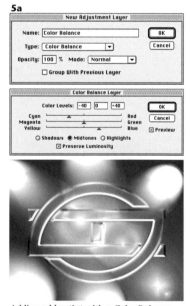
Adding a blue tint with a Color Balance Adjustment layer

5b
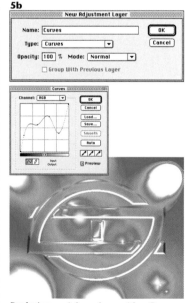
Producing a rainbow sheen with a Curves Adjustment layer

6

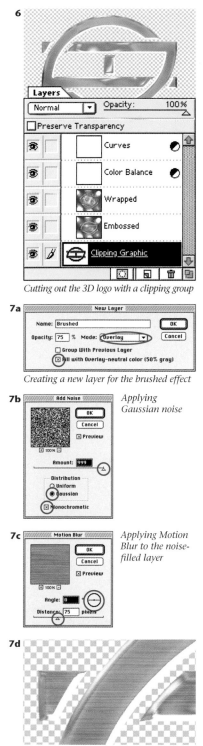

Cutting out the 3D logo with a clipping group

7a

Creating a new layer for the brushed effect

7b

Applying Gaussian noise

7c

Applying Motion Blur to the noise-filled layer

7d

A contracted layer mask eliminates the brushed effect from the bevel.

7 Brushing the steel. To create the surface texture for the steel, start by adding another new layer, this one filled with gray: With the Curves Adjustment layer active, Alt-click the New Layer icon. Name the new layer and put it in Overlay mode. Click in the check box for Fill With Overlay-Neutral Color 50% Gray. Also check the Group With Previous Layer box to include it within the clipping group. Finally, click OK. With the new layer active, choose Filter, Noise, Add Noise and add Mono-chromatic Gaussian noise at the highest setting. Then choose Filter, Blur, Motion Blur and set up a horizontal blur.

The developing file should now show a "brushed" surface over the entire logo. To remove the tex-ture from the bevel, you can use a layer mask: Press Ctrl-Alt-4 to load channel #4 as a selection; then choose Select, Modify, Contract and enter the same setting you used at step 2. With the brushed layer active, click the Add Layer Mask icon, on the left at the bot-tom of the palette. A "constricted graphic" layer mask will be cre-ated, allowing the brushed texture to show on the flat surface of the 3D logo but eliminating it from the beveled edge.

8 Adding finishing touches. To add a shadow, or dark "halo,' we duplicated the Clipping Graphic layer; the copy auto-matically became the new clip-ping layer. The original Clipping Graphic layer was now below the clipping group. We renamed this layer "Halo," Gaussian Blurred it, and duplicated it to darken the shadow. To subdue the rainbow sheen, we lowered the Opacity of the Curves Adjustment layer. A multipointed star created in Adobe Illustrator was dragged and dropped into the file to finish the logo shown at the top of page 262.

8

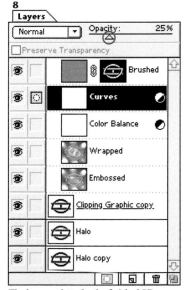

The layers palette for the finished 3D graphic, with Opacity for the Curves layer reduced to diminish the rainbow effect

UNIFORM MOTION BLURS

The Motion Blur filter, applied to a noise-filled layer, can be useful for making textures like brushed metal. But the blur isn't complete at the edges. To make the blur uniform, use the rectangular marquee to select the uniform center of the layer, press Ctrl-T (for Free Trans-form) and Alt-drag a middle handle to stretch the uniform part to the edge of the layer. (The Alt key scales the selected area from the center outward.) Double-click in the selected area to complete the transformation.

Working with Widgets

Overview *Drag and drop an image into a Widgets **hs** file; apply the Displace filter to the Picture layer, using the matching **disp** file.*

JHD

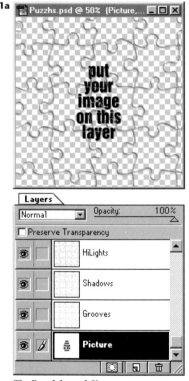

1a

*The **Puzzlehs.psd** file*

PHOTODISC, PEOPLE & LIFESTYLES

1b

Original photo

THE WIDGETS ON THE WOW CD-ROM are "ready-to-wear" special effects that you can apply to any grayscale or color image, simply by inserting your own photo as the bottom layer of the file. The built-in Highlights layer (in Screen mode), the Shadows layer (in Multiply mode), and in some cases other layers interact to create the effect. Then apply the matching displacement map to "mold" the effect into your picture. In addition to the Puzzle shown here, there are five more Widgets on the disc. Examples of these other Widgets applied to the same photo are shown on the facing page.

1 Importing your photo. Choose a Widget from **goodies\widgets** on the Wow! CD-ROM. Open the "**hs**" file for that Widget — for example, the **Puzzlehs.psd** file in this case. Choose File, Save As to make a copy to work in, leaving the original untouched. Open the Layers palette and activate the Picture (bottom) layer by clicking on its name. Then open a photo and drag it with the move tool into the Widget file. At this point you'll be able to see your image with the special-effect highlights and shadows in place. If necessary, resize your imported image (you can choose Layer, Transform, Scale and hold down the Shift key as you drag on a corner handle to scale it proportionally). Once the image is in place, crop it (Choose Select, All and then Image, Crop) to get rid of any "big data" that extends beyond the edges of the canvas. You can reduce file size by merging your image with the original Picture layer below (Ctrl-E).

2 Running the Displacement filter. Now, with your new layer active, choose Filter, Distort, Displace and set both of the Scale factors at 5% or less. (The Displacement Map and Undefined Areas settings are irrelevant, since the displacement map you'll be using exactly fits the file.) Click OK and then pick the matching "**disp**" file — in this case **Puzzdisp.psd** — to complete the Widget effect.

Using Widgets on larger images. If your image is larger than the Widget file (as ours was), you can apply the Widget as a repeating pattern for a result like that shown at the top of this page: Open both your image file and the Widget's **hs** file. Then in the **hs** file, activate

1c

Photo dragged and dropped and merged with the Picture layer

2

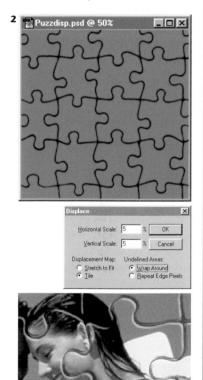

Molding the surface with the Displace filter

the Shadows layer by clicking on its name in the Layers palette. Turn off the eye icons for all the other layers. Then Select All, and choose Edit, Define Pattern.

Back in your image file, add a new layer above the image by Alt-clicking the New Layer icon, in the middle at the bottom of the Layers palette, naming the layer "Shadows." With this new Shadows layer active, choose Edit, Fill, Pattern. Now you'll construct the other two puzzle-piece layers of the Wow Puzzle Widget (HiLights and Grooves) within your image file, as follows. For each of these layers repeat the process of defining a pattern in the hs file, creating and naming a new layer in the image file, and pattern-filling the new layer. Finally, run the Displace filter on the image layer of your file, choosing Tile for the Displacement Map setting in the Displace dialog box. Whether you choose Repeat Edge Pixels or Wrap Around as the setting for the Undefined Areas, you'll probably need to crop the image to get rid of artifacts at the edges.

Variations. To finish the image at the top of page 266, we activated the Grooves layer, and for each piece we wanted to remove from the puzzle image, we clicked the magic wand in the transparent interior of the piece, then activated the Picture layer, and pressed Backspace. We repeated the deleting process for the highlights, shadows, and grooves layers. (Some touch-up with the eraser was required.) To rotate a piece, we made a selection as described above, then chose Edit, Copy Merged. After deleting the original piece as described above, we pasted (Ctrl-V) and rotated (Layer, Free Transform). We merged the layers (Layer, Merge Visible) and added a drop shadow as described in steps 3 and 4 of "Casting a Shadow" on page 241. ⌐Wow⌐

Wow Big Drops (**Drophs.psd** and **Dropdisp.psd**)

Wow Rough (**Roughhs.psd** and **Rghdisp.psd**)

Wow Ice Cubes (**Icehs.psd** and **Icedisp.psd**)

Wow Tiles (**Tilehs.psd** and **Tiledisp.psd**)

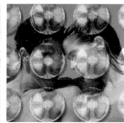

Wow Balls (**Ballhs.psd** and **Balldisp.psd**)

For his series *Kane, Kani, Ki,* **Russell Sparkman** created the textured backgrounds from two scanned photos layered together using the Layers palette's Opacity slider and the Layer Options dialog box.

After the combined texture was completed, the two layers were merged into one. This texture layer was then duplicated. An object — metal, crab shell, or driftwood — was dragged from another file into the texture file to create a third layer. A drop shadow was created under the object (see "Casting a Shadow" in this chapter), and then the object, shadow, and top texture layer were merged, reducing the file to two layers again.

Sparkman created a new layer, specifying Overlay mode and Fill With Overlay-Neutral Color (50% Gray) in the New Layer dialog box. ▶*To open the New Layer dialog box when you add a layer so you can set the blending mode and Opacity and name the layer, Alt-click the New Layer icon in the middle at the bottom of the Layers palette.*

A bevel highlight and shadow were created on this layer, and the neutral layer was then merged with the object-shadow-texture layer.

Sparkman applied a Gaussian Blur to the underlying layer and darkened it using Image, Adjust, Levels. Then he used a combination of feathered selections and layer masks to delete parts of the upper layer to transparency, to partially reveal the underlying blurred and darkened original texture layer.

All layers were then merged and a duplicate of this layer was made. A Gaussian blur was applied to the top layer and then it was darkened with the Output slider of the Levels dialog box. Then, using Layer Options in the top layer, Sparkman held down the Alt key and dragged the left-hand portion of the "This Layers" white point slider over to a setting between 20 and 25. This began to reveal the brighter, sharper underlying layer through the darker, blurred upper layer.

Using heavily feathered selections, he made small "amoeba-like" selections of the upper layer and deleted these areas to transparency, revealing more of the underlying layer. After many areas had been selected and deleted, the end result was an effect of mottled light, with areas of sharpness and softness.

PHOTO: TOM COLLICOTT / ART DIRECTION FOR THE CATALOG: MATTHAEUS, DONAHOE, HALVERSON (SEATTLE)

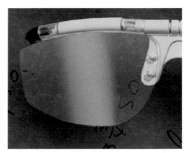

For his images in the award-winning ***Industrial Strength Eyewear catalog***, **Jeff McCord** constructed the transparency and reflectivity of the clear lenses, and the drop shadow beneath the glasses, in Photoshop. He started with product shots of glasses on glass against a neutral backdrop. McCord worked with prepress consultant Doug Peltonen to select the gray background (Select, Color Range works well for this kind of selection) and inverted the selection (Select Inverse) to isolate the glasses. The next step was to make the drop shadow. ("Casting a Shadow" on page 240 describes a tech-nique for producing a drop shadow, as well as a cast shadow.)

With the shadow in place, McCord brought the glasses into his background image. He adjusted the Opacity to 60% to let the background and shadow show through.

To restore the highlight that had been lost in making the lenses transparent, McCord layered another copy of the glasses on top of the first, this time setting the blending mode to Lighten. He used Image, Adjust, Levels to increase the contrast until he achieved the specular highlights he wanted. ▶*Applying tonal changes like*

Levels through an Adjustment layer keeps options open for experimenting with different settings. To change the parameters for an Adjustment layer, double-click on its name *or its* black-and-white circular symbol *in the Layers palette. To restrict the adjustment to a single layer, Alt-click the border between the Adjustment layer and the layer below it in the Layers palette to form a clipping group. To make the adjustment apply to only part of the tonal range of the layers it affects, or to certain colors, double-click the Adjustment layer's* thumbnail *in the Layers palette to open the Layer Options dialog box.*

Stephen King imported PostScript line work to serve as the basis for the neon profile and other shapes in this *Imagitrek Ad*. The line work for each element was first placed in an alpha channel of the background image file. Then each channel was duplicated to another alpha channel by dragging its name to the New Channel icon at the bottom of the Channels palette. A Gaussian Blur was applied to this channel. Then, working in the RGB composite channel, King loaded the blurred channel of the face as a selection and filled it with a bright blue. The line work channel (#4) was loaded in a layer above the glow and filled with the same color. King painted highlights on the neon squiggles with a small paintbrush and lighter tints of paint. The paint could be confined to the lines by loading the line work alpha channels as selections and painting within them on the line work layer. The process was repeated for the other neon shapes.

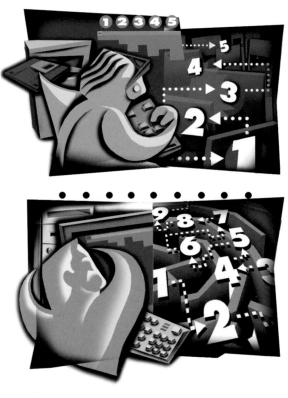

Francois Guerin created the *Steps 1, 2, 3* series of illustrations almost entirely in Photoshop; only the type was imported from Adobe Illustrator. After drawing the shapes with the pen tool, lasso, and polygon lasso, he stored them in alpha channels so he could load them as selections again later. He filled the shapes with color and used the airbrush and eraser to create depth with shadows and highlights. To partially "lift" a shape away from another shape beneath it to get a "cut paper" effect, such as the jaw line or the right arm (above right), he used the shape of the lifted element as a frisket: He loaded the alpha channel as a selection, inverted the selection, and airbrushed the shadow, fine-tuning with the eraser where necessary. He connected the numbers with dotted and dashed lines. ▶*One way to paint a dotted line is to use a hard-edged brush from the top row of the Brushes palette with Spacing adjusted. Double-click the brush's footprint in the palette to open the Brush Options dialog box, and set the spacing to 200% or more. To paint the dots in a straight line that turns a corner, hold down the Shift key and click at the corner point and the ending point of one line segment. Then release the Shift key, click on the corner dot, hold down the Shift key, and click at the endpoint for the second segment.*

To make the type for the *cover of The Photoshop 4 Wow! Book*, **Jack Davis** used the method described in "Creating Crystal" on page 255, with a few differences. For instance, instead of using a clipping group to mask the embossed-and-Plastic-Wrapped type (in Overlay mode) and the "glassified" (distorted) type, he trimmed them as follows: With the glassified layer active, he loaded the original alpha channel as a selection, inverted it, and deleted the background. For the Plastic-Wrapped channel, he loaded the same alpha channel, expanded the selection (Select, Modify, Expand), and then feathered the selection slightly, inverted it, and deleted; this retained a little of the "plasticized" edge effect that extended outside the lettering (above, top). Then he merged the plastic and glassified layers (above, bottom). To color the "4," he selected it and Ctrl-clicked the New Layer icon to make a Hue/Saturation Adjustment layer with an automatic mask that restricted the color change to the "4."

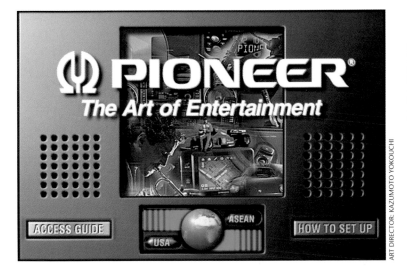

ART DIRECTOR: KAZUMOTO YOKOUCHI

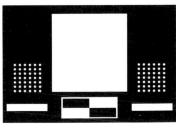

For this *home page* for a World Wide Web site, **Jack Davis**'s client wanted a dramatically lit high-tech look. Davis created the surface of the device by embossing with the Lighting Effects filter,

turning off White Is High and using as the Texture Channel an alpha channel made with artwork created in Adobe Illustrator (the alpha channel is shown at the right). This was then layered with the screen

collage image and a shadow. The frames for a 3D animation of a rotating globe were composited on a square section of the background so the animated element, created with an alpha channel, would blend seamlessly with its surroundings. The small type for the "Access Guide" and "How To Set Up" buttons, which had to be provided in several different languages, was created with a "quick emboss" — the white type layer was duplicated, the new layer was offset, and Shift-Alt-Backspace filled the type with black to make a shadowed edge.

3D, MULTI-MEDIA, AND THE WEB

ALTHOUGH MANY OF THE SAME BASIC RULES of design and composition apply whether you're designing for the screen or for print, in some ways creating images for multimedia or for the World Wide Web is fundamentally different from creating images for the printed page.

- Almost anyone can **"navigate"** a book or magazine, but getting around in a multimedia program or a Web site is a much less familiar and intuitive process for most people. So part of the design of many on-screen presentations is to make it clear how to get somewhere else. Buttons and other "controls" become important. In this chapter "Making Buttons from Photos," "Making a Panel of Pushbuttons," and "Popping Buttons Off the Screen" provide methods for button design and manufacture, and the Actions on the Wow! CD-ROM can automate the production of some simple beveled buttons.

- The typical **format** for on-screen images is horizontal, to match the aspect ratio of the monitor, rather than vertical, to fit the most typical printed page. Many of the elements you use in a design for the screen will need to be horizontal to fit within this format.

- **Three-dimensional graphics** can be an important component of interactive environments for multimedia and the Web. "Photoshop and the Third Dimension" on page 274 describes how Photoshop images can be used in creating 3D objects and how models developed in 3D programs can be incorporated into Photoshop images.

- Making artwork for Multimedia and the Web opens up the opportunity to use not only a third dimension but a fourth — motion. **Animation** is discussed in "Video and Multimedia" on page 276. In addition, the three button-making techniques described on pages 285–294 include alternate states for buttons so that they can be animated by Shockwave or other Web animation software. "Onion-Skinning a GIF Animation" and "Rotoscoping a QuickTime Movie" demonstrate some of the ways Photoshop can help in creating dynamic imagery.

- **Color** in on-screen images sometimes requires designing graphics to look good when displayed with the limited color depth of 8-bit color systems. Or if one of your design goals is to keep

continued on page 274

WEB RESOURCES

Preparing static or animated World Wide Web pages requires more software than Photoshop alone and more Photoshop technique than a single chapter of this book can cover. New Web books appear weekly, but as this book goes to press, two that we find particularly useful for making Web graphics in Photoshop are *Creating Killer Web Sites* and *Photoshop Web Techniques*. These and other useful references are listed in the Appendix.

The Ray Dream Designer 3D program can produce a distance mask with background surfaces and objects in white, foreground objects in black, and intermediate objects in shades of gray. In Photoshop you can adjust the mask using Levels or Curves to get the desired range from black (near) to white (far). Then load the distance mask as a selection in the color image and apply a filter or other effect. Mitch Anthony rendered this image (top left) in Ray Dream Designer, where he saved it, also saving the distance mask as an alpha channel (top right). In Photoshop this channel was loaded as a selection and the Clouds filter was applied (bottom).

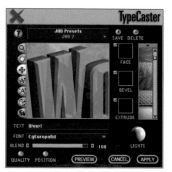

Xaos Tools' TypeCaster plug-in for Photoshop gives type a three-dimensional treatment, with separate control of face, bevel, and edge, as well as textures and colored light sources.

images for the Web small so they can be downloaded quickly, you may need to restrict color depth even more, as described in "Preparing Art for the Web," starting on page 276.

- The **resolution** of on-screen images is a lot lower than that used for print. That means that the files are smaller, so you can work faster in Photoshop and without running out of RAM for memory-intensive operations. But it also means that you can't get the smooth, high-resolution type and graphics typical of print work. This low resolution is one of the reasons that type on-screen has to be bigger than type in print in order to be readable. For low-resolution display type and graphics, you can get more flexibility in the design process and better-looking results if you design them at twice or four times the size you need and then scale them down with Image, Image Size. The limited resolution of on-screen images is often expressed in terms of pixel dimensions — 640 x 480 pixels, for instance.

- Certain **file formats** are used for on-screen images: PICT is the standard for many multimedia applications. For the Web, GIF and JPEG, which is also used extensively to compress large images for transport and archiving, are the standards, with the new PNG showing promise for the future. "Choosing a Format" on page 277 discusses the advantages of each of the formats Photoshop provides for World Wide Web graphics.

PHOTOSHOP AND THE THIRD DIMENSION

In addition to length and width, a third dimension — depth — is implied in almost all photographs and in many illustrations. To make an image look more three-dimensional and real, the Levels command, applied to selected areas, can create shadows and highlights that add depth to a scene. In addition, three of Photoshop's Layer, Transform functions (Skew, Perspective, and Distort) allow you to select part or all of an image and telescope or "bend" it to exaggerate perspective; the Spherize filter can also create depth illusions.

Filters supplied by other developers can also add dimensionality, such as the KPT Glass Lens and Andromeda's Series 2 Three-D (described in Chapter 5). And several filters let you turn type into 3D graphics — for instance, Xaos Tools' TypeCaster and Vertigo 3D's Hot Text. But usually it takes a stand-alone 3D program to actually *model* — to *extrude* or *revolve* a two-dimensional element into a 3D shape, and even to move points to modify the solid object. Three-D programs also allow you to *stage* an entire scene, arranging the models you make, and then quickly change the viewpoint or lighting to produce a new perspective. Most 3D programs can also *render*, producing a photo-like view of the scene that assigns surface characteristics to the models and includes the interaction of light and shadows with these textures.

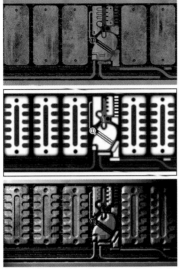

To quickly test this alpha channel (center) as a bump map before committing to a time-consuming 3D rendering process, Frank Vitale and E. J. Dixon of Presto Studios ran Photoshop's Lighting Effects filter on the painted RGB image shown at the top, using the alpha channel as the Texture Channel.

Vertigo's 3D Hot Text plug-in (top) applies 3D effects to type. The 3D Dizzy plug-in, also from Vertigo, allows you to import models saved in 3DMF format directly into Photoshop, then manipulate their orientation and lighting.

Photoshop can work with the artwork from 3D programs in two kinds of ways. It can serve as the recipient of an object or scene modeled and rendered in three dimensions, so it can then be retouched or enhanced. Or it can serve as a generator for images to be used as surface maps to add color, texture, and detail to a model in a stand-alone 3D program.

Photoshop to 3D

All 3D programs accept color files that can be applied to 3D models as flat surface textures (called *texture maps*) or for tactile effects (called *bump maps*). Photoshop's Lighting Effects filter can be useful to quickly test out *bump maps* to be used in 3D images, as in the example at the left. Some programs (such as MetaTools' Bryce) can also generate 3D models from grayscale images, translating the shades of gray as different distances above or below a surface, to create mountains, canyons, or other 3D models.

3D to Photoshop

Programs like Adobe Dimensions are designed to make relatively simple 3D models from type or from artwork drawn in PostScript programs such as Adobe Illustrator, Macromedia FreeHand, or CorelDraw. They can extrude or revolve models around the height, width, or depth axes and they can create perspective views, but they can't provide the complex texture, lighting, and shadowing effects of more powerful 3D programs. Effects such as highlights, shadows, and embossed textures can be added by hand to Dimensions artwork with Photoshop's filtering and layering techniques.

Even if you use a more sophisticated 3D program with advanced modelling and rendering functions for print applications, starting and ending with Photoshop can still save you time. Setting up your models, lighting, and camera angles in a 3D program is time-consuming, and rendering can take a long time. So if you find that you want to change the color or brightness of a 3D image once it's rendered, it may make sense to adjust Color Balance or Hue/Saturation for all or part of the image in Photoshop instead of going back to the 3D program to change the lighting and rerender the scene. Also, some kinds of shadows and other details look more convincing if applied "by hand" with Photoshop's airbrush or masking techniques than by a 3D program's rendering algorithms.

In addition to full-color rendered images, most 3D programs can produce a mask that accompanies the file, appearing as an alpha channel when the file is opened in Photoshop. This channel can then be used in any of the ways Photoshop masks are applied — for instance, to isolate parts of an image so the color can be changed, to apply a blur or another filter selectively as shown on page 274, or to composite the image into a new background.

If you plan to do a lot of preparation of Web graphics in Photoshop, some utilities that will make your life easier are the HVS ColorGIF and JPEG plug-ins and AutoF/X's WebVise Totality, which allow more flexibility in setting color depth for GIF and JPEG conversion, and Debabelizer, a stand-alone file-conversion program that produces more Web-efficient files than Photoshop and with more control in creating Adaptive palettes.

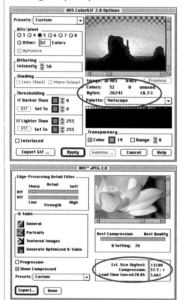

The HVS ColorGIF and HVS JPEG plug-ins for Photoshop are powerful utilities for interactively fine-tuning palette and dithering options and compression ratios for the two most popular Web graphics formats.

VIDEO AND MULTIMEDIA

Photoshop includes filters and functions designed specifically for adapting both still and animated images for display on computer screens or on television. For example, Photoshop can open and save files in Adobe Premiere's Filmstrip format for QuickTime animations (see page 282). Photoshop 4's Batch Actions (see page 47) and Adjustment layers make it quick and easy to apply the same Curves, Levels, and other Photoshop corrections to a series of related image files. And Photoshop documents can be opened directly in Adobe After Effects, with layers and alpha channels intact, ready for animating and compositing with video.

For video, the NTSC Colors filter (under Video in the Filter menu) restricts images to the standard color gamut used for television. The De-interlace filter (also under Video) can smooth video-grabbed images.

Also, creating Photoshop images to be viewed on-screen sometimes involves color restrictions. For instance, PICT files used in multimedia are often produced using a standard 8-bit palette. This reduces file size by two-thirds and can also prevent the "color flashing" that can happen when images with different 8-bit palettes follow each other in a presentation.

PREPARING ART FOR THE WEB

Almost any effect you can create in Photoshop can be adapted for use on World Wide Web sites. Special effects treatments for text and graphics like those in Chapter 8 make excellent styling for the buttons that operate Web links. Photo treatments like those in Chapter 3 and montages like those in Chapter 4, adapted to meet the special challenges of downloading from the Web, can be ideal for background illustrations or for *image maps,* which are bitmapped graphics whose territory can be divided up to allow several links from a single image file.

When you prepare artwork to be included in World Wide Web pages, you're aiming for good image quality and fast downloading. You want the image to be attractive and the colors to be as accurate as possible (the latter is especially important in fine art or in online catalog images, for instance, or in displaying a logo). Speedy downloading is important so that viewers won't give up in frustration waiting for the graphics to be transferred across the Internet and downloaded to their computers.

Colors can change when you convert a Photoshop RGB image to the NTSC color system used for television. To keep surprises to a minimum when you're preparing graphics that will be used on TV, stay away from using pure white or saturated shades of red, green, and blue. If you get color bleeding when the graphics are tested on TV, try dropping Saturation by 10 points or the Output Levels white point by 10 points, or both.

In run-length encoding, which is the type of compression scheme used in the GIF file format, color data is compressed by reading across the image, one row of pixels at a time, and storing information about color *changes* rather than storing the color of each individual pixel. The fewer color changes there are — or the more *color redundancy* — the more the file can be compressed. So, for example, a vertical color gradient — one that changes color from top to bottom — contains only one color per row and can be compressed quite small. But a horizontal or diagonal gradient — changing color from side to side or corner to corner — involves many color changes per row and therefore can't be compressed as much. Solid colors also compress better than dithered colors, since a color change has to be recorded with each color change in the "dotted" mix.

When you choose the Adaptive palette for a conversion from RGB Color to Indexed Color, Photoshop tries to pick a set of colors that best represents the colors in the original image. But the way Photoshop makes the conversion can lead to a problem if you're converting a graphic that you've put on the background color of your Web page. Even though the image may contain more pixels of the background color than of any other single color, this color may not be preserved exactly when an Adaptive palette is generated. So when your graphic goes onto the Web page, it may stand out on a block of slightly mismatched color. If you can, it's safer to use one of the transparency options offered in the GIF89a Export, eliminating the background from your graphic altogether.

Unfortunately, image quality and speed tend to work against each other, exerting exactly opposite pressures on the development of artwork. The more detail and color subtlety in an image, the bigger the file tends to be, and thus the slower to download.

Keeping Files Small

Here are some general tips for reducing the bulk of the images you prepare for the Web:

- **Reduce the dimensions.** Make the image as small as you can and still get the impression you want.

- **Avoid horizontal or diagonal gradients.** Because of *run-length encoding* methods used to compress images in the GIF format, vertical gradients compress much smaller than horizontal or diagonal ones. (See "Run-Length Encoding" at the left.)

- If you use Indexed color, **avoid dithering** whenever you can. Dithering is the interspersing of dots of two different colors to create the illusion of a third color; Photoshop provides it as an option when you convert to Indexed color. Again because of run-length encoding, dithering increases the size of a compressed file. Sometimes, though, color rendition is so much better with dithering that the extra file size is worth it.

- When you convert an RGB color image to the more limited (216-color) browser-safe Web color palette, you may be able to reduce the file size without further reducing the number of colors used in the artwork if you **use an Exact palette.** "'Slimming' the Palette" on page 281 tells how to this.

- When you convert from RGB to Indexed color, choosing Adaptive lets you **try out palettes with less color depth,** such as 4 or 5 bits per pixel rather than the standard 8-bit (256 colors). See "Adaptive Color Caution" at the left and "Targeted Adaptation" on page 279 for advice on working with Adaptive palettes.

- **Use tiled backgrounds.** For a Web background, instead of making an entire image, you can make a *tile* that a Web browser can use to fill the screen (see "Tiling Backgrounds" on page 281).

Choosing a Format

Among the file formats Photoshop can save or export are three that are compact and useful for preparing graphics for web pages. With all three of these formats, you have the option of displaying a blurry or chunky version of the image first, which then builds to a complete detailed version. This is done through *interlacing* or *progressive display*:

- **JPEG** (for *Joint Photographic Experts Group*) uses a compression method designed for **photographs**. It allows 24-bit color, so that people whose computer systems can display this color (or

Because getting the best combination of small file size (for quick downloading) and good color and detail is a trial-and-error process, you may often find yourself comparing several versions of the same image, saved in different ways. Here are some tips to help with that process:

• To evaluate the degradation caused by JPEGing a file, you have to close it after saving and then open it again. (GIFs saved with the GIF89a plug-in are automatically saved closed and have to be opened again also.)

• Saving files without preview icons or thumbnails gives you a better basis for comparing file sizes. To turn off previews, choose File, Preferences, Saving Files.

• You can't accurately compare download times by checking the file size in the lower left corner of an open Photoshop window, or even by comparing Size listings on the desktop. Instead, select the file on the desktop and then choose File, Get Info. In the Size listing, read the number in parentheses.

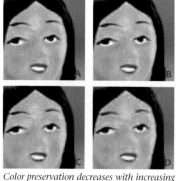

Color preservation decreases with increasing JPEG compression. The following standard settings were used for these images: (A) 3; (B) J2; (C) 1; (D) 0.

16-bit) will see the file at its best (or close to it). (Those with 8-bit systems will see a dithered version.) But JPEG doesn't allow you to make part of the image transparent to let the background of the Web page can show through. And if applied with too high a degree of compression, JPEG can cause serious image degradation, especially around edges.

• **GIF89a** (for *graphics* interchange file, and pronounced "Jif") is great for flat-color artwork, but poor for photos because it supports only 8-bit color or less. It allows transparency, so you can have graphics that are silhouetted against the Web page background.

• **PNG** (pronounced "ping") is the relatively new Portable Network Graphics format that allows both full color and precise control of transparency (through the use of alpha channels, which can be full grayscale masks), as well as a smaller file size (in some cases about 30% smaller than a GIF). It also takes into consideration the different gamma characteristics (brightness) of the monitors used on Mac, Windows, and Unix platforms, so that images created on one system are less likely to look too light or too dark when viewed on another platform.

The new PNG format holds great promise for the future, with big improvements in graphics-handling for the Web. But so far not many browsers support it. So for general distribution, Photoshop's GIF89a and JPEG formats are currently the best bets.

When deciding whether to use GIF89a or JPEG and figuring out how to set up the graphic, you'll need to answer a series of questions about the artwork. The first is: What kind of artwork are you starting with? Your approach will be different depending on whether you're working with (1) a full-color image like a photo or artwork with color gradients, where it's important to preserve the full color range (see "Starting with a Full-Color Image" on page 279), (2) monochromatic artwork (see "Grayscale or Other Monochromatic Art" on page 279), (3) existing flat-color artwork (see "Adapting Existing Flat-Color Artwork" on page 279), or (4) flat-color artwork that you're creating from scratch in Photoshop by importing and coloring elements from Adobe Illustrator, making and filling selections, or drawing with Photoshop's painting tools (see "Type or Flat-Color Artwork Built from Scratch" on page 281).

To some extent, choosing a format (GIF or JPEG) and within that format a degree of color detail reduction (either through limiting the number of colors in the indexed palette of a GIF or through choosing a level of compression for JPEG) is a trial-and-error process of saving a file in several versions of both GIF and JPEG, then comparing the appearance and size of the different results, and choosing the best compromise for each Web-destined image. (If you like making Actions, consider automating the process of saving files in JPEG using the Save A Copy command.)

An image "vignetted" against the background color of a Web page by converting a transparent layer from an RGB file to GIF, using File, Export, GIF89a Export

TARGETED ADAPTATION

To get better color results with an Adaptive palette of less than 8 bits per pixel, you can select the area of the image where color fidelity is most important before you make the conversion from RGB to Indexed color. For example, selecting the face in a portrait will cause Photoshop to used more of the 32 colors of a 5-bit palette for skin tones, leaving fewer for the less important variegated background.

Original 24-bit RGB Color image

Converted with Image, Mode, Indexed Color, Adaptive, 5 bits/pixel, Diffusion

Converted as above, but after an area of important skin tones was selected

Starting with a Full-Color Image

If you want to preserve the quality of a full-color photo or painting destined for the Web, your options will differ, depending on whether your image is partly transparent — a vignette, for example, with soft edges that let the Web page background show through — and whether it's a shape other than rectangular.

If your image is rectangular and it doesn't have any areas that need to be transparent, you can use JPEG. Try several Quality settings, comparing the resulting files for quality and loading time with various browsers. Often medium or low quality will work for images, while medium or high is needed for gradients. Photoshop 4's JPEG option lets you set quality on a sliding scale. You can also choose Optimized Baseline to avoid the blurred edges and "chunked" color that JPEG can produce. Or choose Progressive for a display that appears quickly (though blurred) and then builds sharp detail.

If your image has a shape other than rectangular, especially if it has a soft, feathered edge, you may want to use the GIF89a format, realizing that you'll have to compromise color depth for the appearance of transparency. While still in RGB mode, isolate the artwork on a transparent layer of its own and turn off visibility for all other layers. Choose File, Export, GIF89a Export; choose Adaptive (unless Exact is available), and choose a background color the same as that of the Web page by clicking on the color square and then entering the R, G, and B values for the color of the page, so the background of image and page will blend invisibly.

If your image is nonrectangular and hard-edged or has to appear over a patterned background, over several backgrounds, or over an unknown background, you can use the GIF conversion process described in "Adapting Existing Flat-Color Artwork," below.

Grayscale or Other Monochromatic Art

Often you can get decent-looking monochromatic artwork with many fewer than the 256 shades that a full Indexed Color Adaptive palette would provide. Follow the directions below for flat-color art, but try setting the number of colors as low as 5 or even 4 bits per pixel when you convert to an Adaptive palette.

Adapting Existing Flat-Color Artwork

As mentioned in "Choosing a Format" on page 277, GIF is often the best format for flat-color artwork. Starting in RGB mode, choose Image, Mode, Indexed Color. To get color that will be consistent regardless of which platform the image is viewed on, you can choose Web palette; use None for the Dither setting if it gives acceptable results, or use Diffusion. Then, since your artwork may not need all the colors of the Web palette, you may be able to reduce file size further by switching to an Exact palette, using the method described in "'Slimming' the Palette" on page 281.

TILING BACKGROUNDS

To get a textured background for a Web page and still reduce the time needed for downloading, you can use a background tile — a small, repeating element with which a Web browser fills the screen, starting at the top left corner and proceeding across and down. As usual with Web graphics, tiles require a balance between quick downloading and appealing graphics: The smaller the tile, the less time it will take to download. But very small tiles can cause a perceptible "filling" effect as the browser builds the screen. If you make Web background tiles in Photoshop, be sure to try them out with the common browsers at typical download speeds. (For tips on making tiles for seamlessly repeating patterns, see "Defining a Pattern" on page 197 and "Creating a Canvas Texture" on page 212.)

MAKING WEB-SAFE SWATCHES

You can make a Swatches palette that includes only the 216 browser-safe colors of the Web palette, as follows:

Choose Image, Mode, Indexed Color and choose the Web palette. Then choose Image, Mode, Color Table, and click the Save button. Once the palette is saved, you can open the Swatches palette (Window, Show Swatches) and choose Replace Swatches from the palette's pop-out menu, choosing the Web color table you saved.

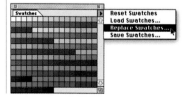

If you need transparency so the background of the Web page can show through your artwork, you'll need to check your image carefully to see whether the color you want to replace with transparency also occurs in other places, where you don't want it to be transparent.

- If the color needs to be transparent in some places but not in others, use Photoshop's selection functions to make a selection of all the pixels that need to be *nontransparent*, and save it as an alpha channel (Select, Save Selection, New). Then choose File, Export, GIF89a Export and choose the name of the channel as the transparency selection. The black areas of the channel will make the corresponding areas of the image transparent in the GIF. Note that in Indexed Color files, alpha channel masks are strictly black and white — there are no shades of gray. So the mask will have a pixelated edge.

- If, on the other hand, the color should be transparent everywhere it exists, you won't need an alpha channel. Just choose File, Export, GIF89a Export. Click the dialog box's plus-eyedropper on the color you want to be transparent. Drag the dropper over any other colors you want to also make transparent; if you accidentally eliminate a color you want to retain, restore it by

"SCREENS" FOR TYPE OR GRAPHICS

You can use the Andromeda Series 3 Screens filter (see Chapter 5) for a distinctive treatment for photos, illustrations, or large, bold display type for use on the Web. Start with a grayscale file (or a color file converted to grayscale) and run a low-resolution Pattern, Special Effect, or Text-Preset effect on it. The result is a black-and-white image, with no grays. To convert it to color, switch to RGB mode (Image, Mode, RGB Color); choose the magic wand (with Anti-aliasing turned off in the Magic Wand Options palette); click on a black pixel; choose Select, Similar to add the rest of the black pixels to the selection; then choose a bright Foreground color from the Web Swatches palette (see "Making Web-Safe Swatches" at the left), and Alt-Backspace to replace the black. Now convert the file to Indexed color, choosing the Exact palette (Image, Mode, Indexed Color, Exact); and finally, export the file via the GIF89a plug-in, for a stylized, monotone image or type treatment, with the option of replacing the white pixels with transparency, and with a very tiny file size. (Instead of using the Andromeda Screens filter, you can get a similar effect by converting to Bitmap mode using a very low-resolution Halftone Dither. You'll need to convert back to Grayscale to use the magic wand in the next step of the process, as described above.)

The "Travel" type shown here was set at 60 points filled with a gradient from black to light gray before the file was flattened, and Andromeda Series 3's Patterns, Wavy Horizontal Lines—20 was applied with settings of 16 lines per inch and Threshold 124. The file was

converted to RGB mode, and a Web color was substituted for black; then the file was converted to Indexed mode (Exact palette), and exported via the GIF89a plug-in, with white designated as the Transparency color. The final size of the file was about 1K.

When you convert an Indexed Color file to GIF using the GIF89a plug-in, you can choose one or more colors to become transparent, so that when the graphic is placed on a Web page, the background will show through. By default a light gray indicates transparent areas, but you can change the indicator color by clicking the Transparency Index Color swatch.

"SLIMMING" THE PALETTE

If you convert a graphic from full RGB color to the 216-color "browser-safe" Web palette, you may end up with more colors than you need — colors that occur in the Web palette but that aren't used in your artwork. If you can drop those colors from the file, the file size can be reduced further, without any further reduction in color depth. Here's how to do it: After you've converted to the Web palette (Image, Mode, Indexed Color, Web), convert back to RGB (Image, Mode, RGB Color). Then convert to Indexed color again, this time using an Exact palette (Image, Mode, Indexed Color, Exact), to retain only those Web colors used in the image. Then choose File, Export,

GIF89a Export to set up transparency if you need it and to save the file.

holding down the Ctrl key and clicking the dropper tool's icon; then click the resulting minus-eyedropper on the swatch of the color you want to restore. When transparency is complete, save the file.

Type or Flat-Color Artwork Built from Scratch

If you're building artwork by importing shapes from Illustrator and filling them with color, or by making selections and filling them, or by drawing directly in Photoshop, you can ensure that all your colors are "browser-safe" by creating your artwork with colors chosen from a browser-safe Swatches palette, made as described in "Making Web-Safe Swatches" on page 280.

Start out working in RGB Color mode with your Web Swatches palette open. Will your graphics appear on a single-color background? If so, start with a rectangle of your background color. Choose the colors for your graphics by sampling from the Swatches palette with the eyedropper tool — you can toggle to the eyedropper from any painting tool simply by moving the tool over the Swatches palette. Import files from Adobe Illustrator (File, Place) with Anti-aliasing turned on (the default) and fill them with color, by pressing Alt-Backspace. Or make antialiased selections and fill them with color. Or paint new lines and shapes, using hard-edged rather than soft brush tips — for example, use the ones from the top row of the default Brushes palette. Photoshop will antialias the artwork, using colors in the Web palette that are intermediate between the colors you're painting with, including the background color.

If you don't know what the background color will be, or if the background might have more than one color, or if your artwork will have to appear over more than one background, it makes sense to prepare the file without antialiasing, so that you don't end up with a halo of color around the art. So that you can import artwork from Illustrator without automatically antialiasing it, choose File, Preferences, General and turn off Anti-alias PostScript. Then place and color artwork as described above. Before you make selections to fill with color, make sure antialiasing is turned off for the selection tool. And when you paint lines or shapes, use the pencil tool, since it's the only painting tool that isn't antialiased.

When you've finished the artwork, choose File, Export, GIF89a and use the Exact palette. Or you can try reducing the number of colors in the GIF by choosing Adaptive and setting the number of bits per pixel to a lower number than the Exact palette would use. The GIF89a conversion will use Web palette colors to achieve the smoothest color transitions it can where colors overlap, simulating the antialiasing that working in RGB Color allowed. 🖌

Rotoscoping a QuickTime Movie

Overview *Export an Adobe Premiere clip as a Filmstrip; open it in Photoshop; add a layer for rotoscoping; paint the special effects; save in Filmstrip format.*

Three frames from the middle of the time-travelling clip, exported from Adobe Premiere as a Filmstrip file and opened in Photoshop

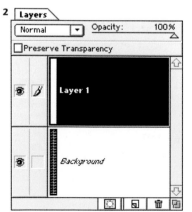

Rotoscoping layer added to Filmstrip file

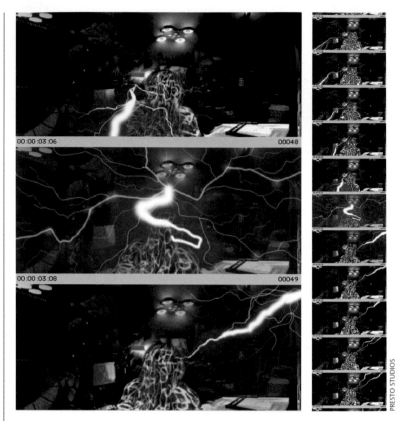

ADOBE PREMIERE AND PHOTOSHOP can work hand-in-hand, so animations created in Premiere can be imported into Photoshop for *rotoscoping* — painting, drawing, or adding a special effect to the individual frames of an animation or video sequence. Victor Navone of Presto Studios used Photoshop's rotoscoping power on several animated scenes from *Buried in Time*, the sequel to the photorealistic interactive adventure game *The Journeyman Project*. The rotoscoping techniques for two of the animations are described here, and the animations themselves are included in the "Buried in Time clips" folder inside the Wow Goodies folder on the Wow CD ROM, so you can play them with the Adobe Premiere demo program (also included on the CD ROM) to see how they turned out.

1 Exporting files from Premiere. Open an animation or video clip in Adobe Premiere and choose Make, Movie, Output Options, Filmstrip to save the file in the Filmstrip format that can be opened in Photoshop. For the animation showing time travel, in which a man is transported from one time and place to another, Navone started with a clip composited in Premiere from live video and a computer-generated background. He exported this animation as several 3-to-4-second Filmstrips, breaking it into these parts because the smaller files would be easier to handle in Photoshop.

3a

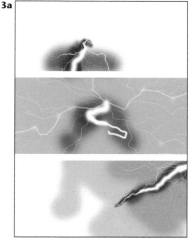

Lightning bolts painted with large, soft airbrushes with purple paint and varied Pressure settings, and a small, hard paintbrush with white paint

3b

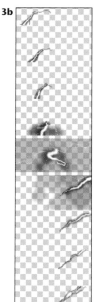

Layer 1 after the lightning bolts have been added to each frame

4

Saving a copy of the rotoscoped file in Filmstrip format

OPENING PART OF A FILMSTRIP

Film Strip Quick Edit 3.0, an Adobe plug-in for Photoshop that allows you to open part (rather than all) of a file in Filmstrip format and then save the part back into the original Filmstrip file, is provided on the Wow! CD-ROM. It makes rotoscoping and other Photoshop changes to animations easier to manage.

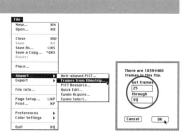

2 Adding a layer. In Photoshop, choose File, Open and choose the Filmstrip file by name. Open the Layers palette and create a new layer (Layer 1) by clicking on the New Layer icon, in the middle at the bottom of the palette. With both *Background* and Layer 1 visible (eye icons turned on) and Layer 1 active, you'll be able to use Layer 1 to experiment, painting and correcting mistakes without permanently changing the original frames.

3 Painting the frames. Now use any of Photoshop's tools to work on the top layer. You don't have to worry about the gray bars between frames; painting on them will have no effect on the animation. To create the bolts of electricity needed for the transmogrification, Navone used a large, soft-edged paintbrush to paint the glow and a smaller, hard-edged brush to paint the bolts themselves.

4 Exporting the Filmstrip. If you have an extended keyboard, you can check the effect of your painting on the animation by

GETTING PRECISE ALIGNMENT

Photoshop's "understanding" of the Filmstrip format makes it possible to repeat a selection or selection outline from one frame to the next, situating it in exactly the same position in the next frame:

- **To move a selection border, without its contents,** from one frame to the next (or previous) frame, hold down the Shift key and press the up (or down) arrow key.

- **To cut a selected element** from one frame and move it to the same position in the next (or previous) frame, use Ctrl-Shift-arrow.

- **To copy a selected element** to the same position in the next (or previous) frame, use Ctrl-Alt-Shift-arrow.

These maneuvers don't work with the current Film Strip Quick Edit (see "Opening Part of a Filmstrip," above).

Copying a selection from one frame to the next using Ctrl-Alt Shift-arrow

Moving a selection border, without its contents, from frame to frame using Shift-arrow

Four frames from the cannon-firing sequence from Buried in Time *before the explosion and retouched cannon ball were added*

The same four frames as above, after the explosion and cannon ball were added in Photoshop. Varying the Opacity of the rotoscoping layer helped create the illusion of dissipating smoke. "Before" and "after" versions of the animation are in the Buried in Time Clips *folder on the Wow! CD-ROM.*

shortening the height of the Window to one frame and then holding down the Shift key and the Page Up key or Page Down key to simulate forward or reverse animation. When you have a result that looks promising, check it in Premiere: Choose Save A Copy from Photoshop's File menu and save in Filmstrip format. Then open the Filmstrip in Premiere, convert it back to a clip by choosing Make, Movie, and view the clip. If you need to make additional changes, export the file in Filmstrip format again and go back into Photoshop for more editing.

Another way of working. Photoshop's ability to vary a layer's Opacity can come in handy for animating effects that dissipate over time, such as explosions. For an animation of a cannon blast, Navone created a puff of smoke and then cleared it away slowly. Again he used a top layer for painting in Photoshop, but this time he did the work on a series of PICT files rather than a Filmstrip. That way he could use the top layer's Opacity control to help dissipate the smoke; if he had used a Filmstrip, all the frames would have been included in one file, varying the Opacity setting of the top layer would have affected the smoke in all the frames equally.

With the individual PICT files, he could airbrush the smoke in the first frame and then copy it to the next frame by dragging the layer name from that PICT's Layers palette to the working window of the next PICT in the series. There he expanded the smoke with Layer, Transform, Scale; blurred it; and then reduced the Opacity to thin it. Dragging and dropping this expanded, thinner smokeburst to the next PICT, he applied the same techniques to dissipate it more. Since the animation involved the camera panning across a stationary object — a model created in Form Z and rendered in Electric Image — one of the most difficult aspects of the job was aligning the smoke from frame to frame. Navone picked elements in the model to use as reference points for alignment.

To make a Premiere movie clip into a series of PICTs, choose Make, Movie. In the Project Output Options dialog box, specify how much of the project to Output (Entire Project or Work Area) and choose Numbered PICT Files from the "as" pop-out menu. Each file will be saved with a suffix of a period followed by a number indicating its order in the sequence. After you've finished the work in Photoshop, the PICTs can be saved together in a folder and then opened and automatically reassembled into an animation in Premiere by choosing File, Open, selecting the image with the lowest number in the series, and clicking the Open button. *Wow!*

COMPRESSION COMES LAST

Don't compress your clip as you move it between applications — for instance, from the 3D program that created it to Adobe Premiere for editing, to Photoshop for retouching, because compression can degrade the image. Only when it's final should you compress it, to get a faster playback rate and a smaller file size.

Making Buttons from Photos

Overview For each button, crop and silhouette the subject; add matching borders, backgrounds, color treatments, and drop shadows; change button color and position to create an "active" state.

1a

The three original photos

1b

Each photo should consist of a single layer that is not "Background."

2   **3a**

Each of the photos was cropped close.

Removing the background from each photo left only the subject.

3b

Similarly cropped and without their backgrounds, the three photos looked more alike.

NOW THAT PEOPLE ARE ACCUSTOMED to clicking on-screen buttons, it's no longer necessary for every set of navigational tools to look like the controls of a VCR. As long as people can distinguish the buttons that make things happen from the informational elements around them, buttons for World Wide Web sites and other interactive projects can be created from a wide variety of imagery.

When you plan to craft on-screen buttons from photos or full-color illustrations, sometimes the biggest design challenge is turning a diverse collection of images into a unified set. Here we've unified three photos by applying a consistent series of graphic treatments: cropping, silhouetting, adding a border, desaturating, applying a consistent background, building a glow, colorizing, and adding a shadow. Depending on your particular set of images and Web-site design, you may decide to stop part-way through the process, or skip some steps and carry on with others.

1 Preparing the photos. To begin the process, open all the images in Photoshop that you want to use for making buttons. For each image, choose File, Save A Copy so you'll have the original, untouched version if you need to start over. Each button can be developed in its own file.

Most scanned photos consist of a single opaque background layer, but you'll need transparency for later steps in the process. Open the Layers palette. If any of your photos consists of *Background* only, give that layer the capability for transparency as follows: Double-click to open the Make Layer dialog box. Rename the layer "photo" and click OK to close the box. Now if you delete or erase any part of the image, that part of the layer will become transparent rather than being filled with the current Background color.

For a cohesive design, photo-based buttons work best if their subjects are roughly the same size and orientation. So that you can see their relative sizes, display all the files at the same magnification (50%, for instance), which can be set by selecting the numbers in the lower left corner of each window and typing in a percentage. Press Ctrl-T (for Layer, Free Transform); Shift-drag on a corner handle of the transform box to resize proportionally, and drag outside the box to rotate. Scale the photos so that at 50% magnification they appear at the size you want them to be in your final buttons. This will make the images twice as big as you want them

4

5

Adding a border defined the shape of each button.

Removing all color prepared each element to receive a unifying color scheme.

6a

Gradient Tool Options
Normal ▼	Opacity: 100% △
Gradient: Foreground to Background ▼
Type: Linear ▼ ☒ Mask ☒ Dither
Edit...	

Setting up the gradient

6b

7a

A gradient was added by dragging diagonally with the gradient tool.

A glow helps the image pop.

7b

Layers
Normal ▼	Opacity: 100% △
☐ Preserve Transparency
👁		Border
👁		Photo
👁	🖌	**Glow**
👁		Gradient

With border, glow, and background gradient in place, the layered button file looks like this.

7c

The matching backgrounds and glows make the buttons look more like a cohesive set.

to be when the buttons are finished, but it will give you extra image detail for the silhouetting and other processes that come next. (You can size the buttons down afterwards.) When you have the sizes and orientations you want, complete each transformation by pressing the Enter key.

2 Cropping. Now you'll make a marquee for cropping all the buttons to be the same size and shape. Select the marquee tool in the toolbox and press Enter to open its Options palette. Set the Style to Fixed Size, enter Height and Width values, set Feather to 0, and set Shape to Rectangular. Click the marquee tool to produce the marching ants, and drag the marquee into place to frame each subject the way you want it for the button. While the marquee is still active, complete the cropping by choosing Image, Crop to eliminate pixels outside the marquee.

3 Silhouetting. Now display your buttons at 200% so you can see the detail in the edges of the subjects. Isolate the elements you want by precisely selecting their silhouettes to eliminate dissimilar backgrounds. For instance you can use the pen tool to draw a path around a subject, then save the path by opening the Paths palette (Window, Show Paths) and double-clicking the Work Path name. To turn the path into a selection, click the Make Selection icon at the bottom of the palette (the dotted circle, third from the left). To select the background instead of the subject, press Ctrl-Shift-I (for Select, Inverse), and then press Backspace to remove it.

4 Creating a border. To outline the button, first add a layer for the border by Alt-clicking the New Layer icon at the bottom of the Layers palette and naming the layer "Border." To add the border, press "D" (for "Default colors") to ensure that the Foreground color is set to black, then select all (Ctrl-A), and choose Edit, Stroke, Inside. For our 140-pixel-high buttons we used a 2-pixel stroke Width.

5 Converting to gray. Even if you want to make the buttons more colorful in the long run (as we do later, in step 9), removing the color from them now can be useful as a first step toward a consistent color scheme: Activate the photo layer and choose Image, Adjust, Desaturate.

Duplicating the button elements into a single layer

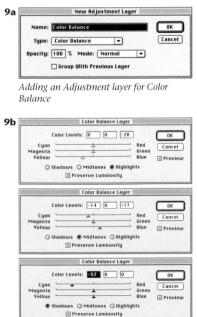

Adding an Adjustment layer for Color Balance

Colorizing a button with Color Balance

6 Adding a background treatment. Using the same background for each button is another unifying technique. Create and name a new layer (we called ours "Gradient," since that would be its content), and move it to be the backmost layer by dragging its name to be lowest in the Layers palette. Then fill the layer with a background; we used the gradient tool inside the selection. To add a diagonal black-to-white gradient, choose the gradient tool; press Enter to open its Options palette; choose Foreground To Background from the Gradient pop-out list and Linear from the Type list; and drag from the corner where you want the background to be black to the diagonally opposite corner, where you want the background to be white. We dragged from lower left to upper right.

7 Adding a glow. To add a glow to each button element, activate the Photo layer, copy this layer by Alt-dragging its thumbnail to the New Layer icon so the Duplicate Layer dialog box will open and you can name it "Glow." In the Layers palette, drag the glow layer between the Photo layer and the Gradient layer. To fill the subject with white, press "D" then "X" (for "eXchange colors") to make white the Foreground color, then press Shift-Alt-Backspace to fill the silhouette shape with white, while leaving the transparent areas unfilled. Then blur the layer to create the glow (Filter, Blur, Gaussian Blur), adjusting the Radius setting until the glow looks the way you want it. (Use the same setting for all the button files.)

8 Merging layers. Now you can merge the Border, Photo, Glow, and Gradient into a single layer: Make sure all four layers are visible (eye icons turned on in the Layers palette). Activate the top layer (press Alt-Shift-]), click the New Layer icon to add an empty layer at the top of the stack, hold down the Alt key, and choose Merge Visible from the palette's pop-out menu. This turns the new empty layer into a merged copy of the developing button. Making a merged copy rather than actually merging the layers themselves lets you keep the layers available for further changes later. Name the new layer something like "Merged."

9 Applying a color scheme. Now add back some color to the highlights, midtones, and shadows of the new merged button layer. In your first button file, add an Adjustment layer at the top of the stack by Ctrl-clicking the New Layer icon. In the New Adjustment Layer dialog box, choose Color Balance and move any or all of the three sliders until the Merged layer is the color you want. Once you've set the Color Balance for one of your photo button files, you can drag and drop the Adjustment layer into the other files. To make the effect of the Adjustment layer permanent in each file, turn on the eye icons for the Color Balance layer and the Merged layer and turn off all others. Then, with the Color Balance layer active, press Ctrl-E to Merge Down.

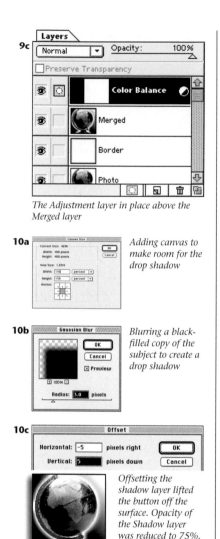

The Adjustment layer in place above the Merged layer

10a *Adding canvas to make room for the drop shadow*

10b *Blurring a black-filled copy of the subject to create a drop shadow*

10c

Offsetting the shadow layer lifted the button off the surface. Opacity of the Shadow layer was reduced to 75%.

11

The inverted color shows that a button is active. With the button centered over its shadow, it looks "pressed."

12a

Reducing the size of a button

10 Adding a drop shadow. To make your buttons stand out from the information elements on a Web page, you can pop them into the third dimension with drop shadows. But first you'll need to add some space. Choose Image, Canvas Size and add enough empty space to accommodate the shadow. Alt-drag the Merged layer to the New Layer icon to duplicate it, and name the copy "Shadow." In the Layers palette, drag the Shadow layer's label below the Merged label. Fill the button shape with black (with black as the Foreground color, press Shift-Alt-Backspace). Then apply a Gaussian Blur to soften the shadow's edge, and use Filter, Other, Offset to shift the shadow. (Apply the same blur and offset values to the shadows in all the button files.)

11 Making an alternate state for the button. If your buttons also need an "active" state — because you want a button's appearance to change when the cursor rolls over it or when it's clicked, for instance — start by duplicating the Merged layer. Turn the color of the new layer negative so the button appears "lit" (Ctrl-I). To make the button appear to be "pressed," you can shift the Merged copy layer so it's centered over the drop shadow: Press Ctrl-F to apply the last filter (Offset) again, with the same values you used in step 11.

12 Saving the buttons. To complete and save each button in each state, you need to make merged copies: Turn on the eye icons for only the Merged and Shadow layers; choose Image, Duplicate, and check the Merged Layers Only box. Make a merged duplicate of the active state button the same way, using the Merged copy and Shadow layers.

Reduce the buttons to their final sizes with Image, Image Size: To actually reduce the size of the file, make sure that Resample Image (Bicubic) is selected; to keep the image in proportion, also turn on Constrain Proportions; set the Height or Width to the pixel size, measurement, or percentage, and the other dimension will change proportionally; click OK to complete the resizing. Experiment with

12b

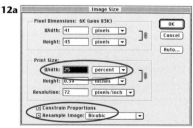

Buttons can be saved in both their original and their active state (as shown here) by duplicating the file with only the appropriate layers visible.

Filter, Sharpen, Unsharp Mask to see if sharpening improves the look of the reduced file.

Now you can save in the standard Web formats (see "Choosing a Format" on page 277). The change from a button's inactive to active state can be orchestrated with an animation utility like Shockwave when your Web page is put together. *WOW!*

Making a Panel of Pushbuttons

Overview *Create alpha channels for engraving and trimming the buttons; emboss the buttons with Lighting Effects; add cast shadows; mount the buttons in a panel; use feathered color fills to create a glow for an "active" state.*

*The **"Buttons"** Actions on the Wow! CD-ROM partially automate a button-making technique similar to this one.*

1

The black-and-white artwork, rasterized in Photoshop

2

Channels	
⬛⬛⬛ Blue copy	⌘4
⬛⬛⬛ Blue copy 2	⌘5
⬛⬛⬛ Blue copy 3	⌘6

The black-and-white art copied into three new alpha channels

3a

Eliminate the icons from channel #4.

3b

Remove the button outlines from channel #5.

3c

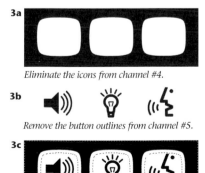

To blur the button outline in channel #6, make a selection that includes some white as well as the black background.

IN THE EFFORT TO HELP WEB SITE VISITORS figure out what's navigational and what's informational, the physical button metaphor has the advantage of already being clearly navigational. Here's a way to turn clip art or type into a set of dimensional pushbuttons.

1 Preparing the artwork. You'll need to start with a black-and-white graphics file. For this example the process started in Adobe Illustrator, but you can also start in Photoshop, using the pen tool and Snap To Grid to make the round-cornered button shapes, and setting type with the type tool instead of using clip art.

In Illustrator a black-filled rectangle was drawn to serve as the bounding box for three buttons. Then we drew a white-filled button shape on top and replicated it twice. Finally, three clip art symbols from Image Club's "Objects & Icons" collection were copied and pasted on top of the button shapes and scaled to fit. The file was saved in EPS format.

Next we rasterized the Illustrator artwork in Photoshop (File, Open, RGB Color, Anti-aliased). We made our panel of buttons 176 pixels high, four times the size it would finally appear on the Web page. Working bigger allows more control over the subtleties of highlight and shadow detail as the buttons develop.

2 Making alpha channels. Next, to make the alpha-channel masks that you'll need to construct your buttons, open the Channels palette and drag the thumbnail for any one of the color channels (we used the Blue, or #3, channel) to the New Channel icon, the second from the right at the bottom of the palette. (Since the artwork started out as strictly black-and-white, the three color channels [Red, Green, and Blue] are the same, and any one of them can be used.) Repeat the channel-copying process two more times so the graphic appears in three alpha channels.

3 Editing the three alpha-channel masks. Next you'll produce three different versions of the artwork — one to use as a "stencil" for cutting out the buttons (channel #4), one that contains only the icon art (channel #5), and a blurred channel (#6) to use with the Lighting Effects filter to raise the buttons off the background and "carve" the icons into the buttons' surfaces.

To make the button outline channel, first activate channel #4 by clicking its name in the Channels palette. Select the first icon

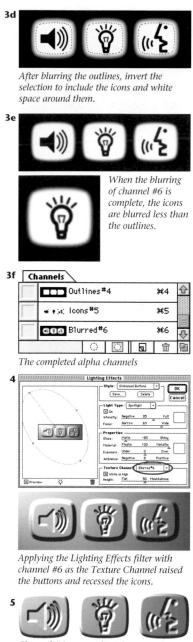

3d

After blurring the outlines, invert the selection to include the icons and white space around them.

3e

When the blurring of channel #6 is complete, the icons are blurred less than the outlines.

3f

The completed alpha channels

4

Applying the Lighting Effects filter with channel #6 as the Texture Channel raised the buttons and recessed the icons.

5

Channel #4 was used to trim away the background.

inside its button outline using the marquee or lasso, and hold the Shift key down as you select the additional icons. Then make white the Background color and press Backspace to remove the icons, leaving the buttons outlines. Leave the selection active.

To make the channel for embossing the icons, with the selection still active, activate channel #5 (Ctrl-5), invert the selection (Ctrl-Shift-I), and with white as the Background color press Backspace to remove everything but the icons.

To make the blurred channel, you'll blur the button outlines and the interior icons at two different settings as the first step in making the carving of the icons look shallower than the overall height of the buttons. First load channel #4 as a selection (press Ctrl-Alt-4) and invert the selection (Ctrl-Shift-I). Then activate channel #6 (Ctrl-6). Choose Select, Modify, Expand and use a setting that will pull the selection boundary into the white area of the button, beyond where you want the dimensional edge of the button outline to extend. We used an Expand By setting of 10. With the selection still active, blur the button outlines; we used Filter, Blur, Gaussian Blur with a setting of 3. Leave the selection active.

Now you'll blur the icons inside the buttons, but at a lower setting than you used for the button outlines. Press Ctrl-Shift-I to invert the selection, selecting the icons and some of the white area around them. Then blur again (Ctrl-Alt-F to repeat the last filter but with the dialog box open so you can change the settings); we used a Gaussian Blur setting of 1. Deselect (Ctrl-D).

4 Raising the buttons and carving the icons. Now the center of activity shifts from the Channels palette to the Layers palette, where the Lighting Effects filter will create the embossed buttons. Completely fill the original artwork layer with white (press Shift-Backspace to open the Fill dialog box, and use White). Run the Lighting Effects filter to raise the buttons from the white background: Choose Filter, Render, Lighting Effects. With channel #6 selected from the pop-out Texture Channel list and with White Is High turned on, set up a wide spotlight with a Matte, Metallic surface. (At this point save the Lighting Effects settings so you can use them again later: Click the Save button and name the new style. If you decide you want to embed the buttons in a panel,

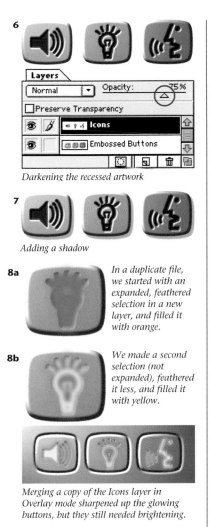

6

Layers

Normal ▾   Opacity: 75%

☐ Preserve Transparency

👁 ✏ ◀ ▮ ▶ **Icons** ⇧

👁 ▮ ⚈⚈⚈ Embossed Buttons ⇩

▣ ⬛ 🗑 ⧉

Darkening the recessed artwork

7

Adding a shadow

8a

In a duplicate file, we started with an expanded, feathered selection in a new layer, and filled it with orange.

8b

We made a second selection (not expanded), feathered it less, and filled it with yellow.

Merging a copy of the Icons layer in Overlay mode sharpened up the glowing buttons, but they still needed brightening.

THE BOTTOM LAYER RULES

When layers are merged together, the name and blending mode of the bottommost layer in the group are adopted for the new layer.

you'll need your Lighting Effects settings again at step 9.)

Click OK to close the Lighting Effects box. The result will be raised buttons with a relatively wide bevel, and recessed symbols with a sharper, narrower groove.

5 Cutting out the buttons. Now you'll isolate the buttons. If your buttons layer is *Background* (without the capacity for transparency), double-click its name in the Layers palette; this opens the Make Layer dialog box and automatically changes the layer so that if you delete or erase part of the image, that part will become transparent rather than being filled with the Background color. Name the layer "Embossed Buttons" and click OK. Load channel #4 as a selection (press Ctrl-Alt-4). Then invert the selection (Ctrl-Shift-I) and press Backspace to trim.

6 Bumping up the contrast. To darken the inscribed symbols on the button faces, create a new layer above the Embossed Buttons layer, and load channel #5 as a selection (Ctrl-Alt-5). Invert the selection (Ctrl-Shift-I) so just the icons are selected, and then fill the selection with black. To let the sculpting of the icons show through the darkening effect, transparency can be adjusted with the Icons layer's Opacity slider.

7 Adding shadows. If you want to use the buttons alone rather than in a panel, shadows will add to the illusion that the buttons are raised off the background. To make shadows, first copy the Embossed Buttons layer by Alt-dragging its name in the Layers palette to the New Layer icon and naming it Shadow. Drag its name below Embossed Buttons in the Layers palette. With black as the Foreground color press Shift-Alt-Backspace to fill the copy of the button shape (but not the surrounding transparent area) with black. Apply a blur (Filter, Blur, Gaussian Blur), then use the move tool and arrow keys to nudge the shadow into position where you want it. The offset and density of the shadow should be consistent with the direction and intensity of the lighting that you set up back in step 4. To lighten the shadow, adjust its Opacity slider.

8 Turning the buttons on. To make an "active" state for the buttons (for animating to attract attention or for a rollover or clicked condition), click the Embossed Buttons thumbnail in the Layers palette to activate it, and then Alt-click the New Layer icon to add a layer between Embossed Buttons and Icons; name the new layer "Glow." In this new layer use channel #5 to create a glow: Load channel #5 as a selection (Ctrl-Alt-5). Expand the selection (Select, Modify, Expand; we used a 5-pixel setting), feather it (Select, Feather; we used 5 pixels), and fill with color (we used orange). Then repeat the loading, feathering, and filling process, this time without the Expand step (we used a feather setting of 3 pixels and a yellow color). To intensify the glow, duplicate the layer (drag it to the New

8c

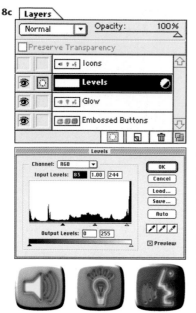

We added an Adjustment layer and used it to increase contrast.

9

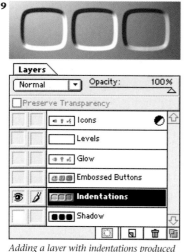

Adding a layer with indentations produced the a panel for the buttons.

10

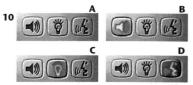

Images B, C, and D were each made by selecting an individual icon from the Glow layer, copying it to its own layer, and then making a merged duplicate from that layer, Levels, Embossed Buttons, and Indentations.

Layer icon at the bottom of the palette) and change the new layer's blending mode to Overlay. Then merge the two glow layers (make only these two layers visible by clicking in the "eye" column, and press Ctrl-E to Merge Down). The merged layer will be in Normal mode.

To add detail to the glowing buttons, we copied the Icons layer by dragging its name to the New Layer icon, put the new layer in Overlay mode, moved it below the Icons layer, and merged it with the Glow layer (Ctrl-E).

To redden the orange and darken the button overall, we added an Adjustment layer (Ctrl-click the New Layer icon), chose Levels as the Type, and moved the Input Levels black- and white-point sliders inward to increase contrast of the layers below. (If you want to affect only the Glow layer, clip the Adjustment layer and the Glow layer together by Alt-clicking the border between their names in the Layers palette.)

9 Putting the buttons in a panel. To get buttons that are inset into a panel rather than raised from the surface, build one more layer: Just add a new white-filled layer below the Embossed Buttons layer. Then in the Channels palette, make a copy of channel #4 by dragging its name to the New Channel icon, and apply a Gaussian blur with the same setting you used to blur the outline in channel #6 (refer to step 3). Then, using the same settings you used in step 4 *except with White Is High turned off,* make a panel by running Lighting Effects on this layer with your new channel (#7) as the Texture Channel.

10 Making each button active. To show the button panel with one button active at a time, you'll need to make four panel files — one with no buttons in the active state and one each for the three active buttons. Before you start, choose File, Save A Copy for safekeeping. Then size the file down to your final on-screen size. We chose Image, Image Size; turned on Constrain Proportions and Resample Image (Bicubic); and changed the Height to 25 percent.

To make the panel with no buttons lit, turn on these layers: Icons, Embossed Buttons, and Indentations. Then choose Image, Duplicate, Merged Layers Only.

For each panel with one glowing button, the process goes like this: Use the rectangular marquee in the Glow layer to select the icon you want to use and copy it to a new layer (Ctrl-J). Then with this new layer turned on as well as Levels, Embossed, Buttons, and Indentations, make a duplicate file (Image, Duplicate, Merged Layers Only). If your small files look a little fuzzy when they're finished, experiment with Filter, Sharpen, Unsharp Mask.

Once you have the four different panels, one way to make the buttons blink is to animate them with GIFConstructionSet (refer to step 5 of "'Onion-Skinning' an Animation" on page 295).

Popping Buttons Off the Screen

Overview *Collect the button graphics in a single file; make shadows, and skew, align, soften, and fade them; add a two-color glow.*

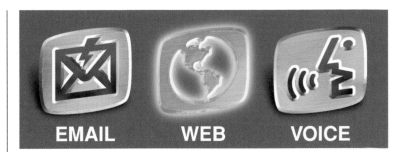

The ***"Cast Shadow"*** *Actions on the Wow! CD-ROM automate the process of making, casting, and fading a shadow; the process is similar to steps 4, 5, 6, and 7 here. The "Glow/Hot" and "Glow/Cold" Actions make a three-color glow similar to the one created in step 8.*

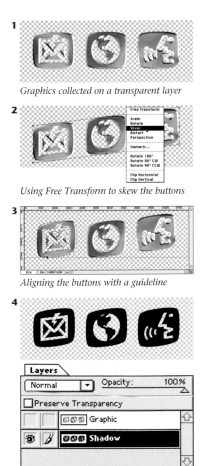

1

Graphics collected on a transparent layer

2

Using Free Transform to skew the buttons

3

Aligning the buttons with a guideline

4

Making shadows in a separate layer

WHEN IT COMES TO NAVIGATIONAL TOOLS for a Web site or other interactive presentation, type or symbols that stand up and announce where a click will take you can be an effective and a relatively simple solution. Photoshop 4's Free Transform command can help make a row of graphic elements into an array of stand-up buttons.

1 Making the graphics. Open a file big enough to accommodate all your graphics in a row, at about two to four times the resolution you want to end up with (File, New, Transparent), and create or drag and drop your graphic elements into it, leaving about half a button-width or more of empty space between buttons so you'll be able to select each one easily in step 3. We made a file 1000 pixels wide with three pieces of clip art, turned into beveled metal cut-outs with one of the "Brushed Steel" Actions from the Wow! CD-ROM that comes with this book. But you can start with anything — elements imported from a 3D program, graphics created in Photoshop, or even type, set as single characters or as words, treated with a 3D filter or left flat. Then open the Layers palette (Window, Show Layers) so you'll be able to watch the file develop.

2 Angling the buttons. To put the buttons at an angle, use Free Transform: Press Ctrl-T, then click the right mouse button and choose Skew from the context-sensitive menu. Drag the right-hand side handle up until the buttons are angled the way you want them, double-click inside the box to finalize the change.

3 Aligning the buttons. Next, you'll set up your buttons beside each other on a horizontal baseline. With the rulers displayed (Ctrl-R) and guidelines visible (View, Show Guides), drag a guideline down from the top ruler to use as a base. Select one of your buttons (you can use the rectangular marquee tool). Then hold down the Ctrl key to toggle to the move tool and drag the button until its lowest point is aligned along the guideline. Repeat the process for the other buttons. Deselect (Ctrl-D).

4 Making shadows. To create shadows to make the buttons look more three-dimensional, duplicate the buttons layer (in the Layers palette, Alt-drag the buttons layer's thumbnail to the New Layer icon, in the middle at the bottom of the palette). In the Duplicate Layer dialog box, name the layer "Shadow" and click OK. Drag the

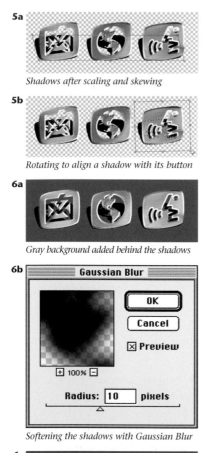

5a

Shadows after scaling and skewing

5b

Rotating to align a shadow with its button

6a

Gray background added behind the shadows

6b

Softening the shadows with Gaussian Blur

6c

A button with its blurred shadow

7a

Setting up the gradient tool to fill the layer mask

Shadow layer below the buttons layer in the Layers palette, and fill the shadows with black (pressing "D" restores the default Foreground and Background colors; pressing Shift-Alt-Backspace fills only the nontransparent areas of the layer with the Foreground color).

5 Casting the shadows. Reshaping the shadows so they fall behind the standing buttons involves scaling, skewing, and rotating, all of which you can do with Free Transform. With the Shadow layer active, press Ctrl-T and then drag the top center handle down until the box is as short as you want the shadow to be. Next use the context-sensitive menu as you did in step 2, choosing Skew again. Drag a top handle sideways to skew the shadows so they seem to fall behind the buttons. If you want each button and its shadow to ultimately be a separate piece of art, be careful not to let the shadow from one button overlap with another button, or it will be tricky to separate them. When the skew is done, double-click in the box to accept the scaling and skewing. Select each individual shadow and rotate it (use Ctrl-T and drag outside the bounding box to rotate) until its bottom edge aligns with the bottom edge of its button. If necessary, drag inside the bounding box to move the shadow. Then double-click inside to accept the changes.

6 Softening the shadows. Once the positions of the shadows are fine-tuned to your liking, you can soften the edges. To get a better idea of shadow transparency, which can't be seen so well against Photoshop's checkerboard representation of transparency, add a background, as follows: Alt-click the New Layer icon, and name the new layer "Background." Drag this layer to the bottom of the stack and choose a Foreground color from the Color palette; if you know the color of the interface where the buttons will be used, you can choose that color; or you can choose a stand-in color (we chose a medium gray) and swap out the background layer later. Press Alt-Backspace to fill the Background layer. Now click on the Shadow layer's thumbnail and soften the shadows by choosing Filter, Blur, Gaussian Blur and adjusting the Radius.

7 Fading the shadows. To make the shadows fade with distance, add a layer mask (click the Add Layer Mask icon, on the left at the bottom of the palette). The mask (rather than the shadows image itself) will be active, and you can fill it with a gradient as follows: Double-click the gradient tool in the toolbox to open the Gradient Tool Options palette. Set black as the Foreground color, choose Foreground To Background and Linear, and drag the gradient tool from the top of the Shadow layer down to the level where you want the full density of the shadow to show.

8 Making "active" states. You may want your Web site to show buttons in one or more "action states" (a different look that appears when the cursor rolls over a button or when a button is clicked.

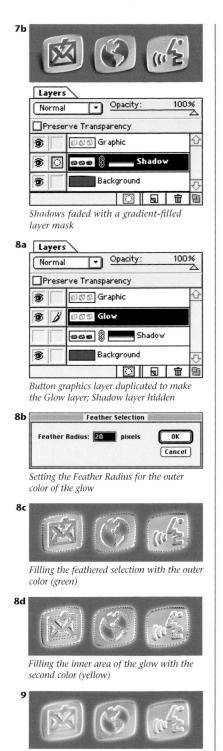

7b

Shadows faded with a gradient-filled layer mask

8a

Button graphics layer duplicated to make the Glow layer; Shadow layer hidden

8b

Feather Selection

Feather Radius: 20 pixels   OK   Cancel

Setting the Feather Radius for the outer color of the glow

8c

Filling the feathered selection with the outer color (green)

8d

Filling the inner area of the glow with the second color (yellow)

9

The buttons with both colors of the glow in place and the buttons layer "eroded" to let the glow spread inward

The change of states can be set up with an animation program such as ShockWave or a Java applet, but you can make the alternative button graphics — glowing buttons, for instance — in Photoshop.

By making a series of feathered selections and filling with color, you can make buttons whose glow changes color as it spreads out. Duplicate the buttons layer by Alt-dragging its name to the New Layer icon and naming the new layer "Glow." Drag this new layer below the buttons layer in the Layers palette, and Ctrl-click its name to load its transparency mask as a selection. Feather the selection (Select, Feather); we used a Feather Radius of 20 for our 1000-pixel-wide file). Then choose a color for the outside of the glow by clicking in the Color palette (we chose a green) and Alt-Backspace to fill the soft selection with the color.

To make the inside of the glow, you'll need to load the buttons' outlines as a selection again. But the Glow layer's transparency mask has been changed by the first stage of the glow. So Ctrl-click the original buttons layer's name to load *its* transparency mask. Again, choose Select, Feather, but this time use a Feather Radius that's about half what you used the first time; we used a setting of 10. Choose another color (we used a yellow) and Alt-Backspace to fill the inside of the glow. Don't drop this second feathered selection.

9 Intensifying the glow. Finally, to soften the edge of the buttons so the glow seems to be coming from the buttons themselves rather than from somewhere behind them, activate the buttons layer. With the second feathered selection still active, click the Add Layer Mask icon. This will make a layer mask that automatically turns the edges of the buttons layer partly transparent, letting the glow in the layer below spread inward.

10 Producing the buttons. To make buttons with and without glows or shadows, you can selectively turn on or off different layers' eye icons and the layer mask (to turn off a layer mask, hold down the Shift key and click on the mask's thumbnail). Then use the rectangular marquee to select the button (or buttons) you want, and choose Edit, Copy Merged. Make a new file, and paste (Ctrl-V) to bring the merged button into a document as a layer.

10

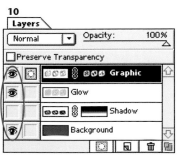

Final layers palette, set up to produce glowing buttons without shadows

Final layers palette, set up to produce shadowed buttons without the glow

"Onion-Skinning" a GIF Animation

Overview *Prepare artwork as a series of sequential layers in a Photoshop file; make changes to the artwork to create individual animation frames, temporarily reducing Opacity settings to see several layers at once; export the individual layers as GIFs; assemble in GIFConstructionSet to animate.*

1a

The original EPS clip art

1b

Heads cropped and resized

2

Line work thickened and Web color applied

3a

Aligning the second head. A 50% Opacity setting reveals the layer below (left). Restoring Opacity to 100% shows the finished artwork.

GRAPHICS: HAVANA STREET, IN THE MOOD

THERE ARE CERTAINLY MORE SOPHISTICATED WAYS of doing animation for the Web. But creating frames in layers using the Photoshop equivalent of the old animator's onion-skinning process and turning the layers into an animated GIF can produce a simple animation that can be viewed by any browser that supports graphics. Here we started with clip art and produced an eight-frame "cartoon."

1 Preparing the graphics. You'll build each frame of your animation in a Photoshop layer. We started with a series of clip art images, opening each of the dogs as an RGB file in Photoshop and selecting and deleting everything but the head.

2 Coloring the artwork. To thicken the line work, the black-and-white artwork was slightly blurred and then treated with Image, Adjust, Brightness/Contrast, using the method described in "Cleaning Up Masks" on page 64. Color was added to the artwork with the paintbrush with hard-edged brush tips (from the top row of the default Brushes palette), and with Multiply mode chosen in the Paint Brush Options palette so that painting onto the black lines wouldn't change their color. Colors were chosen by clicking the paintbrush on colors in the Swatches palette, which had been loaded with Web-safe colors as described in "Making Web-Safe Swatches" on page 280.

3 Using the "onion-skinning" process. Our aim was to animate a sequence of the "space dog" watching a rocket fly over, so we first had to get all the parts into one file at roughly the right size. We selected and dragged and dropped each head into the space dog file to become a layer of its own, arranging the layers in the appropriate order for the animation.

Visibility was turned off (by clicking the eye icons in the Layers palette) for all but the bottom layer and the next layer up. The second layer's Opacity setting was reduced to 50% so that we could see through to the full dog underneath. The head on the second

296 CHAPTER 9: 3D, MULTIMEDIA, AND THE WEB

3b

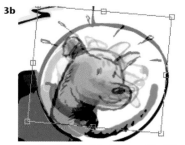

Aligning the last of the heads, with all but the bottom layer at 50% Opacity

3c

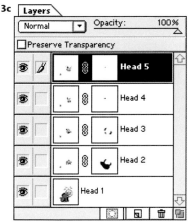

Heads aligned and masked; file cropped

3d

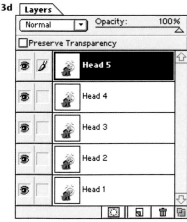

Body composited with all layers

4a

Rocket clip art with Web colors added

layer was selected and moved by dragging inside the Transform box, scaled by dragging the handles inward or outward, and rotated by dragging around the outside of the Free Transform box, until it aligned with the dog on the bottom layer. Being able to see through the layer helped in the aligning. We made a layer mask by clicking the Add Layer Mask icon and painting with black paint to make a smooth transition from the new head to the dog body. Then we turned on visibility for the next layer up, reduced its Opacity to 50%, aligned its head with the body on the bottom layer, and added another layer mask. This process was repeated for the other two heads, and a copy of the tail was also positioned on each layer.

Once all the heads and tails had been moved into position, we added a body to the head and tail on the second layer by selecting the body on the bottom layer and duplicating it to a new layer (Ctrl-J), which appeared between the bottom layer and the Head 2 layer. We clicked the Head 2 layer to activate it, and then pressed Ctrl-E to merge Head 2 with the body copy.

The process of duplicating the body, moving it up the Layers palette until it was under a head layer, and then merging it with the head layer was continued until all heads had bodies.

4 Using a guide for motion. If your animation involves an object moving through the frame, it can be helpful to have a guide — an arc for a bouncing ball or for a rocket flying overhead, for instance. To make a guide for our rocket, we activated the top layer of our file, clicked the New Layer icon to add a layer on top of that, and used the pen tool to form an arc. To make the arc easier to see, you can stroke the path with paint as we did by choosing a color from the Swatches palette, clicking the path name in the Paths palette to activate it, choosing the paintbrush tool, and pressing Enter.

Another aid in aligning moving elements is Photoshop's Grid. We turned on the Grid (View, Show Grid) to help gauge the horizontal distance to move the rocket in each frame.

MAKING IT MOVE!

Michael Gilmore of CyberFlix uses the Layers palette to preview an animation whose cels have been created as a stack of Photoshop layers before taking the file into an animation system for final preparation. Set the Layers palette's thumbnails to the largest size (choose Palette Options from the palette's pop-out menu). Shorten the

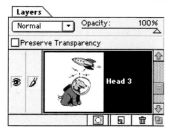

palette until only one layer's thumbnail shows, and move the scroll box up or down the scroll bar, or press and hold the palette's up or down scrolling arrow, to run the movie as a kind of digital flipbook. If your first frame is in the bottom layer of your file and your last frame is in the top layer, scrolling with the up arrow will run the animation forward; using the bottom arrow will run it backwards.

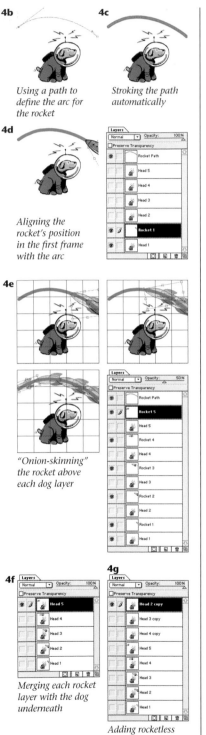

4b **4c**

Using a path to define the arc for the rocket

Stroking the path automatically

4d

Aligning the rocket's position in the first frame with the arc

4e

"Onion-skinning" the rocket above each dog layer

4f *Merging each rocket layer with the dog underneath*

4g *Adding rocketless dog layers to return the head to its starting position*

We opened a clip art file of a rocket and colored it as we had the dogs. Then we clicked on the name of the bottom layer of the dog file in the Layers palette to activate it, and dragged the rocket into the file. We used Layer, Free Transform, dragging around the outside of the box to rotate the rocket so its nose lined up with the green arc. We duplicated the rocket layer, moved the copy up the Layers stack above the next dog, changed its Opacity to 50% so we could see through it to the rocket below, and used Free Transform to move it, rotate it, and scale it.

We continued making copies of the rocket, moving up the stack of layers to the top. Then we merged each rocket layer with the dog layer below it (Ctrl-E). To return the dog's head to its starting position, we added duplicate dog layers, deleting the rocket. Finally, we deleted the layer with the green arc by dragging its thumbnail to the palette's trash can icon. We turned off the Grid (View, Hide Grid).

5 Exporting the frames and assembling the animation.

Once you have a layered Photoshop file, export the frames as follows: Turn on visibility for the bottom layer only and choose File, Export, GIF89a Export. Choose an Adaptive palette, turn off Interlace, and select the color depth (number of Colors; to see the results of your Colors setting, press the Preview button); click OK to save the GIF file. Repeat the export process for all layers of the file. Then open GIFConstructionSet for Windows. Choose File, Animation Wizard and follow directions for importing your series of GIF files. After you press the Done button to finish the import process, in the GIFConstructionSet window, click View to run your animation; press the Esc key to stop. You can also edit the animation. For instance, double-click a "Control" line to open the Edit Control Block dialog box, where you can designate a color as transparent, change the delay before the next frame, and so on. *Wow!*

5

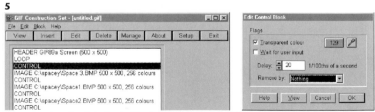

Once an animation is built, double-clicking an individual "Control" line lets you change the amount of time the image list in the line above will stay on the screen, among other settings.

For *Sky Pool*, an illustration for the Japanese edition of *Step-By-Step Electronic Design*, **Jack Davis** created a 3D environment with elements generated from grayscale images. He began with a scan of a hand placed flat on a desktop scanner. The grayscale file was touched up in Photoshop, saved in PICT format, and opened in MetaCreations' Bryce, where it was extruded into a 3D form. A ball, one of Bryce's 3D primitive objects, was added. Textures were applied, lighting was set up, and the scene was rendered. The "well" was modelled and rendered separately in Bryce from another grayscale image, with the same lighting and relative placement as the ball, and then composited with the ball in Photoshop.

ART DIRECTOR: KAZUMOTO YOKOUCHI

To make the *Crystal Hands Ad* for Kenwood's CyberTitler, **Jack Davis** began with two photos, one of the device alone and one with hands in typing position on the keyboard. He used the second photo as a reference for the size and orientation of the crystal hands, and the first as a background in Strata StudioPro, to help create realistic reflections and refractions in the crystal. The hands themselves were made from a purchased articulated model. In

StudioPro, the hands were arranged to match the photo and then fused so they would look solid when rendered with raytracing. Davis rendered the hands twice, once in front of the CyberTitler photo, and once with no background photo. He needed the second rendering to create an alpha channel that could be used to select the hands from the first rendering, so they could be layered above a silhouetted version of the original high-resolution photo, since the

rendering process had degraded the photo used in StudioPro.

Davis made a drop shadow for the hands and then used the smudge tool to bend the shadow as it fell over the various edges of the keyboard. He also used Levels to exaggerate the highlights and shadows on the CyberTitler and enhanced the front edge of the keyboard with purple to match the lighting on the hands and in the background image.

W hen **Louis Fishauf** designed the *I Am Online Web site graphics* for Molson Canadian Ale, he used the company's red maple leaf logo as one element to tie the web pages together. On the home page, the top part of which is shown above, small logotypes act as buttons for connecting with other parts of the site. A set of buttons at the bottom of every page (see the Concert Calendar at the lower right) also provides a visually consistent way of connecting from any page to any other. The header graphics that appear at the tops of other pages (some are shown at right) are unified by the appearance of the maple leaf (in most cases) and a soft-edged oval background shape.

Type is an important part of every page. Much of the type was set in Adobe Illustrator and then imported into Photoshop, where it was treated with various special effects:

A white glow like the one around "ONLINE" on the home page can be made by duplicating the type layer, moving the duplicate below the original, filling the type with white, and blurring the layer.

Although Fishauf used the Trixie typeface for "I Am" on the home page and "The Word" on the page header at right, similarly "distressed" type can be produced by choosing Filter, Brush Strokes, Spatter and experimenting with the Spray Radius and Smoothness settings.

A drop shadow like the one behind the "Outer Limits" type or the type in the Concert Calendar or Hockey Net in Canada can be produced the same as the white glow, except that black is used for the fill, and the blurring step is followed by offsetting the shadow layer. Use Filter, Other, Offset if you will need to repeat exactly the same offset on several elements on different layers. Or use the move tool and use the arrow keys to nudge the layer until the shadow looks right.

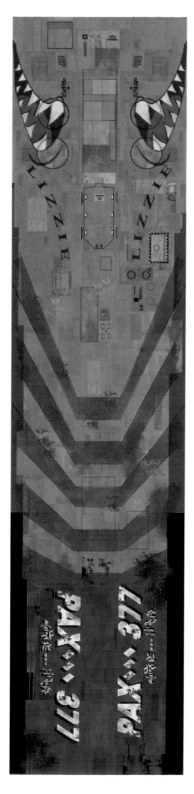

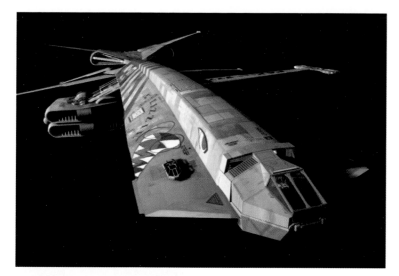

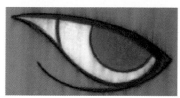

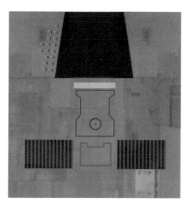

To design the *Sling Ship* for the science-fiction television series *Space Rangers*, **John Knoll** of Industrial Light & Magic, and a co-developer of Photoshop, used a 3D program to translate ILM art director Ty Ellingson's sketches into a 3D model. Then he used Photoshop to create texture maps (the flat artwork to be applied to the surfaces of the model to make it look like it's made of real materials) to turn the vehicle into a beat-up spaceship for chasing criminals for this futuristic show about an understaffed, underfunded police outpost. Knoll scanned several photos of the side panels of military aircraft and cut and pasted these elements, turning them into the "paint" he needed to assemble a patchwork image of dull gray metal with rivets, small doors, and scuff marks from which to build the more than 2000-pixel-long texture map for the fuselage. Because he knew that the front end of the ship would be used in several close-up shots, Knoll created the fuselage at a higher resolution than the wings and back of the plane. The shark's teeth that "personalized" the ship were scanned directly from sketches by Ellingson. Knoll rendered the ship, applying the texture maps to the model, and animated its motion in Electric Image.

Appendix A: Image Collections

A list of addresses and phone numbers of the publishers of these recently published collections on CD-ROM, appears on page 314. Image sizes are for open, flat RGB files (or CMYK as noted) without alpha channels. Images are for both Windows and Mac platforms. Letter codes (explained below) refer to the rights conferred on the buyer of the disc.

Letter codes* used in disc descriptions in Appendix A:

A *Unlimited or nearly unlimited reproduction rights for print and digital publications other than electronic or printed image collections or other products (for instance, photo calendars, postcards, and posters) for which the primary value is in the images themselves*

B *Unlimited or nearly unlimited rights for print and digital publications other than image collections or other products for which the primary value is in the images themselves, with credit to the photographer/artist*

C *Some size, distribution, or usage limits on reproduction; may require credit to the photographer or special copyright notice*

D *For use on screen and in design presentations; other rights by negotiation*

* The codes used here are general indications of license agreements; confirm all rights with the image publisher. Usage agreements vary greatly from one supplier to another. Some license agreements have unusual restrictions; be sure you understand the limitations on the photos you want to use.

WebTools
Thousands of design elements for Web page design: icons, multistate buttons and dials, bars, sounds, and seamless pattern tiles, created by statmedia and Artbeats; GIF, JPEG, BMP, and PICT; A; Artbeats

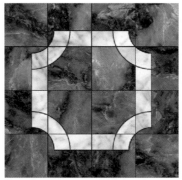

Seamless Textures, Volume 1
300 seamless tiles of a variety of different surfaces such as bark, brick, cork, marble, decorator floors, and marbled paper; mostly 128, 256, and 512 pixels; many with bump maps; 8- and 24-bit; PICT; A; Artbeats

Everyday Animals
120 animals from backyard to barnyard on plain backgrounds; to 28 MB; JPEG; A; CMCD

Exteriors
80 seamless textures designed for 3D rendering: stucco, wood, stone, brick, block, siding, mosaic tile, metal, and concrete; 1024, 512, and 256 pixels; many with bump maps; 8- and 24-bit; PICT; A; Artbeats

Doors & Windows
120 images on plain backgrounds, including a classic elevator cage, a bay window, and stained glass; to 28 MB; JPEG; A; CMCD

Active Lifestyles 2
100 images of activities including skiing, boating, waterskiing, hiking, jogging, cycling, golf, and tennis; to 18 MB; Kodak Photo CD format with custom Kodak Color Management System profile; C; Digital Stock

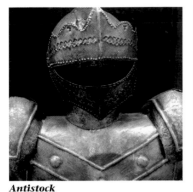

Antistock
100 surreal scenes and abstract still-lifes, including money, drinks, mannequins, and neon; to 18 MB; Kodak Photo CD format with custom Kodak Color Management System profile; C; Digital Stock

Business & Commerce
100 images, including construction, oil, logging, agriculture, and people in business settings; to 18 MB; Kodak Photo CD format with custom Kodak Color Management System profile; C; Digital Stock

Business & Industry 3
100 images of communications, oil, transport, agriculture, electronics, currency, and stock market; to 18 MB; Kodak Photo CD format with custom Kodak Color Management System profile; C; Digital Stock

Characters & Expressions
100 posed portraits of individuals and groups, showing a wide range of costumes (e.g., Girl Scout, graduate, Shakespearean) and emotions; to 18 MB in Kodak Photo CD format; C; Digital Stock

Children & Teens
100 photos (including 10 black-and-white shapshots); individuals and groups; wide range of ages and races; to 18 MB; Kodak Photo CD format with custom Kodak Color Management System profile; C; Digital Stock

Conceptual Backgrounds
100 colorful hand-painted backgrounds, including abstracts, hearts, star of David, spirals, and landscapes; to 18 MB; Kodak Photo CD format with custom Kodak Color Management System profile; C; Digital Stock

Cyberstock
100 surreal scenes, with reflective surfaces, light beams, planets, and 3D geometrics; to 18 MB; Kodak Photo CD format with custom Kodak Color Management System profile; C; Digital Stock

Fire & Ice
100 images, half of volcanic eruptions and half of polar ice, penguins, and other arctic and antarctic subjects; to 18 MB; Koduk Photo CD format with custom Kodak Color Management System profile; C; Digital Stock

Manufacturing & Industry
100 photos of high-tech manufacturing, including chocolate, coffee, clothing, paper, and printing industries; to 18 MB; Kodak Photo CD format with custom Kodak Color Management System profile; C; Digital Stock

Medicine & Healthcare
100 photos of modern medicine, including surgery, pills, scans, labs, x-rays, and doctors with patients; to 18 MB; Kodak Photo CD format with custom Kodak Color Management System profile; C; Digital Stock

Modern Cuisine
100 glamour shots, including deli platters, sandwiches, popular international dishes, desserts, and champagne; to 18 MB; Kodak Photo CD format with custom Kodak Color Management System profile; C; Digital Stock

Natural Textures
100 photographic backgrounds, including sea animals, rock, wood, ocean, sky, and leaves; to 18 MB; Kodak Photo CD format with custom Kodak Color Management System profile; C; Digital Stock

Natural World
100 images of nature, from tranquil landscapes to majestic wildlife, insects, flowers, and leaves; to 18 MB; Kodak Photo CD format with custom Kodak Color Management System profile; C; Digital Stock

Painted Backgrounds
100 backgrounds by Gregory Ochocki in bright and subtle colors, some showing brushstrokes and canvas; to 18 MB; Kodak Photo CD format with custom Kodak Color Management System profile; C; Digital Stock

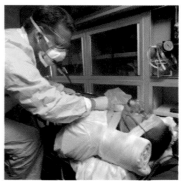

Real Life Medicine
100 images of emergency care and medical personnel with patients, including elderly and people in wheelchairs; to 18 MB; Kodak Photo CD format with custom Kodak Color Management System profile; C; Digital Stock

Skylines of North America
100 skylines of large and mid-size cities U.S. and Canada coast-to-coast, and Hawaii; to 18 MB; Kodak Photo CD format with custom Kodak Color Management System profile; C; Digital Stock

Southern California
100 landmarks, freeways, and skylines from San Diego, Los Angeles, Catalina, Santa Barbara, and elsewhere; to 18 MB; Kodak Photo CD format with custom Kodak Color Management System profile; C; Digital Stock

Space Exploration
100 images of spacecraft, earth, sun, planets, moons, and outer space; to 18 MB; Kodak Photo CD format with custom Kodak Color Management System profile; C; Digital Stock

Sport & Leisure
100 favorite holiday spots and recreational activities, including beach and carnival scenes and ballooning; to 18 MB; Kodak Photo CD format with custom Kodak Color Management System profile; C; Digital Stock

Tranquility
100 landscapes, seascapes and other peaceful and evocative scenes; to 18 MB; Kodak Photo CD format, with custom Kodak Color Management System profile; C; Digital Stock

Urban Graffiti
100 expressive examples of brightly colored, sophisticated street art; mostly portrait and abstract art; to 18 MB; Kodak Photo CD format, with Kodak Color Management System profile; C; Digital Stock

Urban Textures
100 photos including walls, peeling paint, textured metal, tiled pavement, fencing, and window grids; to 18 MB; Kodak Photo CD format with custom Kodak Color Management System profile; C; Digital Stock

Washington D.C.
100 photos including Capitol, White House, Supreme Court, monuments, museums, and Arlington Cemetery; to 18 MB; Kodak Photo CD format with custom Kodak Color Management System profile; C; Digital Stock

Water Sports
100 photos of thrills, spills, sunshine, and sandy beaches, including surfing, kayaking, wake boarding, and scuba; to 18 MB; Kodak Photo CD format with custom Kodak Color Management System profile; C; Digital Stock

Photogear Vol. 7: Fancy Fabrics
32 images of fabrics, most softly bunched, including satins, silks, velvets, suedes, laces, smocking, fleece, metallics, and floral and paisley patterns; to 21 MB; TIFF; A; Image Club Graphics

Photogear Vol. 8: Everyday Fabrics
32 images of fabrics, most softly bunched, including corduroy, flannel, canvas, raw silk, vinyl, stripes, plaids, polka dots, and denim with blue jeans seams, ; to 21 MB; TIFF; A; Image Club Graphics

Photogear Vol. 9: Underwater Life
84 Undersea images including colorful fish (singles and schools), anemones, lobster, shrimp, crab, starfish, coral formations, scuba divers, and shipwrecks; to 7.5 MB; TIFF; A; Image Club Graphics

Photogear Vol. 10: Texture Work
29 photographs of backgrounds hand-painted by Gary Bozeman; diverse colors and textures; to 21 MB; TIFF; A; Image Club Graphics

Photogear Vol. 11: Old Country Collages
32 background photos by CCC Studios of collages of unusual elements, including books, clocks, cameras, buttons, and duck decoys; to 21 MB; TIFF; A; Image Club Graphics

Photogear Vol. 12: Barkgrounds
30 rustic background images of bark, shot close-up by Jim Wetje; birch trees, spruce, pines, eucalyptus, and others, to 21 MB; TIFF; A; Image Club Graphics

Object Gear: Amusements
85 close-cropped photos of knickknacks, toys, and collectibles; includes clipping paths, drop shadows (shown here) and cast shadows; to 4.4 MB; TIFF; A; Image Club Graphics

Object Gear: Antiquities
85 close-cropped images of nostalgic objects from the early 1900s, including clocks, phone, and musical instruments; includes clipping paths and drop and cast shadows; to 4.3 MB; TIFF; A; Image Club Graphics

Object Gear: Business Elements
95 close-cropped images of objects used in offices, including furniture, desktop computers, and office supplies; includes clipping paths and drop and cast shadows; to 6.8 MB; TIFF; A; Image Club Graphics

Object Gear: Clay Buffet
85 photos of food and table settings stylized in clay, from bread to broccoli and hot dogs to hot chocolate; includes clipping paths and drop and cast shadows; to 5 MB; TIFF; A; Image Club Graphics

Object Gear: Culturals
85 visual metaphors for international culture and holidays, including masks, coins, and figurines; includes clipping paths, and drop and cast shadows; to 5 MB; TIFF; A; Image Club Graphics

Aged & Weathered Surfaces
100 images of worn and aged surfaces, including cracked masonry, peeling paint, rusted and oxidized metal, and moss-covered walls; to 24 MB; JPEG and TIFF; A; Image Farm

The Antique Frame Collections
50 images of unique frames, from ornate gilded frames to hand-crafted sterling silver; all with clipping paths; to 48 MB; JPEG; A; Image Farm

Arizona Desert
100 desert textures and backgrounds, including colorful sand and rock, dry grasses, stone walls, tiles, basket weaves, and cactus; to 18 MB; Kodak Photo CD format; A; Image Farm

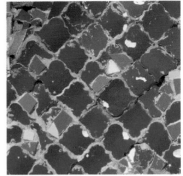

Berlin Walls
100 photographs of urban surfaces in Berlin, including graffiti, mosaic tile, distressed and weathered masonry and more; to 18 MB, Kodak Photo CD format; A; Image Farm

Cottage & Country
100 photographic textures of the countryside, including foliage, moss-covered tree bark, woven mats and baskets, and wood and rock walls; to 18 MB; Kodak Photo CD format; A; Image Farm

Hand-Painted Backgrounds
100 photos of painted surfaces; from textured brushstrokes to smooth finishes painted by artists in acrylics, oils and watercolors; to 24 MB; JPEG; A; Image Farm

Industrial Backgrounds & Objects
130 photos, including stamped metal and hardware such as bolts, gears, and springs; objects include clipping paths; to 24 MB; JPEG; A; Image Farm

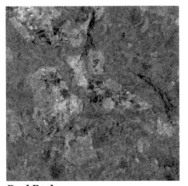

Real Rock
100 photographs of vividly colored and unusual rock textures; from the Canadian Rocky Mountains, Great Britain, and private and museum collections; to 18 MB; Kodak Photo CD format; A; Image Farm

Skies & Cloudscapes
100 photos, from cloud-spotted brilliant skies to dark and ominous thunderclouds, cloud reflections in windows, sunsets, aerial vistas, and cloudless blue skies; to 26 MB; JPEG; A; Image Farm

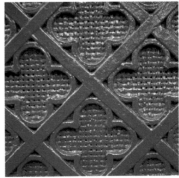

Streets of London
100 photos of textures from the architecture of London, including aged stone facades, sculptured reliefs, inlaid rock, and mosaics; to 18 MB; Kodak Photo CD format; A; Image Farm

American Fine Art and Illustration
100 scans of original turn-of-the-century illustrations featuring modern people, licensed from The La Palma Collection; to 28 MB; JPEG; C; PhotoDisc

Antique Maps and Heraldic Images
100 detailed maps on textures of faded parchment; colorful heraldic images with clipping paths; licensed from Fototeca Storica Nazionale; to 28 MB; JPEG; C; PhotoDisc

Beyond Retro
336 black-and-white studio shots of men, women, and children posed for ads, as well as people interacting in daily commerce; to 10 MB; JPEG; C; PhotoDisc

Business Metaphors and Details
100 images of familiar objects that help get the job done; shot by Thomas Brummet with a monochromatic color scheme; to 28 MB; JPEG; C; PhotoDisc

Business Today
336 images of people at work, juggling numerous projects in home offices or corporate conference rooms and other settings; to 10 MB; JPEG; C; PhotoDisc

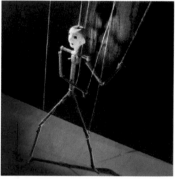

Colorful Contrasts
100 photographs of common objects such as tools, toys, office supplies, American flag, and money, dramatically cropped and lit; photographed by Nick Koudis; to 28 MB; JPEG; C; PhotoDisc

Cultural Arts
100 elements of performance and visual arts, such as dance slippers, sheet music, and musical instruments; photographed by Steve Cole; to 28 MB; JPEG; C; PhotoDisc

Details of Nature
100 images photographed by Jim Linna showing natural subjects shot in natural colors with directional lighting; including leaves, starfish, flowers and more; to 28 MB; JPEG; C; PhotoDisc

European Paintings
100 photos of masterpieces by Da Vinci, Raphael, Botticelli, and others, licensed from Fototeca Storica Nazionale; to 28 MB; JPEG; C; PhotoDisc

Everyday People
100 expressive portraits of people of diverse cultures, ages and emotions; shot by Barbara Penoyar; to 28 MB; JPEG; C; PhotoDisc

Evocative Landscapes
100 landscape scenes shot in moody light; all images convey a sense of place; photographed by Kaz Chiba; to 28 MB; JPEG; C; PhotoDisc

Festivities
120 images of decorations used with most Western parties and holidays; shot on white backgrounds; with clipping paths; to 28 MB; JPEG; C; PhotoDisc

In Character
120 images of people in costume; from the classic American tourist to a fairy princess; shot on white backgrounds; with clipping paths; 28 MB; JPEG; C; PhotoDisc

Industrial Sidestreets
100 images of details from alleys to city streets; windows, oxidized metals, eroded surfaces and more; to 28 MB; JPEG; C; PhotoDisc

Mature Lifestyles
336 images of people, showing the vitality and richness of maturity today; including active retirees, vibrant business leaders, passionate hobbyists and more; to 10 MB; JPEG; C; PhotoDisc

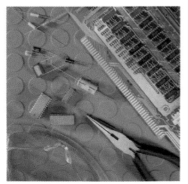

Modern Technologies
336 images that document emerging technologies and research specialties, including biotechnology, medical and telecommunications; to 10 MB; JPEG; C; PhotoDisc

Panoramic Landscapes
100 images including fall colors; clouds above the plains; long stretches of road; and more; shot by Gary Irving; to 28 MB; JPEG; C; PhotoDisc

Retro Relics
100 images of toys and other objects; complied by designer Glenn Mitsui; photographed on a white backgrounds; with clipping paths; to 28 MB; JPEG; C; PhotoDisc

Skan/9 Abstractions
100 soft-focused images, mostly urban abstractions; includes 100 x 100-pixel seamless tiles; to 28 MB; JPEG; C; PhotoDisc

Spacescapes
336 images of space including an M16 star birth, Haley's comet, aurora australis, and more; a combination of photographic and computer generated images; to 10 MB; JPEG; C; PhotoDisc

Studio Geometry
100 well-designed photographs of geometric forms as seen in construction details, paper constructions, metal, cloth, and light, rich in color and texture; to 28 MB; JPEG; C; PhotoDisc

Vintage Vignettes
100 photographs of antique objects, such as a telephone, a clock, and spectacles, enhanced by warm romantic lighting; by Design Photo Image; to 28 MB; JPEG; C; PhotoDisc

World Religions
336 photographs of people, activities, icons and architecture; including Christianity, Islam, Judaism and others; to 10 MB; JPEG; C; PhotoDisc

Syberia: Volume 1
101 unique backgrounds hand-painted by Fisher Bessi in rich and subtle colors; including gold, silver, cracked whitewash, earth tones, thick paint and more; to 18 MB; Kodak PhotoCD format; A; Syberia

Characters and Occupations
100 portraits including stereotypes and humorous images; all with clipping paths; to 30MB; JPEG ; CMYK; C; RubberBall Productions

Portraits of Everyday People
100 portraits of people of all ages and backgrounds; to 30MB; JPEG ; CMYK; C; RubberBall Productions

Lifestyle Portraits
100 portraits of people at work and play; to 30MB; JPEG; CMYK; C; Rubber Ball Productions

Visuality, Volume 1
100 beautifully composed photographs; mostly urban and pastoral scenes; to 28 MB; JPEG; C; RubberBall Productions

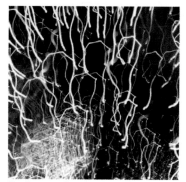

Backgrounds
200 images of unique photographic backgrounds; to 9 MB; JPEG; A; Seattle Support Group

Civil War Memorabilia
100 images of Union and Confederate flags, uniforms, rifles, swords, and accessories used in the Civil War; to 49 MB; JPEG; A; Seattle Support Group

Classic American Automobiles
100 images of classic American cars; to 49 MB; JPEG; A; Seattle Support Group

Floral
200 images of a variety of flowers, landscapes, gardens, pathways and more; to 9 MB; JPEG; A; Seattle Support Group

Planes
200 images of air shows, commercial, military, private, and foreign airplanes; to 9 MB; JPEG; A; Seattle Support Group

Radiant Roses
100 images of many varieties of roses single flowers and groups; to 49 MB; JPEG; A; Seattle Support Group

Space and Space II
400 images of astronaut shuttles, launches, planets, satellites and more; to 9 MB; JPEG; A; Seattle Support Group

Trains of the World
100 images of many types of trains including historic steam and contemporary diesel engines; to 49 MB; JPEG; A; Seattle Support Group

Underwater
200 images of fish and shellfish, divers, sea shells, coral formations, and more; to 9 MB ;JPEG; A; Seattle Support Group

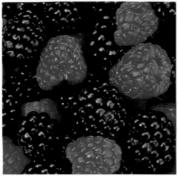

KPT Power Photos: Series One
5 CD ROMs with 500 images of natural backgrounds and textures, food, urban textures and backgrounds, sky, water, landscapes, sports, and recreation, with various kinds of built-in masks and clipping paths; to 24 MB; TIFF; A; MetaCreations

KPT Power Photos: Series Two
5 CD ROMs with 375 images of kids' toys and backgrounds, hot rods, bugs and butterflies, nostalgia, and fall and winter holidays, with various kinds of masks and clipping paths; to 24 MB; TIFF; A; MetaCreations

KPT Power Photos: Series Three
5 CD ROMs with 375 images, each disc contains a different subject, retro toys, tropical paradise, junkyards, frames, and spring and summer holidays, with various kinds of masks and clipping paths; to 24 MB; TIFF; A; MetaCreations

KPT Power Photos: Series Four
5 CD ROMs with 375 images; each disc contains a different subject; Africa, business elements, flowers, fall foliage and paper textures; images have various kinds of built-in masks and clipping paths; to 24 MB; TIFF; A; MetaCreations

MetaPhotos: Professionals Collection
4 CD ROMs with 240 photographs of professionals in different poses with still lifes and backgrounds that relate to the professions; with various kinds of built-in masks and clipping paths; to 24 MB; TIFF; A; MetaCreations

Photo Image Objects: Business Equipment Vol. 1
20 photos of vintage business tools "from when business was done without computers"; images include clipping paths; to 17 MB; TIFF; A; Classic PIO Partners

Photo Image Objects: Classic Sampler CD
20 photographic images with a nostalgic theme (not repeated in other Classic PIO collections), with masks; to 28 MB; TIFF; A; Classic PIO Partners

Photo Image Objects: Entertainment, Volume 1
20 unique photos of vintage movie, TV and theater related objects; images include clipping paths; to 15 MB; TIFF; A; Classic PIO Partners

Photo Image Objects: Fabrics Volume 1
40 photos of unique classic prints from the 1930s, '40s and '50s atomic and floral eras; with masks; to 21 MB; TIFF; A; Classic PIO Partners

Photo Image Objects: Microphones
20 photographic image objects of vintage microphones, with masks; to 16 MB; TIFF; A; Classic PIO Partners

Photo Image Objects: Nostalgic Memorabilia, Volume 1
20 unique photographic image objects of nostalgic treasures, with masks; to 15 MB; TIFF; A; Classic PIO Partners

Photo Image Objects: Radios
20 photographic image objects of vintage radios, with masks; to 15 MB; TIFF; A; Classic PIO Partners

Photo Image Objects: Telephones
20 photographic image objects of vintage telephones, with masks; to 15 MB; TIFF; A; Classic PIO Partners

Terra Botanica
100 digitally manipulated images of leaves, flowers, grasses, trees, undersea plants, and more; some with ghosted text boxes; to 18 MB; Kodak PhotoCD format; C; Texture Farm

Terra Firma
100 digitally manipulated images of the oceans, forests, grasslands, skies and more; some with ghosted text boxes; to 18 MB; Kodak PhotoCD format; C; Texture Farm

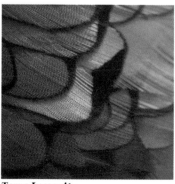

Terra Incognita
100 digitally manipulated images of common textures and abstracts found in nature; some with ghosted text boxes; to 18MB; Kodak PhotoCD format; C; Texture Farm

B & W, Volume 6
56 grayscale photos of marble, leather, clouds, and sunsets; to 9MB; TIFF; A; Vivid Details

B & W, Volume 12
60 grayscale photos of slate, granite, flowers, rustic wood, and old paint; to 9MB; TIFF; A; Vivid Details

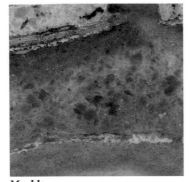

Marble
48 photos of various kinds of marble; to 37MB; TIFF; CMYK; A; Vivid Details

The Stock Solution
Over 200,000 photos; initiate search via World Wide Web site; download thumbnails (free) and comps; high-res delivered as film or digital files; The Stock Solution

Contact information for the photo discs listed in Appendix A. Don't miss the samples on the CD ROM disc that accompanies this book.

Artbeats Software, Inc.
P.O. Box 709
Myrtle Creek, OR 97457
800-444-9392, 541-863-4429
541-863-4547 fax
www.artbeats.com
www.artbeatswebtools.com

Classic PIO Partners
87 East Green Street, Suite 309
Pasadena, CA 91105
800-370-2746, 818-564-8106
818-564-8554 fax
classicpio@earthlink.net
www.classicpartners.com

CMCD
℅ **PhotoDisc, Inc.**
2013 Fourth Avenue, Suite 402
Seattle, WA 98121
800-664-2623, 206-441-9355
206-441-9379 fax
www.photodisc.com

Digital Stock Corp.
750 Second Street
Encinitas, CA 92024
800-545-4514, 760-634-6500
760-634-6510 fax
www.digitalstock.com

Image Farm Inc.
110 Spadina Avenue, Suite 309
Toronto, Ontario
M5V 2K4 Canada
800 438 3276, 416 504 4161
416 504 4163 fax
www.imagefarm.com
email: image-info@imagefarm.com

Image Club Graphics
Suite 800
8334 Fourth Avenue SW
Calgary, Alberta, Canada T2P3T5
800-661-9410, 403-262-8008
403-261-7013 fax
www.imageclub.com
email: info@imageclub.com

MetaCreations
6303 Carpinteria Avenue
Carpinteria, CA 93013
805 566 6200
805 566 6385 fax
www.metacreations.com/products/
metaphotos

PhotoDisc, Inc.
2013 Fourth Avenue, Suite 402
Seattle, WA 98121
800-528-3472, 206-441-9355
206-441-9379 fax
www.photodisc.com

RubberBall Productions
44 North Geneva Road
Orem, Utah 84057
800 888 224 3472
801 224 6886, 810 224 3353 fax
www.rubberball.com
email: photos@rubberball.com

Seattle Support Group
20420 84th Avenue South
Kent, WA 98032
800-995-9777, 253-480-1001
206-480-1006 fax
www.ssgrp.com
email: sales@sssgrp.com

Syberia LLC
97 Pine Street
Columbia, CT 06237
860-228-9028
860-228-9028 fax

The Stock Solution
307 West 200 South, No. 1003
Salt Lake City, UT 84101
800-777-2076, 801-363-9700
801-363-9707 fax
www.tssphoto.com
E-mail: info@tssphoto.com

Texture Farm
P.O. Box 460417
San Francisco, CA 94146-0417
415-284-6180, 415-561-9720 orders
415-285-5359 fax
email: wass@netcom.com

Vivid Details
82 Sulphur Mountain Road
Ojai, CA 93023
800-948-4843, 805-646-0217
805-646-0021
www.vividdetails.com/Phtintro.html

Xaos Tools, Inc.
600 Townsend Street, Suite 270 East
San Francisco, CA 94103
800-289-9267, 415-477-9300
415-558-9303 fax
www.xaostools.com

Appendix B Software Information

Software of potential interest to readers of The Photoshop 3 Wow! Book

Adobe Systems, Inc.
P. O. Box 1034
Buffalo, NY 14240
800-833-6687

After Effects: Digital video editing software with film-quality special effects

Dimensions: Software for adding depth and perspective to type and line art

Illustrator: Design tool with powerful illustration and text-handling capabilities

PageMaker: Desktop publishing software that integrates text and graphics, allowing users to write, design, and produce professional-quality printed communications

Premiere: Digital video editing software

Alien Skin Software
2522 Clark Avenue
Raleigh, NC 27607
919-832-4124

Eye Candy: A set of customizable plug-in filters that produce special effects

Andromeda Software Inc.
699 Hampshire Road, Suite 109
Westlake Village, CA 91361
805-379-4109
805-379-5253 fax

Series 1 Photography Filters: A set of plug-in filters that produce optical lens effects

Series 2 Three-D Filter: A plug-in filter that provides 3D surface mapping onto primitive objects

Series 3 Screens Filter: A plug-in filter that provides preset and customizable mezzotint treatments

Series 4 Techtures Filter: A plug-in filter for blending its library of hand-rendered textures with images

Velociraptor: A plug-in for creating motion trails

Auto F/X
888-828-8639

Photo/Graphic Edges: A plug-in for applying edge treatments to rectangular, nontransparent images.

Typo/Graphic Edges: A plug-in for applying edge treatments to type and graphics on transparent layers

Corel Corporation
1600 Carling Avenue
Ottawa, Ontario K1Z 8R7
Canada
613-728-8200
613-761-9176 fax

CorelDraw: Design and illustration program with text-handling and page layout capabilities

Macromedia, Inc.
600 Townsend Street
San Francisco, CA 94103
415-252-2000

Director: A multimedia and Web content development application

FreeHand: Design and illustration tool for graphics professionals; combines easy-to-use interface with exceptional power

MetaCreations
6303 Carpinteria Avenue
Carpinteria, CA 93013
805-566-6200
805-566-6385

Bryce An application for creating photorealistic 3D environments

Kai's Power Tools: A set of plug-in filters for special effects designed by Kai Krause

KPT Convolver: A plug-in that makes it easier and faster to do sharpening and color correction, and also provides special effects treatments in a highly visual interactive interface

Ray Dream Designer: A program for creating 3D graphics that allows you to build 3D objects, assign surface textures to them, arrange them in a scene, light the scene and render the scene to produce photorealistic illustrations

Quark, Inc.
1800 Grant Street
Denver, CO 80203
800-788-7835
970-894-3398 fax

QuarkXPress: Desktop publishing software. Integrates text and graphics, allowing users to write, design, and produce professional-quality printed communications.

**Symantec Corporation,
Peter Norton Group**
2500 Broadway
Suite 200
Santa Monica, CA 90404
800-441-7234

Norton Utilities: A set of applications for system maintenance

Xaos Tools, Inc.
300 Montgomery, 3rd Floor
San Francisco, CA 94104
415-487-7000
415-477-9303 fax

Paint Alchemy: A "brush engine" plug-in for painterly effects

Appendix C
Publications

Books and other publications of potential interest to readers of The Photoshop 4 Wow! Book

Adobe Systems, Inc.
P. O. Box 1034
Buffalo, NY 14240
800-833-6687

Adobe Technical Notes: Free by fax or mail (or find them on the Photoshop 3 Deluxe Edition CD ROM); on such Photoshop-related topics as The Lab Color Mode; Scanning Basics; Working with Type in Adobe Photoshop, Creating predictable Separations, Maximizing Performance, The Adobe Photoshop Raw File Format, Questions to Ask Your Printer, Adobe Photoshop Tips, Using Separation Tables, and many more.

Agfa Prepress Education Resources
P.O. Box 7917
Mt. Prospect, IL 60056
800-395-7007

An Introduction to Digital Color Prepress and *Digital Color Prepress Volume 2:* Short, colorful technical publications on digital color prepress; also available as 35mm slide shows

Hayden Books
201 W. 103rd
Indianapolis, IN 46290

Creating Killer Web Sites by David Siegel: A guide to designing and creating Web graphics

New Riders
201 West 103rd Street
Indianapolis, IN 46290

Photoshop Web Techniques by J. Scott Hamlin: A guide to using Photoshop as a Web graphics tool, as well as putting graphics into motion with Shockwave, JavaScript, and GIF animation software

Peachpit Press
1249 Eighth Street
Berkeley, CA 94710
800-283-9444

The Non-Designer's Web Book by Robin Williams and John Tollett: A guide to creating, designing, and posting your own Web site

Design Editorial Pty Ltd
11 School Road, Ferny Creek
Victoria, Australia 3786
61-3755-1149
fax: 61-3755-1155

Design Graphics: A bimonthly magazine with how-to's, case studies, hardware and software reviews, and interviews, all tailored to the needs of graphic design professionals. Subscription rates are the same in the United States and Australia.

Appendix D Artists and Photographers

Mitch Anthony 274

Jim Belderes 95

Jeff Brice 146, 147
2416 NW 60th Street
Seattle, WA 98107
206-706-0406
cypsy@aol.com

Jeff Burke 131, 150, 151
Burke/Triolo Productions
8755 Washington Blvd.
Culver City, CA 90232
310-837-9900
foodpix@aol.com

Doug Chang 50

Eric Chauvin 50
Industrial Light & Magic

Jack Cliggett 136
College of Design Arts
Drexel University
Philadelphia, PA 19104
cliggejj@duvm.ocs.drexel.edu

Nino Cocchiarella 232
Cocchiarella Design
201 NW 4th Street, Suite 103
Evansville, IN 47708
812-423-2500

Tom Collicott 239

E. J. Dixon 275
1044 Passiflora Avenue
Encinitas, CA 92024
760-942-3940
ej@hotmail.com

Katrin Eismann 90, 91, 108, 148, 149
PRAXIS.Digital Solutions
3400 Ben Lomond Place #218
Los Angeles, CA 90027
213-663-5626
75720.1334@compuserve.com

Ty Ellingson 259
Industrial Light & Magic

Diane Fenster 190
Computer Art and Design
287 Reichling Avenue
Pacifica, CA 94044
415-355-4205, 415-338-1409
fenster@sfsu.edu

Louis Fishauf 49, 233, 300
Reactor Art + Design Ltd.
51 Camden Street
Toronto, Ontario, Canada, M5V1V2
416-703-1913, ext. 241

Michael Gilmore 161, 297
CyberFlix
4 Market Square
Knoxville, TN 37902
615-546-1157
mjgilmore@aol.com

Francois Guérin 213, 215, 270
33 Rue Alexandre Dumas
Paris 75011, France
43-73-36-62
74067.1513@compuserve.com

Eric Hanauer 130, 149
EHanauer@aol.com

Lance Hidy 89, 230
190A High Street
Newburyport, MA 01950
978-465-1346
LHidy@hbsp.harvard.edu

Phil Howe 219
542A First Avenue South
Seattle, WA 98104
206-682-3453

Peter Kaye 28

Stephen King 270
1097 Oceanic Drive
Encinitas, CA 92024
760-944-8914
kinghome@aol.com

Douglas Kirkland 108

John Knoll 301
Industrial Light & Magic

Ed Lowe 219

Jeff McCord 269
Free-Lancelot
4218 SW Alaska Street, Suite G
Seattle, WA 98116
206-933-9699
freelancet@aol.com

Bert Monroy 231
11 Latham Lane
Berkeley, CA 94708
510-524-9412
waldus@aol.com

Victor Navone 282
Presto Studios, Inc.
5414 Oberlin Drive, Suite 200
San Diego, CA 92121
619-622-0500
presto@presto.com

Doug Peltonen 269

Donal Philby 128

Richard Ransier 131
Classic PIO Partners
87 East Green Street, Suite 309
Pasadena, CA 91105
800-370-2746, 818-564-8106
cpio@ix.netcom.com

Eric Reinfeld 51
Digital Design
87 Seventh Avenue
Brooklyn, NY 11217
718-783-2313
Reinfeld@aol.com

Roy Robinson 121

Max Seabaugh 190
MAX
302 23rd Avenue
San Francisco, CA 94121
415-750-1373

Mark Siprut 193
School of Art, Design, and Art History
San Diego State University
San Diego, CA 92182
619-594-5446
siprut@aol.com

Russell Sparkman 90, 268
2-100 Issha
Meito-ku, Nagoya
Japan 465
052-703-6305
vfe04663@niftyserve.or.jp

Sharon Steuer 219
Bethany, CT
203-393-3981
wowartist@bigfoot.com

Anna Stump 203
School of Art, Design, and Art History
San Diego State University
San Diego, CA 92182
619-594-5446
astump@aol.com

Cher Threinen-Pendarvis 172, 218
475 San Gorgonio Street
San Diego, CA 92106
619-226-6050
ctpendarvs@aol.com

Lorraine Triolo 131, 150, 151
Burke/Triolo Productions
8755 Washington Blvd.
Culver City, CA 90232
310-837-9900
foodpix@aol.com

Frank Vitale 191, 275
1833 11th Street, #2
Santa Monica, CA 90404
Vitalef@earthlink.net

Tommy Yune 74, 206
Ursus Studios
P.O. Box 4858
Cerritos, CA 90703-4858
tommyyune@aol.com

Index

Actions Index

All of these treatments and more can be "automated" in Photoshop with the **Wow! Actions** provided on the CD-ROM that comes with this book. The disc also includes all the original PhotoDisc images (and the graphics), so you can use the Actions as little **"tutorials."** Run each Action with a click and then "dissect" the resulting layers, layer masks, Adjustment layers, clipping groups, and alpha channels in the finished file. Make changes to blending modes, layer opacity, and Adjustment layer settings and see what happens.

Then run the Action on an image of your own, customizing it to taste. **If your image is very different** from ours — in tonal range, contrast, proportions, or size — you may have to adjust the Action to get a desirable result.

The Actions are divided into four categories, according to what you need to run them, as shown on the next five pages.

A note from the authors: We put a lot of time and effort into developing these Wow! Actions, and we hope you enjoy them. **Please be considerate of our rights, and don't distribute the Wow! Actions, either for sale or free of charge, to anyone else.** "Free samples" are available at www.peachpit.com/wow. Thanks.

— Jack and Linnea

Actions That Work on Selections

To run the Actions shown on this page, you need to select an area of an image. You can use Photoshop's selection tools or commands to make the appropriate selection, or if the file has a built-in path or alpha channel, you can load that as a selection. Other specific requirements and instructions are given in the **Stop boxes** in the Actions. **Be sure to read them!**

Blur Background

Cast Shadow

Drop Shadow

Drop Shadow / Motion

Photo Glow / Cold

Photo Glow / Hot

Text Panel

LOADING WOW! ACTIONS

Before you load the Wow! Actions, save the set currently in your Actions palette (choose **Save Actions** from the palette's pop-out menu). Then choose **Load Actions** (to *add* the Wow! Actions to the current set) or **Replace Actions** (to load the Wow! Actions *instead of* the current set.

Actions That Work on Alpha Channels

To run the Actions shown on this page, you need a white graphic on a black background, stored in channel #4 of an RGB file. The channel should be named **Graphic** *with a capital "G." Typically you'll also need a background image or a white Background layer. Any other instructions you need will appear in the* **Stop boxes** *in the Actions.* **Be sure to read them!**

Button Emboss / Bevel

Button Emboss / Round

Distressed Type / Graphic

Graphic Emboss / Color Prep

Graphic Glow / Cold

Graphic Glow / Cold / Hue Interior

Graphic Glow / Hot

Graphic Glow / Hot / Hue Interior

Graphic Stand Out / On Regular

Graphic Stand Out / On Light

Graphic Stand Out / On Dark

Mercury

Recessed / Shadow

Memory-Intensive Actions

To run the Actions shown on this page, you need you need **a file like the one described on the facing page.** You also need enough RAM to run the Lighting Effects or Glass filter, which can be extremely RAM-intensive. Anything else you may need to know about running a particular Action can be found in its **Stop boxes**. **Be sure to read them!**

Chrome / Bright / Background 1

Chrome / Bright / Background 2

Chrome / Light / Background 1

Chrome / Light / Background 2

Crystal

Gold

Metal

Plastic

Silver

AN "EMBOSSING" TUTORIAL

To start with "raw materials" and develop your own embossed or debossed effect, you can use the **Embossing Sampler Action**. It generates alpha channels for all the embossing styles shown on pages 237–238, except the "chiseled" look, which requires MetaCreations' KPT Gradient Designer.

Steel / Brushed

Steel / Brushed / Oiled

Actions That Work with Photos

To run the Actions shown on these two pages for painterly or photographic effects, you'll start with a photograph, scanned artwork, or some other continuous-tone image. If there's anything else you need to know in order to run a particular Action, **Stop boxes** within the Action will alert you. **Be sure to read them!**

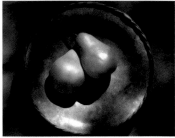
Antiquing Color

Antiquing Color / Light

Antiquing Color / Soft

Artistic Noise

Color "Mezzo" / Dark

Color "Mezzo" / Dithering

Color "Mezzo" / Light

Color "Mezzo" / Medium

Deco Shading

Diffuse Glow / Hard Light

Diffuse Glow / Lighten

Diffuse Glow / Screen

Diffuse Glow / Soft Focus